ARISTOTLE
THE POLITICS

ARISTOTLE

THE
POLITICS

Translated and with an Introduction,
Notes, and Glossary by
Carnes Lord

The University of Chicago Press
Chicago and London

CARNES LORD has taught political science at the University of
Virginia and has served in the U.S. government, most recently on
the staff of the National Security Council. He is the author of
Education and Culture in the Political Thought of Aristotle.

The University of Chicago Press, Chicago 60637
The University of Chicago Press, Ltd., London

93 92 91 90 89 88 87 86 85 84   54321

LIBRARY OF CONGRESS CATALOGING IN PUBLICATION DATA

Aristotle.
    The politics.

    Translation of: Politica.
    Includes index.
1. Political science—Early works to 1700. I. Lord,
Carnes. II. Title.
JC71.A41L67 1984   320.1   84-215
ISBN 0-226-02667-1

CONTENTS

INTRODUCTION

To say that Aristotle's *Politics* is a classic work of political thought is to understate considerably the achievement and significance of this remarkable document. The *Politics* is a product of that singular moment in the history of the West when traditional modes of thinking in every area were being uprooted by the new mode of thinking that had made its appearance in the Greek world under the name of philosophy. It was in and through the elaboration of a philosophic-scientific approach to natural and human phenomena by the ancient Greeks—above all, by Plato and Aristotle—that the intellectual categories of the Western tradition took shape. The significance of Aristotle's *Politics* lies in the first instance in the fact that it represents the earliest attempt to elaborate a systematic science of politics.

The subject matter of the *Politics* is "politics" in its original sense—the affairs of the polis, the classical city-state. The word *polis* cannot be translated by the English "state" or its modern equivalent because polis is a term of distinction. It denotes a political form that is equally distant from the primitive tribe and from the civilized monarchic state of the ancient East. The polis, the form of political organization prevailing in the Greek world during its greatest period (roughly the eighth to the third century B.C.), was an independent state organized around an urban center and governed typically by formal laws and republican political institutions. It is in important respects the forerunner, if not the direct ancestor, of the constitutional democracies of the contemporary West.

Politics in its original sense is at once narrower and broader than politics in the contemporary sense. It is narrower in virtue of its association with an essentially republican political order, but broader by the fact that it encompasses aspects of life which are today regarded as both beyond and beneath politics. The *Politics* trespasses on ground that would today be claimed by the disciplines of economics, sociology, and urban planning, as well as by moral philosophy and the theory of education.

Yet the scope and range of the *Politics* represents more than a passive reflection of its historical moment. By exhibiting the complex unity of the elements of human life and the manner of their fulfillment in the polis and the way of life it makes possible, Aris-

1

totle provides at once an articulation of the phenomenon of politics in the fullness of its potential and a powerful defense of the dignity of politics and the political life. For this reason above all, the *Politics* is an original and fundamental book—one of those rare books that first defines a permanent human possibility and thereby irrevocably alters the way men understand themselves.

This much may be said at the outset regarding the general character and significance of the work before us. Before entering on a fuller consideration of the *Politics*, it is essential to present a more detailed account of Aristotle himself and the age in which he lived and wrote.

I

Aristotle's life is frequently presented as one of virtually uninterrupted devotion to study, with little connection to the great events of the age. To the extent that his well-attested relationship with the rulers of Macedon is acknowledged, it tends to be viewed as a sort of historical curiosity with few implications for Aristotle's own activity. Yet a good case can be made for quite a different interpretation. Although the evidence bearing on Aristotle's life is very incomplete and often conflicting and unreliable, it seems highly likely that he was more active politically on behalf of Macedon, and that his fortunes were more intimately bound up with those of its rulers, than is commonly supposed. At the same time, it appears that the traditional picture of Aristotle as a close associate and admirer of Alexander and his works is, at best, very overdrawn.[1]

Aristotle was born in 384 B.C. in the town of Stagira, in the Chalcidic peninsula of northern Greece. His father Nicomachus was court physician to Amyntas III of Macedon, and is said to have become the king's close friend and advisor; hence it would appear that Aristotle was brought up primarily in Macedonia itself. At the age of seventeen, Aristotle was sent to Athens to pursue his education. Most reports indicate that he immediately joined the Platonic Academy, though some evidence suggests that he may have enrolled initially in the rhetorical school of Isocrates, which was then better known throughout the Greek world.[2] He remained in Athens, in close association with Plato, for the next twenty years.

The circumstances of Aristotle's departure for Athens are of some interest. Amyntas III had died in 370/69. His eldest son and successor, Alexander, was murdered shortly thereafter by Amyntas' brother-in-law, Ptolemy of Alorus, thus initiating a dynastic struggle that was only resolved with the accession of Amyntas' younger son, Philip, in 359. It is possible that Aristotle's father was killed at the time of the assassination of Alexander or subsequently. At all events, it may well be that the dispatch of Aristotle to Athens in 367 had more to do with the political turbulence at home than with the intrinsic attractions of that great center of culture and learning.

Similar considerations are likely to have played a role in Aristotle's departure from Athens in 348/47. It is usually assumed that Aristotle left the Academy after the death of Plato because of disappointment at the choice of Plato's nephew Speusippus as the new head of that institution rather than himself, and possibly because of sharpening philosophical disagreements with the followers of Plato generally. Another explanation is, however, at least equally plausible. Ten years of Philip's rule had brought internal stability to Macedon, and the beginnings of the aggrandizement of Macedonian power and influence that was shortly to make it the most formidable state in the Greek world. Athens, its traditional interests in the north of Greece menaced by these developments, found itself increasingly at odds with Philip, though its own preoccupations (notably the Social War of 357–55, which resulted in the collapse of the second Athenian naval league) prevented effective opposition. In the summer of 348, with the capture and sack of Olynthus, the capital of the Chalcidic Federation, Philip succeeded in bringing all of the neighboring Greek cities under his control, in spite of a belated Athenian intervention stimulated by the fiercely anti-Macedonian oratory of Demosthenes. Given the atmosphere then prevailing in Athens, it would not be surprising if Aristotle had chosen to remove himself from the city. In fact, there is some evidence that Aristotle actually left the city before the death of Plato; and one account explicitly states that the reason for his departure was that he was "frightened by the execution of Socrates"—which is to say, by the prospect of a revival of politically motivated popular hostility to philosophy.[3] Some forty years later, during another outburst of anti-Macedonian feeling in Athens, allegations of treasonous activity by Aristotle during the Olynthian crisis could still be used to support a motion to banish all alien philosophers from Athens.[4]

Aristotle's next five years were spent in Asia Minor. Two former members of the Platonic Academy, Erastus and Coriscus, had established a school at Assos in the Troad under the patronage of the local ruler, Hermias of Atarneus; it was here that Aristotle first settled. While no doubt attracted to Assos primarily by the opportunities for study, it would not be surprising if Aristotle went as more than a private individual. There is no direct evidence that Philip had begun to contemplate the possibility of an invasion of Asia Minor at this time, but the Atarnian state, which had been created at Persian expense during a period of imperial weakness and retrenchment, was a natural ally and staging area for any such undertaking. Philip soon received Persian exiles at his court in Pella, and when Hermias was captured in 341 by the treachery of a Greek mercenary captain and brought to the Persian capital, the torture to which he was subjected appears to have had the purpose of laying bare the nature of Macedonian intentions in Asia. Given these circumstances, it seems quite possible that Aristotle had been instructed by Philip to make contact with Hermias and to act as unofficial ambassador to his court, and that he succeeded in forging an understanding of some sort between the two men. There is also evidence that Aristotle traveled to Macedonia prior to going

3

to Assos in connection with the affairs of his native Stagira, which had been captured and razed by Philip in the previous year; it may have been at this time that his relationship with the son of his father's patron was first firmly established.[5]

In any event, Aristotle soon became an intimate of Hermias. This remarkable man—a eunuch, according to report, who had risen from the status of slave to become a wealthy businessman before taking power in Atarneus and consolidating and expanding the borders of that fragile principality—appears to have shared at least in some measure Aristotle's philosophical interests. The personal attachment that existed between the two men is reflected in Aristotle's marriage to Hermias' niece and adopted daughter, Pythias, and in the warm admiration expressed by Aristotle in a poem composed in his memory.

Possibly because of the increasing precariousness of Hermias' position in the face of the revival of Persian power under Artaxerxes Ochus, Aristotle left Assos in 345/44 for nearby Mytilene on the island of Lesbos. There is evidence that Aristotle devoted his time there to the study of biology, perhaps in conjunction with Theophrastus, a native of Lesbos who was to become Aristotle's successor as head of the Peripatetic school. Then, in 343/42, Aristotle was invited by Philip to take up residence in Macedonia and—according to tradition—undertake the education of his son Alexander.

At the time of Aristotle's arrival, Alexander was thirteen years old. Within two years he would be heavily engaged in the affairs of the kingdom as regent during Philip's prolonged absence in Thrace, and subsequently as one of his military commanders in the campaign that culminated in the battle of Chaeronea in 338. In view of these circumstances, it is difficult to imagine that the influence of Aristotle can have been as decisive in the formation of Alexander's outlook as is often assumed. Moreover, there is reason to wonder whether the traditional account of their relationship can actually be sustained on the basis of the evidence available. That Aristotle acted as the personal tutor of Alexander by no means represents the consensus of the biographical tradition of Aristotle, and is not supported by any near-contemporary source. Indeed, there is a competing tradition according to which Alexander's principal tutors were Leonidas, a relative of his mother Olympias, and a certain Lysimachus of Acarnania.[6] As regards philosophical affiliation, Alexander appears to have been at least as exposed to Cynic as to Academic or Peripatetic influence, and it has been persuasively argued that his own political ideas were closer to Cynic cosmopolitanism than to the views of Aristotle.[7]

The most probable explanation is that Aristotle was summoned by Philip to establish a school for the education of the sons of the high Macedonian aristocracy, and only secondarily, if at all, for the sake of Alexander. Philip appears to have been greatly concerned to inspire a spirit of unity and loyalty in the fractious nobles of his large and heterogeneous domains. One of his most significant measures to this end was the creation of a body known as the Royal Pages, adolescent sons of the nobility who were brought to Philip's court to prepare them for service to the monarchy. Though evidence is lacking, it makes sense to assume that Aristotle was charged with the education—an education centering principally, it may be imagined, on literary and rhetorical rather than philosophical subjects—of this select and influential group. Among his students may have been the sons of Antipater, the regent of Macedonia during Aristotle's first several years there as well as subsequently, and Ptolemy, the founder of the Lagid dynasty in Egypt, who was to be an important patron of the Peripatetic school after Aristotle's death. Aristotle evidently formed a close friendship with Antipater during these years, a friendship which seems to have been maintained through a regular correspondence after Aristotle's return to Athens.[8]

The extent of Aristotle's association with Philip himself is not known. Philip was absent from Pella on campaign in the north during much of the period of Aristotle's stay. When Philip again turned his attention to Greek affairs, however, Aristotle may well have played some advisory role, particularly with respect to Athens. One of the Arabic biographies of Aristotle records an inscription supposed to have been set up on the Acropolis honoring Aristotle's benefactions, and specifically his intervention with Philip on Athens' behalf. It makes sense to connect this information with the circumstances of the Amphissan war of 338 and the aftermath of the battle of Chaeronea, when Philip behaved with great leniency toward defeated Athens.[9] And we shall see that there is some evidence linking Aristotle to the political settlement imposed by Philip on the Greeks under the name of the League of Corinth. If Aristotle did have a hand in facilitating the reconciliation of the Athenians with Philip, it would help to explain his decision to return permanently to Athens in 335. In spite of the renewed fighting that followed the assassination of Philip in 336 and Alexander's decidedly less gentle handling of the rebellious Greeks, Aristotle could still count on a store of popular good will sufficient to neutralize at least in part the resentment generated by his Macedonian associates. It may also be that Aristotle felt less welcome in a Macedonia dominated by the partisans of Alexander.[10]

The next twelve years, during which Alexander destroyed the Persian Empire and extended Macedonian power as far as India and Uzbekistan, were relatively uneventful ones in Greece. Antipater presided effectively over the settlement of Greek affairs arranged by Philip and Alexander; the most serious challenge to that settlement, the movement organized by the Spartan king Agis in 331/30, was crushed in a single battle near Sparta's borders. Athens continued as an independent state under a democratic regime, and even enjoyed something of a revival in consequence of the financial and military reforms of Lycurgus, its leading politician; but its foreign policy remained at best highly circumscribed. It was during this period that Aristotle founded his own school there, the Lyceum, established a program of systematic research and teaching in virtually every area of knowledge, and composed many if not most of the works currently extant under his name.

5

The relative tranquility of these years was shattered by the death of Alexander in 323. News of this event led to a general anti-Macedonian uprising throughout Greece, in which Athens played a prominent role. A force under the Athenian general Leosthenes defeated Antipater in Thessaly and beseiged his army in the town of Lamia; only the arrival of reinforcements from Asia permitted the Macedonians to recover their position. In this atmosphere, Aristotle was indicted on a charge of impiety in connection with the poem he had composed years before honoring Hermias of Atarneus. Remarking that he did not wish Athens to sin a second time against philosophy, Aristotle withdrew to the city of Chalcis on the nearby island of Euboea, where his mother's family owned property and a Macedonian garrison offered protection. He died there in 322. In the year following, Antipater brought the Lamian War to a close with the forced surrender of Athens, the suppression of its democratic regime, and the installation of Macedonian troops in the fort of Munychia.

The *Politics* itself is singularly uninformative concerning Aristotle's view of Macedon and the two men who were responsible for its rise to greatness. In spite of the wealth of detail he provides on the political events and circumstances of the contemporary or near-contemporary Greek world, Aristotle refers explicitly only once to Philip, and never to Alexander, although the reference to Philip in book 5 as already dead indicates that Alexander must have attained considerable prominence by the time the *Politics* (or at least substantial portions of it) was written. There is one passage, however, which is of great interest in this connection, although its bearing has been very generally missed. In the course of a discussion of the relative rarity of the regime based on the "middling" element in a city as distinct from the rich or poor, Aristotle notes that "those who have achieved leadership in Greece" (he appears to think of Athens and Sparta) have looked only to their own regimes and established democracies or oligarchies, with the result that the middling regime has come into being infrequently if at all. He then adds: "For of those who have previously held leadership, one man alone was persuaded to provide for this sort of arrangement, whereas the custom is established now even among those in the cities not to want equality, but either to seek rule or endure domination." In spite of the absence of a learned consensus as to the identity of the individual in question, consideration of the context of the reference and the absence of plausible alternatives can leave little doubt, I believe, that Philip is meant. Philip was officially designated "leader" (*hēgemōn*) in his capacity as head of the League of Corinth, and the constitution of the League contained measures that were designed to moderate the struggle of rich and poor within member cities. Moreover, Aristotle's use of the word "persuaded" in this connection seems intended to suggest some involvement in the matter on the part of Aristotle himself.[11]

If this interpretation is correct, the implications are considerable. Apart from the (generally overlooked) indication of Aristotle's personal participation and of his influence with Philip, it would appear that Aristotle looked with some sympathy on the quasi-federal League of Corinth, and regarded the Macedonian hegemony in Greece not as a necessary evil but as a potential instrument for remedying the historic defects of the domestic politics of the cities. There is every reason to believe that Aristotle would have welcomed in principle the restricted democracy (which seems to have resembled in critical respects the "middling" regime he calls "polity") imposed on Athens first by Antipater in 321 and then by Demetrius of Phaleron—a politician schooled in Aristotle's Lyceum—in the name of Antipater's son Cassander in 317.

Does Aristotle's apparent closeness to Philip and his views also mean that he approved the tendency of Philip's foreign policy, in particular his projects of conquest in the East? To what extent can he be supposed to have favored the growth of Macedonian imperialism? When Aristotle remarks, in book 7 of the *Politics*, that the Greek nation has the capacity to rule all men "if it should unite in a single regime," [12] he has been frequently understood as endorsing both the political integration of Greece under Macedonian leadership and Alexander's war of conquest against the Persian Empire. A similar meaning is often found in the advice Aristotle is said to have given Alexander to treat the Greeks "after the fashion of a leader but the barbarians after the fashion of a master, demonstrating concern for the former as friends and kin, but behaving toward the latter as toward animals or plants." [13] Apart from the very questionable authenticity of this citation, the evidence of the *Politics* hardly bears out the notion that Aristotle supported the conquest and subjugation of foreign peoples as a principle of policy. Indeed, he is explicitly critical of such a view of international behavior, and is at pains to distinguish between the legitimate use of military force for the acquisition and maintenance of "hegemony" and its illegitimate use for unprovoked conquest. [14] As regards the "chauvinism" with which Aristotle is regularly taxed, it must be noted that Aristotle has high praise for the political accomplishments of the non-Greek Carthaginians. That barbarians and slaves were indistinguishable for him, as is often asserted on the basis of several remarks in the *Politics*, cannot be seriously maintained. [15]

This is by no means to argue that Aristotle was indifferent to the Persian threat to Greece or unsympathetic to Philip's efforts to counter it. There was, however, a considerable difference between eliminating or diminishing the Persian presence in Asia Minor and overthrowing the entire Persian Empire. Although little is known about Philip's intentions in this respect, there is reason to believe that his ambitions were more limited than his son's. [16] When Isocrates, in his exhortation to Philip to turn his energies against Persia, canvassed the strategic possibilities available to the king, he identified three: the conquest of the entire empire, the detachment of Asia Minor "from Cilicia to Sinope," and the liberation of the Greek cities of the coast. After the battle of Issus in 333, the Persian king Darius twice offered Alexander a settlement essentially corresponding to the second of these alternatives. Alexander was urged to accept the offer by his senior commander, Parmenion, who appears to have been intimately involved in Philip's planning of the enterprise, and this may well be reflective of the original intention. It is possible and even likely that Aristotle was privy to this intention.

As regards the relationship between Macedon and Greece, there is good evidence that Philip was committed to a genuinely hegemonial rather than an imperial role with respect to the Greek cities (though it must be admitted that strategic considerations had somewhat eroded this distinction even in his own lifetime). By contrast, it is clear that Alexander became increasingly disinclined to treat Greece or Greeks on a privileged basis, whether out of a high-minded devotion to Cynic principles or a fascination with the trappings of oriental despotism. Alexander's execution of Aristotle's nephew Callisthenes in 328 for his refusal to do obeisance in Persian style, a pathological symptom of this development, permanently poisoned the relationship between Alexander and the Peripatetic school,[17] but it should not be assumed to have been the governing factor in Aristotle's view of Alexander. Unsatisfactory as the evidence is, it seems relatively clear that Aristotle's political orientation was from the beginning closer to Philip's, and that neither man succeeded in educating or taming the strong-willed and altogether extraordinary Alexander.

II

If the *Politics* is less studied today than might seem appropriate for a work of its unchallenged eminence, much of the reason surely lies in the unresolved tangle of questions bearing on the character and composition of the *Politics* and of Aristotle's writings generally. It is convenient to imagine that such questions do not fundamentally touch the substance of Aristotle's thought, and may therefore safely be left to the care of philologists. Yet, to begin with, an interpretation of the *Politics*, as of any work of political theory, must depend importantly on one's view of the kind of work it is and the audience for which it was composed, or what might be called the literary character of the work in a broad sense. Is the *Politics* a finished book composed with at least ordinary care? Or is it an accretion of notes used by Aristotle (and possibly by his successors) as the basis of a course of lectures? Is the *Politics* a theoretical treatise addressed only to advanced students within Aristotle's school? Or is it more in the nature of a technical handbook addressed primarily to less advanced students, or to a wider audience whose concerns are predominantly practical? In the second place, the specific difficulties posed by the text of the *Politics* continue to be regarded by many as convincing evidence of a lack of coherence and unity in the work as a whole and its basic argument. According to the very influential view originated by Werner Jaeger, the *Politics* is essentially an amalgam of two separate treatises or collections of treatises written at widely separated intervals and embodying very different approaches to the study of political phenomena. Jaeger's view, and the interpretation of Aristotle's intellectual development on which it rests, amounts in effect to a denial of the very existence of Aristotelian political theory as a single and self-consistent body of thought. To what extent, then, is the *Politics* really a book in the familiar sense of that term?

The corpus of writings that has come down to us under the name of Aristotle represents only a portion of his original output. According to evidence supplied by various ancient sources and confirmed by references in the extant writings themselves, Aristotle's works fall into two broad categories: finished literary productions intended for circulation or use with a general audience, and a variety of more specialized works intended to support the research and teaching activities of his school. To the first category belong dialogues and treatises dealing primarily with moral, political, and literary subjects. Some or all of these writings are generally supposed to be identical with the so-called exoteric discourses (*hoi exōterikoi logoi*) cited on a number of occasions in the treatises now extant, though it has also been argued that this expression refers to rhetorical or dialectical exercises which formed part of Aristotle's early teaching activity.[18] With the exception of a treatise in defense of philosophy—the *Protrepticus*—which has been reconstructed in substantial part from other ancient sources,[19] these works have been almost entirely lost. To the second category belong a series of "catalogues" or compilations of historical and other information, and a large number of more or less elaborate and finished treatises on all subjects. Apart from a study of Athenian constitutional history discovered less than a century ago, and generally assumed to form part of the massive catalogue of "constitutions" (*politeiai*) that was produced by Aristotle and his students,[20] most of the catalogue material has also been lost. The Aristotelian corpus as it exists today consists overwhelmingly, then, of the specialized treatises. What is the character of these works?

It is generally agreed that the specialized treatises were not intended to be "books" within the contemporary or the classical meaning of that term, but rather were connected in some way with the educational activities of the Lyceum. The precise nature of this connection remains, however, highly uncertain. The most common assumption is that the treatises represent "notes" which served as the basis for "lectures" given by Aristotle to students of the Lyceum. It is sometimes maintained that they represent notes or records of Aristotle's lectures made by students. Though most scholars regard the second possibility as most unlikely given the uniformly high quality of the treatises, it may be the correct explanation in a few cases. In the ancient library catalogues of the writings of Aristotle and other members of the Peripatetic school, there are a few entries which expressly mention "notes" (*hypomnēmata*) or "course of lectures" (*akroasis*), but for the most part only the title or subject matter of a work is given.[21] Of all the works appearing in the catalogues, only the *Politics* is invariably described as a "course of lectures," but it is not clear what inference is to be drawn from this fact. In any case, it makes sense to suppose that the treatises served also, or even primarily, as reference works which were treated to some extent as the common property of the school and were available for the use of students.

The fact that the specialized treatises appear to be distinguished by Aristotle from the "exoteric discourses" has suggested to some interpreters that the former were intended only for the private use of students of the Peripatetic school. According to an extreme version of this view which acquired currency in late antiquity, the specialized treatises are deliberately written in a crabbed and obscure style in order to make them unintelligible to all but those who had been personally instructed by Aristotle or his associates.[22] Yet the term "esoteric" is never used by Aristotle or any early Peripatetic, and there is no contemporary evidence to support the notion that the specialized treatises contain a secret doctrine as such, or that there were significant differences between the doctrine of the specialized treatises and that of the corresponding popular works.[23] Nor, for that matter, is there any real evidence that the lectures given by Aristotle on the basis of the specialized treatises were always restricted to members of the Lyceum. According to one account, Aristotle regularly lectured to students of the Lyceum in the morning, while in the afternoon he would give lectures for a public audience.[24] But even if this story were true (the source is in fact highly suspect), it would not prove that Aristotle's "exoteric" lectures were based only on the "exoteric discourses" and not at all on the specialized treatises.

But whatever the situation with respect to the other specialized treatises, a good case can be made that the *Politics*, together with the closely linked ethical writings, was intended for an audience not limited to students of the Lyceum. That the *Politics* alone is consistently described in the ancient catalogues as a "course of lectures" has already been mentioned; this may indicate that the work enjoyed a special and more public status. The assumption that the *Nicomachean Ethics* was intended for a wider audience is very helpful in explaining Aristotle's otherwise curious insistence that the subject of ethics is not one that can be profitably taught to the young.[25] More importantly, the fact that Aristotle's ethical and political writings generally are expressly distinguished by a concern to benefit action or practice rather than simply to advance knowledge strongly suggests that their intended effect was conceived as reaching beyond the confines of the school.[26] Generally speaking, the ethical and political writings appear to be addressed less to philosophers or students of philosophy than to educated and leisured men who are actual or potential wielders of political power.

Such a view of the character of the *Politics* is supported by the evidence of Aristotle's own political involvement, and by what little is known of his early intellectual activity. One of the earliest of Aristotle's writings was a dialogue on rhetoric, and Aristotle is said to have given lectures on or instructions in rhetoric during the time of his association with Plato's Academy. If any reliance may be placed on the fragmentary and polemical testimony of the Epicurean philosopher Philodemus, it seems that Aristotle undertook to teach rhetoric out of dissatisfaction with the rhetorical education offered in the school of Isocrates, and that he taught rhetoric in connection with an education in "political science" (*politikē*) that was designed to prepare students for a life of active participation in politics.[27] That Aristotle may actually have enrolled in the school of Isocrates on his arrival in Athens as a young man was indicated earlier. It was also suggested that Aristotle's invitation to Macedonia may have been stimulated by Philip's desire to establish a school for the political education of the Macedonian nobility. In view of all this, it would seem that Aristotle's interest in political matters was from the beginning—contrary to what is usually assumed—eminently practical in nature. Indeed, the fact that Aristotle undertook a practically oriented course of instruction in rhetoric may reflect a certain dissatisfaction not only with the school of Isocrates but with the school of Plato as well.[28] If Isocrates' teaching was for Aristotle uninformed by genuine philosophy, it may be that Aristotle thought the Academy insufficiently concerned with the presentation of political philosophy in a form capable of being assimilated and used by political men.[29]

The character and composition of the *Politics* cannot be adequately discussed without some consideration of the vexed question of the early history of the Aristotelian corpus. After Aristotle's death, the manuscript originals of the treatises and other uncirculated works remained in the Lyceum as the property of Aristotle's successor as head of the school, Theophrastus. According to the famous tale recounted by Strabo and Plutarch,[30] Theophrastus' library, or such of it as included his own writings and those of Aristotle, was willed to a certain Neleus, who removed it from Athens to the town of Scepsis in Asia Minor. There it was hidden in a cellar by Neleus' heirs, then neglected and virtually forgotten until the beginning of the first century B.C., when it was discovered and purchased by Apellicon, a rich book collector and enthusiast of Aristotle, who brought it back to Athens. Apellicon, we are told, attempted to repair the damage done to the manuscripts during their sojourn in Scepsis by filling in gaps in the text, in effect producing a kind of edition which was "full of errors." Subsequently, Apellicon's collection was acquired by Sulla on the conquest of Athens in 86 B.C. and brought to Rome. There it came to the attention of the grammarian Tyrannion (and through him of Cicero), and eventually was acquired by a certain Andronicus, who undertook to bring order to the entire collection and to produce definitive editions of the works both of Aristotle and of Theophrastus.

This story, at least in its main outlines, has been generally accepted as providing the most plausible explanation for the rapid eclipse of the Peripatetic school after the middle of the third century, and for the absence of widespread knowledge of the specialized treatises of Aristotle throughout the Hellenistic period, as well as for the sudden reappearance of a flourishing Aristotelianism during the first century B.C. Other evidence seems to confirm that Andronicus played a key role in the Peripatetic revival. According to some accounts, he was actually a scholarch (official head of the school) in direct line of succession from Aristotle, and there is reason to believe that his editorial activity involved a considerable degree of substantive judgment regarding the nature of the individual treatises, their relationship to one another, and their authenticity.

One later source reports that Andronicus organized separate books into larger groupings (*pragmateiai*) of related materials; this appears to be supported by the evidence of the ancient book catalogues, and is now generally taken for granted. Whether he also contributed editorial additions—particularly transitions between books and cross-references—is not directly attested, but is often assumed.[31]

The implications of all this for the current condition of the Aristotelian writings are obvious and important. If the works of Aristotle existed in Roman times only in a disordered, unedited, and physically damaged form, were tampered with to an undetermined extent by a philosophic dilettante, and were then subjected to drastic editing and reorganization, the likelihood that the corpus as we now have it is something quite different from the corpus as it existed at the time of Aristotle's death would seem great indeed. Nor is this all. The very fact that Aristotle's writings descended to Andronicus as part of a collection of writings very similar to them in subject and style must inevitably create doubt as to the authenticity of the works or of parts of works included in his edition. If nothing else, the inordinate length of the Theophrastus catalogue preserved by Diogenes Laertius suggests that other contemporary Peripatetics may also be included in it. Accordingly, it has sometimes been suggested that the edition of Andronicus may actually represent a kind of general compendium of the writings of the early Peripatos.[32]

But how credible is the traditional account of the transmission of the Aristotelian writings? That certain features of the story are extremely puzzling has always been acknowledged. Above all, the claim that the manuscripts suffered much damage as well as inexpert repair efforts before coming into the hands of Andronicus is hardly borne out by the condition of our Aristotelian texts. But recent research has gone some way toward demonstrating that the story is in fundamental respects implausible and misleading, and that at least some crucial details are almost certainly incorrect.[33] In the first place, there is incontrovertible evidence that many of the specialized treatises were known and enjoyed some circulation outside the Peripatetic school during the period when they are supposed to have languished at Scepsis. Second, a good case can be made that the definitive edition of the works of Aristotle and Theophrastus was produced by Andronicus not at Rome in the years 40–20 B.C., as is implied in the traditional account, but at Athens perhaps some fifty years earlier. While very little is known with certainty of Andronicus himself, such evidence as does exist suggests that he was a regular head of the Lyceum, and hence might naturally have been occupied in assembling scattered writings of the founders of the school with a view to preparing an edition. Apellicon's discovery of Theophrastus' library, or a portion of it, may or may not have played an important role in this enterprise; it does not seem necessary to believe that it played the crucial role. To the extent that Andronicus was able to utilize an existing library of Aristotelian materials, or to collect copies of works which formed part of a continuous Peripatetic tradition, his editorial activity is likely to have been less drastic than is often imagined.

The chief evidence for the condition of the Aristotelian writings in antiquity is supplied by the library catalogues preserved in several biographies of Aristotle surviving from late Roman times. One of these (the Ptolemy catalogue) clearly presupposes the edition of Andronicus, and is reasonably similar to the Aristotelian corpus as presently constituted. The other two (the catalogues of Diogenes Laertius and Hesychius) are now generally agreed to derive from a source predating Andronicus, probably from the last quarter of the third century B.C.[34] These catalogues—particularly the latter two—present many strange features, and their relationships to one another and to the edition of Andronicus have never been satisfactorily explained. While they include many works that are now lost, there are a number of major works of the corpus that do no appear in them at all, even if one assumes that such works may have originally existed as separate treatises under different titles. It is tempting to dismiss the catalogues as curiosities which are today essentially unintelligible, or else to use them with extreme selectivity to support particular arguments deriving from the texts themselves. They are, however, an invaluable source, and provide many important clues for understanding the early history of Aristotle's writings.

Of all the major Aristotelian works, the *Metaphysics* and the *Politics* have been particularly singled out as evidence of Andronicus' editorial intervention. It is one of the oddities of the catalogues, however, that both works are cited under their present titles in at least one of the older lists. The case of the *Politics* is particularly striking. Almost alone among the major works, the *Politics* is cited by name and assigned the correct number of books in all of the ancient lists. There is a strong presumption, therefore, that the *Politics* existed in something closely resembling its present form prior to the edition of Andronicus—indeed, in the lifetime of Aristotle himself.[35]

Of the works on political subjects listed by Diogenes and Hesychius, most appear to have been dialogues, exoteric treatises, or catalogue materials. Diogenes lists a work entitled *Politics* (*politika*) in two books, and this has sometimes been identified with some version of the last two books of our *Politics*. But the parallel entry in Hesychius makes it highly likely that it was merely a collection of dialectical theses on political subjects, similar to other collections listed in the early catalogues and now lost. It is of considerable interest that the *Politics* itself appears in the list of Diogenes as "a course of lectures on politics like that of Theophrastus" (*politikē akroasis hōs hē Theophrastou*) in eight books. At first sight, this could seem to support the view that Theophrastus had some part in the composition of our *Politics*; yet it actually shows the opposite. Theophrastus himself is reported to have written a *Politics* (*politika*) in six books, and it is clear that the catalogue entry is a description of Aristotle's work with reference to the presumably similar work of Theophrastus, which would appear to have been better known to the cataloguer.

Discussion of the composition of the *Politics* and its early history has been dominated throughout most of this century by the interpretation of Aristotle's intellectual development pioneered by Werner Jaeger.[36] This interpretation rests largely on the view that the key to understanding Aristotle's thought lies in Aristotle's progressive estrangement from the doctrines and approach characteristic of the Platonic Academy in which he had been trained. As originally developed by Jaeger, this view drew a considerable part of its power from the explanations it seemed to provide of the compositional problems connected with Aristotle's ethical and political writings. The *Eudemian Ethics*, formerly regarded by many as the work of Aristotle's student Eudemus of Rhodes, was now revealed as an early, "Platonizing" work of Aristotle himself. This identification could plausibly explain, among other things, the appearance of three books of the *Nicomachean Ethics* (5–7) in manuscripts of the *Eudemian Ethics*, as well as anomalies within the former work itself (notably the double treatment of pleasure in books 7 and 10). As for the *Politics*, Jaeger was able to argue that the textual and interpretive difficulties which had caused many earlier editors to print books 7–8 before books 4–6 actually reflect the composite nature of the *Politics* as a collection of materials written at different periods of Aristotle's career for different purposes, and embodying very different approaches to the study of politics. According to Jaeger, books 7–8, reflecting the Platonic concern with a single ideal form of government, were composed during Aristotle's stay in Assos, when the influence of the Academy was still strong. Jaeger also assigns a relatively early date to books 2–3 (in spite of the extensive criticism of the ideal regime of Plato's *Republic* in book 2), while placing books 4–6, with their detailed anatomy of existing regimes, toward the end of Aristotle's career, when his characteristically empirical or practical approach had most fully asserted itself.

This is not the place to address the general validity of Jaeger's approach, though it is fair to say that that approach has come increasingly under question in recent years. Yet even if Jaeger is right that Aristotle's rejection of the Platonic doctrine of ideas was the decisive event of his intellectual career, Jaeger assumed rather than proved that a rejection of Platonic metaphysics necessarily entails a rejection of Platonic politics, to say nothing of the fact that Jaeger's presentation of Platonic political philosophy can hardly be held to be satisfactory. To mention only one point, Jaeger fails completely to do justice to the place of the *Laws* in Plato's thought, or to acknowledge the close connection between that in many ways eminently practical work and the *Politics* as a whole. This is by no means to deny that there are important differences between Aristotle and Plato concerning politics or the study of politics; indeed, it was suggested earlier that Aristotle's early interest in rhetoric may have been symptomatic of a certain dissatisfaction with the manner of presentation if not the substance of political science or political philosophy in the Academy. It is only to question whether those differences are well enough understood at present to permit their use as a benchmark for determining the relative dates of different portions of the *Politics*.

Our *Politics* in its current form may be divided into six distinct units of inquiry, which may be characterized briefly in the following way: the city and the household (1); views concerning the best regime (2); the city and the regime (3); the varieties of regime and what destroys and preserves them (4–5); the varieties of democracy and of political institutions (6); education and the best regime (7–8). References throughout the *Politics* to an "inquiry" (*methodos*) appear to be to one or another of these divisions of the work, which are also as a rule clearly marked by introductory and summary statements.

That there are differences of emphasis, style, and manner of argumentation in the different parts of the *Politics* will be denied by no one. Yet Jaeger never succeeded in showing that these differences could not be adequately accounted for by the differences in subject matter of the various sections. In particular, he never showed that there is a necessary incompatibility between Aristotle's concern with the best regime in books 7–8 and his concern in books 4–6 with the variety of existing regimes. That Aristotle himself was not aware of any such incompatibility seems quite clear from the introductory remarks to book 4, where the study of the regime that is best simply and the study of the regime that is best (or of regimes that are generally acceptable) for most societies are treated as equally necessary parts of political science.[37] Jaeger's assumed disjunction between "idealistic" and "practical" elements of the *Politics* appears to rest finally on a failure to appreciate the extent to which the *Politics* is a fundamentally practical book, or the implications of Aristotle's assertion that political science is a practical science directed to action rather than a theoretical science pursued for the sake of knowledge.

In what sense the account of the simply best regime in the final books of the *Politics* may be considered necessary to a practical science of politics cannot be adequately discussed here. Yet an excellent case can be made that the treatment there, with its emphasis on education and its striking neglect of political institutions and activities, complements the account of inferior regimes in books 4–6, and is equally addressed to practical questions of contemporary political life. In large measure, it seems intended to provide practical guidance to leisured aristocrats, even—indeed, particularly—in regimes where they do not constitute a ruling class.[38] As regards the question of dating, there are no historical references in the *Politics* that require a date prior to Aristotle's Lyceum period, and book 2 appears to contain two allusions to events of the year 333.[39] More importantly, the attention given throughout the work to democracy strongly suggests that its primary audience was an Athenian one.

There remains the question of the textual condition of the *Politics*, particularly as regards the order of its books. The chief difficulties are that book 3 breaks off with a sentence which is repeated practically verbatim at the beginning of book 7, that the brief chapter concluding it (3. 18) provides a very problematic transition between books 3 and 4 but makes sense as an introduction to book 7, and that book 4 appears in several places to refer back to the discussion of the best regime in books 7–8. In addition, it is obvious that the last book is incomplete as it stands, and the same seems to be true of book 6.

15

I believe that the most satisfactory solution is to recognize that books 7 and 8 do indeed belong between books 3 and 4, and to understand the dislocation as the result of a mechanical accident rather than as the work of Aristotle or a later editor such as Andronicus. It is customary to assume that the *Politics* was left by Aristotle in an unfinished state. Yet such a view does little to explain the frequency and specificity of forward references not satisfied by the existing text (particularly when they occur in "early" strata of the work), and the fact that the missing material can generally be brought into plausible relation with the existing portions of book 6 and 8 lends strong support to an explanation of the kind suggested. That the book rolls constituting the original *Politics* could have been exposed to disturbance and damage is certainly plausible given the history of Aristotle's library, and the fact that the *Politics* seems to have remained wholly unknown throughout the Hellenistic period suggests that it was indeed among the works recovered from Scepsis. It is also possible that an accident could have occurred in the course of the political disorders taking place in Athens at relatively frequent intervals in the period following Aristotle's death. Since these disturbances resulted from attempted Athenian resistance to Macedonian domination, and since the Lyceum was known for its close ties with Macedon, it would not be remarkable if the Lyceum had become the target of occasional public hostility. And, in fact, there is evidence that the interior of the school suffered damage not long before the death of Theophrastus—probably in connection with the anti-Macedonian revolt of 288.[40]

It is worthwhile considering briefly the cross-references within the *Politics*. Jaeger appeals to these references in order to establish the unity and early date of books 2–3 and 7–8, but he is able to do so only by arguing that references to book 1 in 3 and 7 are later additions by an editor. Moreover, Jaeger overlooks a reference in 2 which is almost certainly to 4,[41] as well as a reference in 1 to a lost discussion that would seem to have belonged originally within the "inquiry" of 7–8. The latter passage is peculiarly important with respect both to Jaeger's argument and to the organization of the *Politics* generally, as it indicates that books 7–8 should be viewed as belonging to a larger unit—termed by Aristotle "the [discourses] connected with the regimes"—which would appear to contain 4–6.[42] As was noted earlier, there are several references in 4 to a previous discussion of "aristocracy" which can only be sensibly interpreted as applying to the discussion of the best regime in 7–8.[43] Finally, it may be observed that most of the forward references not satisfied by our current text seem to point to a very extensive discussion originally following book 8 on the general subject of education and the household.[44]

Some remarks are in order at this point concerning the question of interpolation in the text of the *Politics* and in Aristotle's writings generally. Since Jaeger, it has been fashionable to regard as misguided the attempts of philologists of the last century to identify passages of doubtful authenticity in the Aristotelian corpus. Jaeger's assumption that inconsistencies and anomalies existing in a work composed over a period of time would have been over-looked or permitted to stand by Aristotle is not, however, inherently persuasive, at least if such a work is to be imagined as being in continuous use for purposes of teaching and research. The fact that inconsistencies and anomalies do exist in fact is therefore a strong argument in favor of assuming non-Aristotelian authorship in cases where interpretation is otherwise baffled. If Aristotle's treatises indeed served not only as lecture notes but as reference works for students, there is every reason to suppose that, once no longer controlled and used by Aristotle himself, they would come to be annotated with glosses and addenda of various sorts.

Although proof in such matters is difficult or impossible, the *Politics* would appear to contain a number of passages of the kind just described. In general, the endings of books are likely places for interpolation, and there are lengthy passages at the end of books 2 and 5 that arouse suspicion; the final paragraph of book 8 is also highly dubious. Historical and schematic excursions in the manner of the later Peripatos must also be questioned, particularly if they are not clearly related to the main line of argument. The eleventh chapter of book 1 is perhaps the most important instance of such a passage, but there are others of varying length scattered throughout the *Politics*.[45]

While it is necessary to recognize the existence of these and other textual problems in the *Politics*, there would appear to be little basis for the wholesale transpositions, reconstructions, and excisions practiced on Aristotle's text by some nineteenth-century scholars. Generally speaking, the text of the *Politics* is in good condition, the style and texture are very much of a piece, and the overall argument is consistent to a high degree, though the organization of the work as a whole and the various turns of the argument give rise to many questions. In this sense, at any rate, the *Politics* may for all practical purposes be considered and read as a book—a book composed by a single author over a continuous period and governed by a single conception of its subject matter.

III

It remains to clarify and elaborate what has been said concerning the character of Aristotle's "political science," and to consider the relationship between the *Politics* and Aristotle's ethical writings as well as the work of his predecessors. An understanding of the intention and scope of Aristotle's enterprise is essential if the *Politics* is to be appreciated in its own terms rather than on the basis of current preconceptions of the nature of its subject.

Aristotle distinguishes in several places between three fundamental types of science or knowledge (*epistēmē*): theoretical science, practical science, and productive science or "art" (*technē*).[46] This distinction is nowhere systematically developed, however, and Aristotle's conception of practical science in particular remains a matter of controversy. Generally speaking, practical science appears to differ from theoretical science in its objects, its method, its

17

purpose, and the faculty it engages. The objects of theoretical science are things not subject to change, or things of which the principle of change lies in themselves; its method is analysis of the principles or causes of things and demonstration based on those principles or causes; its purpose is knowledge or understanding; its faculty is the scientific or theoretical portion of the rational part of the soul. Among the theoretical sciences recognized and pursued by Aristotle are metaphysics or theology, mathematics, physics, biology, and the science of the soul. Man is an object of several of these sciences under a variety of aspects. Man is uniquely the object of the practical sciences, but only insofar as he is a subject or cause of "action" (praxis). The objects of the practical sciences are the things acted upon or done (ta prakta) by man; because they depend on human volition, these things are essentially changeable. The purpose of the practical science is not knowledge but the betterment of action; its characteristic faculty is the calculative or practical segment of the rational part of the soul, or what Aristotle terms "prudence" (phronēsis). As for the method of the practical sciences, while it is difficult to summarize with any confidence Aristotle's sparse and cryptic statements on this subject, he appears to conceive it as a mode of analysis leading not to an understanding of causes so much as to clarification of the phenomena of human action, through a dialectical examination and refinement of men's opinions concerning those phenomena.[47]

At all events, it is a mistake to expect Aristotle's practical or political writings to display the same degree of conceptual precision that can be found in his theoretical works. Aristotle expressly cautions against demanding such precision on account of the inherent uncertainty and variability of matters of action.[48] Accordingly, he does not proceed by deduction from immutable principles of human nature or laws of human behavior, and he retains the language and respects the manner of thinking of ordinary political men. Aristotle's frequent reliance on dialectical argumentation—that is, on a quasi-conversational mode of inquiry that begins from the probable premises embedded in common opinion—must be understood in relation to the purpose of practical science. Precisely because practical science is in the service of action, it must be centrally concerned with the presentation of its subject in a way that will engage and affect the opinions of its audience. This is not to say that practical science is in no way related to theoretical science as Aristotle conceives it. In several passages, he indicates that "theoretical philosophy" will have a place in his practical writings wherever it is proper to the inquiry, and his argument is informed throughout by assumptions deriving from theoretical psychology in particular. Equally clear, however, is Aristotle's view that practical science cannot or should not depend directly on theoretical science. At least part of the reason for this view appears to lie in Aristotle's certainty that men of experience and practical ability are constitutionally vulnerable to the influence of philosophical arguments put forward by intellectuals lacking practical intelligence.[49] Anticipating, it would seem, the invasion of politics by theory in modern times, Aristotle insists on preserving an area of autonomy for "prudence," the intellectual virtue proper to political men.[50]

The most extensive treatment of prudence and practical science occurs in book 6 of the *Nicomachean Ethics*. There Aristotle indicates that practical science is in a sense coextensive with both prudence and political science (*politikē*). Practical or political science has three main branches: ethics or the science of character, the science of household management, and political science in a more proper sense. It is of the utmost importance to bear in mind that the science of character is considered by Aristotle an integral part of political science in its broadest sense. For Aristotle, the good of the individual cannot be conceptually separated from the good of the community; political science is the "architectonic" or master science of practice because it establishes the framework within which all individual action takes place, or more precisely, because the city or the regime necessarily affects in fundamental ways the private behavior of individuals. By the same token, it must be remembered that politics in the narrower sense necessarily involves or presupposes a consideration of the characters and virtues of individuals. The *Politics* is incomplete, then, not only in the mechanical sense discussed earlier, but in the more important sense that it forms one part of a larger inquiry.[51]

An interesting and difficult question is whether the *Politics* and Aristotle's ethical writings are wholly of a piece in terms of the mode of analysis and the audience for which they were intended. At one point in the *Politics*, Aristotle appears to refer to a passage in book 5 of the *Nicomachean Ethics* in a way that suggests that he distinguished between the ethical writings as "discourses based on philosophy" (*logoi kata philosophian*) and the *Politics* as a work of a more popular nature.[52] That the title given the *Politics* in the ancient book catalogues may point in the same direction was suggested earlier. The context of the reference is significant, since the issue under discussion—the nature of justice—is in fact more systematically and more fully treated in the ethical writings than in the *Politics*, where it might be thought more germane. It is entirely characteristic of the manner of the *Politics* that it contains no discussion of the just or right by nature; but such a discussion is provided, albeit in compressed form, in the ethical writings. It is also striking that the *Politics* is almost entirely devoid of methodological reflections. This fact would be easier to explain if it could be assumed that the *Politics* must be read as the second part of a single treatise on political science. Although the *Politics* appears to be referred to in the concluding paragraph of the *Nicomachean Ethics*, this passage is sufficiently problematic that it is by no means certain that such an assumption can be safely made.[53] A further complicating fact is that study of the references to Aristotle's ethical writings in the *Politics* (where the expression generally used is "our [discourses] on ethics") shows that all are demonstrably or arguably to the *Eudemian* rather than the *Nicomachean Ethics*, although there are no references in the *Eudemian Ethics* to the *Politics*.[54] It is probably best to assume that the *Politics* was composed by Aristotle as an independent work intended to be intelligible in its own terms without depending essentially on the ethical writings.

In book 6 of the *Nicomachean Ethics*, Aristotle suggests a further articulation of the content of political science which is of particular importance for understanding the scope and character of the discussion in the *Politics*. He distinguishes between an "architectonic" sort of prudence to which he gives the term "legislative" (*nomothetikē*), and a prudence concerned with particulars, of an "active and deliberative" sort, which he calls "political" in yet another sense of that term.[55] In the narrowest sense, it seems, *politikē* is the "political expertise" men acquire and manifest in dealing with the deliberative issues that are the stuff of everyday politics. Elsewhere, Aristotle repeats and elaborates this distinction. In a passage in the first book of the *Rhetoric*, he asserts that there are five important matters about which men particularly deliberate: revenues and expenditures, war and peace, defense of the territory, imports and exports, and legislation.[56] In regard to "legislation" (*nomothesia*), Aristotle makes the following remark: "the preservation of the city lies in its laws, so it is necessary to know how many kinds of regimes there are, which are advantageous to each sort of city, and through what things they are naturally apt to be destroyed—both of things proper to the regimes and of their opposites."[57]

It is clear from these passages that the inquiry contained in the *Politics* does not correspond to the full range of subjects belonging to political science or political expertise. Although there are scattered discussions throughout the *Politics* that touch on virtually all the subjects of political deliberation mentioned in the *Rhetoric*, Aristotle makes no attempt to deal with any of these subjects but the last in anything approaching a systematic fashion. Political science or political expertise in what may be called its operational sense must include some knowledge of (to substitute modern terminology for Aristotle's expressions) trade, finance, defense, and foreign policy; but it is not this knowledge that the *Politics* undertakes to provide. The science or expertise that Aristotle teaches in the *Politics* is limited to that category of political knowledge to which he gives the special name of legislation or legislative expertise.

It must be said at once that Aristotle's terminology is somewhat misleading. In the *Politics* itself, Aristotle makes clear that his primary interest is not laws or legislation as such, but only what one might call (again with a view to equivalent modern terminology) "constitutional law," or more generally, the legal and customary institutions and practices that define a city's political constitution or "regime" (*politeia*).[58] It is important to be clear on this point, as it is crucial to understanding the specific character and the originality of Aristotle's political teaching. Toward the end of the *Nicomachean Ethics*, Aristotle remarks on the absence in contemporary Greece of any genuine instruction in political or legislative expertise. As for those among the sophists who profess to offer it, "generally speaking," he says, "they do not even know what it is or what matters it concerns, for otherwise they would not have regarded it as the same as rhetoric or inferior to it, nor would they have supposed it is easy to legislate by collecting the most renowned laws."[59] The great defect of the sophistic approach to "legislation" is precisely its overconcentration on laws as such—that is, laws abstracted from the context of the regime. Legislation is not easy because cities differ in fundamental ways and because they give rise to a variety of regimes with fundamentally different requirements. Just as Aristotle is at pains to argue that rhetoric should be ministerial to a substantive science of politics from which its own effectiveness must in large measure derive,[60] so he insists that laws and institutions suit and support particular regimes. Not law but the regime is the fundamental political phenomenon.

The dissatisfaction Aristotle here expresses with the political science of his day would appear not to be limited to the sophists alone. When he goes on to remark that "since our predecessors [*hoi proteroi*] have left unexplored what concerns legislation, it is perhaps best if we investigate it ourselves, and in general therefore concerning the regime," Aristotle cannot be supposed to have forgotten that his predecessor and teacher had written a lengthy treatise on law. In his brief critique of Plato's *Laws* in the *Politics*, Aristotle notes that the *Laws* has little to say about the actual character of the regime it presents as the best practical political order.[61] Plato was by no means unaware of the phenomenon of the regime and its central importance for political analysis: "regime" is the Greek title of Plato's *Republic*, and books 8 and 9 of that work contain a detailed account of the varieties of existing regimes and their social and psychological bases. But the preoccupation of the *Republic* is a best regime whose realization Plato admits to be highly unlikely if not impossible, while the *Laws*, which is more concerned with the possible and practicable, makes little attempt to analyze the varieties of cities or societies and the regimes corresponding to them. In this sense, Aristotle can reasonably say that Plato left the subject of "legislation" unexplored, in spite of the fact that particular laws are elaborated and discussed in the *Laws* to an extent that the *Politics* does not begin to approach. Whatever Aristotle's final view of Plato's thinking on these questions, he is implicitly critical at least of its emphasis and manner of presentation. For Aristotle, the primary requirement of a practical science of politics is a knowledge of the varieties of regimes and of the things that create, support, preserve, and destroy them.

The fact that the *Politics* is devoted almost entirely to regimes of the polis is frequently taken as indicative of a certain narrowness of outlook or lack of imagination on Aristotle's part. It is surely a striking historical irony that the *Politics* was composed precisely during the period when Philip and Alexander of Macedon were constructing the basis of a new political order that would permanently eclipse the polis in its classical form. In spite of the personal association between Aristotle and the Macedonian royal house, there is little or no discussion in the *Politics* of the political possibilities of a semihellenized territorial monarchy along the lines of Macedon or its successor states. Was

Aristotle's preoccupation with the polis merely the expression of a blind nostalgia for a world already in the process of dissolution?

The evidence available to us in the *Politics* suggests that Aristotle's preference for the polis over other political forms rests on a thorough and carefully reasoned analysis of its advantages. While leaving open the theoretical possibility that monarchy might be the best form of government for an advanced society under certain conditions, Aristotle makes abundantly clear that monarchy is not naturally or normally suited to such a society. Why Aristotle did not devote more attention to monarchy and its various forms, or to states larger than the polis, is a different question, to which a number of answers are possible. It is not at all evident that Aristotle was convinced—or should have been convinced—that the extension of Macedonian imperialism represented an inexorable development or a permanent change in the political geography of the ancient world. It could also be that Aristotle did not believe such information was relevant to his (predominantly Athenian) audience, or that the subject was too sensitive politically given Aristotle's Macedonian ties and existing international realities.

To assume that Aristotle only mirrors or defends the historical phenomenon of the Greek city is, in any event, to make a fundamental error. In the first place, Aristotle makes quite plain that the polis is not an essentially Greek phenomenon: he treats the Phoenician colony of Carthage as superior in its form of government to virtually all existing Greek cities. Second, Aristotle maintains a resolute silence about many features of the Greek city that were of considerable historical importance. It suffices to refer to the matter of religion, which is almost entirely ignored in the *Politics* as we have it—in sharp contrast, for example, to the extensive treatment it receives in the *Laws* of Plato. Finally, Aristotle is highly critical throughout the *Politics* of both Athens and Sparta, the cities that had acted at various times as leaders and symbols of the two most powerful political tendencies in classical Greece. In the place of the narrow oligarchies and partisan democracies that dominated contemporary political practice, Aristotle holds up the alternative of the polity, the mixed regime that rests in the best case on a strong middle class. In the place of the Spartan model, which continued to dominate contemporary theorizing about politics, he holds up the alternative of a best regime ruled by a cultured aristocracy dedicated to the pursuits of peace and leisure rather than to war.

IV

It is the peculiar mark of greatness in a work of political theory that it speaks to the timeless requirements of human life while addressing the most pressing concerns of its time. The *Politics* exhibits this paradox in an acute form. For in spite of its deliberately "practical" and therefore contemporary orientation, the *Politics* succeeds in articulating large areas of the experience of political life with a richness and fidelity that is matched by few works written yesterday. For a variety of reasons, however, Aristotle's treatise on politics has not had the historical impact of many of his other writings, or of some other major works of political theory.

While little is known of the place accorded to the study of politics in the Peripatetic school after Aristotle's death, it does not appear to have been a prominent one. As has been mentioned, from all indications, the *Politics* itself was unknown during the Hellenistic period—quite possibly because it belonged to the part of Aristotle's library that found its way from Athens to the cellar in Scepsis. The rapid development at this time of monarchic states and ideologies no doubt served to dampen whatever interest there may have been in impartial analysis of the varieties of regimes. The *Politics* surfaced again at Rome in the first century B.C. by way of the edition of Andronicus, but seems to have attracted little notice—perhaps in part for similar reasons. No commentary on it survives from later antiquity. The emperor Julian shows knowledge of it, and in the fifth century the Neoplatonic philosopher Proclus undertook a refutation of the critique of Plato in its second book.[62] But other commentators of this period refer to the work in a way that indicates it was not available to them, and no further mention of it occurs until the eleventh century, in the writings of the Byzantine scholar Michael of Ephesus. Unlike most other works of Aristotle and Plato, the *Politics* did not reach the Arabic world, and thus had no impact on the great flowering of Arabic and Jewish philosophic thought in the eleventh and twelfth centuries.[63] Manuscripts of the *Politics* first arrived in the West from Byzantium only in the thirteenth century.

The first Latin translation of the *Politics* was produced around 1250 by William of Moerbeke at the request of Thomas Aquinas. Yet the comprehensive synthesis of Aristotle and Christian thought undertaken by Aquinas had no real place for politics in the Aristotelian sense, beginning as it did from the notion of a natural law that prescribes universal standards of moral and political action; and Aquinas did not attempt to challenge the prevailing forces favoring monarchic and imperial forms of governance. Aristotelian arguments were utilized, however, in the historic vindication of the independence of the Italian city-states against the Holy Roman Empire undertaken by the legist Bartolus of Saxoferrato; and the *Politics* would play a significant role in the revival of republican political thought in Italy throughout the early Renaissance.[64] But the most faithful and influential adaptation of the *Politics* within the context of Christian Europe was the work of Marsilius of Padua, the principal political thinker of the philosophical movement that has come to be known as Latin Averroism. Marsilius' *Defender of the Peace*, in its bold attack on the political role of the Church and the priesthood, anticipated by two centuries a key theme of the Protestant Reformation, and developed a theory of political sovereignty that has strikingly popular overtones.[65]

Marsilius' use of Aristotle was not initially helpful to the assimilation of the *Politics* to the dominant currents of political thinking in Europe. With the le-

23

gitimacy bestowed on all of Aristotle's works by Thomas Aquinas, however, the *Politics* eventually came to assume a prominent place in the traditional curriculum of philosophic studies as taught in universities throughout the continent, and as late as the middle of the eighteenth century it continued to be widely read.[66]

Yet what the *Politics* gained in academic respectability during this period, it lost in real intellectual authority and influence. The displacement of Aristotle as the authoritative exponent of practical or political philosophy in the West had begun in the early years of the sixteenth century, with Machiavelli's declaration that the "imagined republics and principalities" of the past could no longer be taken as a guide to political action, and his call for a new political science that would be firmly grounded in the "effectual truth" about man. The declining fortunes of republican government throughout the sixteenth and seventeenth centuries surely contributed to the eclipse of Aristotle's political teaching. The decisive factor, however, was the broad movement of thought inspired by Machiavelli and developed by such figures as Bacon, Hobbes, and Montesquieu, which would revolutionize men's understanding of politics and profoundly shape the character of modern societies. Under its impact, the *Politics* eventually ceased to be a work of living importance.

Because we are heirs to the modern movement, our categories of thought and our concerns differ in fundamental ways from the categories and concerns of Aristotle or of the classical philosophers generally. For this very reason, however, the encounter with Aristotle's *Politics* can provide an invaluable perspective on the intellectual underpinnings of modern political philosophy and its offspring, contemporary social science. It can certainly be questioned whether those early modern thinkers who sought to ground political action in self-interested motives and passions succeeded as well as has often been assumed in disposing of the arguments of their older rivals. Of all the classical political thinkers, Aristotle is the least open to the charge of utopianism. In their haste to identify a formula for politics that would be applicable to all circumstances and all men, the modern thinkers tended to forget and obscure the lessons Aristotle had so carefully taught concerning the essential diversity of human societies and the indispensability of prudent statesmanship. The moderns have not only proven unable to lay to rest the human impulses that stimulate utopian thinking, but have themselves fostered forms of utopianism more virulent and more destructive of sensible politics than anything known to the premodern world. From this point of view, Aristotelian political science—a political science that steers a deliberate course between "value-free" analysis of political phenomena and ideological prescription—provides an alternative model to current approaches that is of more than merely historical interest.

NOTE ON THE TEXT
AND TRANSLATION

The present translation differs from other versions of the *Politics* currently available by having as its aim to produce as literal and faithful a rendering of this frequently difficult work as is compatible with contemporary English usage. It is hoped that the advantages of this procedure for serious study of Aristotle's text are sufficiently obvious not to require elaborate justification, and are not outweighed by the inevitable loss in readability.

Except where a Greek word has more than one distinct meaning, I have translated key terms in the original by a single English word. In dealing with Aristotle's elliptical and compressed style, I have translated words not appearing in the text but clearly understood; in doubtful cases, and wherever it seemed desirable in order to improve the intelligibility of the translation, words or phrases elaborating the argument are added in square brackets. I have not always observed Aristotle's punctuation, and have not tried to reproduce in mechanical fashion the particles that contribute so much of the nuance in classical Greek; at the same time, I have made a serious effort to preserve the tone and style of the original, in the belief that the intention of Aristotle's work is not properly understood if it is meant to sound like a ponderous academic treatise. Obviously, the requirements of literalness have imposed limits on this effort, and on occasion have no doubt produced jarring effects not intended by the author.

I have tried as much as possible to avoid technical philosophical language or transliterations of Greek words. A glossary at the end of this volume is intended to provide the reader with working definitions of the key terms in Aristotle's philosophical-political vocabulary as well as a guide to linguistic relationships that are not always reflected in equivalent English terms.

Additional explanatory material is provided in the notes to the translation. I have generally resorted to annotation only to provide literary and historical references, to call attention to textual problems, and to supply such other information or interpretation as seems essential to the understanding of the argument. Scholarly commentaries and other secondary works on the *Politics* are not cited or discussed, though I have profited throughout from the labors of numerous learned predecessors.

The translation is based on the text of the *Politics* edited by

Alois Dreizehnter, *Aristoteles' Politik*, Studia et Testimonia Antiqua VII (Munich, 1970). I have, however, given fresh consideration to all important textual problems and variant readings, and have not hesitated to deviate from Dreizehnter where this seemed appropriate; all such deviations are indicated in the notes. Generally speaking, I have been more conservative than Dreizehnter in retaining the consensus reading of the manuscripts or of the best manuscripts (the family Π^2). At the same time, I have been readier to accept the existence of lacunae in the text, and in a number of passages I believe I have identified lacunae not previously noticed by scholars. Supplements are marked in the translation by square brackets.

The division of the text of the *Politics* by numbered chapters and sections and by paragraphs has no authority. The numbers in the margins of the translation refer to the pages, columns, and lines of the edition of Aristotle's works prepared for the Prussian Academy by Immanuel Bekker and published in Berlin in 1831.

ANALYSIS OF THE ARGUMENT

The analysis of the *Politics* provided here is intended for the convenience of the reader; the divisions of the argument and the titles assigned them are wholly the responsibility of the translator. Book and chapter numbers of the *Politics* are given in parentheses. The analysis follows the order of the books as they are found in the manscript tradition.

I. The City and the Household (Book 1)
    A. The City and Man (1. 1–2)
    B. The Household (1. 3–13)
        1. The household in general (1. 3)
        2. Slavery (1. 4–7)
        3. Property and business (1. 8–11)
        4. Household rule in general (1. 12–13)

II. Views concerning the Best Regime (Book 2)
    A. Best Regimes in Speech (2. 1–8)
        1. The regime of Plato's *Republic* (2. 1–5)
        2. The regime of Plato's *Laws* (2. 6)
        3. The regime of Phaleas of Chalcedon (2. 7)
        4. The regime of Hippodamus of Miletus (2. 8)
    B. Regimes Held to Be Well Managed (2. 9–11)
        1. The Spartan regime (2. 9)
        2. The Cretan regime (2. 10)
        3. The Carthaginian regime (2. 11)
    C. Regimes and Legislators (2. 12)

III. The City and the Regime (Book 3)
    A. Citizenship (3. 1–5)
        1. The citizen (3. 1–2)
        2. The identity of the city (3. 3)
        3. The good citizen and the good man (3. 4)
        4. The limits of citizenship (3. 5)
    B. Regimes and Their Basis (3. 6–8)
    C. The Nature of Political Justice (3. 9–13)
        1. The end of the city (3. 9)
        2. The claims to rule (3. 10)

The GREEK WORLD

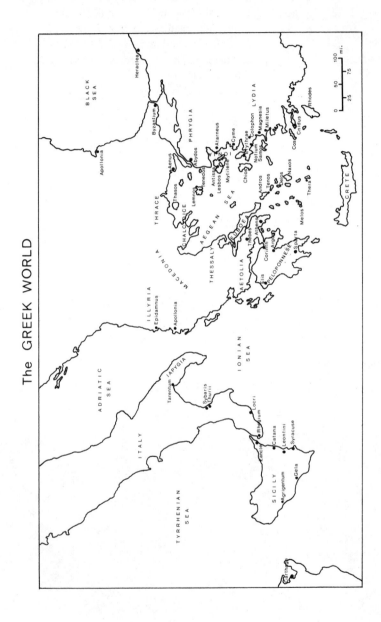

GREECE circa 330 B.C.

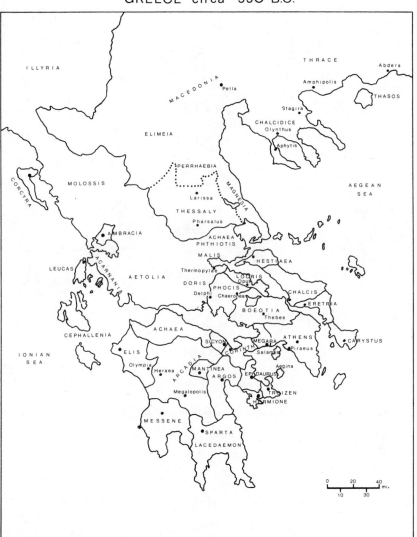

ILLYRIA

THRACE

Abdera

MACEDONIA

Pella

Amphipolis

THASOS

Stagira

CHALCIDICE

ELIMEIA

Olynthus

Aphytis

CORCYRA

MOLOSSIS

PERRHAEBIA

AEGEAN
SEA

MAGNESIA

Larissa

THESSALY

Pharsalus

AMBRACIA

ACHAEA
PHTHIOTIS

LEUCAS

MALIS

HESTIAEA

ACARNANIA

AETOLIA

Thermopylae

DORIS

LOCRIS
Opus

PHOCIS

CHALCIS

Delphi

Chaeronea

ERETRIA

BOEOTIA

Thebes

CEPHALLENIA

ACHAEA

SICYON

MEGARA

ATHENS

CARYSTUS

CORINTH

Piraeus

IONIAN
SEA

ELIS

Salamis

Olympia

ARCADIA

MANTINEA

Aegina

Heraea

ARGOS

EPIDAURUS

Megalopolis

TROIZEN

HERMIONE

MESSENE

SPARTA

LACEDAEMON

0   20   40
     mi.
  10   30

THE POLITICS

BOOK 1

CHAPTER 1

(1) Since we see that every city is some sort of partnership, and 1252a1 that every partnership is constituted for the sake of some good (for everyone does everything for the sake of what is held to be good), it is clear that all partnerships aim at some good, and that the partnership that is most authoritative of all and embraces all the others does so particularly, and aims at the most authoritative good of all. This is what is called the city or the political partnership.

(2) Those who suppose that the same person is expert in political [rule], kingly [rule], managing the household and being a master [of slaves] do not argue rightly.[1] For they consider that each of these differs in the multitude or fewness [of those ruled] and not in kind—for example, [the ruler] of a few is a master, of more a household manager, and of still more an expert in political or kingly [rule]—the assumption being that there is no difference between a large household and a small city; and as for the experts in political and kingly [rule], they consider an expert in kingly [rule] one who has charge himself, and in political [rule] one who, on the basis of the precepts of this sort of science, rules and is ruled in turn.[2] But these things are not true. (3) This will be clear to those investigating in accordance with our normal sort of inquiry.[3] For just as it is necessary elsewhere to divide a compound into its uncompounded elements (for these are the smallest parts of the whole), so too by investigating what the city is composed of we shall gain a better view concerning these [kinds of rulers] as well, both as to how they differ from one another and as to whether there is some expertise characteristic of an art that can be acquired in connection with each of those mentioned.

CHAPTER 2

(1) Now in these matters as elsewhere it is by looking at how things develop naturally from the beginning that one may best study them. (2) First, then, there must of necessity be a conjunc-

30

1252b1

5

10

15

20

25

tion of persons who cannot exist without one another: on the one hand, male and female, for the sake of reproduction (which occurs not from intentional choice but—as is also the case with the other animals and plants—from a natural striving to leave behind another that is like oneself); on the other, the naturally ruling and ruled, on account of preservation. For that which can foresee with the mind is the naturally ruling and naturally mastering element, while that which can do these things with the body is the naturally ruled and slave; hence the same thing is advantageous for the master and slave. (3) Now the female is distinguished by nature from the slave. For nature makes nothing in an economizing spirit, as smiths make the Delphic knife,[4] but one thing with a view to one thing; and each instrument would perform most finely if it served one task rather than many. (4) The barbarians, though, have the same arrangement for female and slave. The reason for this is that they have no naturally ruling element; with them, the partnership [of man and woman] is that of female slave and male slave. This is why the poets say "it is fitting for Greeks to rule barbarians"[5]— the assumption being that barbarian and slave are by nature the same thing.

(5) From these two partnerships, then, the household first arose, and Hesiod's verse is rightly spoken: "first a house, and woman, and ox for ploughing"[6]—for poor persons have an ox instead of a servant. The household is the partnership constituted by nature for [the needs of] daily life; Charondas calls its members "peers of the mess," Epimenides of Crete "peers of the manger."[7] The first partnership arising from [the union of] several households and for the sake of nondaily needs is the village. (6) By nature the village seems to be above all an extension of the household. Its members some call "milk-peers"; they are "the children and the children's children."[8] This is why cities were at first under kings, and nations are even now. For those who joined together were already under kings: every household was under the eldest as king, and so also were the extensions [of the household constituting the village] as a result of kinship. (7) This is what Homer meant when he says that "each acts as law to his children and wives"; for [men] were scattered and used to dwell in this manner in ancient times.[9] And it is for this reason that all assert that the gods are under a king—because they themselves are under kings now, or were in ancient times. For human beings assimilate not only the looks of the gods to themselves, but their ways of life as well.

(8) The partnership arising from [the union of] several villages that is complete is the city. It reaches a level of full self-sufficiency,

so to speak; and while coming into being for the sake of living, it exists for the sake of living well. Every city, therefore, exists by nature, if such also are the first partnerships. For the city is their end, and nature is an end: what each thing is—for example, a human being, a horse, or a household—when its coming into being is complete is, we assert, the nature of that thing. (9) Again, that for the sake of which [a thing exists], or the end, is what is best; and self-sufficiency is an end and what is best.

From these things it is evident, then, that the city belongs among the things that exist by nature, and that man is by nature a political animal. He who is without a city through nature rather than chance is either a mean sort or superior to man; he is "without clan, without law, without hearth," like the person reproved by Homer; (10) for the one who is such by nature has by this fact a desire for war, as if he were an isolated piece in a game of chess.[10] That man is much more a political animal than any kind of bee or any herd animal is clear. For, as we assert, nature does nothing in vain; and man alone among the animals has speech. (11) The voice indeed indicates the painful or pleasant, and hence is present in other animals as well; for their nature has come this far, that they have a perception of the painful and pleasant and indicate these things to each other. But speech serves to reveal the advantageous and the harmful, and hence also the just and the unjust. (12) For it is peculiar to man as compared to the other animals that he alone has a perception of good and bad and just and unjust and other things [of this sort]; and partnership in these things is what makes a household and a city.

The city is thus prior by nature to the household and to each of us. (13) For the whole must of necessity be prior to the part; for if the whole [body] is destroyed there will not be a foot or a hand, unless in the sense that the term is similar (as when one speaks of a hand made of stone), but the thing itself will be defective. Everything is defined by its task and its power, and if it is no longer the same in these respects it should not be spoken of in the same way, but only as something similarly termed. (14) That the city is both by nature and prior to each individual, then, is clear. For if the individual when separated [from it] is not self-sufficient, he will be in a condition similar to that of the other parts in relation to the whole. One who is incapable of participating or who is in need of nothing through being self-sufficient is no part of a city, and so is either a beast or a god.

(15) Accordingly, there is in everyone by nature an impulse toward this sort of partnership. And yet the one who first constituted [a city] is responsible for the greatest of goods. For just as man is

the best of the animals when completed, when separated from law and adjudication he is the worst of all. (16) For injustice is harshest when it is furnished with arms; and man is born naturally possessing arms for [the use of] prudence and virtue which are nevertheless very susceptible to being used for their opposites. This is why, without virtue, he is the most unholy and the most savage [of the animals], and the worst with regard to sex and food.[11] [The virtue of] justice is a thing belonging to the city. For adjudication is an arrangement of the political partnership,[12] and adjudication is judgment as to what is just.

CHAPTER 3

1253bl

(1) Since it is evident out of what parts the city is constituted, it is necessary first to speak of household management; for every city is composed of households. The parts of household management correspond to the parts out of which the household itself is constituted. Now the complete household is made up of slaves and free persons. Since everything is to be sought for first in its smallest elements, and the first and smallest parts of the household are master, slave, husband, wife, father, and children, three things must be investigated to determine what each is and what sort of thing it ought to be. (2) These are expertise in mastery, in marital [rule] (there is no term for the union of man and woman), and thirdly in parental [rule][13] (this too has not been assigned a term of its own). (3) So much, then, for the three we spoke of. There is a certain part of it, however, which some hold to be [identical with] household management, and others its greatest part; how the matter really stands has to be studied. I am speaking of what is called business expertise.

Let us speak first about master and slave, so that we may see at the same time what relates to necessary needs and whether we cannot acquire something in the way of knowledge about these things that is better than current conceptions. (4) For some hold that mastery is a kind of science, and that managing the household, mastery, and expertise in political and kingly [rule] are the same, as we said at the beginning. Others hold that exercising mastery is against nature; for [as they believe] it is by law that one person is slave and another free, there being no difference by nature, and hence it is not just, since it rests on force.

38

CHAPTER 4

(1) Now possessions are a part of the household, and expertise in acquiring possessions a part of household management (for without the necessary things it is impossible either to live or to live well); and just as the specialized arts must of necessity have their proper instruments if their work is to be performed, so too must the expert household manager. (2) Now of instruments some are inanimate and others animate—the pilot's rudder, for example, is an inanimate one, but his lookout an animate one; for the subordinate is a kind of instrument for the arts. A possession too, then, is an instrument for life, and one's possessions are the multitude of such instruments; and the slave is a possession of the animate sort. Every subordinate, moreover, is an instrument that wields many instruments, (3) for if each of the instruments were able to perform its work on command or by anticipation, as they assert those of Daedalus did, or the tripods of Hephaestus (which the poet says "of their own accord came to the gods' gathering"),[14] so that shuttles would weave themselves and picks play the lyre, master craftsmen would no longer have a need for subordinates, or masters for slaves. (4) Now the instruments mentioned are productive instruments, but a possession is an instrument of action. For from the shuttle comes something apart from the use of it, while from clothing or a bed the use alone. Further, since production and action differ in kind and both require instruments, these must of necessity reflect the same difference. (5) Life is action, not production; the slave is therefore a subordinate in matters concerning action.

A possession is spoken of in the same way as a part. A part is not only part of something else, but belongs wholly to something else; similarly with a possession. Accordingly, while the master is only master of the slave and does not belong to him, the slave is not only slave to the master but belongs wholly to him.

(6) What the nature of the slave is and what his capacity, then, is clear from these things. For one who does not belong to himself by nature but is another's, though a human being, is by nature a slave; a human being is another's who, though a human being, is a possession; and a possession is an instrument of action and separable [from its owner].

25

30

35

1254a1

5

10

15

CHAPTER 5

(1) Whether anyone is of this sort by nature or not, and whether it is better and just for anyone to be a slave or not, but rather all slavery is against nature, must be investigated next. It is not diffi-
20 cult either to discern [the answer] by reasoning or to learn it from what actually happens. (2) Ruling and being ruled belong not only among things necessary but also among things advantageous. And immediately from birth certain things diverge, some toward being ruled, others toward ruling. There are many kinds both of ruling and ruled [things], and the better rule is always that over
25 ruled [things] that are better, for example over a human being rather than a beast; (3) for the work performed by the better is better, and wherever something rules and something is ruled there is a certain work belonging to these together. For whatever is con-stituted out of a number of things—whether continuous or dis-
30 crete—and becomes a single common thing always displays a rul-ing and a ruled element; (4) this is something that animate things derive from all of nature, for even in things that do not share in life there is a sort of rule, for example in a harmony. But these matters perhaps belong to a more external sort of investigation.[15] But an animal is the first thing constituted out of soul and body, of
35 which the one is the ruling element by nature, the other the ruled. (5) It is in things whose condition is according to nature that one ought particularly to investigate what is by nature, not in things that are defective. Thus the human being to be studied is one whose state is best both in body and in soul—in him this is clear; for in the case of the depraved, or those in a depraved condition, the
1254bl body is often held to rule the soul on account of their being in a condition that is bad and unnatural.

(6) It is then in an animal, as we were saying, that one can first discern both the sort of rule characteristic of a master and political rule. For the soul rules the body with the rule characteristic of
5 a master, while intellect rules appetite with political and kingly rule; and this makes it evident that it is according to nature and advantageous for the body to be ruled by the soul, and the pas-sionate part [of the soul] by intellect and the part having reason, while it is harmful to both if the relation is equal or reversed. (7) The same holds with respect to man and the other animals:
10 tame animals have a better nature than wild ones, and it is better for all of them to be ruled by man, since in this way their preser-vation is ensured. Further, the relation of male to female is by na-

ture a relation of superior to inferior and ruler to ruled. The same must of necessity hold in the case of human beings generally. 15

(8) Accordingly, those who are as different [from other men] as the soul from the body or man from beast—and they are in this state if their work is the use of the body, and if this is the best that can come from them—are slaves by nature. For them it is better to be ruled in accordance with this sort of rule, if such is the case 20 for the other things mentioned. (9) For he is a slave by nature who is capable of belonging to another—which is also why he belongs to another—and who participates in reason only to the extent of perceiving it, but does not have it. (The other animals, not perceiving reason, obey their passions.[16]) Moreover, the need for them differs only slightly: bodily assistance in the necessary things is 25 forthcoming from both, from slaves and from tame animals alike.

(10) Nature indeed wishes to make the bodies of free persons and slaves different as well [as their souls]—those of the latter strong with a view to necessary needs, those of the former straight and useless for such tasks, but useful with a view to a political 30 way of life (which is itself divided between the needs of war and those of peace); yet the opposite often results, some having the bodies of free persons while others have the souls. It is evident, at any rate, that if they were to be born as different only[17] in body as the images of the gods, everyone would assert that those not so 35 favored merited being their slaves. (11) But if this is true in the case of the body, it is much more justifiable to make this distinction in the case of the soul; yet it is not as easy to see the beauty of the soul as it is that of the body. That some persons are free and 1255a1 others slaves by nature, therefore, and that for these slavery is both advantageous and just, is evident.

CHAPTER 6

(1) That those who assert the opposite are in a certain manner correct, however, is not difficult to see. Slavery and the slave are 5 spoken of in a double sense. There is also a sort of slave or enslaved person according to law, the law being a certain agreement by which things conquered in war are said to belong to the conquerors. (2) This [claim of] justice is challenged by many of those conversant with the laws—as they would challenge an orator—on 10 a motion of illegality,[18] on the grounds that it is a terrible thing if

what yields to force is to be enslaved and ruled by what is able to apply force and is superior in power. And there are some of the wise as well who hold this opinion, though some hold the other. (3) The cause of this dispute—and what makes the arguments converge—is that virtue, once it obtains equipment, is in a certain manner particularly able to apply force, and the dominant element is always preeminent in something that is good, so that it is held that there is no force without virtue, and that the dispute concerns only the justice of the matter; (4) for on this account some hold that justice consists in benevolence, while the others hold that this very thing, the rule of the superior, is just. At any rate, if these arguments are set on one side, the other arguments—which assume that what is better in virtue ought not to rule or be master—have neither strength nor persuasiveness.[19] (5) Those who regard the slavery that results from war as just adhere wholly, as they suppose, to a sort of justice (for law is just in a certain sense); yet at the same time they deny [implicitly that it is in fact always just]. For the beginnings of wars are not always just, and no one would assert that someone not meriting enslavement ought ever to be a slave. Otherwise, the result will be that those held to be the best born will become slaves and the offspring of slaves if they happen to be captured and sold. (6) Accordingly, they do not want to speak of these as slaves, but rather of barbarians. When they say this, however, they are in search of nothing other than the slave by nature of which we spoke at the beginning; for they must necessarily assert that there are some persons who are everywhere slaves, and others who are so nowhere. (7) It is the same way with good birth as well; for they consider themselves well born not only among their own but everywhere, but barbarians only at home—the assumption being that there is something well born and free simply, and something not simply [but relatively], as Theodectes' Helen says:

> As offshoot of divine roots on either side
> Who would dare call me serving-maid?[20]

(8) When they speak in this way, it is by nothing other than virtue or vice that they define what is slave and what is free, who well born and who ill born. For they claim that from the good should come someone good, just as a human being comes from a human being and a beast from beasts. But while nature wishes to do this, it is often unable to. (9) That there is some reason in the dispute, therefore, and that it is not [simply] the case that the ones are slaves by nature and the others free, is clear; and also that such a distinction does exist for some, where it is advantageous as well

as just for the one to be enslaved and the other to be master; and that the one ought to be ruled and other to rule, and to rule by the sort of rule that is natural for them, which is mastery, (10) while bad rule is disadvantageous for both. For the same thing is advantageous for the part and the whole and for body and soul, and the slave is a sort of part of the master—a part of his body, as it were, animate yet separate. There is thus a certain advantage—and even affection of slave and master for one another—for those [slaves] who merit being such by nature; but for those who do not merit it in this way but [who are slaves] according to law and by force, the opposite is the case.

CHAPTER 7

(1) It is evident from these things as well that mastery and political [rule] are not the same thing and that all the sorts of rule are not the same as one another, as some assert. For the one sort is over those free by nature, the other over slaves; and household management is monarchy (for every household is run by one alone), while political rule is over free and equal persons. (2) Now the master is so called not according to a science [he possesses] but through being a certain sort, and similarly with the slave and the free person. Yet there could be a science characteristic both of mastery and of slavery. The science characteristic of slavery would be the sort of thing provided through the education offered by the fellow in Syracuse—for someone there used to receive pay for teaching slave boys their regular serving chores; (3) and there might be additional learning in such matters, for example in cookery and other service of this type. For certain works are more honored or more necessary than others, and as the proverb has it, "slave before slave, master before master." [21] (4) All things of this sort, then, are sciences characteristic of slavery; but the science characteristic of mastery is expertise in using slaves, since the master is what he is not in the acquiring of slaves but in the use of them. This science has nothing great or dignified about it: the master must know how to command the things that the slave must know how to do. (5) Hence for those to whom it is open not to be bothered with such things, an overseer assumes this prerogative, while they themselves engage in politics or philosophy. Expertise in acquiring [slaves] is different from both of these—that is, the just sort of acquiring, which is like a certain kind of expertise in

10

15

20

25

30

35

40 war or hunting. Concerning slave and master, then, let the discussion stand thus.

CHAPTER 8

1256a1 (1) But let us examine generally, in accordance with our normal sort of approach, possessions as such and expertise in business, since the slave too turned out to be a part of one's possessions. In the first place, then, one might raise the question whether expertise in business is the same as expertise in household management, a part of it, or subordinate to it; and if subordinate, whether

5 it is so in the way expertise in making shuttles is to expertise in weaving, or in the way expertise in casting bronze is to expertise in sculpture. For these are not subordinate in the same way, but the one provides instruments, the other the matter. (2) (By the matter I mean the substance out of which some work is performed—for example, wool for the weaver or bronze for the

10 sculptor.) Now it is clear that expertise in household management is not the same as expertise in business, for it belongs to the latter to supply and the former to use. For what is the expertise that uses the things in the house if not expertise in household management? But whether expertise in business is a part of it or different in kind is a matter of dispute. (3) For if it belongs to the expert business-

15 man to discern how to get goods and possessions, and if possessions and wealth encompass many parts, [one must consider] in the first place whether expertise in farming is part of business expertise[22] or different in kind, and [whether this is the case for] the concern with sustenance generally and the possessions connected with it. (4) There are indeed many kinds of sustenance, and there-

20 fore many ways of life both of animals and of human beings. For it is impossible to live without sustenance, so that the differences in sustenance have made the ways of life of animals differ. (5) For of beasts some live in herds and others scattered—whichever is advantageous for their sustenance, on account of some of them

25 being carnivorous, some herbivorous, and some omnivorous; so that it is with a view to their convenience and their predilections in these matters that nature has determined their ways of life. And because the same thing is not pleasant to each [species of animal] according to nature but different things to different [species], among the carnivorous and the herbivorous themselves their ways of life differ from one another. (6) The same is the case for human

44

beings as well; for there are great differences in their ways of life. The idlest are nomads: they derive sustenance from tame animals without exertion and amid leisure, though as it is necessary for their herds to move about on account of their pastures, they are compelled to follow along with them, as if they were farming a living farm. (7) Others live from hunting, and different sorts from different sorts of hunting. Some, for example, live from piracy; others from fishing, if they dwell near lakes, marshes, rivers, or a sea that is suitable; others from birds or wild beasts. But the type of human being that is most numerous lives from the land and from cultivated crops.

(8) The ways of life are, then, about this many, or at least those which involve self-generated work and do not supply sustenance through exchange and commerce: the way of life of the nomad, the farmer, the pirate, the fisher, and the hunter. There are also some who live pleasantly by combining several of these in order to compensate for the shortcomings of one way of life, where it happens to be deficient with regard to being self-sufficient. For example, some combine the nomad's with the pirate's, some the farmer's with the hunter's, and similarly with others as well—they pass their time in the manner that need [together with pleasure] compels them to. (9) Now possessions of this sort are evidently given by nature itself to all [animals], both immediately from birth and when they have reached completion. (10) For at birth from the very beginning some animals provide at the same time as much sustenance as is adequate until the offspring can supply itself—for example, those that give birth to larvae or eggs; while those that give birth to live offspring have sustenance for these in themselves for a certain period—the natural substance called milk. (11) It is clear in a similar way, therefore, that for grown things as well one must suppose both that plants exist for the sake of animals and that the other animals exist for the sake of human beings—the tame animals, both for use and sustenance, and most if not all of the wild animals, for sustenance and other assistance, in order that clothing and other instruments may be got from them.[23] (12) If, then, nature makes nothing that is incomplete or purposeless, nature must necessarily have made all of these for the sake of human beings.

Hence expertise in war will also be in some sense a natural form of acquisitive expertise; for one part of it is expertise in hunting, which should be used with a view both to beasts and to those human beings who are naturally suited to be ruled but unwilling—this sort of war being by nature just. (13) One kind of acquisitive expertise, then, is by nature a part of expertise in

30

35

40

1256b1

5

10

15

20

25

household management, and must either be available or be supplied by the latter so as to be available—[expertise in acquiring] those goods a store of which is both necessary for life and useful for partnership in a city or a household.[24] (14) At any rate, it

30 would seem to be these things that make up genuine wealth. For self-sufficiency in possessions of this sort with a view to a good life is not limitless, as Solon asserts it to be in his poem: "of wealth no boundary lies revealed to men."[25] (15) There is such a boundary, just as in the other arts; for there is no art that has an

35 instrument that is without limit either in number or in size, and wealth is the multitude of instruments belonging to expert household managers and political [rulers]. That there is a natural expertise in acquisition for household managers and political [rulers], then, and the cause of this, is clear.

CHAPTER 9

40 (1) But there is another type of acquisitive expertise that they particularly call—and justifiably so—expertise in business, on ac-

1257a1 count of which there is held to be no limit to wealth and possessions. This is considered by many to be one and the same as the sort mentioned because of the resemblance between them; and while it is not the same as the one spoken of, it is not far from it either. The one is by nature, while the other is not by nature but

5 arises rather through a certain experience and art.

(2) Concerning this, let us take the following as our beginning. Every possession has a double use. Both of these uses belong to it as such, but not in the same way, the one being proper and the other not proper to the thing. In the case of footwear, for example, one can wear it or one can exchange it. Both of these are uses of

10 footwear; (3) for the one exchanging footwear with someone who needs it in return for money or sustenance uses footwear as footwear, but not in respect of its proper use; for it did not come to be for the sake of exchange. The same is the case concerning other possessions as well. (4) For there is an expertise in exchange for

15 all things; it arises in the first place from something that is according to nature—the fact that human beings have either more or fewer things than what is adequate. Thus it is also clear that expertise in commerce does not belong by nature to expertise in business; for it was necessary to make an exchange in order to obtain what was adequate for them. (5) In the first partnership,

then—that is, the household—it is evident that exchange has no   20
function, but only when the partnership has already become more
numerous. For those [in the household] were partners in their own
things, while persons separated [into different households] were
partners in many things of others as well, and it was necessary to
make transfers of these things according to their needs, as many
barbarian nations still do, through exchange. (6) For they ex-   25
change useful things for one another and nothing besides—giving, for example, wine and accepting grain, and similarly for
other such things. This sort of expertise in exchange is not contrary to nature, nor is it any kind of expertise in business, for it
existed in order to support natural self-sufficiency. (7) However,   30
the latter arose from it reasonably enough. For as the assistance of
foreigners became greater in importing what they were in need
of and exporting what was in surplus, the use of money was necessarily devised. (8) For the things necessary by nature are not in
each case easily portable; hence with a view to exchanges they
made a compact with one another to give and accept something   35
which was itself one of the useful things and could be used flexi-
bly to suit the needs of life, such as iron and silver and whatever
else might be of this sort. At first this was something [with its
value] determined simply by size and weight, but eventually they
impressed a mark on it in order to be relieved of having to mea-   40
sure it, the mark being put on as an indication of the amount.
(9) Once a supply of money came into being as a result of such
necessary exchange, then, the other kind of expertise in business 1257bl
arose—that is, commerce. At first this probably existed in a simple fashion, while later through experience it became more a
matter of art—[the art of discerning] what and how to exchange
in order to make the greatest profit. (10) It is on this account that   5
expertise in business is held to be particularly connected with
money, and to have as its task the ability to discern what will
provide a given amount [of it]; for it is held to be productive of
wealth and goods. Indeed, they often define wealth as a given
amount of money, since this is what expertise in business or commerce is connected with. (11) At other times, however, money   10
seems to be something nonsensical and [to exist] altogether [by]
law, and in no way by nature, because when changed by its users
it is worth nothing and is not useful with a view to any of the necessary things; and it will often happen that one who is wealthy in
money will go in want of necessary sustenance. Yet it would be
absurd if wealth were something one could have in abundance and   15
die of starvation—like the Midas of the fable, when everything
set before him turned into gold on account of the greediness of his

prayer. (12) Hence they seek another [definition] of wealth and expertise in business, and correctly so. For the expertise in business and the wealth that is according to nature is something different: this is expertise in household management, while the other is commercial expertise, which is productive of wealth not in every way but through trafficking in goods, and is held to be connected with money, since money is the medium and goal of exchange. (13) And the wealth deriving from this sort of business expertise is indeed without limit. For just as expertise in medicine has no limit with respect to being healthy, or any of the other arts with respect to its end (for this is what they particularly wish to accomplish), while there is a limit with respect to what exists for the sake of the end (since the end is a limit in the case of all of them), so with this sort of expertise in business there is no limit with respect to the end, and the end is wealth of this sort and possession of goods. (14) But of expertise in household management as distinguished from expertise in business there is a limit; for that is not the work of expertise in household management. Thus in one way it appears necessary that there be a limit to all wealth; yet if we look at what actually occurs we see that the opposite happens—all who engage in business increase their money without limit. (15) The cause of this is the nearness to one another of these [forms of expertise in business]. For they converge in the matter of use, the same thing being used in the case of either sort of expertise in business. For possessions serve the same use,[26] though not in the same respect, but in the one case the end is increase, in the other something else. So some hold that this is the work of expertise in household management, and they proceed on the supposition that they should either preserve or increase without limit their property in money. (16) The cause of this state is that they are serious about living, but not about living well; and since that desire of theirs is without limit, they also desire what is productive of unlimited things. Even those who also aim at living well seek what conduces to bodily gratifications, and since this too appears to be available in and through possessions, their pursuits are wholly connected with business, and this is why the other kind of business expertise has arisen. (17) For as gratification consists in excess, they seek the sort that is productive of the excess characteristic of gratification; and if they are unable to supply it through expertise in business, they attempt this in some other fashion, using each sort of capacity in a way not according to nature. For it belongs to courage to produce not goods but confidence; nor does this belong to military or medical expertise, but it belongs to the former to produce victory, to the latter, health. (18) But all of these they make forms of expertise in business, as if this were the end and everything else had to march toward it.

Concerning the unnecessary sort of expertise in business, then, both as regards what it is and why we are in need of it, enough has been said; and also concerning the necessary sort—that it is different from the other, being expertise in household management according to nature (the sort connected with sustenance), and is not without limit like the other, but has a defining principle. 15

CHAPTER 10

(1) It is also clear what the answer is to the question raised at the beginning whether business expertise belongs to the expert household manager or political [ruler] or not, but should rather be available to him. For just as political expertise does not create human beings but makes use of them after receiving them from nature, so also should nature provide land or sea or something else for sustenance, while it befits the household manager to have what comes from those things in the state it should be in. (2) For it does not belong to expertise in weaving to make wool, but to make use of it, and to know what sort is usable and suitable or poor and unsuitable. Otherwise one might raise the question why expertise in business should be a part of household management but not medical expertise, since those in the household ought to be healthy, just as they must live or do any other necessary thing. (3) But just as seeing about health does indeed belong to the household manager and the ruler in a sense, but in another sense not but rather to the doctor, so in the case of goods it belongs to the household manager in a sense, but in another sense not but rather to the subordinate expertise. This should be available above all, as was said before, by nature. For it is a work of nature to provide sustenance to the newly born, everything deriving sustenance from what remains of that from which it is born. (4) Expertise in business relative to crops and animals is thus natural for all. But since it is twofold, as we said, part of it being commerce and part expertise in household management, the latter necessary and praised, while expertise in exchange is justly blamed since it is not according to nature but involves taking from others, usury is most reasonably hated because one's possessions derive from money itself and not from that for which it was supplied. (5) For it came into being for the sake of exchange, but interest actually creates more of it. And 20 25 30 35 40 1258b1

5   it is from this that it gets its name: offspring are similar to those who give birth to them, and interest is money born of money.[27] So of the sorts of business this is the most contrary to nature.

CHAPTER 11

(1) Since we have discussed adequately what relates to knowl-
10   edge, what relates to practice must be treated. All things of this sort have room for a free sort of study, but experience in them is a necessity. The useful parts of expertise in business are: to be experienced regarding livestock—what sorts are most profitable in which places and under what conditions (for example, what sort of horses or cattle or sheep ought to be kept, and similarly with the other animals, (2) for one needs to be experienced as regards
15   those that are most profitable both compared with one another and in particular places, since different kinds thrive in different areas); next, regarding farming, both of grain and fruit; and finally, regarding beekeeping and the raising of other animals, whether fish or fowl, from which it is possible to derive benefit. (3) Of expertise in business in its most proper sense, then, these are the parts
20   and primary elements. Of expertise in exchange the greatest part is trade, of which there are three parts: provisioning the ship, transport, and marketing (these differ from each other by the fact that some are safer while others provide greater remuneration); the second is moneylending; and the third is wage labor, (4) of
25   which one sort involves the vulgar arts, while the other [is performed by] those who lack any art but are useful only for their bodies. There is a third kind of expertise in business between this and the first, since it has some part both of the sort that is according to nature and of expertise in exchange: [this deals with] things
30   from the earth and unfruitful but useful things that grow from the earth, [and includes activities] such as lumbering and every sort of mining (5) (this now encompasses many different types, as there are many kinds of things mined from the earth).

      A general account has now been given of each of these things; a detailed and exact discussion would be useful in undertaking
35   the works themselves, but to spend much time on such things is crude. (6) The most artful of these works are those which involve chance the least; the most vulgar, those in which the body is most damaged; the most slavish, those in which the body is most used; the most ignoble, those which are least in need of virtue.

50

(7) Since some have written on these matters—as Chares of Paros and Apollodoros of Lemnos on farming both of grain and fruit, for example, and others on other things—they may be studied there by anyone concerned with them; but, in addition, what has been said in various places concerning the ways some have succeeded in business should be collected.[28] (8) For all these things are useful for those who honor expertise in business. There is, for example, the [way] of Thales of Miletus.[29] This is a business scheme which is attributed to him on account of his wisdom, yet it happens to be general in application. (9) For they say that when some on account of his poverty reproached him with the uselessness of philosophy, Thales, observing through his knowledge of astronomy that there would be a good harvest of olives, was able during the winter to raise a small sum of money to place in deposit on all the olive presses in both Miletus and Chios, which he could hire at a low rate because no one was competing with him; then, when the season came, and many of them were suddenly in demand at the same time, he hired them out on what terms he pleased and collected a great deal in the way of funds, thus showing how easy it is for philosophers to become wealthy if they so wish, but it is not this they are serious about. (10) Thales, then, is said to have made a display of his wisdom in this manner, though, as we said, this piece of business expertise is universal, if someone is able to establish a monopoly for himself. Thus even some cities raise revenue in this way when they are short of funds; they establish a monopoly on things being sold. (11) In Sicily, a man used some money deposited with him to buy all the iron from the iron foundries, and when traders came from their trading places he alone had it to sell; and though he did not greatly increase the price, he made a hundred talents' profit out of an original fifty. (12) When Dionysius heard of this, he ordered him to take his funds and leave Syracuse, on the grounds that he had discovered a way of raising revenue that was harmful to Dionysius' own affairs.[30] Yet the insight was the same as that of Thales, for both artfully arranged a monopoly for themselves. (13) It is useful for political [rulers] also to be familiar with these things. For many cities need business and revenues of this sort, just as households do, yet more so. Thus there are some even among those engaged in politics who are concerned only with these matters.

40

1259a1

5

10

15

20

25

30

35

51

CHAPTER 12

(1) Since there are three parts of expertise in household management—expertise in mastery, which was spoken of earlier, expertise in paternal [rule], and expertise in marital [rule]—[the latter two must now be taken up. These differ fundamentally from the former, since one ought][31] to rule a wife and children as free persons, though it is not the same mode of rule in each case, the wife being ruled in political, the children in kingly fashion. For the male, unless constituted in some respect contrary to nature, is by nature more expert at leading than the female, and the elder and complete than the younger and incomplete. (2) In most political offices, it is true, there is an alternation of ruler and ruled, since they tend by their nature to be on an equal footing and to differ in nothing; all the same, when one rules and the other is ruled, [the ruler] seeks to establish differences in external appearance, forms of address, and prerogatives, as in the story Amasis told about his footpan.[32] The male always stands thus in relation to the female. (3) But rule over the children is kingly. For the one who generates is ruler on the basis of both affection and age, which is the very mark of kingly rule. Homer thus spoke rightly of Zeus when he addressed as "father of men and gods" the king of them all. For by nature the king should be different, but he should be of the same stock; and this is the case of the elder in relation to the younger and the one who generates to the child.

CHAPTER 13

(1) It is evident, then, that household management gives more serious attention to human beings than to inanimate possessions, to the virtue of these than that of possessions (which we call wealth), and to the virtue of free persons rather than that of slaves. (2) First, then, one might raise a question concerning slaves: whether there is a certain virtue belonging to a slave besides the virtues of an instrument and a servant and more honorable than these, such as moderation and courage and justice and the other dispositions of this sort, or whether there is none besides the bodily services. (3) Questions arise either way, for if there is [such a virtue], how will they differ from free persons? But if there is not, though they are human beings and participate in reason, it is odd. Nearly the

same question arises concerning a woman and a child, whether
there are virtues belonging to these as well—whether the woman   30
should be moderate and courageous and just, and whether a child
is [capable of being] licentious and moderate or not. (4) And in
general, then, this must be investigated concerning the ruled by
nature and the ruler, whether virtue is the same or different. For if
both should share in gentlemanliness, why should the one rule
and the other be ruled once and for all? For it is not possible for   35
them to differ by greater and less, since being ruled and ruling
differ in kind, not by greater and less; (5) but that one should
[have such virtue] and the other not would be surprising. For unless the ruler is moderate and just, how will he rule finely? And
unless the ruled is, how will he be ruled finely? For if he is licentious and cowardly he will perform none of his duties. It is evident, then, that both must of necessity share in virtue, but that   1260a1
there are differences in their virtue, as there are in [that of] those
who are by nature ruled. (6) Consideration of the soul guides us
straightway [to this conclusion]. For in this there is by nature a   5
ruling and a ruled element, and we assert there is a different virtue of each—that is, of the element having reason and of the irrational element. It is clear, then, that the same thing holds in the
other cases as well. Thus by nature most things are ruling and
ruled. (7) For the free person rules the slave, the male the female,
and the man the child in different ways. The parts of the soul are   10
present in all, but they are present in a different way. The slave is
wholly lacking the deliberative element; the female has it but it
lacks authority; the child has it but it is incomplete. (8) It is to be
supposed that the same necessarily holds concerning the virtues
of character: all must share in them, but not in the same way, but   15
to each in relation to his own work. Hence the ruler must have
complete virtue of character (for a work belongs in an absolute
sense to the master craftsman, and reason is a master craftsman);
while each of the others must have as much as falls to him. (9) It is
thus evident that there is a virtue of character that belongs to all   20
these mentioned, and that the moderation of a woman and a man
is not the same, nor their courage or justice, as Socrates supposed, but that there is a ruling and a serving courage, and similarly with the other virtues. (10) This is further clear if we investi- 25
gate the matter in more detail. For those who say in a general way
that virtue is a good condition of the soul or acting correctly or
something of this sort deceive themselves. Those who enumerate
the virtues, like Gorgias, do much better than those who define it
in this way.[33] (11) One should thus consider that matters stand with
everyone as the poet said of woman: "to a woman silence is an

ornament," [34] though this is not the case for a man. Since the child is incomplete, it is clear that its virtue too is not its own as relating to itself, but as relating to its end and the person leading it. (12) The same is true of that of the slave in relation to a master. We laid it down that the slave is useful with respect to the necessary things, so that he clearly needs only a small amount of virtue—as much as will prevent him from falling short in his work through licentiousness or cowardice. One might raise the question whether, if what has just been said is true, artisans too will need virtue, since they often fall short in their work through licentiousness. (13) Or is the case very different? For the slave is a partner in [the master's] life, while the other is more remote, and shares in virtue only so far as he also shares in slavery. For the vulgar artisan is under a special sort of slavery, and while the slave belongs among those [persons or things that are] by nature, no shoemaker does, nor any of the other artisans. (14) It is evident, therefore, that the master should be responsible for [instilling] this sort of virtue in the slave; he is not merely someone possessing an expertise in mastery which instructs the slave in his work. Those who deny reason to slaves and assert that commands only should be used with them do not argue rightly: admonition is to be used with slaves more than with children. (15) But concerning these matters let our discussion stand thus. Concerning husband and wife and children and father and the sort of virtue that is connected with each of these, and what is and what is not fine in their relations with one another and how one should pursue what is well and avoid the bad, these things must necessarily be addressed in the [discourses] connected with the regimes. [35] For since the household as a whole is a part of the city, and these things of the household, and one should look at the virtue of the part in relation to the virtue of the whole, both children and women must necessarily be educated looking to the regime, at least if it makes any difference with a view to the city's being excellent that both its children and its women are excellent. (16) But it necessarily makes a difference: women are a part amounting to a half of the free persons, and from the children come those who are partners in the regime. So since there has been discussion of these matters, and we must speak elsewhere of those remaining, let us leave off the present discourses as having reached an end and make another beginning to the argument. Let us investigate in the first instance the views that have been put forward about the best regime.

BOOK 2

CHAPTER 1

(1) Since it is our intention to study the sort of political partnership that is superior to all for those capable of living as far as possible in the manner one would pray for, we should also investigate other regimes, both those in use in some of the cities that are said 30
to be well managed and any others spoken about by certain persons that are held to be in a fine condition, in order that both what is correct in their condition and what is useful may be seen—and further, that to seek something apart from them may not be held wholly to belong to those who wish to act the sophist, but that we may be held to enter into this inquiry because those regimes now available are in fact not in a fine condition. (2) We must make a 35
beginning that is the natural beginning for this investigation. It is necessary that all the citizens be partners either in everything, or in nothing, or in some things but not in others. Now it is evident that to be partners in nothing is impossible; for the regime is a certain sort of partnership, and it is necessary in the first instance 40
to be partners in a location: a single city occupies a single location, and the citizens are partners in the single city. (3) But, of the things in which there can be participation, is it better for the city 1261a1
that is going to be finely administered to participate in all of them, or is it better to participate in some but not in others? For it is possible for the citizens to be partners with one another in respect 5
to children and women and property, as in the *Republic* of Plato; for there Socrates asserts that children and women and property should be common.[1] Which is better, then, the condition that exists now or one based on the law that is described in the *Republic*?

CHAPTER 2

(1) Having women common to all involves many difficulties; but a 10
particular difficulty is that the reason Socrates gives as to why there should be legislation of this sort evidently does not result

from his arguments. Further, with respect to the end which he asserts the city should have, it is, as has just been said, impossible; but how one should distinguish [a sense in which it is possible] is not discussed. (2) I mean, that it is best for the city to be as far as possible entirely one; for this is the presupposition Socrates adopts. And yet it is evident that as it becomes increasingly one it will no longer be a city. For the city is in its nature a sort of multitude, and as it becomes more a unity it will be a household instead of a city, and a human being instead of a household; for we would surely say that the household is more a unity than the city, and the individual than the household. So even if one were able to do this, one ought not do it, as it would destroy the city. (3) Now the city is made up not only of a number of human beings, but also of human beings differing in kind: a city does not arise from persons who are similar. A city is different from an alliance. The latter is useful by its quantity, even if [its parts are] the same in kind (since an alliance exists by nature for mutual assistance), as when a greater weight is added to the scale. In this sort of way, too, a city differs from a nation, when the multitude is not separated in villages but rather is like the Arcadians.[2] Those from whom a unity should arise differ in kind. (4) It is thus reciprocal equality which preserves cities, as was said earlier in the [discourses on] ethics.[3] This is necessarily the case even among persons who are free and equal, for all cannot rule at the same time, but each rules for a year or according to some other arrangement or period of time. (5) In this way, then, it results that all rule, just as if shoemakers and carpenters were to exchange places rather than the same persons always being shoemakers and carpenters. (6) But since that condition is better also with respect to the political partnership, it is clear that it is better if the same always rule, where this is possible; but in cases where it is not possible because all are equal in their nature, and where it is at the same time just for all to have a share in ruling (regardless of whether ruling is something good or something mean), there is at least an imitation of this.[4] (7) For some rule and some are ruled in turn, as if becoming other persons. And, in the same way, among the rulers different persons hold different offices. It is evident from these things, then, that the city is not naturally one in this sense as some argue, and what was said to be the greatest good for cities actually destroys them; yet the good of each thing is surely what preserves it. (8) It is evident in another way as well that to seek to unify the city excessively is not good. For a household is more self-sufficient than one person, and a city than a household; and a city tends to come into being at the point when the partnership formed by a multitude is self-sufficient. If, therefore, the more self-sufficient is more choiceworthy, what is less a unity is more choiceworthy than what is more a unity. 15

CHAPTER 3

(1) But even if it is best for the partnership to be as far as possible a unity, even this does not appear to be proved by the argument [that it will follow] if all say "mine" and "not mine" at the same time; for Socrates supposes this is an indication of the city being completely one. (2) For "all" has a double sense. If it means "each 20 individually," perhaps this would be closer to what Socrates wants to do, for each will then speak of the same boy as his own son and the same woman as his own wife, and similarly with regard to property and indeed to everything that comes his way. But those who have wives and children in common will not speak of them in 25 this way, but as "all" [collectively] and not individually; (3) and similarly with respect to property, as "all" [collectively] but not individually. It is evident, then, that a certain fallacy is involved in the phrase "all say"—indeed, the double sense of "all," "both," "odd," and "even" produces contentious syllogisms in arguments as well.[5] Therefore that "all say the same thing" is in one way 30 fine, though impossible, while in another way it is not even productive of concord.

(4) Furthermore, the formula is harmful in another way. What belongs in common to the most people is accorded the least care: they take thought for their own things above all, and less about things common, or only so much as falls to each individually. For, apart from other things, they slight them on the grounds that 35 someone else is taking thought for them—just as in household service many attendants sometimes do a worse job than fewer. (5) Each of the citizens comes to have a thousand sons, though not as an individual, but each is in similar fashion the son of any of them; hence all will slight them in similar fashion. 1262a1

Further, each says "mine" of a citizen who is acting well or ill only in this sense, that he is one of a certain number: each really says "mine or his," meaning by this every individual of the thousand or however many the city has. And even then he is in doubt, for it is unclear who has happened to have offspring, or whether any have survived. (6) Yet which is superior—for each of two 5 thousand (or ten thousand) individuals to say "mine" and address

57

the same thing, or rather the way they say "mine" in cities now? (7) For now the same person is addressed as a son by one, by another as a brother, by another as a cousin, or according to some other sort of kinship, whether of blood or of relation and connection by marriage—in the first instance of himself, then of his own; and further, another describes him as clansman or tribesman. It is better, indeed, to have a cousin of one's own than a son in the sense indicated.

(8) Actually, though, it is impossible to avoid having some suspect who their brothers and sons or fathers and mothers really are; for they will of necessity find proofs of this in the similarities that occur between children and their parents. (9) Indeed, some of those who have composed accounts of travels[6] assert that this in fact happens; for they say that some inhabitants of upper Libya have women in common, yet the children they bear are distinguishable according to their similarities. There are some women [and some females] of other animals such as horses and cattle that are particularly inclined by nature to produce offspring similar to the parents, like the mare at Pharsalus called the Just.

CHAPTER 4

(1) Further, it is not easy for those establishing this sort of partnership to avoid such difficulties as outrages or involuntary homicides, for example, or voluntary homicides, assaults, or verbal abuse. None of these things is holy when it involves fathers, mothers, or those not distant in kinship, as distinct from outsiders; yet they must necessarily occur more frequently among those who are ignorant [of their relatives] than among those who are familiar [with them], and when they do occur, only those who are familiar [with their relatives] can perform the lawful expiations, while the others cannot. (2) It is also odd that while sons are made common, only sexual intercourse between lovers is eliminated, but love is not forbidden, or other practices which are improper particularly for a father in relation to his son or a brother in relation to his brother, as indeed is love by itself. (3) It is also odd that sexual intercourse is eliminated for no other reason than that the pleasure involved is too strong, it being supposed that it makes no difference whether this occurs between a father and a son or between brothers.[7]

(4) It would seem to be more useful for the farmers to have women and children in common than for the guardians.[8] For there will be less affection where children and women are common; but the ruled should be of this sort if they are to obey their rulers and not engage in subversion. (5) In general, there must necessarily result from a law of this sort the very opposite of what correctly enacted laws ought properly to cause, and of what caused Socrates to suppose that the matter of children and women should be arranged in this way. (6) For we suppose affection to be the greatest of good things for cities, for in this way they would least of all engage in factional conflict; and Socrates praises above all the city's being one, which is held to be, and which he asserts to be, the work of affection—just as in the discourses on love[9] we know that Aristophanes speaks of lovers who from an excess of affection "desire to grow together," the two of them becoming one. (7) Now here it must necessarily happen that both, or one of them, disappear [in the union]; in the city, however, affection necessarily becomes diluted through this sort of partnership, and the fact that a father least of all says "mine" of his son, or the son of his father. (8) Just as adding much water to a small amount of wine makes the mixture imperceptible, so too does this result with respect to the kinship with one another based on these terms, it being least of all necessary in a regime of this sort for a father to take thought[10] for his sons as sons, or a son for his father as a father, or brothers for one another [as brothers]. (9) For there are two things above all which make human beings cherish and feel affection, what is one's own and what is dear; and neither of these can be available to those who govern themselves in this way.

There is also considerable uncertainty concerning the manner in which children are to be transferred from the farmers and artisans to the guardians as well as from the latter to the former; at any rate, those who transfer and assign them necessarily know who has been assigned to whom. (10) Further, what was mentioned before must necessarily result above all in these cases— that is, outrages, love affairs, homicides; for those who have been assigned to the other [class of] citizens will no longer address the guardians as brothers, children, fathers, or mothers, nor will those among the guardians so address the other [class of] citizens, so that they avoid doing any of these things on account of their kinship. Concerning the partnership in children and women, then, let our discussion stand thus.

1262b1

5

10

15

20

25

30

35

CHAPTER 5

(1) Next after this it remains to investigate the manner in which possessions should be instituted for those who are going to govern themselves under the best regime—whether possessions should be common or not. (2) This may be investigated even apart from the legislation concerning children and women. I mean, as regards what is connected with possessions, even if the former are held separately, which is the way all do it now, [one may investigate in particular whether] it is better for both possessions and uses to be common[, or whether one should be held in common and the other separately].¹¹ For example, farmland could be held separately while the crops are brought into a common [store] and consumed [in common], as some [barbarian] nations do; or the opposite could happen, land being held and farmed in common and the crops divided for private use (some barbarians are said to have this mode of partnership as well); or both farmland and crops could be common. (3) Now if the farmers were [of a] different [class than the citizens] the mode would be different and easier, but if they undertake the exertion for themselves, the arrangements concerning possessions would give rise to many resentments. For if they turn out to be unequal rather than equal in the work and in the gratifications deriving from it, accusations against those who can gratify themselves or take much while exerting themselves little must necessarily arise on the part of those who take less and exert themselves more. (4) In general, to live together and be partners in any human matter is difficult, and particularly things of this sort. This is clear in the partnerships of fellow travelers, most of whom are always quarreling as a result of friction with one another over everyday and small matters. Again, friction particularly arises with the servants we use most frequently for regular tasks. (5) Having possessions in common involves, then, these and other similar difficulties, and the mode that prevails now—if provided with the adornment of character and an arrangement of correct laws—would be more than a little better. For it would have what is good in both—by both I mean what comes from having possessions in common and what from having them privately. For they should be common in some sense, yet private generally speaking. For they should be common in some sense, yet private generally speaking. (6) Dividing the care [of possessions] will cause them not to raise these accusations against one another, and will actually result in improvement, as each applies himself to his own; and it will be through virtue that "the things of friends are common," as the proverb has it, with a view to use.

Even now this mode can be found in outline in some cities, so it is not impossible; in finely administered cities especially some of these things already exist, while others could be brought into being. (7) [In these cities] everyone has his own possessions, but he makes some of them useful to his friends, and some he uses as common things. In Lacedaemon, for example, they use each other's slaves, as well as their horses and dogs, as practically their own, and anything they need by way of provisions from the fields [when they travel] in their territory. (8) It is evident, then, that it is better for possessions to be private, but to make them common in use. That [the citizens] become such [as to use them in common]—this is a task peculiar to the legislator. 35

Further, it makes an immense difference with respect to pleasure to consider a thing one's own. It is surely not to no purpose that everyone has affection for himself; this is something natural. (9) Selfishness is justly blamed; but this is not having affection for oneself [simply], but rather having more affection than one should—just as in the case of the greedy person; for practically everyone has affection for things of this sort. Moreover, it is a very pleasant thing to help or do favors for friends, guests, or club mates; and this requires that possessions be private. (10) Those who make the city too much of a unity not only forfeit these things; in addition, they manifestly eliminate the tasks of two of the virtues, moderation concerning women (it being a fine deed to abstain through moderation from a woman who belongs to another) and liberality concerning possessions. For it will not be possible to show oneself as liberal or to perform any liberal action, since the task of liberality lies in the use of possessions. 40

1263bl

5

10

(11) This sort of legislation has an attractive face and might be held humane; he who hears of it accepts it gladly, thinking it will produce a marvelous affection in all for each other, especially when it is charged that the ills that now exist in regimes come about through property not being common—I am speaking of lawsuits against one another concerning contracts, trials involving perjury, and flattery of the rich. (12) Yet none of these things comes about because of the lack of partnership [in property], but through depravity. For it is precisely those who possess things in common and are partners whom we see most at odds,[12] not those who hold their property separately; but those at odds as a result of their partnerships are few to observe in comparison with those who own possessions privately. (13) Further, it is only just to speak not only of the number of ills they will be deprived of by being partners, but also the number of goods. Indeed, it is a way of life that appears to be altogether impossible. 15

20

25

The cause of Socrates' going astray one should consider to be
the incorrectness of the presupposition. (14) Both the household
and the city should be one in a sense, but not in every sense. On
the one hand, as the city proceeds [in this direction], it will at
some point cease to be a city; on the other hand, while remaining
a city, it will be a worse city the closer it comes to not being a
city—just as if one were to reduce a consonance to unison, or a
meter to a single foot.[13] (15) Rather, as was said before, [the city,]
being a multitude, must be made one and common through education. It is odd that one who plans to introduce education[14] and
who holds that it is through this that the city will be excellent
should suppose it can be corrected by things of that sort, and not
by habits, philosophy, and laws, just as the legislator in Lacedaemon and Crete made common what is connected with possessions by means of common messes.[15] (16) Nor should one ignore
the fact that it is necessary to pay attention to the length of time
and the many years during which it would not have escaped notice
if this condition were a fine one; for nearly everything has been
discovered, though some things have not been brought together,
while others are known but not practiced. (17)[That it is not fine]
would become evident above all if one could see such a regime
actually being instituted; for it will not be possible to create a city
without splitting and separating these things, on the one hand into
common messes, on the other into clans and tribes. So nothing
else will result from the legislation except that the guardians will
not farm; yet the Lacedaemonians attempt to do this even now.[16]

(18) Neither, for that matter, has Socrates told us what the mode
[of organization] of the regime as a whole will be for those participating in it; nor is it easy to say. At all events, the bulk of the
city is the multitude of the other citizens, and yet there is no discussion of whether the farmers too should have possessions in
common or each individual should have private possessions as
well, or further, whether women and children should be private or
common. (19) If everything is to be common to all in the same
manner, how will these differ from the guardians? What more will
they get by submitting to their rule? Or how will they be forced to
submit[17] to it, unless the guardians act the sophist and devise
something like the Cretans have? For these allow their slaves to
have the same things as themselves, except that they forbid them
exercises and the possession of arms. (20) But if [the farmers]
have those things, as they do in other cities, what will the mode of
their partnership be? For there must necessarily be two cities in
the one, and these opposed to one another. For he makes the guar-

dians into a sort of garrison, while the farmers and artisans and the others are the citizens.[18] (21) Accusations and lawsuits and whatever other ills he asserts exist in cities—all will exist among these as well. And yet Socrates speaks[19] as if they will have little need for ordinances—urban or market ordinances, for example, or others of this sort—on account of their education, although he assigns education only to the guardians. (22) Further, he gives the farmers authority over the possessions and has them pay a tax;[20] but then they are much more likely to be difficult and filled with high thoughts than the helots or serfs that some hold today,[21] or than slaves. (23) Whether the same things are necessary in a similar way [for this class] or not is in fact nowhere discussed, nor matters connected with this—what regime and education they have, and what laws. It is not easy to discover what sort of people these are, yet it makes no little difference with a view to the preservation of the partnership of guardians. (24) But if he is going to make women common and possessions private, who will manage the household while the men work in the fields? (Or, for that matter, if possessions and the wives of the farmers are both common?) Moreover, it is odd that in order to show that women should have the same pursuits as men he makes a comparison with the animals,[22] among whom household management is nonexistent.

(25) Also, the way Socrates selects the rulers is hazardous; for he has the same persons always ruling. This can become a cause of factional conflict even in the case of those possessing no particular claim to merit, not to speak of spirited and warlike men. (26) That it was necessary for him to make the same persons rulers is evident; for the gold from god is not mixed in the souls of some at one time and others at another, but always in the same—he says that directly at birth gold is mixed with some, silver with others, and bronze and iron with those who are going to be artisans and farmers.[23] (27) Further, he even destroys the guardians' happiness, asserting that the legislator should make the city as a whole happy.[24] But it is impossible for it to be happy as a whole unless most [people], or all or some of its parts, are happy. For happiness is not the same kind of thing as evenness: this can exist in the whole but in neither of its parts, but happiness cannot. (28) But if the guardians are not happy, which others are? For the artisans and the multitude of the vulgar surely are not, at any rate. The regime which Socrates spoke about raises, then, these questions, as well as others no less considerable than these.

CHAPTER 6

(1) Very similar is the case of the *Laws*, which was written later, so it is best to investigate briefly the regime there as well. In the *Republic*, after all, Socrates has discussed very few matters—how things should stand concerning the partnership in women and children, possessions, and the arrangement of the regime; (2) for he divides the mass of inhabitants into two parts, the farmers and the military part, and from these [latter arises] a third that is the deliberative and authoritative part of the city. (3) As for the farmers and artisans, whether they share in rule to some extent or not at all, or whether they should possess arms and join in warfare themselves, is nowhere discussed by Socrates; yet he supposes that the women should join in warfare and share in the same education as the guardians.[25] Otherwise, he has filled out the argument with extraneous discourses, particularly concerning the sort of education the guardians should have.

(4) The *Laws* deals for the most part with laws, and little is said about the regime. As to this, although he wishes to make it more attainable by cities, he gradually brings it around again toward the other regime. (5) For apart from the partnership in women and possessions, the other things he assigns it are the same for both regimes: education is the same, as is the life of abstention from necessary work and of common messes; only here he asserts that there should be common messes for women as well, and that the number of those possessing arms should be five thousand, whereas it is a thousand there.[26] (6) All the discourses of Socrates are extraordinary: they are sophisticated, original, and searching. But it is perhaps difficult to do everything finely. With regard to the multitude just mentioned, it should not be overlooked that so many will need the territory of Babylon[27] or some other that is unlimited in extent to sustain in idleness five thousand of them and a crowd of women and attendants about them many times as large. (7) Now one's presuppositions should indeed accord with what one would pray for; yet nothing should be impossible. It is said that the legislator should look to two things in enacting laws, the territory and the human beings [who inhabit it].[28] But, further, one would do finely to add that he should look to the neighboring regions, in the first place if the city is to lead a political way of life and not one of isolation; for it is necessary that it use for war the arms that are useful not only on its own territory but in foreign regions as well. (8) But if one does not accept this way of life either as one's own or as the common way of life of the city, still

64

[men] should be formidable to their enemies not only when these enter their territory but also when they leave it.

As regards the extent of possessions, too, one should see whether it would not be better to determine this differently and more clearly. For he asserts that there should be as much as is needed to live with moderation,[29] which is as if one were to say "to live well": (9) it is too general. Moreover, it is possible to live with moderation but wretchedly. A better defining principle would be "with moderation and liberally" (for when separated the one will tend toward luxury, the other toward a life of hardship), since these alone are the choiceworthy dispositions concerning the use of property: it is not possible to use property gently or courageously, but it is possible to use it with moderation and liberally, so the dispositions connected with it must be these.

(10) It is also odd that while possessions are equalized, nothing is instituted in connection with the number of the citizens, but procreation is left unrestricted, on the grounds that it will remain sufficiently close to the same number through childlessness [on the part of some] no matter how many births there may be,[30] because this is held to be the result in cities now. (11) But the precision this requires is not the same there and in cities now; for now no one becomes poor, on account of the splitting of properties to accommodate any number [of heirs], but there, as properties are indivisible, persons who are in surplus must necessarily have nothing, whether they are more or fewer in number. (12) One would suppose that procreation should be restricted sooner than property, so that there would not be births beyond a certain figure, and that the whole number would be fixed by looking to the chances of some of those born dying and of childlessness on the part of others. (13) To leave it alone, as in most cities, must necessarily cause poverty among the citizens, and poverty produces factional conflict and crime. Pheidon of Corinth, one of the very ancient legislators, in fact supposed that the households and the number of citizens should be kept equal, even if the allotments of all were originally unequal in size; in the *Laws* it is just the opposite of this. (14) But about these matters and how we suppose they could be better handled we will speak later.[31]

Also omitted in the *Laws* is the matter of the rulers, and how they will differ from the ruled. For he asserts that just as the warp is made of a different kind of wool from the woof, so the rulers should stand with respect to the ruled.[32] (15) And since he permits the whole of one's property to increase as much as fivefold,[33] why should this not be allowed up to a certain point with respect to [ownership of] land? It needs also to be investigated whether the

65

25

separation of housing sites is not disadvantageous for household management; for he assigned two housing sites to each individual and made them separate and distinct,[34] yet it is difficult to administer two houses.

(16) The organization [of the regime] as a whole is intended to be neither democracy nor oligarchy, but the one midway between them which is called a polity; for it is based on those who bear [heavy] arms.[35] Now if he institutes this as being the most attain-

30

able of all the regimes for cities, he has perhaps argued rightly; but if as being the best after the first sort of regime, not so.[36] For one might well praise that of the Spartans more, or some other that is more aristocratic. (17) Now there are certain people who say that the best regime should be a mixture of all the regimes,

35

and who therefore praise that of the Lacedaemonians. Some of them assert it is a mixture of oligarchy, monarchy, and democracy, calling the kingship monarchy, the rule of the senators oligarchy, and saying it is democratically run by virtue of the rule of the overseers, on account of the overseers' being drawn from

40

the people; but others call the board of overseers a tyranny, and find it democratically run by virtue of the common messes and the rest of their everyday way of life. (18) In the *Laws*, on the other

1266a1

hand, it is said that the best regime should be composed out of democracy and tyranny[37]—which one might regard either as not being regimes at all or as the worst of them all. More nearly right, then, are those who mix more [of the regimes], for the regime that

5

is composed out of more is better. Actually, though, [the regime of the *Laws*] manifestly lacks a monarchic element; its characteristics are oligarchic and democratic, although its tendency is to incline more toward oligarchy. (19) This is clear from the system of selecting officials.[38] Selection by lot from among persons previously elected is common to both [oligarchy and democracy]; but for those who are better off to be compelled to attend the assem-

10

bly, vote for officials, and perform other political [tasks], while the others are let off, is oligarchic, as is the attempt to have the majority of officials from among the well off, and the greatest officials from among [those with] the greatest assessments. (20) He also makes election of the council oligarchic. It is compulsory for

15

all to elect—from the first assessment, and then from the second in equal number, and then from the third; except it is not compulsory for those from the first and second to elect from the fourth; (21) and he then says that from among those [elected in this way] they should designate an equal number from each as-

20

sessment. Hence those who are from the highest assessments and

66

better will be more numerous,[39] since some from the popular [classes] will not elect because it is not compulsory.

(22) That a regime of this sort should not be constituted out of democracy and monarchy, then, is evident from these things and from what will be said later, when the investigation turns to this sort of regime.[40] Also, with regard to the election of officials, it is dangerous to have them elected from persons previously elected; for if even a relatively few are willing to combine, the election will always take place in accordance with their wishes. This, then, is the way matters stand concerning the regime in the *Laws*.

25

30

CHAPTER 7

(1) There are certain other regimes as well, some of private individuals, others of philosophers and political [rulers]; but all of them are closer than either of those [just discussed] to established regimes under which [men] are now governed. For no one else has shown originality regarding community of women and children or regarding common messes for women; they begin rather from the necessary things. (2) For some of them hold that a fine arrangement concerning property is the greatest thing: it is about this, they assert, that all factional conflicts arise. The first to introduce this was Phaleas of Chalcedon,[41] who asserts that the possessions of the citizens should be equal. (3) He supposed this would not be difficult to do in [cities] just being settled; in those already settled he supposed it would be troublesome, but that a leveling could be quickly brought about by having the wealthy give dowries but not receive them, and the poor receive but not give them. (4) Plato, when writing the *Laws*, supposed [increase in properties] should be allowed up to a certain point, no citizen being permitted to possess [a property] more than five times the size of the smallest one, as was said earlier.[42] (5) But those who legislate in this fashion should not overlook—what they overlook now—that an arrangement concerning the extent of property should properly include an arrangement concerning the number of children as well. If the number of children outstrips the size of the property, the law will surely be abrogated; and, abrogation aside, it is a bad thing to have many of the wealthy become poor, for such persons are apt to become subversives. (6) Thus the leveling of property does indeed have a certain power to affect the political partner-

35

40
1266b1

5

10

15

ship. This was plainly recognized by some of former times, as in the legislation of Solon,[43] and others have a law which forbids the acquisition of land in whatever amount one wishes. Similarly, some laws forbid the sale of property, for example among the Locrians, where there is a law against sale unless one can show he has suffered manifest misfortune; (7) and some attempt to preserve original allotments [of land in colonies]. It was the abrogation of this [sort of law] at Leucas that led to their regime becoming overly popular; for the result was that offices were no longer filled from the designated assessments.[44] Yet it is possible to have equality of property, but for [the amount of property] to be either too great (so that luxury results) or too little (so that they live in penury). It is clear, then, that it is not enough for the legislator to make property equal; he must also aim at a mean. (8) Yet even if one were to arrange a moderate level of property for all, it would not help. For one ought to level desires sooner than property; but this is impossible for those not adequately educated by the laws. Phaleas would perhaps object that this is what he himself is saying; for he supposes that cities must have equality in these two things, possessions and education. (9) But one ought to say what the education is to be: having it one and the same is no help, for it is possible for it to be one and the same, and yet of such a sort that they intentionally choose to aggrandize themselves with respect to goods or honor or both. (10) Further, factional conflict occurs not only because of inequality of possessions, but also because of inequality of honors, though in an opposite way in each case; for the many [engage in factional conflict] because possessions are unequal, but the refined do so if honors are equal—hence the verse "in single honor whether vile or worthy."[45] (11) Nor do human beings commit injustice only because of the necessary things—for which Phaleas considers equality of property a remedy, so that no one will steal through being cold or hungry; they also do it for enjoyment and the satisfaction of desire. For if they have a desire beyond the necessary things, they will commit injustice in order to cure it—(12) and not only for this reason, for they might desire merely the enjoyment[46] that comes with pleasures unaccompanied by pains.

What remedy is there, then, for these three things? For the one, a minimum of property and work; for the other, moderation. As for the third, if certain persons should want enjoyment through themselves alone, they should not seek a remedy except in connection with philosophy; for the other [pleasures] require human beings. (13) The greatest injustices are committed out of excess, then, not because of the necessary things—no one becomes a tyrant in order to get in out of the cold (hence the honors too are great if one kills a tyrant rather than a thief). So it is only with a view to minor injustices that the mode of Phaleas' regime is of assistance.

(14) Further, most of what Phaleas wants to institute is designed to enable them to engage in politics finely among themselves; but they should do so also with a view to their neighbors and all foreigners. Therefore it is necessary that the regime be organized with a view to military strength, and he has said nothing about this. (15) And similarly concerning possessions: they should be adequate not only for political uses but also for foreign dangers. Hence the extent of them should neither be so much that those near at hand and superior will desire them and those having them will be unable to ward off the attackers, nor so little that they will be unable to sustain a war even against those who are equal and similar. (16) Although he has not discussed this, then, one should not overlook the extent of possessions that is advantageous.[47] Perhaps the best defining principle is that [there should be just so much that] those who are superior will not gain if they go to war because of the excess, but [will go to war only under such circumstances] as they would even if their property were not so great. (17) For example, when Autophradates was about to beseige Atarneus, Euboulus bid him examine how much time would be required to take the place and calculate what the expense for this time would be, as he was willing to abandon Atarneus at once for less than this; and by saying this he caused Autophradates to have second thoughts and give up the seige.[48]

(18) For the property of the citizens to be equal, then, is indeed an advantage with a view to avoiding factional conflict between them, but it is by no means a great one. For the refined may well become disaffected, on the grounds that they do not merit [mere] equality, and for this reason they are frequently seen to attack [the people] and engage in factional conflict. (19) Further, the wickedness of human beings is insatiable: at first the two obol allowance was adequate, but now that this is something traditional, they always ask for more, and go on doing so without limit.[49] For the nature of desire is without limit, and it is with a view to satisfying this that the many live. (20) To rule such persons, then, [requires[50]] not so much leveling property as providing that those who are respectable by nature will be the sort who have no wish to aggrandize themselves, while the mean will not be able to, which will be the case if they are kept inferior but are done no injustice.

(21) But not even what he has said about equality of property is right. For he equalizes only the possession of land; but there may

15

20

25

30

35

40

1267b1

5

69

10   also be wealth in slaves, livestock, or money, and there is a great
     supply of it in so-called furnishings. Either, then, equality is to be
     sought in all these things, or some moderate arrangement, or all
     are to be left alone. (22) It is also evident from this legislation that
     he is instituting a small city; at any rate, all the artisans will be
15   public slaves and will not contribute to the full complement of the
     city. (23) But if there should be public slaves at all, it is those who
     work at common tasks who should be in this condition, as at Epi-
     damnus, or as Diophantus once tried to institute at Athens.[51] Con-
     cerning the regime of Phaleas, then, whether he happens to have
     argued rightly in some respect or not may be discerned from what
20   has been said.

CHAPTER 8

(1) Hippodamus, the son of Euryphon, of Miletus, who invented
the division of cities and laid out Peiraeus—and who was extraordinary in other aspects of his life through ambition, so that he
seemed to some to live in a rather overdone manner, with long
25   hair and expensive ornaments, and furthermore with cheap and
warm clothing which he wore not only in winter but also in summer weather, and who wished to be learned with regard to nature
as a whole—was the first of those not engaged in politics to undertake to give an account of the best regime.[52] (2) He wanted to
30   institute a city of ten thousand men, divided into three parts, and
to make one part artisans, one farmers, and the third the military
part and that possessing arms. (3) He also divided the territory
into three parts, one sacred, one public and one private:[53] the sacred to provide what custom requires to be rendered to the gods,
35   the public for the warriors to live off of, and the private that belonging to the farmers. (4) He supposed that there are three kinds
of laws as well, since the things concerning which cases arise are
three in number—arrogant behavior, injury, and death.[54] He also
wished to legislate a single authoritative court, to which all cases
40   that are held not to have been rightly judged should be appealed;
this he wanted to institute out of a certain number of elected elders. (5) He supposed that decisions in the courts should not be
1268a1   rendered by a ballot, but that each should deposit a tablet on
which, if he condemned simply, he should write the verdict, or if
he acquitted simply, leave it blank, but if neither, he should make
5   distinctions. For he supposed current legislation is not fine in this

regard, as it compels [men] to perjure themselves if they judge one way or the other. (6) He also wanted to enact a law concerning those who discover something useful to the city, so that they might obtain honor, and one providing that the children of those who die in war should receive sustenance from public funds (he supposed this had never been legislated by others, although such a law exists now both in Athens and in other cities). (7) The rulers were all to be elected by the people, the people being the three parts of the city; those elected were to take care of common matters, matters affecting aliens, and matters affecting orphans.

These are most of the elements of Hippodamus' arrangement and those most deserving mention. The first question one might raise concerns the division of the multitude of the citizens. (8) The artisans and the farmers and those possessing arms all participate in the regime, although the farmers have no arms and the artisans neither land nor arms—so that they become virtually slaves of those possessing arms. (9) It is impossible, then, for them to share in all the prerogatives, since the generals and regime guardians[55] and practically all the authoritative offices will necessarily be selected from among those possessing arms; yet if they do not share in the regime, how will they feel any affection toward the regime? Those possessing arms would then have to be superior to both of the other parts; but this would not be easy unless there were many of them. (10) Yet if that is to be the case, why should the others share in the regime and have authority with respect to the selection of rulers? Furthermore, what use are the farmers to the city? It is necessary that there be artisans, for every city needs artisans, and they can subsist, as they do in other cities, from their arts. It would have been reasonable to make the farmers a part of the city if they provided sustenance to those possessing arms; as it is, however, they have private [land] and are to farm this privately. (11) As for the common land, from which the warriors are to have their sustenance, if they are to farm it themselves there would be no difference between the fighting and the farming element, contrary to the wish of the legislator; but if there are to be others different from both those farming privately and from the fighters, this will be an additional fourth part of the city which shares in nothing and is hostile to the regime. (12) On the other hand, if one makes the same persons farm both the private and the public land, will not the amount of crops from each one's farming be insufficient for two households? Or why is it they do not simply take sustenance for themselves from the land and their own allotments and also provide it to the fighters? In all of these things there is much confusion.

10

15

20

25

30

35

40

1268b1

(13) Nor is the law concerning judging a fine one—to require the one judging to make distinctions when the indictment in a case is simple, thus making the juror an arbitrator. This can be done in an arbitration, even by many persons, since they may confer together over the judgment; but it is not possible in courts where most legislators have made provision for the opposite of this— that the jurors do not confer together. (14) But further, how will the judgment be other than confused, when the juror finds something owed, but not as much as claimed by the plaintiff? He claims twenty minas, but a juror judges ten minas (or the one more and the other less), another judges five, another four—it is clear they will split in this way; but others will condemn for all, and others for nothing. (15) How then will they calculate the votes? Moreover, no one compels the one who simply acquits or condemns to perjure himself, at least if the indictment is simple (and justly so). For the one acquitting does not judge that he owes nothing, but that he does not owe the twenty minas, though the one indeed perjures himself who condemns without believing he owes the twenty minas.

(16) Concerning the matter of those who discover something advantageous for the city, to legislate that they receive some honor is not safe, though it sounds appealing: it would involve harassments[56] and, it might well happen, changes of regime. But this leads into another problem and a different investigation. For some raise the question whether it is harmful or advantageous for cities to change traditional laws, if some other one should be better. (17) If indeed it is not advantageous, it would not be easy to agree readily with what has been said; but it is not impossible that some might propose the dissolution of the laws or the regime as something in the common good. Since we have made mention of this, it will be best to expand a bit further on it. (18) For it involves, as we said, a question, and change might seem to be better. This has been advantageous, at any rate, in the other sciences—medicine, for example, has changed from its traditional ways, and gymnastic, and the arts and capacities generally, so that as political expertise too is to be regarded as one of these, it is clear that the same must necessarily hold concerning this as well. (19) One might assert that evidence is provided by the facts themselves: the laws of ancient times were overly simple and barbaric. For the Greeks used to carry weapons and purchase their wives, (20) and whatever other ancient ordinances still remain are altogether foolish. At Cyme, for example, there is a law concerning cases of homicide, to the effect that the accused shall be guilty of

murder if the plaintiff can provide a certain number of witnesses   1269a1
from among his own relatives. (21) In general, all seek not the
traditional but the good. The first [human beings], whether they
were earthborn or preserved from a cataclysm, are likely to have   5
been similar to average or even simpleminded persons [today], as
indeed is said of the earthborn;[57] so it would be odd to abide by the
opinions they hold. In addition to this, it is not best to leave written [laws] unchanged. (22) For just as in the case of the other arts,
so with respect to political arrangements it is impossible for ev-   10
erything to be written down precisely; for it is necessary to write
them in universal fashion, while actions concern particulars.
From these things it is evident, then, that some laws must be
changed at some times; yet to those investigating it in another
manner this would seem to require much caution. (23) For when
the improvement is small, and since it is a bad thing to habituate   15
people to the reckless dissolution of laws, it is evident that some
errors both of the legislators and of the rulers should be let go; for
[the city] will not be benefited as much from changing them as it
will be harmed through being habituated to disobey the rulers.
(24) And the argument from the example of the arts is false.
Change in an art is not like change in law; for law has no strength   20
with respect to obedience apart from habit, and this is not created
except over a period of time. Hence the easy alteration of existing
laws in favor of new and different ones weakens the power of law
itself. (25) Further, if they are indeed to be changeable, are all to
be, and in every regime? And by anyone, or by whom? For these   25
things make a great difference. Let us therefore set aside this investigation for the present; it belongs to other occasions.[58]

CHAPTER 9

(1) Concerning the regime of the Lacedaemonians[59] and the Cretan regime, and indeed virtually all other regimes, there are two   30
investigations [to be made]: one, whether some aspect of the legislation is fine or not with respect to the best arrangement; the
other, whether it is opposed to the presupposition and the mode of
the regime they actually have. (2) Now it is agreed that any [city]
that is going to be finely governed must have leisure from the necessary things; but in what manner it should have this is not easy to   35
grasp. For the serfs of Thessaly have often attacked the Thes-

salians, and similarly with the Spartans' helots, who are constantly awaiting their misfortunes as if in ambush.[60] In the case of the Cretans, however, nothing of this sort has happened. The cause of this is perhaps that neighboring cities there, even when at war with one another, never ally themselves with those in revolt, since as possessors of subjects[61] themselves it would not be to their advantage; but all the neighbors of the Spartans—the Argives, Messenians, and Arcadians—have been their enemies. In the case of the Thessalians, too, they revolted in the beginning when there was still war with those in adjacent territories—Achaeans, Perrhaebeans, and Magnesians.[62] (4) But it would appear that, apart from anything else, supervision of them is troublesome in itself—what the mode of one's relations with them should be; for if it is lax, they become arrogant and claim to merit equality with those in authority, and yet if harshly treated they come to hate and conspire against them. It is clear, then, that those who have this happen to them in connection with helotry have not discovered the mode that is best.

(5) Furthermore, their laxness concerning women is harmful with a view both to the intention of the regime and to the happiness of the city. For just as man and woman are a part of the household, it is clear that the city should be held to be very nearly divided in two—into a multitude of men and a multitude of women; so in regimes where what is connected with women is poorly handled, one must consider that legislation is lacking for half of the city. (6) This very thing has happened there; for the legislator[63] wished the city as a whole to be hardy, and this is manifest in terms of the men; but he thoroughly neglected it in the case of the women, who live licentiously in every respect and in luxury. (7) Wealth will necessarily be honored in a regime of this sort, particularly if they are dominated by the women, as is the case with most stocks that are fond of soldiering and war (excluding the Celts and any others that openly honor sexual relations among males). (8) For the one who first told the myth was not unreasonable in pairing Ares and Aphrodite:[64] all those of this sort are possessed, as it were, when it comes to relations with either men or women. This was the case with the Spartans, and many matters were administered by the women during the period of their [imperial] rule.[65] (9) And yet what difference is there between women ruling and rulers who are ruled by women? For the result is the same. Boldness is something useful in war (if then) rather than in everyday matters; but the Spartan women have been very harmful even in this respect. (10) This became clear during the Theban in-

vasion: they were not only wholly useless, like women in other cities, but they created more of an uproar than the enemy.[66]

Now this laxness concerning women appears to have arisen among the Spartans in a way that is quite reasonable. (11) They spent much time away from their own land when they were at war with the Argives, and later with the Arcadians and Messenians; and thus once they had leisure they could place themselves in the hands of the legislator having been well prepared by the soldiering life—for it involves many of the parts of virtue. As for the women, they say Lycurgus attempted to lead them toward the laws, but they were resistant, and he gave it up.[67] (12) The causes of what has happened, then, and of this error of theirs, are these; but we are not investigating whom to excuse in this matter, but what is correct or incorrect. (13) That what is connected with the women is not finely handled would seem not only to create an inappropriateness in the regime in its own terms, as was said earlier, but to contribute to their greed. For next to what has just been said, one might censure what pertains to the disparity in possessions. (14) For it has happened that some of them possess too much property, and others very little; hence the territory has come into the hands of a few. This too was poorly arranged in the laws. For [the legislator] made the buying or selling of existing [property in land] something not noble, and correctly so; but he left it open to them to give or bequeath it if they wished, although the result must be the same in this case as in that. (15) Indeed, nearly two-fifths of the entire territory belongs to women, both because many have become heiresses and because large dowries are given. It would have been better to have none, or to arrange for a dowry to be small or even moderate. As it is now, [not only is there no limit on its size, but everyone] is permitted to give an heiress in marriage to whomever he wishes, and if he dies intestate, his heir can give her to anyone he pleases.[68] (16) Accordingly, although the territory was capable of sustaining fifteen hundred cavalrymen and thirty thousand heavy-armed troops, they were [reduced to] less than a thousand in number. But it became clear through the facts themselves how poor their condition was as a result of this arrangement; for the city could not bear up under a single blow, but was ruined through its lack of manpower.[69] (17) It is said that at the time of the earlier kings they gave others a share in the regime, and so had no lack of manpower then even though they were at war for a long time; indeed, they say there were once ten thousand Spartiates. But regardless of whether these things are true or not, it is better for the city to have an abundance of men

40 through the leveling of possessions. (18) The law concerning procreation is also an obstacle to correcting this. For the legislator,

1270b1 wishing there to be as many Spartiates as possible, encourages
the citizens to have as many children as possible; for there is a law
that one who has fathered three sons is exempted from garrison
duty,[70] and one with four is exempted from all taxes. (19) Yet it is
evident that if many are born and the territory remains divided as

5 it is, many of them will be poor.

Also poorly handled is the matter of the overseers. This office
has authority by itself over the greatest matters among them, yet it
is filled entirely from the people,[71] so that the board is often entered by very poor men who because of their poverty can be

10 bought. (20) They have often made this clear both in the past and
now in the Andros matter, where some of them, having been corrupted by silver, did all that was in them to ruin the city as a
whole.[72] Also, because the office is overly great—like a tyranny,

15 in fact—even the kings are compelled to try to become popular
with them; this has done added harm to the regime, for from an
aristocracy it has become a democracy. (21) It is indeed the case
that this board holds the regime together: the people keep quiet
because they share in the greatest office, and so whether it was
through the legislator or by chance that this came about, it is ad-

20 vantageous for their affairs.[73] (22) If a regime is going to be preserved, all the parts of the city must wish it to exist and continue
on the same basis. Now the kings are in this condition because of
the honor accorded them, the gentlemen on account of the senate

25 (for this office is a prize of virtue), and the people on account of
the overseers, who are selected from all. (23) This office should
have been elected from all, to be sure, but not in the way it is now,
which is overly childish.[74] Further, although they are of an average sort, they have authority in the most important [judicial] decisions.[75] Hence it would be better if they judged not at discretion

30 but in accordance with written [rules] and the laws. (24) Also, the
comportment of the overseers does not agree with the inclination
of the city: it is overly lax, though in other respects [the city] goes
to excess in the direction of harshness—with the result that they
cannot endure it, but secretly run away from the law and seek

35 gratification in the pleasures of the body.

The matter of the office of senator is also not finally handled by
them. (25) Now if these were respectable persons adequately educated with a view to the qualities of a good man, one would
probably say it is advantageous to the city, though doubts could be
raised about their having authority in important [judicial] deci-

sions throughout their lifetime (since old age affects the mind as
well as the body). Yet when their education is such that even the
legislator himself lacks trust in them as not being good men, it is
not safe. (26) It is evident that many who have participated in this
office have been thoroughly affected by bribery and favoritism in
handling many common matters. Hence it is better that they not
go unaudited; now they do. The office of overseer might be held
[to be the proper one] to audit all the offices; but this is too great a
gift to the overseers, and it is not in this way that we say the auditing ought to be carried out. (27) Further, the election they hold of
senators is childish in its manner of decision,[76] and to have the one
who claims to merit the office ask for it himself is not correct; for
the one who merits the office should rule whether he wishes to or
not. (28) As it is, the legislator is evidently doing what he has
done with respect to the rest of the regime; it is with a view to
making the citizens ambitious that he has used this [device] in the
election of the senators—for no one would ask for office unless he
were ambitious. And yet most voluntary acts of injustice among
human beings result from ambition or from greed.

(29) Concerning kingship and whether it is better for it to exist
in cities or not, there will be discussion later;[77] but it is surely better in any event not to have it as at present, [a hereditary office,]
but to judge each king on the basis of his own [manner of] life.
(30) Now it is clear that the legislator did not himself suppose it
possible to make [the Spartan kings] gentlemen. At any rate, he
lacks trust in them as not being sufficiently good men; and it is on
this account that they repeatedly send them on embassies accompanied by their enemies, and hold that factional conflict between
the kings means preservation for the city.[78]

The legislation concerning common messes—the so-called
friends' messes[79]— was also not finely handled by the one who
first established it. (31) The support for this should have come primarily from the common [treasury,] as in Crete; but among the
Spartans everyone must contribute, even though some of them are
very poor and unable to afford the expense. Hence the result is the
opposite of the legislator's intention; (32) for he wants the institution of common messes to be a democratic one, but it is least of
all democratic as a result of the legislation being handled this way.
For it is not easy for the very poor to share in it, and yet this is the
traditional defining principle of the regime among them—that
whoever is unable to contribute this fee does not share in the
regime.[80]

(33) The law concerning admirals has been criticized by others,

40

and correctly so. It is a cause of factional conflict: the position of admiral has been established almost as another kingship over against the kings, who are generals in perpetuity.[81]

1271b1

(34) Moreover, one may criticize the presupposition of the legislator, in the way Plato criticizes it in the *Laws*:[82] the entire organization of the laws is with a view to a part of virtue—warlike virtue; for this is useful with a view to domination. Yet while they preserved themselves as long as they were at war, they came to ruin when they were ruling [an empire] through not knowing how to be at leisure, and because there is no training among them that has more authority than the training for war. (35) This error is no slight one. They consider that the good things [men] generally fight over are won by virtue rather than vice, and rightly so; but they conceive these things to be better than virtue, which is not right. (36) Also poorly handled among the Spartiates is the matter of common funds. For there is nothing in the common [treasury] of the city in spite of their being compelled to carry on great wars, and they are very backward in paying [special war] taxes. For because most of the land belongs to the Spartiates, they do not scrutinize each other's payments of such taxes. (37) The consequence for the legislator has been the opposite of advantageous: he has created a city lacking in funds, and invididuals greedy for them.

5

10

15

Concerning the regime of the Lacedaemonians, then, let this much be said; for these are the things one might particularly criticize.

CHAPTER 10

20

(1) The Cretan regime[83] is very close to this one, and while it has a few features that are not worse, most of it is less fully finished. It appears, and it is said, that the regime of the Spartans is an imitation of the Cretan in most respects; but most ancient things are less fully articulated than newer things. (2) They say that Lycurgus, when he gave up his stewardship of King Charilaus and left home, spent most of his time in Crete on account of kinship; for the Lyctians were colonists of the Spartans, (3) and those who had gone to the colony had adopted the arrangement of laws that existed among those who dwelt there then. Thus even now the subjects use them in the same manner, and assume that Minos was the first to institute this arrangement of laws.[84]

25

30

The island seems naturally situated for [imperial] rule in Greece.

It lies across the entire sea, and most of the Greeks are settled around the sea: it is not far distant from the Peloponnese on the one side, and on the other from the part of Asia around Cape Triopium and Rhodes. (4) Hence Minos established [imperial] rule over the sea, subduing some of the islands and settling others; and finally he attacked Sicily, and ended his life there near Camicus.[85]

The Cretan arrangement corresponds to the Spartan. (5) For the helots farm for the latter, while the subjects do it for the Cretans; and both have common messes, which the Spartans called "men's messes" rather than "friends' messes" in ancient times, just as the Cretans do now, from which it is clear that they came from there. The same holds for the arrangement of the regime. (6) For the overseers have the same powers as the so-called orderers in Crete, except that the overseers are five in number and the orderers ten. The senators are the equals of their senators, whom the Cretans call the Council. As for kingship, there was one in earlier times, but the Cretans later overthrew it, and the orderers now have leadership in war. (7) All share in an assembly, but it has authority to do nothing other than ratify proposals of the senators and orderers.

The matter of common messes is better handled by the Cretans than the Spartans. In Lacedaemon, each contributes a set amount; otherwise, the law prohibits him from sharing in the regime, as was said earlier. (8) In Crete, it is handled instead in more common fashion: from all the crops and livestock derived from the public land and from the contributions of the subjects, one portion is set aside for the gods and for common sorts of public service, and another for the common messes, so that everyone—women, children, and men—receives sustenance from the common [treasury]. (9) The legislator has shown his love of wisdom in devising many things with a view to ensuring a beneficial scantiness of food; and with a view to segregating the women, so as to prevent them having many children, he has provided for relations between men (whether this was poorly done or not will be investigated on another occasion).[86] That the matter of common messes is better arranged among the Cretans than the Spartans, then, is evident.

The matter of the orderers, however, is even worse than that of the overseers. (10) For whatever is bad in the board of overseers exists in theirs as well (for it consists of average persons); but whereas here it is advantageous for the regime, there it is not. Here, since the election is from all, the people share in the greatest office and hence wish the regime to continue. There, however, they do not elect the orderers from all, but from certain families, and the senators from those who have been orderers. (11) And one

35

40
1272al

5

10

15

20

25

30

35 might make the same arguments about these as about those who become [senators] in Sparta: it is not safe that they should go un-audited, that they should have throughout their lifetime a privilege which is greater than their merit, and that they should rule not by written [rules] but at discretion.[87] (12) Nor is it a sign of a fine arrangement that the people keep quiet and do not share. For the

40 orderers have no source of gain, as the overseers do, since they dwell on an island far away from those who might corrupt them.

1272b1 (13) The cure they have found for this error is an odd one, charac-teristic not of political but of dynastic [rule]. For often the or-derers are expelled by a combination either of their own col-leagues or of private individuals; and it is also open to the orderers

5 to resign the office in the middle of a term. But it is better if all these things are done in accordance with law rather than in accor-dance with human wish, as the latter is not a safe standard. (14) But the worst thing of all is the [condition termed] "lack of or-der," which the powerful frequently establish when they do not wish to submit to punishment[88]—by which it is clear that their

10 arrangement has elements of a regime but is not so much a regime as a dynasty. It is habitual with them to have followings among the people and their friends, create [petty] monarchies, and engage in factional conflict and fighting against one another. (15) Yet how does this sort of thing differ from the city actually ceasing to be such for a certain period, and the political partnership dissolving?

15 A city in this condition is also in great danger from those who wish and are able to attack it. But, as was said, Crete is preserved by its location: distance has acted as the equivalent of a law expel-ling foreigners.[89] (16) On this account too the subjects put up with the Cretans, while the helots frequently revolt. For the Cretans do

20 not participate in external rule, and only recently has foreign war come to the island and made evident the weakness of the laws there.[90] Concerning this regime, then, let us say this much.

CHAPTER 11

(1) The Carthaginians are also held to govern themselves in a way
25 that is fine and in many respects extraordinary compared to oth-ers; but in certain respects they are particularly similar to the Spartans.[91] For these three regimes—the Cretan, the Spartan, and, thirdly, that of the Carthaginians—are very close to one an-other in a sense, and at the same time very different from the oth-

ers. Many of their arrangements are finely handled. (2) It is a sign of a well-organized regime if the people voluntarily acquiesce in   30
the arrangement of the regime, and if there has never been factional conflict worth mentioning, or a tyrant. (3) The common messes of their clubs are similar to the friends' messes of the Spartan regime, and their office of the Hundred and Four to the overseers. And it is by no means worse: the latter are drawn from   35
average persons, but they elect the former on the basis of desert. The kings and the senate are comparable to the kings and senators there; (4) yet it is better [handled in Carthage] insofar as the kings do not derive from the same family, nor an average one, but if any is outstanding whether [in birth or virtue, it is from such families   40
that they are chosen, and the senators too] are elected from these rather than [occupying the office] on the basis of age.[92] For as they have authority in great matters, if they are insignificant persons they do great harm; and they have already done harm to the city of   1273a1
the Lacedaemonians.

(5) Now most of what may be criticized as deviations [from the best regime] happen to be common to all the regimes mentioned. As regards what may be criticized with a view to the presupposition of aristocracy and polity, some features incline toward [rule   5
of the] people, others toward oligarchy. The kings and the senators together have authority to submit or not submit [a proposal] to the people if all are agreed on it, but if not, the people have authority over these things as well. (6) And when the former propose something, it is granted to the people not only to hear out   10
[and approve] the opinions of the rulers, but they have authority to come to a decision of their own, and whoever wishes is permitted to speak against the proposals—something which does not exist in the other regimes. (7) But to have the Committees of Five, which have authority in many great matters, elected by their own [members], to have them elect to the greatest office, the Hundred [and Four],[93] and further, to have them rule for a longer period   15
than the others (for they rule [in effect] even after they have left office and before they enter it)—all this is oligarchic. On the other hand, that [officials] are unpaid and not chosen by lot must be regarded as aristocratic, as well as other things of this sort; and also having all cases tried by boards and not some by other [bodies] as in Lacedaemon.[94]   20

(8) But the Carthaginian arrangement deviates from aristocracy toward oligarchy particularly as regards a certain thought which is held jointly [by the few and] by the many:[95] they suppose that the rulers ought not to be elected on the basis of desert alone but also on the basis of wealth, it being impossible for a poor person to

81

25   rule finely and be at leisure. (9) If, therefore, election on the basis of wealth is oligarchic and election in accordance with virtue aristocratic, the arrangement by which the Carthaginians and others have organized matters pertaining to the regime would be of a third sort. For they look to both of these things when they elect—

30   particularly in the case of the greatest offices, kings and generals. (10) One should consider this deviation from aristocracy an error of the legislator. It is most necessary at the beginning to try to see how the best persons can be at leisure and avoid disgraceful conduct not only when they are ruling but even as private individuals.

35   But if for the sake of leisure one should indeed look to what is needed for being well off, it is a poor thing that the greatest offices—those of both king and general—can be bought. (11) For this law makes wealth something more honored than virtue, and the city as a whole greedy. For whatever the authoritative element

40   conceives to be honorable will necessarily be followed by the opinion of the other citizens. Where virtue is not honored above

1273b1   all, there cannot be a securely aristocratic regime. (12) And it is reasonable that those who have bought [an office] will become habituated to profiting [from it], since they spent so much in order to rule. Therefore, those capable of ruling best should rule. For it would be odd if, when even a respectable person who is poor will want to profit [from office], a worse one will not want to when he

5   has already spent so much. It would be better, if not for the legislator to enable the respectable to be well off [generally], at least to take care that they will have leisure while they are ruling.

(13) It would also seem a poor thing to have the same person hold several offices—something that is held in high repute among the Carthaginians. For one task is best accomplished by one per-

10   son. The legislator should try to see that this happens, and not command the same person to play the flute and make shoes. (14) Except where the city is small, it is more political to have more persons share in offices, and also more popular; for it is more common, as we said, and each of these things[96] is accomplished

15   more finely and more quickly. This is clear in military and maritime matters, for in both cases ruling and being ruled extends through practically everything.

(15) Although the regime is oligarchic, they escape [the consequences of this] in the best way by the fact that a part of the people is always becoming wealthy through being sent out to the

20   cities;[97] for by doing this they heal [the disease of] the regime and make it lasting. But this is really the work of chance, whereas they ought to be free of factional conflict through the legislator.

(16) As it is, should some mischance occur and the multitude of the ruled revolt, there is no medicine that will restore quiet through the laws.

This, then, is the way matters stand concerning the regime of the Lacedaemonians, the Cretan regime, and that of the Carthaginians, which are justly held in high repute.

25

CHAPTER 12

(1) Of those who have put forward some view concerning the regime, some did not participate in political actions of any sort, but led entirely private lives; concerning them, if there is anything that merits mention, it has been spoken about for the most part in the case of all of them. But others became legislators—some for their own cities, others for certain foreigners as well—and engaged in politics themselves; and of these some were craftsmen of laws only, but others of a regime as well—for example, Lycurgus and Solon, who established both laws and regimes. (2) Now the regime of the Lacedaemonians has been spoken of. As for Solon, there are some who suppose him to have been an excellent legislator.[98] For [they say] he dismantled an oligarchy that was too unmixed, put an end to the slavery of the people, and established the traditional democracy, under which the regime was finely mixed— the council of the Areopagus being oligarchic, the element of elective offices being aristocratic, and the courts being popular. (3) It would seem, though, that Solon found these things existing previously—the council and election to offices—and did not dismantle them, but established [rule of] the people by making the courts open to all. Thus there are also some who blame him for dissolving the other [elements of the existing regime] by giving authority to the court, which was to be chosen from all by lot. (4) For once this had become strong, they tried to gratify the people as if it were a tyrant, and [altering] the regime established the current democracy. Ephialtes and Pericles cut back the council of the Areopagus, Pericles established pay for the courts,[99] and in this manner each of the popular leaders proceeded by increasing [the power of the people] in the direction of the current democracy. (5) Yet this appears to have happened coincidentally rather than in accordance with the intention of Solon. For because the people were the cause of [Athenian] naval supremacy during the Persian

30

35

40

1274a1

5

10

83

wars, they began to have high thoughts and to obtain mean persons as popular leaders when they were opposed politically by the respectable.[100] Solon seems, at any rate, to have granted only the most necessary power to the people, that of electing to office and auditing; for if the people did not even have authority over this, they would be enslaved and an enemy [to the regime]. (6) But all the offices established by him were to be chosen from among notable and well-off persons—from the Five-hundred-bushel-men, the Team-men, and the third rating, the so-called Cavalrymen; but the fourth, the Laborers, had no part in any office.[101]

Other legislators were Zaleucus for the Epizephyrian Locrians, and Charondas of Catana for both his own citizens and the other Chalcidic cities in Italy and Sicily. (7) Some persons attempt to connect them, their view being that Onomacritus, a Locrian, was the first to become skilled in legislation, having been trained in Crete when he visited there in connection with [his practice of] the divining art, that Thales became a companion of his, and that Lycurgus and Zaleucus became students of Thales, and Charondas of Zaleucus. (8) But they say these things without much of an investigation of chronology.[102] But Philolaus of Corinth was a legislator for the Thebans. Philolaus was of the Bacchiad family; he became a lover of Diocles the Olympic victor, and when the latter left the city in disgust at his mother Alcyone's love for himself, he went to Thebes, and there both of them ended their lives. (9) And even now they show their tombs, which are in full view of one another, but one has a view toward Corinthian territory and the other does not, the tale being told that they arranged the burial this way—Diocles, out of hatred for the passion [of his mother], so that the territory of Corinth would not be visible from his mound, Philolaus, so that it would be from his. (10) So they settled among the Thebans for this reason, and Philolaus became a legislator for them concerning childbearing among other matters—what they call "adoptive laws"; this is something peculiar to his legislation, its purpose being that the number of allotments should be preserved.[103] (11) Nothing is peculiar to Charondas except trials in cases of perjury, for he was the first to introduce denunciation for this; but in the precision of his laws he is more polished even than current legislators. (12) Peculiar to Phaleas is the leveling of property; to Plato, having in common women and children as well as property; and further, the law concerning drinking—that the sober must act as rulers of drinking parties; and also that aspect of military training which has them develop ambidexterity, the assumption being that they should not have one useful and one useless hand.[104] (13) There are laws of Draco, but he laid them down for an existing regime; there is nothing peculiar to these laws that is worth recalling, except the harshness deriving from the size of the penalties.[105] Pittacus too was a craftsman of laws and not of a regime; peculiar to him is a law that those who are drunk should pay a greater penalty than the sober if they commit an offense. For on account of the fact that more persons commit outrages when drunk than when sober, he did not have regard for an indulgence that should be shown toward those who are drunk, but rather for what is advantageous.[106] (14) Androdamas of Rhegium also was a legislator for the Chalcidians of Thrace in matters concerning homicides and heiresses; but there is nothing peculiar to him that one might mention.[107] What concerns regimes—both those that have authority and those spoken about by certain persons—may be considered to have been studied, then, in this manner.[108]

BOOK 3

CHAPTER 1

(1) For one investigating the regime—what each sort is and what its quality—virtually the first investigation concerns the city, to see what the city actually is. For as it is, there are disputes, some arguing that the city performed an action, others that it was not the city but the oligarchy or the tyrant. We see that the entire activity of the political [ruler] and the legislator is concerned with the city, and the regime is a certain arrangement of those who inhabit the city. (2) But since the city belongs among composite things, and like other composite wholes is made up of many parts, it is clear that the first thing that must be sought is the citizen; for the city is a certain multitude of citizens. Thus who ought to be called a citizen and what the citizen is must be investigated.

There is often much dispute about the citizen, for not everyone agrees that the same person is a citizen. Someone who is a citizen in a democracy is often not one in an oligarchy. (3) Those who happen to be so designated but in some other sense—for example, honorary citizens—must be disregarded; nor is the citizen a citizen by inhabiting a place, for aliens and slaves are partners in the habitation; (4) nor are those sharing in matters of justice to the extent of being subject to lawsuits and adjudication, for this exists even for those who are partners as a result of agreements, since these things exist for them as well. For that matter, in many places not even aliens share completely in these things, but they must necessarily find a patron, so that they share in this sort of partnership in an incomplete sense. (5) Like children who are not yet enrolled because of age and elderly persons who have been relieved,[1] they must be admitted to be citizens in a sense, but not unqualifiedly, but rather with the addition of "incomplete" or "superannuated" or something else of this sort—it makes no difference, as what has been said is clear. We are seeking the citizen in an unqualified sense, one who has no defect of this sort requiring correction, since questions may be raised and resolved concerning such things in the case of those who have been deprived

35

40

1275a1

5

10

15

20

86

of [civic] prerogatives or exiled as well. (6) The citizen in an unqualified sense is defined by no other thing so much as by sharing
in decision and office. Now some offices are divided on the basis
of time, so that in some cases the same person is not permitted to
hold them twice, or only after some definite period of time has   25
passed; but other offices are indefinite, such as that of juror or assemblyman. (7) Perhaps someone might say that the latter are not
rulers and do not share in office on account of these things; yet it
would be ridiculous to deprive those with greatest authority of
[the title of] office. But it should make no difference: the argument is over a term, for what is common to juror and assembly-
man lacks a name that could apply to both. For the sake of defini-   30
tion, then, let it be "indefinite office." (8) We set it down, then,
that citizens are those who share in this way.

The [notion of] citizen that fits best with all those who are
called citizens is, therefore, something of this sort. But it should
not be overlooked that of [types of] things where the constituent
elements differ in kind—one of them being primary, one secondary, another derivative—the common element either is not present at all insofar as they are such, or only slightly. (9) We see that
regimes differ from one another in kind, and that some are prior
and some posterior; for those that are errant and deviant must necessarily be posterior to those that are without error. (In what sense   1275b1
we are speaking of deviant regimes will be evident later.[2]) Hence
the citizen must necessarily differ in the case of each sort of regime. (10) Accordingly, the citizen that was spoken of is a citizen
above all in a democracy; he may, but will not necessarily, be a   5
citizen in the others. In some [regimes] there is no people, nor is
an assembly recognized in law, but [only a consultative meeting
of specially] summoned persons,[3] and cases are adjudicated by
groups [of officials]. In Lacedaemon, for example, different overseers try different cases involving agreements, the senators those   10
involving murder, and another office perhaps others; (11) and it is
the same in the case of Carthage, where certain offices try all
cases.[4] But the definition of the citizen admits of correction. In the
other regimes, it is not the indefinite ruler who is assemblyman or
juror, but one whose office is definite. For of these either all or   15
some are assigned to deliberate and adjudicate, either concerning
all matters or concerning some.

(12) Who the citizen is, then, is evident from these things.
Whoever is entitled to participate in an office involving deliberation or decision is, we can now say, a citizen in this city; and the
city is the multitude of such persons that is adequate with a view
to a self-sufficient life, to speak simply.   20

CHAPTER 2

(1) As a matter of usage, however, a citizen is defined as a person from parents who are both citizens, and not just one, whether the father or the mother; and some go even further back, seeking two or three or more [generations of citizen] forebears. But these being political and offhand definitions, some raise the question of how that third or fourth [generation ancestor] will have been a citizen. (2) Gorgias of Leontini therefore, perhaps partly by way of raising the question and partly in irony, said that just as mortars are made by mortar makers, so Larisaeans are made by craftsmen, since some of them are "Larisa makers."[5] (3) The matter is simple. If they shared in the regime according to the definition that has been given, they were citizens; for, at any rate, it is impossible that the definition from citizen father or mother should fit in the case of the first inhabitants or founders.

But perhaps more of a question is involved in the case of those who came to share in the regime after a revolution—for example, [the citizens] created in Athens by Cleisthenes after the expulsion of the tyrants; for he enrolled in the tribes many foreigners and alien slaves.[6] The dispute about these is not over who is a citizen, but whether [they are so] justly or unjustly. (4) And yet a further question might be raised as to whether one who is not justly a citizen is a citizen at all, the assumption being that "unjust" and "false" amount to the same thing. (5) But since we also see certain unjust rulers, whom we assert do rule but unjustly, and since the citizen is defined by a kind of office (for someone who participates in that sort of office is a citizen, as we said), it is clear that these too must be admitted to be citizens.

CHAPTER 3

(1) The question of [whether some are citizens] justly or unjustly touches on the dispute mentioned previously. For some raise the question of when the city performed an action and when it did not—for example, at the time when a democracy replaces an oligarchy or a tyranny. (2) At these times, some do not want to fulfill [public] agreements on the grounds that it was not the city but the tyrant who entered into them, or many other things of this sort, the assumption being that some regimes exist through domi-

nation and not because they are to the common advantage. However, if some are run democratically in this same fashion, the actions of this regime must then be admitted to belong to the city in just the same way as the actions of the oligarchy or the tyranny.

(3) This argument seems related to the question of the sense in which the city ought to be spoken of as the same, or as not the same but different. Now the most superficial way of examining this question concerns the location and the human beings [constituting the city]; for the location and the human beings can be disjoined, with some inhabiting one location and others another[, and it will still be a city]. (4) The question in this form is to be regarded as a slight one, for the fact that the city is spoken of in several senses makes the examination of such cases easy.[7] And similarly in the case of human beings inhabiting the same location, [if one asks] when the city should be considered one. (5) For it is surely not by the fact of its walls—it would be possible to build a single wall around the Peloponnese. Babylon is perhaps a city of this sort, or any which has the dimensions of a nation rather than a city; at any rate, they say that its capture was not noticed in a certain part of the city for three days.[8] (6) But the investigation of this question will be useful on another occasion.[9] For the size of the city—as regards both quantity and whether it is advantageous to have one or several [locations][10]—should not be overlooked by the political [ruler]. But where the same persons inhabit the same location, must it be asserted that the city is the same as long as the stock of inhabitants remains the same, even though some are always passing away and some being born (as we are accustomed to speaking of rivers and springs as the same even though more water is always coming and flowing away)? Or must it be asserted that the human beings are the same for this sort of reason, but that the city differs? (7) For if the city is a type of partnership, and if it is a partnership of citizens in a regime, if the regime becomes and remains different in kind, it might be held that the city as well is necessarily not the same. At any rate, just as we assert that a chorus which is at one time comic and at another tragic is different even though the human beings in it are often the same, (8) it is similar with any other partnership and any compound, when the compound takes a different form—for example, we would say that the mode is different even when the notes are the same, if it is at one time Dorian and at another Phrygian.[11] (9) If this is indeed the case, it is evident that it is looking to the regime above all that the city must be said to be the same; the term[12] one calls it can be different or the same no matter whether the same human beings inhabit it or altogether different

15

20

25

30

35

40
1276b1

5

10

ones. As to whether it is just to fulfill or not to fulfill [agreements] when the city undergoes revolution into another regime, that is another argument.

CHAPTER 4

(1) Connected with what has been said is the investigation of whether the virtue of the good man and the excellent citizen is to be regarded as the same or as not the same. If we are indeed to examine this, however, the virtue of the citizen must first be grasped in some sort of outline. Now just as a sailor is one of a number of partners, so, we assert, is the citizen. (2) Although sailors are dissimilar in their capacities (one is a rower, another is a pilot, another a lookout, and others have similar sorts of titles), it is clear that the most precise account of their virtue will be that peculiar to each sort individually, but that a common account will in a similar way fit all. For the preservation of the ship in its voyage is the work of all of them, and each of the sailors strives for this. (3) Similarly, although citizens are dissimilar, preservation of the partnership is their task, and the regime is [this] partnership; hence the virtue of the citizen must necessarily be with a view to the regime. If, then, there are indeed several forms of regime, it is clear that it is not possible for the virtue of the excellent citizen to be single, or complete virtue. (4) That it is possible for a citizen to be excellent yet not possess the virtue in accordance with which he is an excellent man, therefore, is evident.

By raising questions in a different manner, the same argument can be made concerning the best regime. (5) For if it is impossible for a city to consist entirely of excellent persons, yet if each should perform his own work well, and this [means] out of virtue, there would still not be a single virtue of the citizen and the good man, since it is impossible for all the citizens to be similar. The virtue of the excellent citizen must exist in all, for it is necessarily in this way that the city is excellent, but this is impossible in the case of the virtue of the good man, unless all the citizens of an excellent city are necessarily good men. (6) Further, since the city is made up of dissimilar persons—as an animal is made up of soul and body, for instance, soul of reason and appetite, and a household of man and woman and master and slave,[13] in the same way a city is made up of all of these, and in addition to these it consists of other dissimilar kinds [of persons]—the virtue of all the citizens is necessarily not single, just as that of a head and a file leader in a chorus is not single. (7) That it is not the same in an unqualified sense, therefore, is evident from these things. But will there be some case, then, in which the virtue of the excellent citizen and the excellent man is the same? We assert that the excellent ruler is good and prudent, while the [excellent] citizen is not necessarily prudent. (8) Indeed, some say that the very education of a ruler is different, as is manifestly the case with the sons of kings who are educated to be expert in riding and in war; and when Euripides says "no subtleties for me, but what is needed for the city," [14] the assumption is that there is a certain education of a ruler. (9) If the virtue of the good ruler and the good man is the same, and if one who is ruled is also a citizen, the virtue of citizen and man would not be the same unqualifiedly, but only in the case of a certain sort of citizen. For the virtue of ruler and citizen is not the same, and it was perhaps for this reason that Jason said he was hungry except when he was tyrant, as one who did not know how to be a private individual. [15]

(10) At the same time, the capacity to rule and be ruled is praised, and the virtue of a citizen of reputation is held [16] to be the capacity to rule and be ruled finely. Now if we regard the virtue of the good man as being of a ruling sort, while that of the citizen is both [of a ruling and a ruled sort], they would not be praiseworthy to a similar extent. (11) Since both [views] are sometimes held— that the ruler and the ruled ought to learn different things and not the same, and that the citizen must know both sorts of things and share in both—the next step becomes visible. There is rule of a master, by which we mean that connected with the necessary things. It is not necessary for the ruler to know how to perform these, but only to use [those who do]; the other [sort of knowledge] is servile (by the other I mean the capacity to perform the subordinate tasks of a servant). (12) Now we speak of several forms of slave; for the sorts of work are several. One sort is that done by menials: as the term itself indicates, these are persons who live by their hands; the vulgar artisan is among them. Hence among some peoples the craftsmen did not share in offices in former times, prior to the emergence of [rule of] the people in its extreme form. [17] (13) Now the works of those ruled in this way should not be learned by the good [man] or the political [ruler] or the good citizen, unless he does it for himself out of some need of his own (for then it does not result in one person becoming master and another slave).

But there is also a sort of rule in accordance with which one rules those who are similar in stock and free. (14) For this is what

10   we speak of as political rule, and the ruler learns it by being ruled—just as the cavalry commander learns by being commanded, the general by being led, and [similarly in the case of] the leader of a regiment or company. Hence this too has been rightly said—that it is not possible to rule well without having been ruled.[18] (15) Virtue in [each of] these cases is different, but the good citizen should know and have the capacity both to be

15   ruled and to rule, and this very thing is the virtue of a citizen— knowledge of rule over free persons from both [points of view]. (16) Both belong to the good man too, as well as whatever kind of moderation and justice is characteristic of ruling. For it is clear that a virtue—[the virtue] of justice, for example—would not be a single thing for [a ruler and for[19]] a ruled but free person who is

20   good, but has different kinds in accordance with which one will rule or be ruled, just as moderation and courage differ in a man and a woman. (17) For a man would be held a coward if he were as courageous as a courageous woman, and a woman talkative if she were as modest as the good man; and household management differs for a man and a woman as well, for it is the work of the

25   man to acquire and of the woman to guard. But prudence is the only virtue peculiar to the ruler. The others, it would seem, must necessarily be common to both rulers and ruled, (18) but prudence is not a virtue of one ruled, but rather true opinion; for the one ruled is like a flute maker, while the ruler is like a flute player, the user [of what the other makes].[20] Whether the virtue of the good

30   man and the excellent citizen is the same or different, then, and in what sense it is the same and in what sense different, is evident from these things.

CHAPTER 5

(1) One of the questions concerning the citizen still remains. Is he only truly a citizen to whom it is open to participate in office, or

35   are vulgar persons also to be regarded as citizens? For if those too are to be so regarded who have no part in offices, then such virtue [as we have discussed] cannot belong to every citizen, as this sort is then a citizen. On the other hand, if none of these sorts is a citizen, in which class is each [sort] to be placed?[21] For he is neither a resident alien nor a foreigner. (2) Or shall we assert that there is nothing odd about this, at least on the basis of this argu-

1278al   ment? Neither slaves nor freedmen belong to those just men-

92

tioned. And this is true: not all those are to be regarded as citizens without whom there would not be a city, since children are not citizens in the same sense that men are; the latter are unqualifiedly, but the former only by way of a presupposition—they are citizens, but incomplete ones. (3) Now in ancient times among some [peoples] the vulgar element was slave or foreign, and for this reason many are such even now; but the best city will not make a vulgar person a citizen. But if this sort is a citizen, the virtue of a citizen, as we have been discussing it at any rate, cannot be spoken of as belonging to everyone or even to every free person, but only to those who have been relieved of necessary sorts of work. (4) Those who perform necessary services for one person are slaves; those who do so for the partnership are vulgar persons and laborers.

If we investigate a bit further from this point it will be evident how matters stand concerning these people. What has already been said will itself make this clear, once it is recalled.[22] (5) Since there are several regimes, there must necessarily be several kinds of citizen, and particularly of the citizen who is ruled. Thus in one sort of regime the vulgar and the laborer must necessarily be citizens, while in others this is impossible—for example, in any of the sort they call aristocratic, in which prerogatives are granted in accordance with virtue and merit; for it is impossible to pursue the things of virtue when one lives the life of a vulgar person or a laborer. (6) In oligarchies, on the other hand, it is not possible for a laborer to be a citizen, for sharing in offices is on the basis of large assessments, but it is possible for a vulgar person, since many artisans become wealthy. (7) In Thebes there used to be a law that one who had not abstained from the market for ten years could not share in office. But in many regimes the law pulls in even some foreigners; for one descended from a citizen mother is a citizen in some democracies, and it is the same way with bastards in many [regimes]. (8) Nevertheless, since it is because of a lack of genuine citizens that they make for themselves citizens of this sort (for they use such laws on account of a shortage of manpower), when they are well off as regards numbers they gradually disqualify first those with a slave as father or mother, then those with citizen mothers [but foreign fathers], and finally they make citizens only those with two native parents.

(9) That there are several kinds of citizens, therefore, is evident from these things, as is the fact that one who shares in prerogatives is particularly spoken of as a citizen—thus, for example, Homer's line "like some vagabond without honor."[23] For one who does not share in prerogatives is like an alien. But wherever this

sort of thing is kept concealed, it is for the sake of deceiving the [excluded] inhabitants.

40

1278b1

(10) As to whether [the virtue] which constitutes the good man and the excellent citizen is to be regarded as the same or different, then, it is clear from what has been said that in one sort of city this person is the same and in another different, and that [even in the former sort] it is not everyone but the political [ruler] and the one having authority or capable of having authority, either by himself or together with others, over the superintendence of common

5

matters.

CHAPTER 6

(1) Since these things have been discussed, what comes after them must be investigated—whether we are to regard there as being one regime or many, and if many, which and how many there are and what the differences are between them. The regime is an arrangement of a city with respect to its offices, particularly the one

10

that has authority over all [matters]. For what has authority in the city is everywhere the governing body, and the governing body *is* the regime. (2) I mean, for example, that in democratic regimes the people have authority, while by contrast it is the few in oligarchies. The regime too, we say, is different in these cases; and we shall speak in the same way concerning the others as well.

15

First, then, we must lay down by way of presupposition what it is for the sake of which the city is established, and how many kinds of rule are connected with man and the partnership in life. (3) It was said in our initial discourses, where household management and mastery were discussed, that man is by nature a political animal. Hence [men] strive to live together even when they

20

have no need of assistance from one another, though it is also the case that the common advantage brings them together, to the extent that it falls to each to live finely. It is this above all, then, which is the end for all both in common and separately; but they also join together, and maintain the political partnership, for the

25

sake of living itself. For there is perhaps something fine in living just by itself, provided there is no great excess of hardships. It is clear that most men will endure much harsh treatment in their longing for life, the assumption being that there is a kind of joy

30

inherent in it and a natural sweetness.

As for the modes of rule that are spoken of, it is easy to distinguish them, and we discuss them frequently in the external discourses.[24] Mastery, in spite of the same thing being in truth advantageous both to the slave by nature and to the master by nature, is still rule with a view to the advantage of the master primarily, and 35 with a view to that of the slave accidentally (for mastery cannot be preserved if the slave is destroyed). Rule over children and wife and the household as a whole, which we call household management, is either for the sake of the ruled or for the sake of something common to both—in itself it is for the sake of the ruled, as we see in the case of the other arts such as medicine and gymnas- 40 tic, but accidentally it may be for [the sake of the rulers] them- 1279al selves. For nothing prevents the trainer from being on occasion one of those engaging in gymnastic, just as the pilot is always one of the sailors: the trainer or pilot looks out for the good of the ruled, and when he becomes one of them himself, he shares acci- 5 dentally in the benefit; for the one is a sailor, and the other becomes one of those engaging in gymnastic, though still a trainer. Hence with respect to political offices too, when [the regime] is established in accordance with equality and similarity among the citizens, they claim to merit ruling in turn. Previously, as accords 10 with nature, they claimed to merit doing public service by turns and having someone look to their good, just as when ruling previously they looked to his advantage. Now, however, because of the benefits to be derived from common [funds] and from office, they wish to rule continuously, as if they were sick persons who were always made healthy by ruling; at any rate, these would perhaps 15 pursue office in a similar fashion.[25]

It is evident, then, that those regimes which look to the common advantage are correct regimes according to what is unqualifiedly just, while those which look only to the advantage of the rulers are errant, and are all deviations from the correct regimes; 20 for they involve mastery, but the city is a partnership of free persons.

CHAPTER 7

(1) These things having been discussed, the next thing is to investigate regimes—how many in number and which sorts there are, and first of all the correct ones; for the deviations will be evident once these have been discussed. (2) Since "regime" and "govern- 25 ing body" signify the same thing, since the governing body is the

authoritative element in cities, and since it is necessary that the authoritative element be either one or a few or the many, when the one or the few or the many rule with a view to the common advantage, these regimes are necessarily correct, while those with a view to the private advantage of the one or the few or the multitude are deviations. For either it must be denied that persons sharing [in the regime] are citizens, or they must participate in its advantages. (3) Now of monarchies, that [form] which looks toward the common advantage we are accustomed to call kingship; [rule] of the few (but of more than one person) we are accustomed to call aristocracy—either because the best persons are ruling, or because they are ruling with a view to what is best for the city and for those who participate in it; and when the multitude governs with a view to the common advantage, it is called by the term common to all regimes, polity. (4) This happens reasonably. It is possible for one or a few to be outstanding in virtue, but where more are concerned it is difficult for them to be proficient with a view to virtue as a whole, but [some level of proficiency is possible] particularly regarding military virtue, as this arises in a multitude; hence in this regime the warrior element is the most authoritative, and it is those possessing [heavy] arms who share in it. (5) Deviations from those mentioned are tyranny from kingship, oligarchy from aristocracy, democracy from polity. Tyranny is monarchy with a view to the advantage of the monarch, oligarchy [rule] with a view to the advantage of the well off, democracy [rule] with a view to the advantage of those who are poor; none of them is with a view to the common gain.

CHAPTER 8

(1) It is necessary to speak at somewhat greater length of what each of these regimes is. For certain questions are involved, and it belongs to one philosophizing in connection with each sort of inquiry and not merely looking toward action not to overlook or omit anything, but to make clear the truth concerning each thing. (2) Tyranny, as was said, is monarchic rule of a master over the political partnership; oligarchy is when those with property have authority in the regime; and democracy is the opposite, when those have authority who do not possess a [significant] amount of property but are poor. (3) The first question has to do with the definition. If a well-off majority has authority, and similarly in the

other case, if it somewhere happened that the poor were a minority with respect to the well off but were superior and had authority in the regime, although when a small number has authority it is called oligarchy, this definition of the regimes would not be held to be a fine one. (4) But even if one were to combine fewness with being well off and number with being poor and described the regimes accordingly (oligarchy being that in which those who are well off and few in number have the offices, and democracy that in which those who are poor and many in number have them), another question is involved. (5) What shall we say of the regimes that were just mentioned—those in which the majority is well off and the poor are few and each has authority in the regime—if there is no other regime beside those we spoke of? (6) The argument seems to make clear, therefore, that it is accidental that few or many have authority in oligarchies on the one hand and democracies on the other, and that this is because the well off are everywhere few and the poor many. Hence it also turns out that the causes of the differences are not what was mentioned. (7) What makes democracy and oligarchy differ is poverty and wealth: wherever some rule on account of wealth, whether a minority or a majority, this is necessarily an oligarchy, and wherever those who are poor, a democracy. (8) But it turns out, as we said, that the former are few and the latter many; for few are well off, but all share in freedom—which are the causes of both [groups] disputing over the regime.

25

30

35

40
1280a1

5

CHAPTER 9

(1) It is necessary first to grasp what they speak of as the defining principles of oligarchy and democracy and what justice is [from] both oligarchic and democratic [points of view]. For all fasten on a certain sort of justice, but proceed only to a certain point, and do not speak of the whole of justice in its authoritative sense. For example, justice is held to be equality, and it is, but for equals and not for all; (2) and inequality is held to be just and is indeed, but for unequals and not for all; but they disregard this element of persons and judge badly. The cause of this is that the judgment concerns themselves, and most people are bad judges concerning their own things. (3) And so since justice is for certain persons, and is divided in the same manner with respect to objects and for persons, as was said previously in the [discourses on] ethics,[26]

10

15

20

they agree as to the equality of the object, but dispute about it for persons. They do this particularly because of what was just spoken of, that they judge badly with respect to what concerns themselves, but also because both, by speaking to a point of a kind of justice, consider themselves to be speaking of justice simply. (4) For the ones, if they are unequal in a certain thing, such as goods, suppose they are unequal generally, while the others suppose that if they are equal in a certain thing, such as freedom, they are equal generally. (5) But of the most authoritative [consideration]

25

they say nothing. For if it were for the sake of possessions that they participated and joined together, they would share in the city just to the extent that they shared in possessions, so that the argument of the oligarchs might be held a strong one; for [they would say] it is not just for one who has contributed one mina to share equally in a hundred minas with the one giving all the rest, whether

30

[he derives] from those who were there originally or the later arrivals.[27] (6) But if [the city exists] not only for the sake of living but rather primarily for the sake of living well (for otherwise there could be a city of slaves or of animals—as things are, there is not, since they do not share in happiness or in living in accordance with intentional choice) and if it does not exist for the sake of an alliance to prevent their suffering injustice from anyone, nor for

35

purposes of exchange and of use of one another—for otherwise the Tyrrhenians and Carthaginians, and all who have agreements with one another, would be as citizens of one city—(7) at any rate, there are compacts between them concerning imports, agreements to abstain from injustice, and treaties of alliance. But no offices

40
1280b1

common to all have been established to deal with these things, but different ones in each [city]; nor do those [in one city] take thought that the others should be of a certain quality, or that none of those coming under the compacts should be unjust or depraved in any way, but only that they should not act unjustly toward one another.

5

(8) Whoever takes thought for good management, however, gives careful attention to political virtue and vice. It is thus evident that virtue must be a care for every city, or at least every one to which the term applies truly and not merely in a manner of speaking. For otherwise the partnership becomes an alliance which differs from

10

others—from [alliances of] remote allies—only by location. And law becomes a compact and, as the sophist Lycophron says, a guarantor among one another of the just things, but not the sort of thing to make the citizens good and just. (9) But that the matter stands thus is evident. For even if one were to bring the locations together into one, so that the city of the Megarians were fastened

to that of the Corinthians by walls,[28] it would still not be a single 15
city. (10) Nor would it be if they practiced intermarriage with one
another, although this is one of the aspects of the partnership that
is peculiar to cities. Nor, similarly, if certain persons dwelled in
separate places, yet were not so distant as to have nothing in common, but had laws not to commit injustice toward one another in
their transactions—for example, if one were a carpenter, one a 20
farmer, one a shoemaker, one something else of this sort, and the
multitude of them were ten thousand, yet they had nothing in
common except things of this sort, exchange and alliance; not
even in this way would there be a city. (11) What, then, is the reason for this? It is surely not on account of a lack of proximity of
the partnership. For even if they joined together while participating in this way, but each nevertheless treated his own household 25
as a city and each other as if there were a defensive alliance
merely for assistance against those committing injustice, it would
not by this fact be held a city by those studying the matter precisely—if, that is, they participated in a similar way when joined
together as they had when separated. (12) It is evident, therefore,
that the city is not a partnership in a location and for the sake of 30
not committing injustice against each other and of transacting
business. These things must necessarily be present if there is to be
a city, but not even when all of them are present is it yet a city, but
[the city is] the partnership in living well both of households and
families for the sake of a complete and self-sufficient life. (13)
This will not be possible, however, unless they inhabit one and the 35
same location and make use of intermarriage. It was on this account that marriage connections arose in cities, as well as clans,
festivals, and the pastimes of living together. This sort of thing is
the work of affection; for affection is the intentional choice of living together. Living well, then, is the end of the city, and these
things are for the sake of this end. (14) A city is the partnership of 40
families and villages in a complete and self-sufficient life. This, 1281a1
we assert, is living happily and finely. The political partnership
must be regarded, therefore, as being for the sake of noble actions, not for the sake of living together. (15) Hence those who
contribute most to a partnership of this sort have a greater part in
the city than those who are equal or greater in freedom and family 5
but unequal in political virtue, or those who outdo them in wealth
but are outdone in virtue.

That all who dispute about regimes speak of some part of justice, then, is evident from what has been said. 10

99

CHAPTER 10

(1) There is a question as to what the authoritative element of the city should be. It is either the multitude, the wealthy, the respectable, the one who is best of all, or the tyrant; but all of these appear to involve difficulties. How could they not? If the poor by the fact of being the majority distribute among themselves the things of the wealthy, is this not unjust? "By Zeus, it was resolved in just fashion by the authoritative element!" (2) What, then, ought one to say is the extreme of injustice? Again, taking all [the citizens] into consideration, if the majority distributes among itself the things of a minority, it is evident that it will destroy the city. Yet it is certainly not virtue that destroys the element possessing it, nor is justice destructive of a city; so it is clear that this law cannot be just. (3) Further, [on such an assumption] any actions carried out by a tyrant are necessarily just: he is superior and uses force, like the multitude with respect to the wealthy.

But is it just, therefore, for the minority and the wealthy to rule? If they act in the same way and rob and plunder the possessions of the multitude, is this just? If so, the other is as well. (4) That all of these things are bad and unjust, then, is evident. But should the respectable rule and have authority over all [matters]? In this case, all the others are necessarily deprived of prerogatives, since they are not honored by [filling] political offices. For we say that offices are honors, and when the same persons always rule the others are necessarily deprived of [these honors or] prerogatives.[29] (5) But is it better for the one who is most excellent of all to rule? But this is still more oligarchic, as more are deprived of prerogatives. One might perhaps assert, however, that it is bad for the authoritative element generally to be man instead of law, at any rate if he has the passions that result [from being human] in his soul. But if law may be oligarchic or democratic, what difference will it make with regard to the questions that have been raised? For what was said before will result all the same.

CHAPTER 11

(1) Concerning the other matters there will be another discourse. That the multitude should be the authoritative element rather than those who are best but few, though, [is a position involving diffi-

culties which] could be held to be [in need of being] resolved,[30] and while questionable, it perhaps also involves some truth. (2) The many, of whom none is individually an excellent man, nevertheless can when joined together be better—not as individuals but all together—than those [who are best], just as dinners contributed [by many] can be better than those equipped from a single expenditure. For because they are many, each can have a part of virtue and prudence, and on their joining together, the multitude, with its many feet and hands and having many senses, becomes like a single human being, and so also with respect to character and mind. (3) Thus the many are also better judges of the works of music and of the poets; some [appreciate] a certain part, and all of them all the parts. (4) But it is in this that the excellent men differ from each of the many individually, just as some assert beautiful persons differ from those who are not beautiful, and things painted by art from genuine things, by bringing together things scattered and separated into one; for taken separately, at any rate, this person's eye will be more beautiful than the painted one, as will another part of another person. (5) Whether this difference between the many and the few excellent can exist in the case of every people and every multitude is not clear. Or rather, [it might be objected,] "by Zeus, it is clear that in some cases it is impossible: the same argument would apply to beasts—for what difference is there between some [multitudes] and beasts, so to speak?" But nothing prevents what was said from being true of a certain kind of multitude.

(6) Through these things, accordingly, one might resolve both the question spoken of earlier [concerning who should rule] and one connected with it—over what [matters] free persons or the multitude of the citizens (these being whoever is neither wealthy nor has any claim at all deriving from virtue) should have authority. (7) For having them share in the greatest offices is not safe: [one might argue that] through injustice and imprudence they would act unjustly in some respects and err in others. On the other hand, to give them no part and for them not to share [in the offices] is a matter for alarm, for when there exist many who are deprived of prerogatives and poor, that city is necessarily filled with enemies. (8) What is left, then, is for them to share in deliberating and judging. Hence Solon and certain other legislators arrange to have them both choose officials and audit them, but do not allow them to rule alone.[31] (9) For all of them when joined together have an adequate perception and, once mixed with those who are better, bring benefit to cities, just as impure sustenance[32] mixed with the pure makes the whole more useful than the small

1281b1

5

10

15

20

25

30

35

amount of the latter, but each separately is incomplete with respect to judging.

(10) But this arrangement of the regime involves questions. In the first place, it might be held that it belongs to the same person to judge whether someone has healed in correct fashion and to heal and make healthy one who is suffering from a particular disease, this being the doctor; and similarly with respect to other kinds of experience and art. Just as a doctor must submit to audit by doctors, then, so must the others submit to audit by those similar to them. (11) But "doctor" [is a term that can be applied to] the [ordinary] craftsman, the master craftsman, and thirdly, the person who is educated with respect to the art; for there are some of this [latter] sort in the case of nearly all the arts, and we assign the task of judging to the educated no less than to those who know [the art]. (12) And it might be held that the case is the same with respect to the choice [of officials]. Choosing correctly is indeed also the work of those who know—for example, choosing a geometer is the work of experts in geometry, and a pilot that of experts in piloting. If certain nonprofessionals share in some of these works and arts, however, they do not do so to a greater extent than those who know. (13) So according to this argument the multitude ought not to be given authority either over the choice of officials or over their auditing. (14) But perhaps not all of these things have been rightly argued, both because of the previous argument, provided the multitude is not overly slavish (for each individually will be a worse judge than those who know, but all when joined together will be either better or no worse), and because there are some [arts] concerning which the maker might not be the only or the best judge, but where those who do not possess the art also have some knowledge of its works. The maker of a house, for example, is not the only one to have some knowledge of it, but the one who uses it judges better than he does, and the one who uses it is the household manager; and a pilot judges rudders better than a carpenter, and the diner, not the cook, is the better judge of a banquet.

(15) This question, then, may perhaps be held to be adequately resolved in this fashion. But there is another connected with it. It is held to be absurd for mean persons to have authority over greater matters than the respectable; but auditing and the choice of officials are a very great thing, and in some regimes, as was said, these are given to the people, for the assembly has authority over everything of this sort. (16) Hence, persons from the lowest assessments and of whatever age share in the assembly and deliberate and adjudicate, while those from the greatest assessments

are the treasurers and generals and hold the greatest offices. Now one might resolve this question as well in a similar way. (17) For perhaps these things too are handled correctly: neither the juror nor the councilman nor the assemblyman acts as ruler, but the court, the council and the people, and each individual is [only] a part of these things just mentioned—I mean by "part" the councilman, the assemblyman, and the juror. (18) So the multitude justly has authority over greater things, for the people, the council, and the court are made up of many persons. Also, the assessment of all of them together is more than that of those who hold great offices, whether taken singly or as a [group of a] few. 35

40

(19) Let the discussion of these things stand thus, then. As regards the first question, it makes nothing more evident than that it is laws—correctly enacted—that should be authoritative and that the ruler, whether one person or more, should be authoritative with respect to those things about which the laws are completely unable to speak precisely on account of the difficulty of making clear general declarations about everything. (20) But as to what the quality of the laws should be if they are to be correctly enacted, it is not at all clear, and the question that was raised previously remains. Laws are necessarily poor or excellent and just or unjust in a manner similar to the regimes [to which they belong]: (21) if nothing else, it is evident that laws should be enacted with a view to the regime. But if this is the case, it is clear that those [enacted] in accordance with the correct regimes are necessarily just, and those [enacted] in accordance with the deviant ones, not just. 1282b1

5

10

CHAPTER 12

(1) Since in all the sciences and arts the end is some good, it is the greatest and primary good in that which is the most authoritative of all; this is the political capacity. The political good is justice, and this is the common advantage. Justice is held by all to be a certain equality, and up to a certain point they agree with the discourses based on philosophy in which ethics has been discussed;[33] for they assert that justice is a certain thing for certain persons, and should be equal for equal persons. (2) But equality in what sort of things and inequality in what sort of things—this should not be overlooked. For this involves a question, and political philosophy. One might perhaps assert that offices should be un- 15

20

103

equally distributed in accordance with a preeminence in any good
even among persons who do not differ in any other respect but
happen to be similar, on the grounds that justice and what accords
with merit is different for those who differ. (3) But if this is true, it
will mean some aggrandizement in [claims to] political justice for
those who are preeminent in complexion, height, or any other
good. (4) Is this not plainly false? That it is false is evident in the
case of the other sciences and capacities: where flute players are
similar with respect to the art, aggrandizement in flutes is not
granted to those who are better born. They will not play the flute
better [on this account]; but it is to one who is preeminent in the
work that preeminence in the instruments should be granted. If
what has been said is in some way not clear, it will be still more
evident if we take it further. (5) If someone were preeminent in
flute playing, but very deficient in good birth or fine looks, even if
each of those goods is greater than flute playing (I mean good
birth and fine looks), and even if they are proportionately more
preeminent with respect to flute playing than he is preeminent in
flute playing, the outstanding flutes nevertheless ought to be given
to him. For preeminence in wealth and good birth should contribute something to the work; but they contribute nothing. (6) Further, according to this argument every good would have to be
commensurable with every other. For if being of a certain height
[provided] more [in the way of a claim],[34] then height generally
would be in rivalry with both wealth and freedom. So if this person is more outstanding in height than that one in virtue, and is
more preeminent generally in respect to height than virtue,[35] everything would be commensurable. For if some amount of height
is superior to some amount [of virtue], it is clear that some amount
is equal. (7) Since this is impossible, it is clear that in political
matters too it is reasonable for them not to dispute over offices on
the basis of every inequality. If some are fast and others slow, they
should not have more or less on this account; it is in gymnastic
contests that being outstanding in these things wins honor. (8) The
dispute necessarily occurs in respect to those things that constitute
a city. It is reasonable, therefore, that the well born, the free, and
the wealthy lay claim to honor. For there must be both free persons and those paying an assessment, since a city cannot consist
wholly of those who are poor, any more than of slaves; (9) yet if
these things are needed, so also, it is clear, are [the virtue of] justice and military virtue. It is not possible for a city to be administered without these things. But whereas without the former elements there cannot be a city, without the latter one cannot be
finely administered.

CHAPTER 13

(1) Now with a view to the existence of a city, all or at least some of these things might be held to have a correct claim in the dispute; but with a view to a good life it is education and virtue above all that would have a just claim in the dispute, as was also said earlier. But since those who are equal in one thing alone should not have equality in everything, nor those who are unequal in a single thing inequality, all regimes of this sort are necessarily deviations. (2) It was also said previously that all dispute justly in a certain way, but not justly in an unqualified sense. The wealthy [have a claim] because they have the greater part of the territory, and the territory is something common; further, for the most part they are more trustworthy regarding agreements. The free and well born [have a claim] as being close to one another; for the better born are more particularly citizens than the ignoble, and good birth is honorable at home among everyone. (3) Further, [the well born have a claim] because it is likely that better persons come from those who are better, for good birth is virtue of a family. In a similar way, then, we shall assert that virtue has a just claim in the dispute, for we assert that [the virtue of] justice is a virtue characteristic of partnerships, and that all the other [virtues] necessarily follow on it.[36] (4) Finally, the majority [has a just claim] in relation to a minority, for they are superior and wealthier and better when the majority is taken together in relation to the minority.

If, therefore, all should exist in a single city—I mean, both the good and the wealthy and well born, as well as a political multitude apart from them—will there be a dispute as to which should rule, or will there not? (5) Now the judgment as to who should rule is not disputed under each of the regimes that have been mentioned, for they differ from one another by their authoritative elements: for one the authoritative element is the wealthy, for another the excellent men, and in the same manner for each of the others. Still, we are investigating how the matter is to be determined when these things are present simultaneously. (6) Now if those possessing virtue were very few in number, in what way should one decide it? Or should the fact that they are few be investigated with a view to the work involved—whether they are capable of administering the city, or whether there is a multitude of them large enough to form a city? But there is a question affecting all of those who dispute over political honors. (7) Those who claim to merit rule on account of wealth could be held to have no argument of justice at all, and similarly with those claiming to merit rule on the basis of family; for it is clear that if there is one person wealthier than all of them, this one person should rule all of them in accordance with the same [claims of] justice, and similarly, that one who is outstanding in good birth should rule those who dispute on the basis of freedom. (8) And this same thing will perhaps result with respect to aristocracies in the case of virtue; for if one man should be better than the others in the governing body, even though they are excellent, this one should have authority in accordance with the same [claims of] justice, and if it is because they are superior to the few that the multitude should have authority, if one or more persons—though fewer than the many—should be superior to the rest, these should have authority rather than the multitude.

(9) All of these things seem to make it evident, then, that none of the defining principles on the basis of which they claim they merit rule, and all the others merit being ruled by them, is correct. (10) For, indeed, multitudes have an argument of some justice to make against those claiming to merit authority over the governing body on the basis of virtue, and similarly also against those claiming it on the basis of wealth: nothing prevents the multitude from being at some point better than the few and wealthier—not as individuals but taken together. (11) Hence also it is possible to confront in this manner a question which certain persons pursue and put forward. For some raise the question whether the legislator who wants to enact the most correct laws should legislate with a view to the advantage of the better persons or that of the majority, when what was spoken of turns out to be the case. (12) But correctness must be taken to mean "in an equal spirit": what is [enacted] in an equal spirit is correct with a view both to the advantage of the city as a whole and to the common [advantage] of the citizens. A citizen in the common sense is one who shares in ruling and being ruled; but he differs in accordance with each regime. In the case of the best regime, he is one who is capable of and intentionally chooses being ruled and ruling with a view to the life in accordance with virtue.

(13) If there is one person so outstanding by his excess of virtue—or a number of persons, though not enough to provide a full complement for the city—that the virtue of all the others and their political capacity is not commensurable with their own (if there are a number) or his alone (if there is one), such persons can no longer be regarded as a part of the city. For they will be done injustice if it is claimed they merit equal things in spite of being so unequal in virtue and political capacity; for such a person would

106

likely be like a god among human beings. (14) From this it is clear
that legislation must necessarily have to do with those who are
equal both in stock and capacity, and that for the other sort of person there is no law—they themselves are law. It would be ridiculous, then, if one attempted to legislate for them. They would per-   15
haps say what Antisthenes says the lions say when the hares are
making their harangue and claiming that everyone merits equality.[37] (15) Hence democratically run cities enact ostracism for this
sort of reason. For these are surely held to pursue equality above
all others, and so they used to ostracize and banish for fixed peri-   20
ods from the city those who were held to be preeminent in power
on account of wealth or abundance of friends or some other kind
of political strength.[38] (16) The tale is told that the Argonauts left
Heracles behind for this sort of reason: the Argo was unwilling to
have him on board because he so exceeded the other sailors.[39]
Hence also those who criticize tyranny and the advice Periander   25
gave to Thrasyboulus must not be supposed to be simply correct
in their censure. (17) It is reported that Periander said nothing by
way of advice to the messenger who had been sent to him, but
merely lopped off the preeminent ears of corn and so leveled the
field. When the messenger, who was in ignorance of the reason   30
behind what had happened, reported the incident, Thrasyboulus
understood that he was to eliminate the preeminent men.[40] (18)
This is something that is advantageous not only to tyrants, nor are
tyrants the only ones who do it, but the matter stands similarly
with respect both to oligarchies and to democracies; for ostracism   35
has the same power in a certain way as pulling down and exiling
the preeminent. (19) And the same thing is done in the case of
cities and nations alike by those with [military] power under their
authority—for example, the Athenians in the case of the Samians, Chians, and Lesbians, for no sooner was their [imperial]   40
rule firm than they humbled these [cities,] contrary to the compacts [they had with them].[41] And the king of the Persians frequently pruned back the Medes and Babylonians and others who   1284b1
harbored high thoughts on account of once exercising [imperial]
rule themselves.

(20) The issue is one that concerns all regimes generally, including correct ones. For the deviant ones do this looking to the
private [advantage of the rulers], yet even in the case of those that   5
look to the common good the matter stands in the same way. (21)
This is clear as well in the case of the other arts and sciences. For
a painter would not allow himself to paint an animal with a foot
that exceeded proportion, not even if it were outstandingly beautiful, nor would a shipbuilder permit himself to build a stern or any   10

107

of the other parts of a ship that exceeded proportion, nor indeed would a chorus master allow someone with a voice louder and more beautiful than the entire chorus to be a member of it. (22) So on this account there is nothing that prevents monarchs from being in consonance with their cities when they do this, provided their own rule is beneficial to their cities. Thus in connection with the [generally] agreed forms of preeminence the argument concerning ostracism involves a certain political justice. (23) Now it is better if the legislator constitutes the regime from the beginning in such a way that it does not need this sort of healing; but the "second voyage," [42] if the contingency should arise, is to try to correct [the regime] with some corrective of this sort. But this is not what used to happen in the case of the cities [that used it]: they did not look to the advantage of their own regime but used ostracisms for purposes of factional conflict.

(24) In the deviant regimes it is evident that ostracism is advantageous [for the rulers] privately [43] and is just; and perhaps that it is not simply just is also evident. In the case of the best regime, however, there is considerable question as to what ought to be done if there happens to be someone who is outstanding not on the basis of preeminence in the other goods such as strength, wealth, or abundance of friends, but on the basis of virtue. (25) For surely no one would assert that such a person should be expelled and banished. But neither would they assert that there should be rule over such a person: this is almost as if they should claim to merit ruling over Zeus by splitting the offices. [44] What remains—and it seems the natural course—is for everyone to obey such a person gladly, so that persons of this sort will be permanent kings in their cities.

CHAPTER 14

(1) Perhaps it is the right thing after these discourses to make a transition and investigate kingship; for we assert that this is one of the correct regimes. What must be investigated is whether it is advantageous for the city or the territory that is to be well administered to be under a kingship or not, or some other regime instead, or whether it is advantageous for some but not others. (2) First, it should be determined whether there is one single type or whether it has several varieties.

This, at any rate, is surely easy to discern—that it encom- 1285a1
passes several types, and that the mode of rule is not the same in
all. (3) For that of the Spartan regime is held to be particularly
[representative] of kingships based on law; it does not have authority over all matters, but when [the king] goes outside their territory he has leadership in matters related to war, and matters re- 5
lated to the gods are further assigned to the kings. (4) This [kind
of] kingship, then, is a sort of permanent generalship of plenipo-
tentiaries. [The king] does not have authority in matters of life
and death, except in certain kingships such as those in ancient
times, [where he could put men to death] on military expeditions 10
by the law of might. Homer makes this clear: Agamemnon en-
dured being spoken ill of in assemblies, but when they went out
to fight he had authority even in matters of life and death. (5) At
any rate, he says: "Anyone I find apart from the battle, he shall
have no hope of escaping the dogs and birds; for death is in my
power." [45] This, then, is one kind of kingship, generalship for life; 15
and some of these are [constituted] on the basis of family, while
others are elective.

(6) Beside this there is another form of monarchy—the kingships that exist among some of the barbarians. All of these are
very near to tyrannies in their power, but are based on law and
hereditary. It is because barbarians are more slavish in their characters than Greeks (those in Asia being more so than those in Eu- 20
rope) that they put up with a master's rule without making any
difficulties. (7) They are tyrannical, then, through being of this
sort; but they are stable because they are hereditary and based on
law. For the same reason, their bodyguard is of a kingly rather
than a tyrannical sort. For the citizens guard kings with their own 25
arms, while a foreign element guards the tyrant, since the former
rule willing persons in accordance with law, while the latter rule
unwilling persons. So the ones have a bodyguard provided by the
citizens, the others one that is directed against them.

(8) These, then, are two kinds of monarchy, but there is another
which existed among the ancient Greeks—[rule by] those they 30
call dictators. [46] This is, to speak simply, an elective tyranny, and
differs from barbarian kingship not by not being based on law but
only by not being hereditary. (9) Some ruled in this office for life,
others for certain fixed periods of time or for [the purpose of per-
forming] certain actions. For example, the Mytilenaeans once
elected Pittacus [to defend them] against the exiles headed by 35
Antimenides and the poet Alcaeus. (10) Alcaeus makes clear in
one of his drinking songs that they elected Pittacus tyrant; for he

40   censures them because "they set up Pittacus, base of lineage, as tyrant of a city lacking bile and heavy with doom, with great praise from the crowd."[47] (11) These are and were like rule of a master on account of their being tyrannical, but like kingship on account of their being elective and over willing persons. But there is another kind of kingly monarchy, those belonging to the times of the heroes, which were willing, hereditary, and arose in accordance with law.[48] (12) For because the first [kings] had been benefactors of the multitude in connection with the arts or with war or by bringing them together [in a city] or providing them land, these came to be kings over willing persons, and their descendants took over from them. They had authority regarding leadership in war and those sacrifices that did not require priests; in addition to this, they were judges in legal cases. Some of them did this under oath and others not; the oath was a lifting up of the scepter.[49] (13) In ancient times they ruled continuously, dealing with city matters, rural matters, and matters beyond the borders. Later, however, some of these things were relinquished by the kings, some were taken away by the mob, and in most cities the kings were left only with the sacrifices. Wherever there was a kingship worth speaking of, they only held the leadership in military matters beyond the borders.

    (14) These, then, are the kinds of kingship, being four in number: one, that of the times of the heroes, which was over willing persons but for certain fixed [purposes], the king being general and juror and having authority over matters related to the gods; second, the barbaric, which is rule of a master in accordance with law, and deriving from family; third, what they call dictatorship, which is elective tyranny; and fourth among them, the Spartan, which to speak simply is permanent generalship based on family. (15) These differ from one another, then, in this manner. But there is also a fifth kind of kingship, when one person has authority over all matters, just as each nation and each city has authority over common matters, with an arrangement that resembles household management. For just as rule of the household manager is a kind of kingship over the house, so [this kind of] kingship is household management for a city or a nation (or several nations).

CHAPTER 15

(1) There are, then, fundamentally two kinds of kingship which must be investigated, this and the Spartan. For most of the others

are between these: they have authority over fewer matters than absolute kingship does, but more than Spartan kingship. (2) So the investigation is fundamentally about two things: one, whether it is advantageous for cities to have a permanent general (whether [chosen] on the basis of family or by turns) or not; the other, whether it is advantageous for one person to have authority over all matters or not. Now to investigate this sort of generalship has the look of [an investigation of] laws rather than the regime, since this is something that can arise in all regimes; so the first may be dismissed. (3) The remaining mode of kingship, however, is a kind of regime, so this should be studied and the questions it involves gone over.

1286a1

5

The beginning point of the inquiry is this: whether it is more advantageous to be ruled by the best man or by the best laws. (4) Those who consider it advantageous to be under a kingship hold that laws only speak of the universal and do not command with a view to circumstances. So to rule in accordance with written [rules] is foolish in any art; and in Egypt it is permissible for doctors to alter the treatment after the fourth day, though before then they may do so at their own risk. It is evident, therefore, for the same reason that the best regime is not one based on written [rules] and laws. (5) Yet that same universal account should also be available to rulers; and what is unaccompanied by the passionate element generally is superior to that in which it is innate. Now this is not present in law, but every human soul necessarily has it. But one might perhaps assert that this is made up for by the fact that he will deliberate in finer fashion concerning particulars. (6) That [the ruler] must necessarily be a legislator, then, and that laws must exist, is clear; but they must not be authoritative insofar as they deviate [from what is right], though in other matters they should be authoritative. But as regards the things that law is unable to judge either generally or well, should the one best person rule, or all? (7) As it is, they [all] come together to adjudicate and deliberate and judge, and the judgments themselves all concern particulars. Any one of them taken singly is perhaps inferior in comparison [to the best man]; but the city is made up of many persons, just as a feast to which many contribute is finer than a single and simple one, and on this account a crowd also judges many matters better than any single person. (8) Further, what is many is more incorruptible: like a greater amount of water, the multitude is more incorruptible than the few. The judgment of a single person is necessarily corrupted when he is dominated by anger or some other passion of this sort, whereas it is hard for all to become angry and err at the same time. (9) But the multitude must be free persons acting in no way against the law, except in

10

15

20

25

30

35

111

those cases where it necessarily falls short. This is certainly not easy for many, but if there were a number who were both good men and good citizens, is the one ruler more incorruptible, or rather the larger number who are all good? Is it not clear that it is the larger number? Yet the latter will have factional conflict, while the former will be without it. (10) But against this should perhaps be set down that they [may be] excellent in soul, just like the single person. If, then, the rule of a number of persons who are all good men is to be regarded as aristocracy, and the rule of a single person as kingship, aristocracy would be more choiceworthy for cities than kingship (whether the office brings power with it or not), provided it is possible to find a number of persons who are similar.

(11) And this is perhaps why [peoples] were under kingships originally—because it was rare to discover men who were very outstanding in virtue, especially since the cities they inhabited then were so small. Also, they selected kings on account of their benefactions, something that is the work of good men. But when it happened that many arose who were similar with respect to virtue, they no longer tolerated [kingship] but sought something common and established a polity. (12) As they became worse and did business at the expense of common [funds,] it was reasonable that oligarchies should arise as a result, for they made wealth a thing of honor. After this there was a change first into tyrannies, then from tyrannies into democracy. For by bringing things into fewer hands through a base longing for profit, they made the multitude stronger, and so it attacked them and democracies arose. (13) Now that it has happened that cities have become even larger, it is perhaps no longer easy for any regime to arise other than a democracy.

But if one were to regard kingship as the best thing for cities, how should one handle what pertains to the offspring? Must the family rule as kings also? But if those born into it are persons of average quality, it would be harmful. (14) Perhaps he will not turn it over to his children in spite of having authority to do so? But it is not easy to believe this either; it would be difficult, and [require] greater virtue than accords with human nature. There is a question also concerning his power—whether one who is going to rule as king should have about himself some force by which he will be able to compel those who do not want to obey, or how otherwise the office can be administered. (15) For even if he had authority in accordance with law and acted in nothing on the basis of his own will contrary to the law, still there must necessarily be available to him some power by which to safeguard the laws. (16)

1286b1

5

10

15

20

25

30

112

In the case of a king of this sort it is perhaps not difficult to determine this: he himself should have a certain force, but the force should be such that it is superior to individuals both by themselves and taking many of them together, but inferior to the multitude. It was thus that the ancients gave a bodyguard whenever they selected someone to be what they called dictator or tyrant of the city; and when Dionysius requested a bodyguard, someone advised the Syracusans to give him a bodyguard of this size.[50]

35

40

CHAPTER 16

(1) The argument has now come around to the king who acts in all things according to his own will, and this must be investigated. Now the king, so-called, [who rules] according to law is not, as we said, a kind of kingship.[51] There can be a permanent general in all [regimes]—in democracy or aristocracy, for example; and many give one person authority over administration—there is an office of this sort at Epidamnus, for instance, and one of somewhat lesser extent at Opus as well. (2) Concerning so-called absolute kingship, on the other hand (this is where the king rules in all matters[52] according to his own will),[53] some hold that it is not even in accordance with nature for one person among all the citizens to have authority,[54] where the city is constituted out of similar persons. For in the case of persons similar by nature, justice and merit must necessarily be the same according to nature; and so if it is harmful for their bodies if unequal persons have equal sustenance and clothing, it is so also [for their souls if they are equal] in what pertains to honors, and similarly therefore if equal persons have what is unequal. (3) Hence it is no more just [for equal persons] to rule than to be ruled, and it is therefore just [that they rule and be ruled] by turns. But this is already law; for the arrangement [of ruling and being ruled] is law. Accordingly, to have law rule is to be chosen in preference to having one of the citizens do so, according to this same argument, (4) and if it should be better to have some of them rule, these must be established as law-guardians and as servants of the laws; for there must necessarily exist certain offices [by which persons rule and not law], but they deny that it is just that this one person [rule], at least when all are similar. For that matter, as regards those things which law is held not to be capable of determining, a human being could not decide them either. (5) Rather, the law educates especially for

1287a1

5

10

15

20

25

113

this, and hands over what remains [undetermined by law itself] to be judged and administered "by the most just decision" of the rulers.[55] Further, it allows them to make corrections in cases where they hold something to be better than the existing [laws] on the basis of their experience. One who asks law to rule, therefore, is held to be asking god and intellect alone to rule, while one who

30   asks man adds the beast. Desire is a thing of this sort; and spiritedness perverts rulers and the best men. Hence law is intellect without appetite. (6) And the argument from the example of the arts may be held to be false—that it is a poor thing [for example] to heal in accordance with written [rules], and one should choose

35   instead to use those who possess the art. (7) For these do not act against reason on account of affection, but earn their pay by making the sick healthy; but those in political offices are accustomed to acting in many matters with a view to spite or favor. In any case, if doctors were suspected of being persuaded by a person's

40   enemies to do away with him for profit, he would be more inclined to seek treatment from written [rules]. (8) Moreover, doc-

1287bl   tors bring in other doctors for themselves when they are sick, and trainers other trainers when they are exercising, the assumption being that they are unable to judge what is true on account of judging both in their own case and while they are in a state of suffering. So it is clear that in seeking justice they are seeking impartiality; for law is impartiality. (9) Further, laws based on

5   [unwritten] customs are more authoritative, and deal with more authoritative matters, than those based on written [rules]; so if it is safer for a human being to rule than laws based on written [rules], this is not the case for laws based on custom. Moreover, it is not easy for one person to survey many things. Accordingly, there will be a need for a number of persons to be selected as rulers

10   under him—but then what difference is there between having them present right from the beginning and having one person select them in this manner? (10) Further, there is what was said earlier: if it is just for the excellent man to rule because he is better, two good persons are better than the one. Thus the saying "two going together," and Agamemnon's prayer for "ten such coun-

15   selors for myself." [56] Even now there are offices (that of juror, for example) which have authority to judge concerning some matters that the law is unable to determine; for in the case of those it is able to determine, at any rate, no one would dispute that the law would be the best ruler and judge concerning them. (11) But because some things can be encompassed by the laws and others

20   cannot, the latter cause the question to be raised and pursued whether the rule of the best law is more choiceworthy than that of

the best man. For to legislate concerning matters of deliberation is impossible. Now their counterargument is not that it is not necessary for a human being to judge in such matters, but rather that there should be many persons instead of one only. (12) For every ruler judges finely if he has been educated by the law; and it would perhaps be held to be odd if someone should see better with two eyes, judge better with two ears, and act better with two feet and hands than many persons would with many. For as it is, monarchs create many eyes for themselves, and ears, feet, and hands as well; for those who are friendly to their rule and themselves they make corulers. (13) If they are not friends, they will not behave in accordance with the monarch's intention, but if they are friends to him and his rule, the friend is someone similar and equal, so if he supposes these should rule, he [necessarily] supposes that those who are similar and equal should rule similarly. The arguments of those who dispute against kingship are, then, essentially these.

CHAPTER 17

(1) And yet while these [arguments] hold in some cases, in others perhaps they do not. For by nature there is a certain [people] apt for mastery, another apt for kingship, and another that is political, and this is both just and advantageous. (Nothing, however, is naturally apt for tyranny, or for the other regimes that are deviations: these cases are contrary to nature.) (2) From what has been said, at any rate, it is evident that among similar and equal persons it is neither advantageous nor just for one person to have authority over all [matters], regardless of whether there are laws or not and he acts as law himself, whether he and they are good or not, and even whether he is better in respect to virtue—unless it is in a certain manner.

(3) What that manner is must now be spoken of, though in a sense it was spoken of previously as well. We must first determine what it is that is apt for kingship, what is aristocratic, and what is political. (4) What is apt for kingship, then, is a multitude of such a sort that it accords with its nature to support a family that is preeminent in virtue relative to political leadership; an aristocratic multitude is one of such a sort that it accords with its nature to support a multitude capable of being ruled in accordance with the rule that belongs to free persons by those whose virtue makes

115

them expert leaders relative to political rule; and a political multitude is one in which there arises in accordance with its nature a military multitude capable of ruling and being ruled in accordance with a law distributing offices on the basis of merit to those who are well off.[57] (5) Now when it happens that a whole family, or even some one person among the rest, is so outstanding in virtue that this virtue is more preeminent than that of all the rest, it is just in that case that the family be a kingly one and have authority over all matters, or that this one person be a king. (6) For as was said earlier, the matter stands thus not only on the basis of the sort of justice that is customarily alleged by those who establish aristocracies and oligarchies, or for that matter democracies—they all[58] claim to merit [rule] on the basis of some preeminence, though not the same preeminence—but [also] in accordance with that [sort of justice] mentioned earlier.[59] (7) For it is surely not proper to execute or exile or ostracize a person of this sort, or claim that he merits to be ruled in turn. It does not accord with nature for the part[60] to be preeminent over the whole, but this is the result in the case of someone having such superiority. (8) So all that remains is for a person of this sort to be obeyed, and to have authority simply and not by turns. Concerning kingship, then, the varieties that it has, and whether it is advantageous for cities or not, and if so, which and in what fashion, let our discussion stand thus.

CHAPTER 18

(1) Since we assert that there are three correct regimes, that of these that one is necessarily best which is managed by the best persons, and that this is the sort of regime in which there happens to be one certain person or a whole family or a multitude that is preeminent in virtue with respect to all the rest, [and this a multitude] of persons capable of being ruled and of ruling with a view to the most choiceworthy way of life, and since in our earlier discourses it was shown that the virtue of man and citizen is necessarily the same in the best city,[61] it is evident that it is in the same manner and through the same things that a man becomes excellent and that one might constitute a city under an aristocracy or a kingship. So the education and the habits that make a man excellent are essentially the same as those that make him a political or kingly [ruler].

116

(2) These things having been determined, we must now attempt to speak about the best regime—in what manner it accords with its nature to arise and to be established. It is necessary, then, for one who is going to undertake the investigation appropriate to it. . . .[62]

5

BOOK 4

CHAPTER 1

10   (1) In all arts and sciences which have not arisen on a partial basis but are complete with respect to some one type of thing, it belongs to a single one to study what is fitting in the case of each type of thing. In the case of training for the body, for example, it belongs to it to study what sort is advantageous for what sort of body; which is best (for the best is necessarily fitting for the body that is naturally the finest and is most finely equipped); which is

15   best—a single one for all—for most bodies (for this too is a task of gymnastic expertise); (2) and further, if someone should desire neither the disposition nor the knowledge befitting those connected with competitions, it belongs no less to the sports trainer and the gymnastic expert to provide this capacity as well. We see a similar thing occurring in the case of medicine, shipbuilding,

20   [the making of] clothing, and every other art.

(3) So it is clear that, with regard to the regime, it belongs to the same science to study what the best regime is, and what quality it should have to be what one would pray for above all, with external things providing no impediment; which regime is fitting for

25   which [cities]—for it is perhaps impossible for many to obtain the best, so neither the one that is superior simply nor the one that is the best that circumstances allow should be overlooked by the good legislator and the political [ruler] in the true sense; (4) further, thirdly, the regime based on a presupposition—for any given regime should be studied [with a view to determining] both how it might arise initially and in what manner it might be preserved for

30   the longest time once in existence (I am speaking of the case where a city happens neither to be governed by the best regime—and is not equipped even with the things necessary for it—nor to be governed by the regime that is [the best] possible among existing ones, but one that is poorer; (5) and besides all these things, the regime that is most fitting for all cities should be recognized.

35   Thus most of those who have expressed views concerning the regime, even if what they say is fine in other respects, are in error

118

when it comes to what is useful. (6) For one should study not only the best regime but also the regime that is [the best] possible, and similarly also the regime that is easier and more attainable for all. As it is, however, some seek only the one that is at the peak and requires much equipment, while others, though speaking of an attainable sort of regime, disregard those that exist and instead praise the Spartan or some other [single one]. (7) But one ought to introduce an arrangement of such a sort that they will easily be persuaded and be able to participate in it [by the fact that it arises directly] out of those that exist, since to reform a regime is no less a task than to institute one from the beginning, just as unlearning something is no less a task than learning it from the beginning. Hence in addition to what has been said the political expert should be able to assist existing regimes as well, as was also said earlier.[1] (8) But this is impossible if he does not know how many kinds of regime there are. As it is, some suppose there is one sort of democracy and one sort of oligarchy; but this is not true. So the varieties of the regimes—how many there are and in how many ways they are combined—should not be overlooked. (9) And it is with this same prudence that one should try to see both what laws are best and what are fitting for each of the regimes. For laws should be enacted—and all are in fact enacted—with a view to the regimes, and not regimes with a view to the laws. (10) For a regime is an arrangement in cities connected with the offices, [establishing] the manner in which they have been distributed, what the authoritative element of the regime is, and what the end of the partnership is in each case;[2] and there are distinct laws among the things that are indicative of the regime—those in accordance with which the rulers must rule and guard against those transgressing them.[3] (11) So it is clear that it is necessary to have a grasp of the varieties of each regime and their number with a view to the enactment of laws as well. For it is impossible for the same laws to be advantageous for all oligarchies or for all democracies, at least if there are several kinds of them and not merely a single sort of democracy or of oligarchy.

40

1289a1

5

10

15

20

25

CHAPTER 2

(1) Since in our first inquiry concerning regimes we distinguished three correct regimes—kingship, aristocracy, and polity—and three deviations from these—tyranny from kingship, oligarchy

30

35

from aristocracy, and democracy from polity;[4] and since aristocracy and kingship have been spoken of—for to study the best regime is the same as to speak about [the regimes designated by] these terms as well, as each of them wishes to be established on the basis of virtue that is furnished with equipment;[5] and further, since the difference between aristocracy and kingship and when [a regime] should be considered kingship[6] were discussed earlier;[7] what remains is to treat polity—that which is called by the name common [to all regimes]—and the other regimes—oligarchy and democracy, and tyranny.

40

1289b1

5

10

(2) Now it is evident also which of the deviations is the worst and which second worst. For the deviation from the first and most divine regime must necessarily be the worst, but kingship must necessarily either have the name alone without being such, or rest on the great superiority of the person ruling as king. So tyranny is the worst, and the farthest removed from [being] a regime;[8] oligarchy is second worst, for aristocracy stands far from this regime; and democracy is the most moderate. (3) Now an earlier [thinker] has expressed this view as well, though without looking to the same thing we do.[9] For he judged them all to be respectable (there being a good sort of oligarchy, for example, as well as of the others), with democracy as the worst, but the best of the bad sorts; but we assert that these are generally thoroughly in error, and that it is not right to speak of one sort of oligarchy as better than another, but rather as less bad.

15

20

25

(4) As regards this sort of judgment, let us dismiss the matter for the present. Instead, we must distinguish, first, the number of varieties of regimes, if indeed there are several kinds both of democracy and of oligarchy; next, which is the most attainable and which the most choiceworthy after the best regime, and if there is some other that is aristocratic and finely constituted but fitting for most cities, which it is; (5) next, which of the others is choiceworthy for which [cities]—for perhaps democracy is more necessary for some than oligarchy, and for others the latter more than the former; after these things, in what manner the one wishing to do so should establish these regimes—I mean, democracy in each of its kinds and likewise oligarchy; (6) and finally, when we have provided as far as possible a concise treatment of all these matters, we must attempt to describe the sources of destruction and preservation for regimes both in general and in the case of each separately, and the reasons for which these things particularly come about in accordance with the nature of the matter.[10]

CHAPTER 3

(1) Now the reason for there being a number of regimes is that there are a number of parts in any city. For, in the first place, we see that all cities are composed of households, and next that of this multitude some are necessarily well off, others poor, and others middling, and that of the well off and the poor there is an armed and an unarmed element. (2) And we see that the people has a farming, a marketing, and a vulgar element. In the case of the notables too there are differences based on wealth and the extent of their property—for example, in the matter of horse breeding, which is not easy to do for those who are not wealthy. (3) Hence in ancient times those cities whose power lay in horses had oligarchies, for they used horses in wars against their neighbors— for example, the Eretrians and Chalcidians, the Magnesians on the Maeander, and many others in Asia. (4) Further, in addition to the differences based on wealth, there is that based on family and that based on virtue, and indeed whatever else was said to be a part of the city in the [discourses] on aristocracy (for there we distinguished how many necessary parts there are in every city);[11] for of these parts all share in the regime in some cases, and in others more or fewer. (5) It is evident, therefore, that there must necessarily be a number of regimes differing from one another in kind, since these parts differ from one another in kind. Now a regime is the arrangement of offices, and all distribute these either on the basis of the power of those sharing [in the regime] or on the basis of some equality common to them—I mean, [the power of] the poor or the well off, or some [equality] common to both.[12] (6) There are necessarily, therefore, as many regimes as there are arrangements based on the sorts of preeminence and the differences of the parts.

But there are held to be two sorts of regimes particularly: just as in the case of winds some are called northern and others southern and the others deviations from these, so [many hold there are] two sorts of regimes, [rule by] the people and oligarchy. (7) They regard aristocracy as a kind of oligarchy on the grounds that it is a sort of rule by the few, and so-called polity as a kind of democracy, just as among the winds the western is regarded as belonging to the northern, the eastern to the southern. It is similar also in the case of harmonies, so some assert: they regard there as being two kinds of these as well, Dorian and Phrygian, while the other modal arrangements they call either "Doric" or "Phrygic."[13] (8)

30

35

40

1290a1

5

10

15

20

[Men] are accustomed particularly, then, to conceive of regimes in this way. But it is truer and better to distinguish as we have, and say that one or two are finely constituted and the others deviations from them—deviations from the well-blended harmony as well as from the best regime, the more taut [of the harmonies] being oligarchic and more like rule of a master, the relaxed and soft being popular.[14]

CHAPTER 4

(1) One should not regard democracy, as some are accustomed to do now, as existing simply wherever the multitude has authority, since in oligarchies and indeed everywhere the major part has authority, nor oligarchy as existing wherever the few have authority over the regime. (2) For if [the male inhabitants of a city] were one thousand three hundred in all, and a thousand of these were wealthy and gave no share in ruling to the three hundred poor, though these were free persons and similar in other respects, no one would assert that they are under a democracy. (3) Similarly, if the poor were few, but superior to a majority of well-off persons, no one would describe this sort of thing as an oligarchy, if the others had no part in the prerogatives although they were wealthy. It must rather be said, therefore, that [rule of] the people exists when [all] free persons have authority, and oligarchy when the wealthy have it; (4) but it turns out that the former are many and the latter few, for many are free but few wealthy. Otherwise, there would be an oligarchy where they distributed offices on the basis of size, as some assert happens in Ethiopia,[15] or on the basis of good looks; for the number of both good-looking and tall persons is few. (5) Yet neither is it adequate to define these regimes by these things alone. But since there are a number of parts both in the case of [rule of] the people and of oligarchy, it must be grasped further that [rule of] the people does not exist even where a few free persons rule over a majority who are not free, as at Apollonia on the Ionian Sea, for example, or Thera (in each of these cities those who were outstanding in good birth on account of descent from the first settlers of the colony—a few among many—held the prerogatives); nor is there [rule of] the people where the wealthy [rule] through being preeminent in number, as was formerly the case at Colophon (there the majority possessed large properties prior to the war against the Lydians).[16] (6) De-

122

mocracy exists when the free and poor, being a majority, have authority to rule; oligarchy, when the wealthy and better born have authority and are few.   20

(7) That there are a number of regimes, then, and the reason for this, has been spoken of. As to why there are more than the ones spoken of, which these are, and how [they come to exist], let us speak of this, taking as our beginning point what was mentioned earlier. We agree that every city has not one part but several. (8) Now if we chose to acquire a grasp of kinds of animals, we would   25 first enumerate separately what it is that every animal must necessarily have—for example, certain of the sense organs and something that can work on and receive sustenance, such as a mouth and a stomach, and in addition to these, parts by which each of them moves; and if there were then only so many kinds,[17] and there were varieties of these (I mean, for example, a certain number of types of mouth and stomach and sense organs, and further   30 of the locomotive parts), the number of combinations of these things will necessarily make a number of types of animals, since it is impossible for the same animal to have a number of varieties of mouth or of ears; so when taken together all the possible pairings of them will make kinds of an animal, and as many kinds of   35 the animal as there are combinations of the necessary parts. (9) [One may proceed] in the same manner in the case of the regimes spoken of. For cities are composed not of one but of many parts, as we have often said.[18] Now one of these is the multitude that is   40 concerned with sustenance, those called farmers. A second is what is called the vulgar element. This is the one that is concerned with the arts, without which a city cannot be inhabited   1291a1 (though of these arts [only] some must exist of necessity, while others are directed toward luxury or living finely). (10) A third is the marketing element, by which I mean that which spends its time concerned with buying and selling and trade and commerce.   5 A fourth is the laboring element; a fifth type is the warrior element—which is no less necessary than the others if they are not to be the slaves of whomever marches against them. (11) For it is impossible that a city that is by nature slavish merits being called such: the city is self-sufficient, but what is slavish is not self-sufficient.   10

Hence what is said in the *Republic*, though sophisticated, is not adequate.[19] (12) For Socrates asserts that a city is composed of the four most necessary persons, and he says these are a weaver, a farmer, a shoemaker, and a builder; and then, on the grounds that these are not self-sufficient, he adds a smith and persons in charge of the necessary herds, and further both a trader and a person en-   15 gaged in commerce. All of these make up the complement of the first city, as if every city were constituted for the sake of the necessary things and not rather for the sake of what is noble, and as if it were equally in need of shoemakers and farmers. (13) But he does not assign it a warrior part until, with the increase in their territory and its encroaching on that of their neighbors, they become involved in war. Moreover, even among four persons, or however many partners there are, there must necessarily be someone who assigns and judges what is just. (14) If, then, one were to regard soul as more a part of an animal than body, things of this sort—the military element and the element sharing in [the virtue of] justice as it relates to adjudication, and in addition the deliberative element, which is the work of political understanding— must be regarded as more a part of cities than things relating to necessary needs. (15) (Whether these belong to certain persons separately or to the same ones makes no difference to the argument; indeed, it often happens that the same persons bear arms and farm.) So if both the former and the latter elements are to be regarded as parts of the city, it is evident that the heavy-armed element, at any rate, is a necessary part of the city.[20]

A seventh is the element that performs public service by means of its property—what we call the well off. (16) An eighth is the magisterial element or that performing public service with respect to offices, since a city cannot exist without officials. There must, then, of necessity be certain persons who are capable of ruling and who perform public service for the city in this connection either continuously or in turn. (17) There remain the things we just happened to discuss, the element that deliberates and [the element that] judges concerning the just things for disputants. If these things must exist in cities, then, and exist in a way that is fine and just, there must necessarily be certain persons who share the virtue of political [rulers].[21] (18) Now the other capacities are held by many to be susceptible of belonging to the same persons. For example, the warriors, farmers, and artisans could be the same persons, and all lay claim even to virtue, and suppose themselves capable of ruling in most offices. But it is impossible for the same persons to be poor and wealthy. (19) Hence these are particularly held to be parts of the city, the well off and the poor. Further, on account of the fact that the former are for the most part few and the latter many, these parts appear [the most] opposed of the parts of the city. Accordingly, regimes are instituted on the basis of the sorts of preeminence associated with these, and there are held to be two sorts of regimes, democracy and oligarchy.

(20) That there are several sorts of regimes, then, and what the

124

reasons are for this, was stated earlier; we may now say that there   15
are also several kinds of democracy and of oligarchy. This is evident from what has been said as well. (21) For there are several
kinds both of the people and of the so-called notables. In the case
of the people, for example, there are the farmers, the element engaged in the arts, the marketing element whose pursuits are buying and selling, and the element connected with the sea; of the   20
latter, there is the military element, the element engaged in business, the ferrying element, and the fishing element. (In many
places one of these elements amounts to a considerable mass—for
example, the fishermen in Tarentum and Byzantium, the warship
crews at Athens, the trading element in Aegina and Chios, and the
ferrying element in Tenedos.) In addition, there is the menial element and that having little property, so as to be incapable of being   25
at leisure; and further, the free element that is not descended from
citizen parents on both sides, and whatever other similar kind of
multitude there may be. (22) In the case of the notables, [there are
kinds distinguished by] wealth, good birth, virtue, education, and
whatever is spoken of as based on the same sort of difference as
these.

The first sort of democracy, then, is that which is particularly
said to be based on equality. The law in this sort of democracy   30
asserts that there is equality when the poor are no more preeminent than the well off, and neither have authority, but they are
both [treated as] similar. (23) For if freedom indeed exists particularly in a democracy, as some conceive to be the case, as well as
equality, this would particularly happen where all participate in   35
the regime as far as possible in similar fashion. But since the people are a majority, and what is resolved by the majority is authoritative, this will necessarily be a democracy. (24) This is one
kind of democracy; another is the kind where offices are filled on
the basis of assessments, but these are low, and it is open to anyone possessing [the amount] to share, while anyone losing it does   40
not share. Another kind of democracy is where all citizens of un-
questioned descent share, but law rules. (25) Another kind of de-   1292a1
mocracy is where all have a part in the offices provided only they
are citizens, but law rules. Another kind of democracy is the same
in other respects, but the multitude has authority and not the law.
This comes about when decrees rather than law are authoritative,   5
and this happens on account of the popular leaders. (26) For in
cities under a democracy that is based on law a popular leader
does not arise, but the best of the citizens preside; but where the
laws are without authority, there popular leaders arise. For the   10
people become a monarch, from many combining into one—for

the many have authority not as individuals but all together. (27) What Homer means when he says "many-headed rule is not good"[22] is not clear—whether it is this sort of rule, or the sort when there are a number of rulers acting as individuals. At any rate, such a people, being a sort of monarch, seek to rule monarchically on account of their not being ruled by law, and become like a master: flatterers and held in honor, and this sort of [rule of] the people bears comparison with tyranny among the forms of monarchy. (28) Hence their character is the same as well: both are like masters with respect to the better persons; the decrees of the one are like the edicts of the other; and the popular leader and the flatterer are the same or comparable. These are particularly influential in each case, flatterers with tyrants and popular leaders with peoples of this sort. (29) These are responsible for decrees having authority rather than the laws because they bring everything before the people. For they become great through the people's having authority in all matters, and through having authority themselves over the opinion of the people, since the multitude is persuaded by them. (30) Moreover, some bring accusations against [certain persons holding] offices and assert that the people should judge; the invitation is gladly accepted, and all the offices are thus overthrown. One may hold it a reasonable criticism to argue that a democracy of this sort is not a regime.[23] For where the laws do not rule there is no regime. (31) The law should rule in all matters, while the offices and the regime[24] should judge in particular cases. So if democracy is one of the sorts of regime, it is evident that such a system, in which everything is administered through decrees, is not even democracy in the authoritative sense, since no decree can be general. This may stand, then, as our discussion of the kinds of democracy.

CHAPTER 5

(1) Of the kinds of oligarchy, one is where the offices are filled on the basis of assessments of such a size that the poor do not share, though they are a majority, while it is open to anyone possessing [the amount] to share in the regime. Another is when the offices are filled on the basis of large assessments, and they themselves elect in filling vacancies (if they do this out of all of these it is held to be more aristocratic, but if from certain special ones, oligarchic).[25] (2) Another form of oligarchy is when father succeeds

son. A fourth is when what was just spoken of occurs, and not law   5
but the officials rule. This is the counterpart among oligarchies to
tyranny among monarchies, and to the sort of democracy we
spoke of last among democracies; they call such an oligarchy a
"dynasty."   10

(3) There are, then, this many kinds of oligarchy and democracy. But it should not be overlooked that it has happened in many
places that, although the regime insofar as it is based on the laws
is not a popular one, it is governed in popular fashion as a result of
the character and upbringing [of the citizens]. Similarly, it has
happened elsewhere that the regime insofar as it is based on the   15
laws tends toward the popular, but through the [citizens'] upbringing and habits tends to be oligarchically run. (4) This happens particularly after revolution in regimes. For the transition is not immediate: they are content at first to aggrandize themselves at the
expense of the others only in small ways, so that the laws that   20
existed before remain, although those who have effected revolution in the regime are dominant.

CHAPTER 6

(1) That there are this many kinds of democracy and oligarchy is
evident from what has been said. For, necessarily, either all the
parts of the people that have been spoken of participate in the regime, or some do and some do not. (2) Now when the farming
element and that possessing a moderate amount of property have   25
authority over the regime, they govern themselves in accordance
with laws. For they have enough to live on as long as they work,
but are unable to be at leisure, so they put the law in charge and
assemble only for necessary assemblies. As for others, it is open
to them to share as soon as they are in possession of the assess-   30
ment defined by the laws; hence it is open to all who possess [the
amount] to share. (3) In general, it is oligarchic when it is not
open to all [actually to share in office in spite of being full citizens,] but that it should be open to them to be at leisure is impossible unless there are revenues.[26] For these reasons, then, this is
one kind of democracy. Another kind arises through the next sort   35
of distinction. For it is possible for it to be open to all of unques-
tioned descent with respect to family [to share in the regime], but
for those [only actually] to share who are able to be at leisure; (4)
hence in a democracy of this sort the laws rule on account of there

not being a revenue. A third kind is when it is open to all who are free persons to share in the regime, but they do not [actually] share for the reason just mentioned, so in this as well the law necessarily rules. (5) A fourth kind of democracy is the one that was the last to arise in cities. For on account of cities' having become much larger than they originally were and having available abundant sources of revenues, all share in the regime on account of the preeminence of the multitude, and all participate and engage in politics, as even the poor are able to be at leisure through receiving pay. (6) A multitude of this sort is indeed particularly at leisure: the care of their private affairs is in no way an obstacle for them, while it is an obstacle for the wealthy, so that the latter frequently do not participate in the assembly or in adjudicating. Hence the multitude of the poor comes to have authority over the regime, and not the laws.

(7) The kinds of democracy, then, are such and so many on account of these necessities. As for the kinds of oligarchy, when a larger number of persons owns property, but in lesser amounts and not overly much, this is the first kind of oligarchy. Sharing [in the regime] they make open to whomever possesses [the amount of the assessment]; (8) and as there is a multitude of persons sharing in the governing body, not human beings but the law necessarily has authority. For the further removed they are from monarchy, and have neither so much property that they can be at leisure without concerning themselves with it, nor so little that they must be sustained by the city, they will necessarily claim to merit having the law rule for them rather than ruling themselves. (9) Now when those who own property are fewer than those mentioned earlier, and the properties greater, the second kind of oligarchy arises. Being more influential, they claim to merit aggrandizement for themselves; hence they themselves elect from the others those who are to enter the governing body. But as they are not yet strong enough to rule without law, they make a law of this sort.[27] (10) If they tighten it by being fewer and having larger properties, the third advance in oligarchy occurs—that where the offices are in their own hands, in accordance with a law requiring that the deceased be succeeded by their sons. (11) When they tighten it excessively with respect to their properties and in the extent of their friendships, this sort of dynasty is close to monarchy, and human beings rule rather than the law. This is the fourth kind of oligarchy, the counterpart to the final kind of democracy.

CHAPTER 7

(1) There are, further, two sorts of regimes besides democracy and oligarchy, one of which is spoken of by all—and we spoke of earlier—as one of the four kinds of regimes (the four they speak of are monarchy, oligarchy, democracy, and fourthly, so-called aristocracy). There is a fifth sort, which is referred to by the term common to all—they call it polity; but because it has not often existed, it is overlooked by those who undertake to enumerate the kinds of regimes, and they use only the four (as Plato does) in the [works of theirs treating] regimes.[28] (2) Now it is right to call aristocracy [the regime] we treated in our first discourses.[29] Only the regime that is made up of those who are best simply on the basis of virtue, and not of men who are good in relation to some presupposition, is justly referred to as an aristocracy; for only here is it simply the case that the same person is a good man and a good citizen, while those who are good in others are so in relation to their regime. (3) Nevertheless, there are certain regimes which differ both from those that are oligarchically run and from so-called polity, and are called aristocracies. For wherever they elect to offices not only on the basis of wealth but also on the basis of desert, the regime itself is different from both of these and is called aristocratic. (4) For, indeed, in [cities] that do not make virtue a common concern there are still certain persons who are of good reputation and held to be respectable. Wherever, therefore, the regime looks both to wealth and to virtue as well as the people, as in Carthage, it is aristocratic; and so also those which, like the Lacedaemonian regime, look to two alone, virtue and the people, and where there is a mixture of these two things, democracy and virtue. (5) There are, therefore, these two kinds of aristocracy besides the first or the best regime. And there is a third: those forms of so-called polity which incline more toward oligarchy.

35

40

1293b1

5

10

15

20

CHAPTER 8

(1) It remains for us to speak of what is termed polity as well as of tyranny. We have arranged it thus, although polity is not a deviation, nor are those sorts of aristocracies just spoken of, because in truth all fall short of the most correct regime, and because [usu-

25   ally] enumerated with them are those which are themselves deviations from them, as we said in our initial [discourses].[30] (2) It is
reasonable to make mention of tyranny last since of all of them
this is least a regime, while our inquiry concerns the regime. The

30   reason it has been arranged in this manner, then, has been spoken
of; now we must set out [our view of] polity. Its power should be
more evident now that we have discussed what pertains to oligarchy and democracy.

(3) Simply speaking, polity is a mixture of oligarchy and democracy. It is customary, however, to call polities those [sorts of

35   polities] which tend toward democracy, and those tending more
toward oligarchy, aristocracies, on account of the fact that education and good birth particularly accompany those who are better
off. (4) Further, those who are well off are held to possess already
the things for the sake of which the unjust commit injustice; this is
why they are referred to as gentlemen and notables. Since aristoc-

40   racy tries to assign preeminence to the best of the citizens, it is
asserted that oligarchies too are made up particularly of gentlemen. (5) Also, it is held to be impossible for a city to be well

1294a1   managed if it is run not aristocratically but by the base, and similarly, for one that is not well managed to be aristocratically run.
For good management does not exist where the laws have been
well enacted yet are not obeyed. (6) Hence one should conceive it

5   to be one sort of good management when the laws are obeyed as
enacted, and another sort when the laws being upheld have been
finely enacted (for it is possible that even badly enacted ones will
be obeyed). This may be done in two ways: [they may obey] either
the laws that are the best of those possible for them, or those that
are the best simply.

(7) Aristocracy is held to be most particularly the distribution
of prerogatives on the basis of virtue; for the defining principle of

10   aristocracy is virtue, as that of oligarchy is wealth, and of [rule
of] the people freedom. (The [principle of] what the major part
resolves is present in all: in an oligarchy, an aristocracy, or in
[regimes ruled by] peoples, what is resolved by the greater part of
those sharing in the regime is authoritative.) (8) Now in most cit-

15   ies the kind of regime [that is commonly called aristocracy is not
correctly so] called.[31] For the mixture aims only at the well off
and the poor, at wealth and freedom, since in most places the well
off are held to occupy the place of gentlemen. (9) Since there are

20   three things disputing over equality in the regime,[32] freedom,
wealth, and virtue (for the fourth—what they call good birth—
accompanies the latter two, good birth being old wealth and virtue together), it is evident that a mixture of the two—of the well

off and the poor—is to be spoken of as polity, while a mixture of the three should (apart from the genuine and first form) be spoken of most particularly as aristocracy. (10) That there are other kinds of regimes apart from monarchy, democracy, and oligarchy, then, has been stated, and it is evident which sorts these are, in what ways aristocracies differ among themselves and polities from aristocracy, and that they are not far from one another.

25

CHAPTER 9

(1) In what manner so-called polity comes into being beside democracy and oligarchy, and how it should be established, we shall speak of now in conformity with what has been said. At the same time, it will be clear also what it is that defines democracy and oligarchy; for the distinction between these must be grasped, and a combination then made out of these, taking from each a tally, as it were.[33] (2) There are three defining principles of this combination or mixture. One is to take elements of the legislation of each, as for example concerning adjudication. In oligarchies they arrange to fine the well off if they do not take part in adjudicating, and provide no pay for the poor, while in democracies they provide pay for the poor and do not fine the well off. (3) What is common to and a mean between these is to have both [arrangements], and hence this is characteristic of polity, which is a mixture formed from both. This, then, is one mode of conjoining them. Another is to take the mean between the arrangements of each. For example, in the one case they attend the assembly on the basis of no assessment at all or a very small one, and in the other on the basis of a large assessment: what is common here is neither of these, but the mean between the assessments. (4) A third is [a selection] from both arrangements, taking some from the oligarchic law and some from the democratic. I mean, for example, it is held to be democratic for offices to be chosen by lot, oligarchic to have them elected, and democratic not [to do it] on the basis of an assessment, oligarchic [to do it] on the basis of an assessment. (5) It is characteristic of aristocracy and polity, therefore, to take an element from each—from oligarchy making offices elected, from democracy not [doing it] on the basis of an assessment.

(6) The manner of mixing them, then, is this. The defining principle of a good mixture of democracy and oligarchy is that it

30

35

40

1294b1

5

10

15   should be possible for the same polity to be spoken of as either a
democracy or an oligarchy, and it is clear that it is because the
mixture is a fine one that those who speak of it do so in this way.
The mean too is of this sort: each of the extremes is revealed in it.
(7) Just this happens in the case of the Lacedaemonian regime.

20   Many attempt to speak of it as if it were a democracy on account
of the fact that the arrangement has many democratic elements. In
the first place, for example, as far as the rearing of children is
concerned, those of the wealthy are reared in similar fashion to
those of the poor, and they are educated in a manner such that the

25   children of the poor can also [afford it]. (8) It is similar as well in
the age following; and when they become men the same mode is
followed. For a wealthy person is in no way marked off from a
poor one: the sustenance they get in the common messes is the
same for all, and the dress of the rich is of a sort that any of the
poor could also provide himself with. (9) Further, [it seems demo-
cratic] by the fact that, of the two greatest offices, one is elected

30   by the people, while they share in the other—for they elect the
senators and share in the board of overseers. On the other hand,
others call it oligarchy on account of its having many oligarchic
elements. For example, all the offices are chosen by election and
none by lot, a few have authority over cases [with penalties] of
death and exile, and many other such things. (10) In a polity that
is finely mixed, [the regime] should be held to be both—and nei-

35   ther. And it should be preserved through itself, not from outside—
through itself not because those wishing [its preservation] are a
majority[34] (since this might be the case even in a base regime),
but because none of the parts of the city generally would wish to
have another regime.

40   In what manner polity should be established, and similarly the
regimes termed aristocracies, has now been spoken of.

CHAPTER 10

1295a1   (1) It remains for us to speak about tyranny; not that there is room
for much argument about it, but that it may have its part in the
inquiry, since we placed it too among the regimes. Now we discussed kingship in our first discourses, where we made an investigation of what is most particularly spoken of as kingship—

5   whether it is disadvantageous or advantageous for cities, who
[should be king], where [he should be drawn] from, and how [the

kingship] should be established.[35] (2) We distinguished two kinds of tyranny while investigating kingship, as their power in a sense overlaps with kingship as well on account of the fact that both of these sorts of rule are based on law. For among some of the barbarians they choose plenipotentiary monarchs, and formerly among the ancient Greeks there arose in this manner certain monarchs who were called dictators. (3) There are certain differences between these; but both were kingly by the fact of being based on law and a monarchic rule over willing persons, and at the same time tyrannical by the rule being characteristic of a master and in accordance with their own will. There is also a third kind of tyranny, the one that is most particularly held to be tyranny, being a sort of counterpart to absolute kingship. (4) Any monarchy must necessarily be a tyranny of this sort if it rules in unchallenged fashion over persons who are all similar or better, and with a view to its own advantage and not that of the ruled. Hence [it is rule over persons who are] unwilling; for no free person would willingly tolerate this sort of rule. The kinds of tyranny, then, are these and this many for the reasons spoken of.

CHAPTER 11

(1) What regime is best and what way of life is best for most cities and most human beings, judging with a view neither to virtue of the sort that is beyond private persons, nor to education, in respect to those things requiring [special advantages provided by] nature and an equipment dependent on chance, nor to the regime that one would pray for, but a way of life which it is possible for most to participate in, and a regime in which most cities can share? (2) For those that are called aristocracies—the ones we were just speaking of—either fall outside [the range] of most cities, or border on so-called polity; hence we may speak of both as one.

Judgment in all these matters rests on the same elements. (3) If it was correctly said in the [discourses on] ethics[36] that the happy life is one in accordance with virtue and unimpeded, and that virtue is a mean, then the middling sort of life is best—the mean that is capable of being attained by each sort of individual. These same defining principles must also define virtue and vice in the case of a city and a regime; for the regime is the way of life of a city. (4) Now in all cities there are three parts of the city, the very

10

15

20

25

30

35

40

1295b1

well off, the very poor, and third, those in the middle between these. Since, however, it is agreed that what is moderate and middling is best, it is evident that in the case of the goods of fortune as well a middling possession is the best of all. (5) For it is readiest to obey reason, while for one who is overly handsome, overly strong, overly well born, or overly wealthy—or the reverse of these things, overly indigent, overly weak, or very lacking in honor—it is difficult to follow reason. The former sort tend to become arrogant and base on a grand scale, the latter malicious and base in petty ways; and acts of injustice are committed either through arrogance or through malice. Moreover, these are least inclined either to avoid ruling or to wish to rule, both of which things are injurious to cities.[37] (6) In addition, those who are preeminent in the goods of fortune—strength, wealth, friends, and the other things of this sort—neither wish to be ruled nor know how to be. This is something that marks them from the time they are children at home, for the effect of living in luxury is that they do not become habituated to being ruled even at school; but those who are excessively needy with respect to these things are too humble. (7) So the ones do not know how to rule but only how to be ruled, and then only in the fashion of rule of a master, and the others do not know how to be ruled by any sort of rule, but only to rule in the fashion of rule of a master. What comes into being, then, is a city not of free persons but of slaves and masters, the ones consumed by envy, the others by contempt. Nothing is further removed from affection and from a political partnership; for partnership involves the element of affection—enemies do not wish to have even a journey in common. (8) The city wishes, at any rate, to be made up of equal and similar persons to the extent possible, and this is most particularly the case with the middling elements. So this city must necessarily be governed in the best fashion if it is made up of the elements out of which we assert the city is by nature constituted. Also, of citizens in cities these most particularly preserve themselves. (9) For neither do they desire the things of others, as the poor do, nor others their [property], as the poor desire that of the wealthy; and as a result of not being plotted against or plotting against others they pass their time free from danger. On this account, the prayer of Phocylides was a fine one: "Many things are best for the middling; I would be of the middling sort in the city."[38]

(10) It is clear, therefore, that the political partnership that depends on the middling sort is best as well, and that those cities are capable of being well governed in which the middling element is numerous—most particularly if it is superior to both [of the other]

parts, but if not, superior to either of them; for when added to one it will tip the scale and prevent the opposing excesses from arising. (11) Thus it is the greatest good fortune for those who are engaged in politics to have a middling and sufficient property, because where some possess very many things and others nothing, either [rule of] the people in its extreme form must come into being, or unmixed oligarchy, or—as a result of both of these excesses—tyranny. For tyranny arises from the most headstrong sort of democracy and from oligarchy, but much less often from the middling sorts [of regime] and those close to them. (12) We will speak of the reason for this later in the [discourses] on revolutions in regimes.[39] But that the middling sort is best is evident. It alone is without factional conflict, for where the middling element is numerous, factional conflicts and splits over [the nature of] the regimes occur least of all. (13) And large cities are freer of factional conflict for the same reason—that the middling element is numerous. In small cities it is easier for all to be separated into two [factions] and have no one left in the middle, and nearly everyone is either poor or well off. (14) And democracies are more stable than oligarchies and more durable on account of those of the middling sort, who are more numerous and have a greater share in the prerogatives in democracies than in oligarchies. When the poor predominate numerically in the absence of these, they fare badly and are quickly ruined. (15) It should be considered an indication of this that the best legislators are from the middling citizens. Solon was one of these, as is clear from his poems, and Lycurgus (for he was not king), Charondas, and most of the others.[40]

(16) It is also evident from these things why most regimes are either democratic or oligarchic. For as a result of the fact that the middling element is often few in them, whichever is preeminent, whether those owning property or the people, oversteps the middle [path] and conducts the regime to suit itself, so that either [rule of] the people comes into being or an oligarchy. (17) In addition to this, on account of the factional conflicts and fights that arise between the people and the well off, whichever of the two succeeds in dominating its opponents does not establish a regime that is common or equal, but they grasp for preeminence in the regime as the prize of victory. (18) Further, those who have achieved leadership in Greece have in either case looked to their own regime in establishing either democracies or oligarchies in cities,[41] having in view not what is advantageous for the cities but rather what is advantageous for themselves. (19) So for these reasons the middling regime has either never arisen or has done so

40

1296a1

5

10

15

20

25

30

35

infrequently and in a few [cities]. For of those who have previously held leadership, one man alone was persuaded to provide for this sort of arrangement;[42] and the custom is now established that those in the cities do not even want equality, but either seek to rule or endure being dominated.

40

1296bl

(20) What the best regime is, then, and for what reason, is evident from these things. As for the other regimes (since we assert that there are several sorts of democracies and several of oligarchies), once the best is defined it is not difficult to see which is to be regarded as first, which second, and so on in the same manner according to whether it is better or worse. (21) The one that is closest to this must of necessity always be better, the one that is more removed from the middle, worse, provided one is not judging with a view to a presupposition. I say "with a view to a presupposition" because while one sort of regime is more choiceworthy, there is often nothing to prevent another regime being more advantageous for certain [cities].

5

10

CHAPTER 12

(1) What regime is advantageous for which [cities], and what sort for which sort [of persons], is to be treated next after what has been spoken of. Now the same thing must first be grasped about all of them generally: the part of the city that wants the regime to continue must be superior to the part not wanting this. Every city is made up of both quality and quantity. By quality I mean freedom, wealth, education, and good birth; by quantity, the preeminence belonging to the multitude. (2) It is possible that, while quality belongs to one part of the city among all those of which a city is constituted, and quantity to another part (for example, the ignoble may be more in number than those of good family, or the poor than the wealthy), [the larger part] is nevertheless not preeminent in quantity to the same extent that it falls short in quality. Hence these [two factors] must be judged in relation to one another. (3) Where the multitude of the poor is preeminent, therefore, with respect to the proportion mentioned, there a democracy is what accords with nature—and each kind of democracy according to the preeminence belonging to each sort of people. If, for example, the multitude of farmers predominates, it will be the first sort of democracy; if that of vulgar persons and wage earners, the last sort, and similarly for the others between these. But

15

20

25

30

where the element of the well off and the notables predominates in quality to a greater extent than it falls short in quantity, there it is oligarchy that accords with nature, and in a similar manner each of its kinds according to the preeminence belonging to the oligarchic multitude.

(4) The legislator should always add those of the middling sort [to the dominant class] in the regime. If he enacts oligarchic laws, he ought to aim at the middling sort; if democratic ones, he ought to attach these to them. Where the multitude of middling persons predominates either over both of the extremities together or over one alone, there a lasting polity[43] is capable of existing. (5) For there is no reason to fear that the wealthy and the poor will come to an agreement against them: neither will want to be the slaves of the other, and if they seek a regime in which they will have more in common, they will find none other than this. They would not put up with ruling in turn on account of their distrust toward one another. The most trustworthy person everywhere is the arbitrator; but the middling person is a sort of arbitrator. (6) The better the mixture in the polity, the more lasting it will be. Many of those who want to set up aristocratic regimes as well [as polities] thoroughly err not only by the fact that they distribute more to the well off, but also by deceiving the people. For in time from things falsely good there must result a true evil, and the aggrandizements of the wealthy are more ruinous to the polity than those of the people.

CHAPTER 13

(1) The devices used in polities[44] as pretexts against the people are five in number, being connected with the assembly, the offices, the courts, armament, and exercise. As regards the assembly, [the device is] that it is open to all to attend assemblies, but either a fine is imposed on the well off alone for not attending, or a much larger one on them; (2) as regards the offices, that it should not be open to those who are assessed to abjure,[45] but it should be to the poor; as regards the courts, that there should be a fine against the well off if they do not attend, but impunity for the poor, or else a large fine for the ones and a small fine for the others, as in the laws of Charondas. (3) In some places it is open to all to enroll themselves for the assembly and courts, but if they do not attend the assembly or adjudicate once they are enrolled they are fined

35

40

1297a1

5

10

15

20

25

heavily—in order that they avoid enrolling, and through not being enrolled do not adjudicate or attend the assembly. (4) They legislate in a similar manner concerning the possession of [heavy] arms and exercising. It is open to those who are poor not to possess them, but the well off are fined if they do not, while if they do not exercise there is no fine for the former, but the well off are fined, so that the ones share in these things on account of the fine, and the others do not share through not being afraid of it.

(5) Now these devices of legislation are oligarchic. In democracies, however, there are counterdevices to them. To the poor they give pay for attending the assembly and adjudicating, and arrange not to have the well off fined [for not attending]. (6) So it is evident that if one wishes to have a just mixture, elements from both must be brought together—[for example,] the ones being provided pay, the others fined; in this way all would participate, while in the other way the regime comes to belong to one side alone.

(7) A polity should be made up only of those possessing [heavy] arms. But it is not possible to define the amount of assessment in simple fashion and say that so much must be available; rather, one should investigate what sort of amount is the largest that would let those sharing in the regime be more numerous than those not sharing, and arrange for it to be this. (8) For the poor are willing to remain tranquil even when they have no share in the prerogatives, provided no one acts arrogantly toward them nor deprives them of any of their property. Yet this is not easy; for it does not always turn out that those sharing in the governing body are the refined sort. (9) And when war comes, they are in the habit of shirking if they are poor, unless they receive sustenance; if someone provides them sustenance, however, they are willing to go to war.

In some cases, the regime [of a polity] is made up not only of those bearing [heavy] arms, but of those who had once done so. Among the Malians the regime was made up of [both of] these, though they elected to offices from those who were actually soldiers. (10) And the first sort of regime that arose among the Greeks after kingships was made up of the warrior elements, and initially of cavalrymen. For strength and preeminence in war then belonged to the cavalrymen: without organization the heavy-armed element is useless, but experience in such matters and tactical arrangements were lacking among the ancients, so that their strength lay in the cavalrymen. But as cities increased in size and those with [heavy] arms provided relatively more strength, more persons shared in the regime. (11) Hence the regimes we now call polities used to be called democracies. That the ancient regimes

138

were oligarchic and kingly is reasonable: on account of a lack of manpower [cities] did not have much of a middling element, so being relatively few both in number and in organizations, [the people] put up with being ruled.

(12) For what reason there are several sorts of regimes, then; why there are other sorts beyond those [generally] spoken of (for democracy is not one in number, and similarly with the others); further, what the varieties are and for what reason it happens [that they are different]; in addition, which is the best of the regimes for the majority of cases, and of the other regimes which sort suits which sort [of city]—this has been spoken of.

30

CHAPTER 14

(1) Let us speak of what comes next again both generally and separately for each [regime], taking the beginning point that is appropriate to it. There are, then, three parts in all regimes with respect to which the excellent lawgiver must attempt to discern what is advantageous for each. As long as these are in a fine condition, the regime is necessarily in a fine condition; and regimes necessarily differ from one another as a result of differing in each of these parts. (2) Of these three things, one is the part that is to deliberate about common matters; the second, the part connected with offices—that is, which offices there should be, over what matters they should have authority, and in what fashion the choice of [persons to fill] them should occur; and the third, the adjudicative part.

35

40

1298a1

(3) The deliberative element has authority concerning war and peace, alliances and their dissolution, laws, [judicial cases carrying penalties of] death or exile or confiscation, and the choosing and auditing of officials. It is necessary either that all these sorts of decision be assigned to all the citizens, that all be assigned to some of the citizens (for example, by assigning all to one particular office or several, or some to some and some to others), or that some of them be assigned to all of the citizens and others to some. (4) Now that all [decide] concerning all is characteristically popular; for the people seek this sort of equality. But there are several modes in which all [decide]. One is by turns rather than all together, as in the regime of Telecles of Miletus; and there are other regimes in which deliberation is carried out by officials meeting jointly, with all entering office by turns from the tribes and the

5

10

15

smallest parts [of the city] until all have been gone through, and they meet [all together] only concerning legislation or matters affecting the regime, or to listen to announcements by the officials.[46] (5) Another mode is when all [decide] together, but meet only with a view to the choosing of officials, legislation, what concerns war and peace, and audits, while in other matters deliberation is carried out through offices arranged to deal with each sort of thing, and the offices are chosen from all by election or by lot. (6) Another mode is when the citizens get together in connection with offices and audits and to deliberate about war and alliance, while other matters are administered by offices that are chosen by election to the extent possible [rather than by lot]— those in which it is necessary to have knowledgeable persons ruling. (7) A fourth mode is when all meet to deliberate on all matters, while the offices decide on nothing but merely make preliminary decisions. This is the mode in which the final sort of democracy—the sort that we assert bears comparison with dynastic oligarchy and tyrannical monarchy—administers itself now.

All these modes, then, are democratic, while having some [decide] in all matters is oligarchic. (8) This too has several varieties. Where they are elected on the basis of moderate assessments and are numerous because of the moderateness of the assessment, where they do not attempt change in matters where the laws forbid it but instead follow [the laws], and where it is open to anyone possessing the assessment to share [in deliberation], such a regime is indeed an oligarchy, but by the fact of its moderateness, a political one. When all do not share in deliberation but only those elected to do so, and they rule in accordance with law, it is oligarchic as before. (9) When those who have authority over deliberation elect themselves, and when son succeeds father [in office] and they have authority over the laws, this arrangement is necessarily oligarchic. (10) But when some [have authority in] some matters [and all in some]—for example, when all have it concerning war and peace and audits, and officials in other matters, these being chosen either by election or by lot—it is aristocracy or polity. If persons chosen by election [have authority] in some matters and persons chosen by lot in others, with those chosen by lot being chosen either simply [from all] or from a preselected group, or if persons chosen by election and by lot [have authority] in common, these are features on the one hand of an aristocratic regime, and on the other of a polity. (11) The deliberative element is distinguished in relation to the regimes in this manner, then, and each regime administers [matters] in accordance with the definition mentioned.

(12) In the sort of democracy which is now most particularly held to be democracy (I mean, the sort in which the people has authority even over the laws), it is advantageous with a view to deliberating better to do the same thing that is done in regard to the courts in oligarchies. For they arrange to fine [for nonattendance] those they want to have adjudicate to ensure that they do adjudicate, while the popular sort provide pay for the poor. This should be done in regard to assemblies as well. For all will deliberate better when they do so in common—the people with the notables and these with the multitude. (13) It is also advantageous if those who deliberate are chosen by election or by lot in equal numbers from the parts [of the city]; and where the popular sort among the citizens greatly exceed [the notables] in number, it is advantageous too either not to provide pay for all but only for as many as will balance the multitude of notables, or else to exclude the majority by lot [from receiving pay].[47]

(14) In oligarchies it is advantageous either to elect additionally certain persons from the multitude [to serve as officials], or to establish an official board of the sort that exists in some regimes, made up of those they call "preliminary councillors" or "law guardians," and to [have a popular assembly that will] take up only that business which is considered in the preliminary council; for in this way the people will share in deliberating but will not be able to overturn anything connected to the regime. (15) Further, it is advantageous to have the people vote on measures which are either the same as those brought before them [by a preliminary council] or not contrary to them, or to allow all to advise but the officials to deliberate. Here the opposite of what occurs in polities should be done: the multitude should be given authority to veto measures but not to pass their own, these being referred to the officials. (16) The converse is done in polities, where the few have authority to veto measures but not to pass them; measures of the latter sort are always referred to the many.

Concerning the deliberative and authoritative element of the regime, then, let our discussion stand in this manner.

15
20
25
30
35
40
1299a1

CHAPTER 15

(1) Next after these things is the distinction among offices. For this part of the regime also involves many differences: how many offices there are, in what matters they have authority, and in re-

5

gard to time, how long each office lasts (for some make them for a year, others for a shorter period, others for a longer one), and whether [permitted tenure in] offices should be perpetual or of long duration or neither, but the same persons [should be permitted to hold them] several times or the same person not even twice but only once, and further in regard to the selection of officials, from which persons they should come, by which persons they should be selected, and how they should be selected. (2) With regard to all of these one should be able to distinguish how many modes can exist, and then fit the sorts of offices to the sorts of regimes for which they are advantageous.

Even to determine which should be called offices, however, is not easy. The political partnership requires many functionaries, so that not all of those chosen by election or lot can be regarded as officials. Priests, for example, in the first place (for this must be regarded as something apart from the political offices), (3) and further, equippers and heralds, and also envoys, are chosen by election [but are not officials]. Of the sorts of superintendence some are political, and are either over all of the citizens with a view to a certain action (as, for example, a general is over them when they are campaigning) or over a part (for example, the manager of women or the manager of children); some are related to management of the household (for they often elect grain measurers[48]); and some are subordinate, and of such a sort that [cities] that are well off arrange to have slaves do them. (4) Simply speaking, those should be most particularly spoken of as offices to which are assigned both deliberation and judgment concerning certain matters and command, but most particularly the latter, for command is more characteristic of ruling. But these things make almost no difference with a view to use, as no judgment has ever been handed down to anyone disputing over the term, though there is room for some further treatment of them in thought.

(5) Which sort and how many offices are necessary for a city to exist, and what sort are not necessary but rather useful with a view to an excellent regime, are questions one can raise in relation to every regime, but especially [in the case of] small cities. (6) In large cities one can and should arrange to have a single office to handle a single task: because there are many citizens, many persons can take up office, the offices being held after a long interval or only once, and each sort of task is better done when the superintendence of it is handled as a single matter rather than together with many other matters. (7) In small cities, however, many offices are necessarily brought under a few persons. Because of the lack of manpower it is not easy to have many per-

sons in the offices, for if this were the case, who will be those who succeed them? Sometimes small cities need the same offices and laws as large ones; but the latter need them often, while the former do only at long intervals. (8) Hence, there is nothing to prevent small cities from mandating that they supervise many things at once. They will not interfere with one another; and on account of the lack of manpower it is necessary for them to make their boards of officials like spit-lamps.[49] If, then, we are able to say how many offices necessarily belong to every city and how many offices should[50] but need not necessarily belong, one who knew this could more easily bring under one office the sorts of offices it is fitting to bring under a single one. (9) It is also fitting not to neglect this—what sort of matters should be supervised by many boards[51] on a local basis and over what sort a single office should everywhere have authority. (In regard to orderliness, for example, should the market-manager have authority over this in the market and another [official] in another place, or should the same one have it everywhere?) Also, whether one should distinguish [offices] on the basis of their activity or of the human beings [they supervise]. (I mean, for example, whether there should be a single office for orderliness, or one for children and another for women). (10) Also, in connection with the kinds of regimes, whether the types of offices too differ for each sort—whether the same offices have authority in, for example, a democracy, an oligarchy, an aristocracy, and a monarchy, but are not made up of equal [numbers of] nor similar sorts of persons, but rather of different sorts in different [regimes] (in aristocracies, for example, of the educated, in oligarchies of the wealthy, and in democracies of the free), or whether it happens that certain of the offices exist as a result of these very differences, and that in some cases the same offices are advantageous, while in others they differ (for it is fitting for the same to be large here, small there). (11) Some offices are indeed peculiar [to particular regimes], such as that of preliminary councillors; this is not democratic, whereas a council is popular. For there should be something of this [latter] sort which takes care of preliminary deliberation for the people, so that they can pursue their occupations; this is oligarchic [only] when they are few in number. But the number of preliminary councillors is necessarily few, and so this is necessarily oligarchic. (12) But where both these offices exist, the preliminary councillors have been established as a counter to the councillors; for the councillor is popular, the preliminary councillor oligarchic. Yet even the power of the council is overturned in those sorts of democracies in which the people themselves meet and transact all

5

10

15

20

25

30

35

1300a1

business. (13) This is usually the result when those coming to the assembly are either well off or get pay;[52] for as they have leisure they can collect together frequently and decide all things themselves. The manager of children, the manager of women, and any other office that has authority for this sort of superintendence is aristocratic, and not democratic. For how is it possible to prevent the wives of the poor from going out? Nor is it oligarchic, for the wives of oligarchs live luxuriously.

(14) Concerning these matters let this much be said for now, and let us make an attempt to treat the selection of officials, beginning from the beginning. The varieties [of selection] depend on three defining principles, which when combined necessarily embrace all the modes. Of these three the first is who selects the officials, the second, from whom [they are selected], and finally, in what manner. (15) In the case of each of these three there are three[53] varieties. For either all of the citizens select or some; [they select] either from all or from certain special persons, [distinguished] by assessment, for example, or family, or virtue, or some other such thing (as in Megara it is from those who returned from exile together and fought in alliance against the people[54]); and [selection is made] either by election or by lot. (16) And these may again be conjoined, by which I mean that some offices may be selected by some and others by all, some may be selected from all and others from some, and some may be selected by election and others by lot. In the case of each of these varieties there will be four modes. (17) For either all select from all by election or all from all by lot (and from all[55] either by turn, for example on the basis of tribes, quarters, or clans, until all the citizens have been gone through, or from all each time), [or all select from some by election or all from some by lot];[56] and[57] [offices can be selected] partly in one way, partly in another. (18) Again, if some are selecting, they may do so either from all by election or from all by lot, or from some by election or from some by lot; or [offices can be selected] partly in one way, partly in another—I mean, [for example,] they can be selected from all partly by election, partly by lot. So twelve modes arise, apart from the [other] two conjunctions.[58]

(19) Of these systems of selection two are popular: for all to select from all by election or by lot[59] (or by both, some of the offices being selected by lot, others by election). When all select but not at the same time, and select either from all or from some, either by lot or by election or both, or select from all and some from some [either by lot or by election or][60] by both (by "both" I mean some offices by lot and others by election), it is characteristic of polity. (20) When some select from all by election or by lot

or by both (some offices by election and others by lot), it is [characteristic of an] oligarchic [polity], though by both is more oligarchic; when some offices are selected [by all] from all and others from some, this is characteristic of a polity [run] in aristocratic fashion, [or offices are selected by election], or some by election and others by lot.[61] (21) It is oligarchic when some select from some [by election],[62] and similarly when some select from some by lot (though this does not occur), and when some select from some by both. It is aristocratic when some select from all, and on occasion all from some, by election.

(22) The modes concerning offices are, then, so many in number, and are distinguished in this manner in accordance with the regimes. Which are advantageous for which regimes, and how their selection should occur, will become evident together with the powers of the offices and which these are.[63] By power of an office I mean, for example, having authority over revenues or having authority over defense. For a different kind of power is involved in generalship and in having authority over agreements in the market.

CHAPTER 16

(1) Of three [parts] it remains to speak of the adjudicative. The modes of these [bodies] too must be grasped in accordance with the same presupposition. There is a difference among courts deriving from three defining principles: from whom [they are selected], on what [matters they decide], and in what manner [they are selected]. By "from whom" I mean whether [they are selected] from all or some; by "on what," how many kinds of courts there are; by "in what manner," whether by lot or election.

(2) Let us first distinguish, then, how many kinds of courts there are. They are eight in number. One is concerned with audits; another is for anyone acting unjustly with respect to common matters; another is concerned with what bears on the regime; a fourth is for both officials and private individuals and concerns disputes over fines; a fifth is that concerned with private transactions of a certain magnitude. Besides these there is one concerned with homicide and one with aliens. (3) The kinds of homicide court, whether having the same persons as jurors or others, are: one concerned with premeditated homicides; one with involuntary homicides; one with cases where there is agreement [on the

fact of homicide] but a dispute over what is just; and a fourth with cases involving those who had been exiled for homicide after their return, as is said to be the case, for example, with the court of Phreatto in Athens, although such cases are few over the whole of time even in large cities.[64] (4) Of the court for aliens, one kind is for aliens [disputing] against aliens, one for aliens against townspeople. Further, besides all these there is one concerned with small transactions—those involving a drachma, five drachmas, or slightly more. For a decision has to be given in such cases as well, but it does not require a multitude of jurors.

(5) But these courts—both those concerned with homicide and those concerned with aliens—may be dismissed; let us speak of the political ones. It is in connection with these that factional conflicts arise when matters are not finely handled, and revolutions in regimes. Now necessarily either all decide on all the matters which have been distinguished [having been selected] by election or by lot, or all decide on all [having been selected] in part by lot and in part by election, or [all decide] on some of the same matters, these [being selected] on the one hand by lot, on the other by election. (6) These modes are, then, four in number; and there are as many again based on a part [of the citizens rather than all]. For those adjudicating may also[65] be [selected] from some and [decide] on all matters by election, or be [selected] from some and [decide] on all matters by lot, or in part by lot and in part by election, or some courts [that decide] on the same matters may be [made up of] persons selected both by lot and election. As was said, these modes [are counterparts[66]] to the ones spoken of. (7) Further, these same ones may be conjoined—I mean, for example, some courts may be [selected] from all, some from some, and some from both (in which case the same court would have some selected from all and some from some), and either by lot or election or both.

(8) How many modes there are for courts has, then, been spoken of. Of these the first—those [selected] from all[67] [that decide] on all matters—are popular. The second—those [selected] from some [to decide] on all matters—are oligarchic. The third are characteristic of aristocracy and polity—those [selected] in part from all and in part from some.

BOOK 5

CHAPTER 1

(1) Nearly everything else that we intended to speak of has been treated. What things bring about revolutions in regimes and how many and of what sort they are; what are the sources of destruction for each sort of regime and into which sort of regime a regime is most particularly transformed; further, what are the sources of preservation both [for regimes] in common and for each sort of regime separately; and further, by what things each sort of regime might most particularly be preserved—these matters must be investigated in conformity with what has been spoken of.

(2) It is necessary first to take as a beginning point the fact that many sorts of regimes have arisen because, while all agree regarding justice and proportionate equality, they err about this, as was also said earlier.[1] (3) [Rule of] the people arose as a result of those who are equal in any respect supposing they are equal simply, for because all alike are free persons, they consider themselves to be equal simply; and oligarchy arose as a result of those who are unequal in some one respect conceiving themselves to be wholly unequal, for as they are unequal in regard to property they conceive themselves to be unequal simply. (4) Then the former claim to merit a share in all things equally on the grounds that they are equal, while the latter seek to aggrandize themselves on the grounds that they are unequal, since "greater" is something unequal.[2] (5) All [regimes of this kind] have, then, a certain sort of justice, but in an unqualified sense they are in error. And it is for this reason that, when either [group] does not share in the regime on the basis of the conception it happens to have, they engage in factional conflict. (6) Those who are outstanding in virtue would engage in factional conflict most justifiably, yet they do it the least of all; for it is most reasonable for these only to be unequal in an unqualified sense. (7) There are also certain persons who are preeminent on the basis of family and claim not to merit equal things on account of this inequality: they are held to be well-born persons, to whom belong the virtue and wealth of their ancestors.

20

25

30

35

40

1301b1

5

These, then, are in a manner of speaking the beginning points and springs of factional conflicts. (8) Hence revolutions also occur in two ways. Sometimes [factional conflict] is with a view to the regime, so that it will be transformed from the established one into another sort, for example from democracy into oligarchy or from oligarchy into democracy, or from these into a polity or aris-

10

tocracy, or from the latter into the former; sometimes it is not with a view to the established regime, and they intend that the system remain the same, but want to have it in their own hands, as in the case of oligarchy or monarchy. (9) Further, [there may be factional conflict] concerning more and less—for example, where there is an oligarchy, to make it more oligarchically run or less, or

15

where there is a democracy, to make it more democratically run or less, and similarly in the case of the remaining regimes, either to tighten or to loosen them. (10) Further, [there may be factional conflict] with a view to changing a part of the regime—for example, to establish or abolish a certain office. Some assert that Lysander tried to eliminate the kingship at Sparta, and King Pausan-

20

ias the board of overseers;[3] in Epidamnus too the regime was altered partially—a council replaced the tribal officials, (11) but it is still compulsory [only] for those of the governing body [who hold] offices to come to the hall when there is voting for an office,

25

and the single [supreme] official was also an oligarchic feature of that regime.[4] Factional conflict is everywhere the result of inequality, at any rate where there is no proportion among those who are unequal (a permanent kingship is unequal if it exists among equal persons); in general it is equality they seek when they engage in factional conflict.

30

(12) Equality is twofold: one sort is numerical, the other is according to merit. By numerical I mean being the same and equal in number or size; by according to merit, [being equal] in respect to a ratio. For example, three exceeds two and two one by an equal amount numerically, whereas four exceeds two and two one by an equal amount with respect to a ratio, both being halves. (13)

35

Now while there is agreement that justice in an unqualified sense is according to merit, there are differences, as was said before: some consider themselves to be equal generally if they are equal in some respect, while others claim to merit all things unequally if they are unequal in some respect.

(14) Hence two sorts of regimes particularly arise—[rule of]

40

1302a1

the people and oligarchy. Good birth and virtue exist among few persons, these things among more: nowhere are there a hundred well-born and good persons, but in many places the well off are many. Yet to have everywhere an arrangement that is based sim-

148

ply on one or the other of these sorts of equality is a poor thing. This is evident from the result: none of these sorts of regimes is lasting. (15) The reason for this is that, once the first and initial error is committed, it is impossible not to encounter some ill in the end. Hence numerical equality should be used in some cases, and in others equality according to merit. Nevertheless, democracy is more stable and freer from factional conflict than oligarchy. (16) In oligarchies two sorts of factional conflict arise, one against each other, the other against the people; in democracies, though, there is only that against the oligarchy, there being none that arises among the people against itself that is worth mentioning. Moreover, the regime made up of the middling elements is closer to [rule of] the people than to [rule of] the few, and this is the most stable of regimes of this sort.

CHAPTER 2

(1) Since we are investigating the things from which both factional conflicts and revolutions affecting regimes arise, one must first grasp their beginning points and causes in a general way. These are, roughly speaking, three in number, and must be discussed first by themselves in outline. One should grasp what condition [men] are in when they engage in factional conflict; for the sake of what they do so; and thirdly, what the beginning points are of political disturbances and of factional conflicts among one another.

(2) The general cause of [men] being in a certain condition with respect to revolution should be regarded as being the one we have spoken of already. Some engage in factional conflict because they aim at equality, if they consider that they have less in spite of being equal to those who are aggrandizing themselves; others, because they aim at inequality and preeminence, if they conceive themselves to be unequal but not to have a greater share, but an equal or lesser one. (3) To strive for these things may be justified; it may also be unjustified. The lesser engage in factional conflict in order to be equal; those who are equal, in order to be greater.

What their condition is when they engage in factional conflict, then, has been spoken of. As for the things over which they engage in factional conflict, these are profit and honor and their opposites (for they may engage in factional conflict in cities in order to avoid dishonor or punishment either for themselves or for their friends).

(4) The causes and beginning points of the changes through which they come to be in a state of the sort spoken of and concerning the things mentioned are in one sense seven in number, but in another sense more. (5) Of these, two are the same as the ones spoken of, though not in the same way. For [men] are stirred up against one another by profit and by honor—not in order to acquire them for themselves, as was said earlier, but because they see others aggrandizing themselves (whether justly or unjustly) with respect to these things. They are stirred up further by arrogance, by fear, by preeminence, by contempt, by disproportionate growth, and further, though in another manner, by electioneering, by underestimation, by [neglect of] small things, and by dissimilarity.

CHAPTER 3

(1) Of these, the power that arrogance and profit have, and the sense in which they are causes, is fairly evident. For it is when those who are in office behave arrogantly and aggrandize themselves that [men] engage in factional conflict—both against one another and against the regimes which provide them license to do so. (Aggrandizement occurs sometimes at the expense of private, sometimes at the expense of common [funds].) (2) It is also clear what the power of honor is, and in what sense it is a cause of factional conflict. [Men] engage in factional conflict both when they themselves are dishonored and when they see others honored. This occurs unjustifiably in cases where certain persons are either honored or dishonored contrary to their merit, and justifiably in cases where it happens in accordance with their merit.

(3) [There is factional conflict] through preeminence when a certain person or persons are greater in power than accords with the city and the power of the governing body; from such persons there customarily arises a monarchy or a dynasty. Hence in some places they have the custom of ostracism—at Argos and Athens, for example. It is better to see to it from the beginning that no one is preeminent to such an extent, however, than to let them arise and to heal [the malady] afterwards.

(4) [Men] engage in factional conflict through fear, both when they have committed injustice and are frightened of paying the penalty, and when they are about to suffer injustice and wish to forestall it—as at Rhodes, where the notables joined together

against the people on account of the suits being brought against them.[5]

(5) Through contempt as well [men] engage in factional conflict and attack on one another—in oligarchies, for example, when those not sharing in the regime are a majority (for they suppose themselves superior), and in democracies, when the well off are contemptuous of the disorder and anarchy. In Thebes, for example, the democracy collapsed as a result of their being badly governed following the battle of Oenophyta, the one at Megara through disorder and anarchy when they were defeated; and [contempt was similarly aroused] in Syracuse prior to the tyranny of Gelo and by the people in Rhodes prior to the revolt [of the notables].[6]

(6) Revolutions in regimes also occur through disproportionate growth [of a part]. A body is composed of parts which must increase in proportion if a balance is to be maintained, and if this does not happen it perishes—[for example,] when a foot is four yards long and the rest of the body two feet high; and sometimes too it may be altered to the shape of another animal, if the increase is not only quantitative but qualitative and contrary to proportion. So too is a city composed of parts; and frequently an increase in one of them is overlooked—for example, the multitude of the poor in democracies and polities. (7) Sometimes this happens also through chance occurrences. At Tarentum, for example, a democracy replaced a polity when many of the notables were defeated and killed by the Iapygians shortly after the Persian War.[7] At Argos, when those of the seventh[8] were killed by Cleomenes of Sparta, they were compelled to accept [in the regime] some of their subjects; and at Athens the notables became fewer as a result of their misfortunes on land, because they campaigned during the Spartan War on the basis of an enrollment list [of citizens].[9] (8) This happens in democracies as well, though to a lesser extent. When there come to be more persons who are well off, or when properties increase, they undergo revolution and become oligarchies and dynasties.

(9) Regimes undergo revolutions without factional conflict too, both through electioneering—as at Heraea, where they had [the officials] chosen by lot instead of by election because those engaging in electioneering were getting elected[10]—and through underestimation, when they allow persons who are not friends of the regime to occupy the authoritative offices. In Oreus, for example, the oligarchy was overthrown when Heracleodorus became one of the officials: he instituted in place of the oligarchy a polity, or rather a democracy.[11]

(10) Further, [regimes undergo revolution] through [neglect of] small differences. I mean that a great shift in usages often occurs unnoticed when a small thing is overlooked. In Ambracia, for example, the assessment was small, and eventually they came to hold office with none at all, the assumption being that there was little or no difference between none and a small one.[12]

(11) Dissimilarity of stock is also conducive to factional conflict, until a cooperative spirit develops.[13] For just as a city does not arise from any chance multitude, so it does not arise in any chance period of time. Hence those who have admitted joint settlers or later settlers [of different stock] have for the most part split into factions. For example, the Achaeans settled Sybaris jointly with the Troezenians, but when the Achaeans came to be more numerous they expelled the Troezenians; this is what gave rie to the curse of the Sybarites.[14] (12) At Thurii, too, the Sybarites [became involved in factional conflict] with those who had settled it jointly with them: they claimed to merit aggrandizement on the grounds that the territory was theirs, and were driven out.[15] The later settlers were discovered conspiring against the Byzantines and were driven out after a battle; the Antissaeans expelled after a battle the Chian exiles they had admitted; the Zanclaeans were themselves driven out by the Samians they had admitted.[16] (13) The Apolloniates (those on the Black Sea) fell into factional conflict after bringing in later settlers; the Syracusans fell into factional conflict and battled one another when they made citizens of foreigners and mercenaries after the period of the tyrants; and the Amphipolitans, after admitting later settlers from among the Chalcidians, were almost all driven out by them.[17]

(14) In oligarchies, as was said earlier, the many engage in factional conflict on the grounds that they are done an injustice because they do not share in equal things in spite of being equal. In democracies the notables engage in factional conflict because they share in equal things although they are not equal.[18]

(15) Cities sometimes fall into factional conflict on account of location, when the territory is not naturally apt for there being a simple city. At Clazomenae, for example, those in Chytrus [engaged in factional conflict] against those on the island; so also the Colophonians and Notians.[19] At Athens too there is dissimilarity: those living in Peiraeus are more of the popular sort than those living in town. (16) For just as in war the crossing of ditches, even if they are very small, splits apart the ranks, so every difference, it appears, makes a factional split. The greatest factional split is perhaps that between virtue and depravity; then there is that between wealth and poverty, and so on with others in varying degree, one of these being that just spoken of.

CHAPTER 4

(1) Factional conflicts arise, then, not over small things but from small things—it is over great things that [men] engage in factional conflict. And even small ones acquire great strength when they arise among those in authority, as happened in Syracuse, for example, in ancient times, when the regime underwent a revolution because two young men who were holding office came into conflict in connection with a love affair. (2) For when one was away, the other, in spite of being his club mate, seduced his lover; the first, enraged at him, induced his wife to commit adultery; afterwards they attached to themselves the entire governing body and created a factional split.[20] (3) Hence one should take precautions when such things are beginning so as to head off factional conflicts among leading and powerful persons. The error arises at the beginning, and the beginning is said to be "half of the whole," so that even a small error there is comparable to any made throughout the other parts.[21] (4) In general, the factional conflicts of the notables are felt jointly by the entire city as well. In Hestiaea after the Persian Wars, for example, it happened that two brothers quarreled over the distribution of their inheritance: the one who was less well off, claiming the other had not declared [the full extent of] the property or the treasure their father had found, enlisted the popular element, while the other, who had much property, enlisted the well off.[22] (5) At Delphi, too, it was a quarrel arising from a marriage that was the beginning of all the later factional conflicts. The bridegroom, having come for the bride, took some accident as a bad omen and went away without her; the bride's relatives, considering this an act of arrogance, subsequently introduced some sacred objects among those he was sacrificing and then killed him for committing sacrilege.[23] (6) At Mytilene as well a factional conflict arising concerning heiresses was the beginning of many of their ills, in particular of the war against the Athenians, during which Paches took their city. Timophanes, one of the well off, left behind two daughters; the person who was treated high-handedly and failed to obtain them for his son, Dexander, initiated factional conflict and stirred up the Athenians, as he was their agent.[24] (7) Among the Phocians a factional conflict also arose from an heiress, involving Mnaseas the father of Mnason and Euthycrates the father of Onomarchus; this factional conflict was the beginning of the Sacred War for the Phocians.[25] The regime in Epidamnus also underwent revolution in connection with a marriage: someone had betrothed his daughter to a person whose father, as one of the officials, imposed a fine on him; feel-

20

25

30

35

1304a1

5

10

15

ing himself insulted, he attached to himself those who were outside the regime.[26]

(8) Regimes also undergo revolution into oligarchy, [rule of]
the people, or polity as a result of an official board or a part of the
city acquiring reputation in some way or growing. The Council of
the Areopagus, for example, as a result of the reputation it acquired during the Persian Wars, was held to have made the [Athe-
nian] regime more strict; but then the seafaring mass, through
being the cause of the victory at Salamis and, as a result of this, of
the leadership [the Athenians exercised] on account of their power
at sea, made the democracy stronger.[27] (9) In Argos too the notables acquired reputation in connection with the battle of Mantinea
against the Lacedaemonians, and undertook to overthrow [the
rule of] the people.[28] In Syracuse, the people, as the cause of victory in the war against the Athenians, effected a revolution from
polity to democracy.[29] At Chalcis the tyrant Phoxus was removed
by the people together with the notables, and the former immediately got hold of the regime.[30] At Ambracia, similarly, the people joined with those who attacked Periander to expel him and
then brought the regime around to themselves.[31] (10) In general,
therefore, this should not be overlooked: those who come to be a
cause of power's [being acquired,] whether private individuals, offices, tribes, or generally a part or multitude of any sort, give rise to
factional conflict. For either those who envy their being honored
initiate factional conflict or they themselves are unwilling to remain on an equal footing on account of their preeminence.

(11) Regimes undergo change also when parts of the city that
are held to be in opposition become equal to one another—for example, the wealthy and the people—and there is nothing or very
little in the middle. For if either of the parts is greatly preeminent,
the one that remains is unwilling to put itself at risk against one
that is manifestly superior. (12) Hence those who are outstanding
for virtue do not engage in factional conflict to speak of; for they
are few against many.

Concerning all regimes universally, then, the beginning points
and causes of factional conflicts and revolutions stand in this manner. Regimes are sometimes changed through force, sometimes
through deceit. Force may be used right at the beginning, or they
may resort to compulsion later on. Deceit is also twofold. (13)
Sometimes they use deceit at first and effect revolution in the regime with the others willing, and then later on keep hold of it by
force when the others are unwilling (at the time of the Four Hundred, for example, they deceived the people by asserting that the
king [of Persia] would provide funds for the war against the Lace-

daemonians, and having put out this lie attempted to keep hold of the regime[32]); but sometimes they both persuade at the beginning and maintain the persuasion later on, and rule over willing persons. In a simple sense, then, revolutions occur in the case of all regimes as a result of the things spoken of.

15

CHAPTER 5

(1) What derives from these things should be split up and studied in the case of each kind of regime.

20

Now democracies undergo revolution particularly on account of the wanton behavior of the popular leaders. On the one hand, by harassing individually those owning property they get them to combine (for common fear brings together even the worst enemies); on the other hand, they egg on the multitude publicly [against them]. One may see many cases where this happened. (2) At Cos the democracy underwent revolution when vicious popular leaders arose there, for the notables revolted.[33] At Rhodes the popular leaders provided pay [to the people] and at the same time prevented the trierarchs' getting what was owed them, while these, on account of the suits brought against them, were compelled to stand together and overthrow [the rule of] the people.[34] (3) [The rule of] the people was also overthrown in Heracleia immediately after the colony was settled on account of the popular leaders: the notables were treated unjustly by them and went into exile, but the exiles later gathered together and returned to overthrow [the rule of] the people.[35] (4) The democracy in Megara was also overthrown in a similar way. The popular leaders, in order to be in a position to confiscate their goods, expelled many of the notables, until they had created many exiles, who then returned, defeated the people in battle, and established an oligarchy.[36] The same thing happened in the case of the democracy at Cyme which was overthrown by Thrasymachus.[37] (5) And one would see in studying other cases as well that revolutions occur just about in this manner. Sometimes, in order to win favor with [the people, popular leaders] treat the notables unjustly and cause them to combine, making them yield up their properties for redivision, or their revenues as a result of public services; sometimes they slander the wealthy in order to be in a position to confiscate their goods.

25

30

35

1305a1

5

(6) In ancient times, when the same person was both popular

leader and general, [democracies] underwent revolution into tyranny; most of the ancient tyrants arose from popular leaders. (7) The reason this happened then but does not now is that the popular leaders then came from those who served as generals, and were not particularly skilled at speaking, whereas now with the growth of rhetoric those who are capable speakers act as popular leaders, but on account of their inexperience in military matters they do not attempt anything, though this may have happened somewhere in rare cases. (8) Tyrannies arose more frequently earlier than now also because great offices were in the hands of individuals—as in Miletus [one arose] from the presidency, for the president had authority over many and great matters.[38] This happened further because cities then were not large: the people lived in the fields and were occupied by their work, while those who were heads of the people, when they became expert in military matters, attempted to set up a tyranny. (9) All of them did this having won the people's trust; this trust was based on their hostility toward the wealthy. At Athens, for example, Pisistratus claimed to merit becoming tyrant as a result of engaging in factional conflict with those of the plain;[39] Theagenes did so at Megara by slaughtering the cattle of the well off when he caught them grazing by the river, (10) and Dionysius by accusing Daphnaeus and the wealthy[40]—all winning trust on account of this enmity as being of the popular sort.

[Democracies] undergo revolution as well from traditional democracy to the most recent sort. Wherever offices are chosen by election, and this is not done on the basis of assessments, and the people elect, those seeking office establish the people as having authority even over the laws in order to make themselves popular. (11) A remedy so that this will not occur, or will occur less, is to have the tribes vote for officials, not the entire people. Nearly all the revolutions in democracies occur, then, for these reasons.

CHAPTER 6

(1) Of the modes in which oligarchies undergo revolution, two in particular are the most evident. One is when they treat the multitude unjustly. Any leader is then adequate [to effect revolution], particularly when the leader comes from the oligarchy itself, as happened in Naxos in the case of Lygdamis, who later became tyrant of the Naxians.[41] (2) Factional conflict that has its begin-

156

ning point from others[42] also involves several varieties. Sometimes the overthrow [of an oligarchy] comes about through the
well off themselves—those not in [the group that holds] the offices, when those who do enjoy prerogatives are very few. This
has happened at Massilia, for example, at Istrus, at Heraclea, and
in other cities. (3) Those who had no share in the offices sought   5
change, until first the elder brothers could take part, and later the
younger as well. (In some places father and son may not hold
offices at the same time, in others an elder and younger brother.)
The result was that the oligarchy in Massilia became more like a   10
polity, at Istrus it ended in [rule of] the people, and at Heraclea it
went from being a small number to six hundred.[43] (4) At Cnidos
too the oligarchy underwent revolution when the notables fell into
factional conflict against one another because few shared [in the
offices]—as was said, if a father shared, the son could not, and if   15
there were several brothers, only the eldest. For as this factional
conflict proceeded the people stepped in, picked one of the notables as their head, attacked them, and conquered—for whatever
is engaged in factional conflict is weak.[44] (5) And at Erythrae during the oligarchy of the Basilids in ancient times, even though
matters were well superintended by those in [charge of] the re-   20
gime, the people chafed at being ruled by a few and effected a
revolution in the regime.[45]

(6) Oligarchies undergo change from within in the first place
through the rivalry of those seeking popularity. Popular leadership
is twofold. One sort involves the few themselves; for a popular
leader may arise even among a very few, as for example the Thirty
at Athens. For Charicles and those around him became strong by   25
seeking popularity with the Thirty, and Phrynichus and those
around him among the Four Hundred in the same manner.[46] The
other is when those in the oligarchy seek popularity with the
mass, as at Larisa, for example, where the regime guardians[47]
sought popularity with the mass on account of their being elected,   30
and in all oligarchies where those who elect to offices are not
those from whom the officials are drawn, but the offices are filled
from those with large assessments or those of certain clubs, and
election is by those having [heavy] arms or by the people (which
was the case at Abydus).[48] (7) [This also happens] wherever the
courts are not drawn from the governing body; for in seeking
popularity with a view to [judicial] decisions they effect revolu-   35
tion in the regime, as occurred at Heracleia on the Black Sea.[49] [It
happens further] when some draw the oligarchy into fewer hands,
for those who seek equality are compelled to bring in the people
to assist them.

40

1306a1

(8) Revolutions in oligarchies also occur when they expend their private [wealth] in wanton living. For such persons attempt sedition, and either aim at tyranny themselves or help institute it for someone else (as Hipparinus did for Dionysius at Syracuse).[50] At Amphipolis, someone named Cleotimus brought in Chalcidian settlers and, once they were there, aroused them to factional conflict against the well off.[51] (9) At Aegina, this sort of thing was the reason for the one who struck the bargain with Chares to attempt revolution in the regime.[52] Sometimes, then, [such persons] immediately attempt some change; sometimes too they steal common [funds], with the result that either they themselves or those who resist their stealing initiate factional conflict against [the oligarchs,] as happened at Apollonia on the Black Sea.[53]

5

10

(10) An oligarchy marked by concord is not easily ruined from within. The regime at Pharsalus is an indication of this: they are few, but they have authority over many because they treat one another finely.[54] But oligarchies are overthrown as well when they make another oligarchy within the oligarchy. (11) This is when, the governing body as a whole being few, not all of these few share in the greatest offices. This happened at one time in Elis. For while their regime was in the hands of a few, very few became senators because there were ninety of them serving for life, and their election was of a dynastic character, similar to that of the senators at Sparta.[55]

15

20

(12) A revolution in oligarchies can occur both in peace and in war. They occur in war when [oligarchs] are compelled to use mercenaries on account of their distrust of the people: if these are handed to a single person [to command,] he often becomes tyrant, as was the case with Timophanes at Corinth;[56] if to several, these set up a dynasty for themselves. Sometimes out of fear of these things [oligarchs] give a share in the regime to the multitude as a result of being compelled to make use of the people. (13) In peacetime, on account of their distrust of one another, they hand over their defense to mercenaries and to a neutral official—who sometimes gains authority over both [groups]. This happened at Larisa in the case of the rule of Simus and his followers among the Aleuads, and at Abydus at the time of the clubs, one of which was that of Iphiades.[57]

25

30

(14) Factional conflicts also arise when some of those in the oligarchy are treated by others in high-handed fashion in connection with marriages or lawsuits and driven into factional conflict. Where the cause is a marriage there are, for example, those spoken of earlier as well as the oligarchy of the cavalrymen at Eretria, which Diagoras overthrew when he was done an injustice

35

concerning a marriage.[58] (15) Factional conflict arose from a judicial decision in Heracleia and at Thebes, where punishment for adultery (in Heracleia of Euetion, in Thebes of Archias) was imposed in a way that was both just and factious: out of rivalry their enemies had them pilloried in the marketplace.[59] (16) Many [regimes] have been overthrown, too, when the oligarchies had too many of the features of rule by a master, by those in the regime who were resentful; this was the case with the oligarchy in Cnidus and with that in Chios.[60]

1306b1

5

Revolutions also occur as a result of accident both in so-called polity and in oligarchies in which they deliberate, adjudicate, and rule in the other offices on the basis of an assessment. (17) For frequently the assessment is arranged at first with a view to existing circumstances, so that the few will share in the oligarchy or middling persons in the polity; and it then happens that the same properties come to merit an assessment many times as great, as a result of prosperity that arises from peace or some other sort of good fortune, so that all [citizens] come to share in all [offices]. Sometimes the revolution happens gradually and is overlooked, but sometimes it happens quickly.

10

15

(18) Oligarchies undergo revolution and factional conflict, then, through causes of this sort. Democracies and oligarchies generally sometimes also undergo alteration not into opposing sorts of regimes, but into those of the same type—for example, from democracies and oligarchies of the sort that are under law into the [sort where the ruling element is wholly] authoritative, and from the latter into the former.

20

CHAPTER 7

(1) In aristocracies factional conflicts arise on the one hand on account of there being few who share in the prerogatives, which was said to be what effects change in oligarchies as well; this is because aristocracy too is in some sense an oligarchy. In both, the rulers are few, and though it is not on account of the same thing that they are few, aristocracy too is at any rate held to be a sort of oligarchy on account of these things. (2) This necessarily results above all when there is a certain multitude of persons who presume themselves to be similar on the basis of virtue—as for example the so-called Partheniae at Sparta, who came from the peers and, when discovered conspiring, were sent off by them to

25

30

Tarentum as settlers.[61] Or it results when those who are great and inferior to no one in virtue are dishonored by persons held in greater honor, as Lysander was by the kings, for example; (3) or when someone of a manly sort does not share in the prerogatives, such as the Cinadon who instigated the attack on the Spartiates in the time of Agesilaus.[62] Further, it results when some persons are very poor and others well off, as happens most particularly during wars. This was the result, for instance, in Sparta at the time of the war with Messene. (4) This is clear from the poem of Tyrtaeus called "Good Management": persons who were hard-pressed on account of the war claimed to merit a redivision of the land.[63] Further, it results if someone who is great and has the capacity to be yet greater [instigates factional conflict] in order to become sole ruler, as Pausanias—the one who was general during the Persian War—is held to have done in Sparta, for example, or Hanno in Carthage.[64]

(5) But both polities and aristocracies are overturned above all through a deviation from justice in the regime itself. The beginning point in polity is when democracy and oligarchy have not been finely mixed, and in aristocracy these things and virtue as well, though above all the two—I mean [rule of] the people and oligarchy; for these are what polities and most of the so-called aristocracies attempt to mix. (6) Aristocracies differ in this from what are termed polities, and it is on account of this that some of these [regimes] are more lasting and others less. For those [regimes] that incline more toward oligarchy they term aristocracies, and those inclining more toward the multitude, polities; it is on this account that those of the latter sort are more stable than the former sort. For the majority is superior, and they are more content, as they have equality; (7) but those who are well off, if the regime gives them preeminence, seek to act arrogantly and aggrandize themselves. In general, to whichever [group] the regime inclines, it is in that direction that it is transformed when either [preeminent group] is able to enhance its position—polity into [rule of] the people, that is, and aristocracy into oligarchy; or it is in an opposite direction, [when either preeminent group weakens itself by acting unjustly,][65]—that is, aristocracy into [rule of] the people, when those who are poorer pull the regime around to its opposite on the grounds that they are being treated unjustly, and polities into oligarchy, [when those who are better off effect revolution on the grounds that] the only lasting thing is equality based on merit and having one's due. (9) What was just spoken of happened at Thurii. Because offices were restricted on the basis of a rather large assessment, there was a shift to a smaller one and to a

160

larger number of official boards; but as the regime still tended toward oligarchy and the notables were able to aggrandize themselves, they acquired between them all the land, contrary to the
law[, and this led to factional conflict and civil war, with the notables operating from garrisoned strong points in the country and
the people holding the city]. But the people, who had been exercised in war, proved superior to the garrisons, until those having
more than their share of the land voluntarily gave it up.[66] (10) Further, as all aristocratic regimes have an oligarchic character, the
notables tend to aggrandize themselves—even in Sparta, for example, properties are always coming into the hands of fewer persons.[67] It is also open to the notables to a greater extent to do
whatever they wish and connect themselves by marriage with
whomever they wish. Hence the city of the Locrians suffered as a
result of the marriage connection with Dionysius—something
that would not have happened in a democracy, or in an aristocracy
that has been well mixed.[68]

(11) Revolutions in aristocracies are particularly apt to be overlooked because they are overturned by small steps, a point made
in the earlier [discourses] universally with respect to all regimes—
that even a small thing can be a cause of revolution.[69] For once
they abandon anything of what pertains to the regime, after this it
is easier to effect another and slightly greater change, until they
change the entire order. (12) This too happened in the case of the
regime of Thurii. There being a law that one could be general
only at five year intervals, some of the younger [men] who had
become expert in war and developed a reputation with the multitude of garrison troops, holding in contempt those who were in
charge of affairs and considering it an easy matter to prevail over
them, undertook first of all to overturn this law, so that it would be
open to the same persons to be general continuously, since they
saw that the people would eagerly vote them in. (13) Those of the
officials who were charged with this—the so-called councillors—
set out at first to oppose this, but were then persuaded, as they
supposed that once these had changed this law they would leave
the rest of the regime alone; yet later, when they wanted to prevent other things from being changed, they were no longer able to
do anything more, and the entire arrangement of the regime underwent a revolution, becoming a dynasty of those who had attempted subversion.[70]

(14) All regimes are overturned sometimes from within themselves and sometimes from outside, when an opposite sort of regime is either nearby or far away but powerful. This is what
happened in the case of the Athenians and the Lacedaemonians:

30

35

40

1307b1

5

10

15

20

the Athenians overthrew oligarchies everywhere, and the Spartans democracies.[71] Where revolutions in regimes come from, then, and factional conflicts, has for the most part been spoken of.

CHAPTER 8

(1) We have to speak next about the preservation of regimes, both in common and separately for each sort. Now in the first place it is clear that if we have an understanding of the things that destroy them, we will also have an understanding of the things that preserve them; for opposites are productive of opposite things, and destruction is the opposite of preservation. (2) In well-blended regimes, then, one should watch out to ensure there are no transgressions of the laws, and above all be on guard against small ones. Transgression of the laws slips in unnoticed, just as small expenditures consume a person's property when frequently repeated. (3) The expenditure goes unnoticed because it does not happen all at once: the mind is led to reason fallaciously by this, as in the sophistical argument "if each is small, so are all." This is so in one sense, but in another sense not. The whole and all things[72] are not something small, but are composed of small things.

(4) One must be on guard in the first instance, then, against this sort of beginning [of destruction]. Next, one should not trust to those things that have been devised against the multitude, for they are thoroughly refuted by the facts. (As to which sort of devices in regimes we mean, this was spoken of earlier.[73])

(5) Further, one should see that not only some aristocracies but even some oligarchies last, not because the regimes are stable, but because those occupying the offices treat well those outside the regime as well as those in the governing body—those who do not have a share, by not acting unjustly toward them and by bringing into the regime those among them who have the mark of leaders, not acting unjustly toward the ambitious by depriving them of prerogatives or toward the many with regard to profit; and themselves and those who do have a share, by treating one another in a popular spirit. (6) For the equality that those of the popular sort seek for the multitude is not only just but advantageous for persons who are similar. Hence where there are a number of persons in the governing body, many legislative measures of a popular sort are advantageous, such as having offices be for six months, so that all

those who are similar may have a share in them. For similar persons are already a people, as it were, and hence popular leaders often arise among them, as was said earlier.[74] (7) Oligarchies and aristocracies will then be less apt to decline into dynasties, for it is not easy for rulers to act as criminally in a short time as over a longer one. Indeed, it is on this account that tyrannies arise in oligarchies and democracies. For those who aim at tyranny in either regime are either the greatest persons—the popular leaders in the one, the powerful in the other—or those who hold the greatest offices, when they rule for a long time.

(8) Regimes are preserved not only through the things that destroy them being far away, but sometimes also through their being nearby; for when [men] are afraid, they get a better grip on the regime. Thus those who take thought for the regime should promote fears—so that they will defend and not overturn the regime, keeping watch on it like a nocturnal guard—and make the far away near.

(9) Further, one should try to guard against the rivalries and factional conflicts of the notables, both through laws and [by guarding against] those who are outside the rivalry getting caught up in it themselves—for to recognize an ill as it arises in the beginning belongs not to an ordinary person but rather to a man expert in politics.

(10) With regard to the revolution from oligarchy and polity that occurs on account of assessments, when this happens while the assessments remain the same but money becomes abundant, it is advantageous to investigate what the amount of the common assessment[75] is compared with that of the past (in cities which assess every year, on the basis of that period; in larger ones, every third or fifth year), and if the amount is many times greater or less than before at the time when the assessment rates for the regime were established, to have a law that tightens or relaxes the assessments—if [the total current amount] exceeds [the old amount], tightening [the assessments] in proportion to the increase, if it falls short, relaxing the rate of assessment and making it less. (11) If this is not done in oligarchies and polities, the result in the one case is that in the latter an oligarchy arises and in the former a dynasty, while in the other case a democracy arises from polity, and from oligarchy a polity or [rule of the] people.[76]

(12) It is a thing common to [rule of the] people and oligarchy and to monarchy[77] and every regime not to allow any person to grow overly [great] contrary to proportion, but to attempt to give small prerogatives over a long period of time rather than great ones quickly[78] (for they become corrupted—it does not belong to

15   every man to bear good fortune), or failing this, at least not to give them all at the same time and then take them back all at the same time, but rather gradually. Above all, one should try to shape matters by means of the laws so that there arises no one especially preeminent by the power of his friends or riches, or failing this, that such persons have sojourns abroad.[79]

20   (13) Since [men] also attempt subversion on account of their private lives, one should create an office to oversee those who live in a manner that is disadvantageous relative to the regime—in a democracy, relative to democracy, in an oligarchy, relative to oligarchy, and similarly for each of the other regimes. For the same

25   reasons the prospering of a part of the city should be guarded against. (14) A remedy for this is always to place actions and offices in the hands of the opposing parts (I speak of the respectable as opposed to the multitude, and the poor as opposed to the well off), and to try either to mix together the multitude of the

30   poor and that of the well off, or to increase the middling element, for this dispels the factional conflicts that result from inequality.

    (15) But a very great thing in every regime is to have the laws and management of the rest arranged in such a way that it is impossible to profit from the offices. This is something that must be looked after particularly in oligarchies. (16) The many do not chafe as much at being kept away from ruling—they are even glad

35   if someone leaves them the leisure for their private affairs—as they do when they suppose that their rulers are stealing common [funds]; then it pains them both not to share in the prerogatives and not to share in the profits. (17) Indeed, the only way it is possible for democracy and aristocracy to exist together is if someone

40   instituted this. For it would then be possible for both the notables

1309al   and the multitude to have what they want. Having it open to all to rule is characteristic of democracy; having the notables in the offices is characteristic of aristocracy. (18) But this is what will happen when it is impossible to profit from the offices. The poor

5   will not want to rule on account of not profiting, but rather will want to attend to their private affairs; the well off will be able to rule because they will need nothing from the common [funds]. The result for the poor is that they will become well off through spending their time at work; for the well off, that they will not be ruled by ordinary persons. (19) To prevent the stealing of common

10   [funds], then, let the transfer of funds occur in the presence of all the citizens, and let records of this be deposited with each clan, company,[80] and tribe. But to ensure profitless rule, there should be legislation assigning honors to those of good reputation.

15   (20) In democracies, the well off should be spared, not only

by not having their possessions redivided, but not even their incomes, which in some regimes happens unnoticed; it is better to prevent them from taking on expensive but useless public services, such as leading choruses, officiating at torch races, and other similar things, even if they are willing. In oligarchy, on the other hand, much care should be taken of the poor, and offices from which gains accrue distributed to them, and if one of the well off behaves arrogantly toward them, the penalty should be greater than if toward one of their own. Also, inheritances should be passed on not by bequest but on the basis of family, and the same person should not receive more than one inheritance. In this way, properties would be more on a level, and more of the poor could establish themselves among the well off. (21) And it is advantageous both in a democracy and in an oligarchy to assign equality or precedence to those who participate least in the regime—in [rule of] the people, to the well off, in oligarchy, to the poor—in all respects other than the authoritative offices of the regime; these should be kept in the hands only or mainly of those from the regime.

20

25

30

CHAPTER 9

(1) Those who are going to rule in the authoritative offices ought to have three things: first, affection for the established regime; next, a very great capacity for the work involved in rule; third, virtue and justice—in each regime the sort that is relative to the regime (for if justice is not the same in all regimes, [the virtue of] justice must also necessarily have varieties). (2) When all of these things do not occur in the same person, the question arises how one ought to make a choice.[81] If, for example, someone were an expert general, but a vicious person and not friendly to the regime, and another were just and friendly, how should one make the choice? It would seem that one should look to two things: which [of these] do all share in to a greater extent, and which to a lesser? (3) In the case of generalship, then, one should look to experience rather than virtue, as all share in generalship to a lesser extent, in respectability to a greater extent. For a guardian [of property] or a treasurer, however, the opposite is the case: this requires more virtue than the many possess, but the knowledge is common to all. (4) One might also raise the question why, if the capacity is present as well as affection for the regime, there is a

35

40
1309b1

5

10 need for virtue; for even the two will provide what is advantageous. Or is it because it is possible for those who possess these two things to lack self-control, so that just as they do not serve themselves by knowing and being friendly to themselves, there is nothing to prevent some persons from being in this condition with respect to the community?[82]

(5) Simply speaking, whatever things in the laws we say are
15 advantageous to the regimes, all these preserve the regimes, as does the great principle that has often been mentioned—to keep watch to ensure that the multitude wanting the regime is superior to that not wanting it.[83]

(6) Besides all these things, one should not neglect—what is neglected now by the deviant regimes—the middling element; for many of the things that are held to be characteristically popular
20 overturn democracies, and many of those held to be characteristically oligarchic overturn oligarchies. (7) Those who suppose this to be the single virtue pull the regime to an extreme, ignorant that just as a nose that deviates from the straightness that is most beautiful toward being hooked or snub can nevertheless still be
25 beautiful and appealing to look at, yet if some [artist] tightens it further in the direction of an extreme he will in the first place eliminate any moderateness in the part and eventually will go so far as to make it not even appear to be a nose, on account of the preeminence and the deficiency of the opposites (and it is the same with the other parts [of the body] as well), (8) so this is what
30 results in the case of regimes too. For it is indeed possible for an oligarchy or a democracy to be in an adequate condition in spite of departing from the best arrangement. But if someone tightens either of them further, he will make the regime worse first of all, and eventually not even a regime.

35 (9) Hence the lawgiver and the expert in politics should not be ignorant of which of the characteristically popular things preserve democracy and which destroy it, and which of the characteristically oligarchic things preserve oligarchy and which destroy it. For neither of these regimes can exist and last without the well off and the multitude, and when a leveling of property occurs, such a
40 regime necessarily becomes a different one, so that in destroying
1310a1 [differences in property] by laws reflecting the preeminence [of the people], they destroy the regime.[84] (10) Errors are made both in democracies and in oligarchies. Popular leaders err in democracies where the multitude has authority over the laws: by always
5 fighting with the well off they make the city two cities, yet they should do the opposite, and always be held to be spokesmen for the well off. And in oligarchies the oligarchic [leaders] should be held to be spokesmen for the people, and they should swear oaths

just the opposite of those oligarchic [leaders] swear now. (11) For there are some cities now where they swear: "I will bear ill will toward the people and take counsel to plan whatever ill I can against them." But they ought both to have and to act as if they had the opposite conception, and declare in their oaths: "I will not act unjustly toward the people." 10

But the greatest of all the things that have been mentioned with a view to making regimes lasting—though it is now slighted by all—is education relative to the regimes. (12) For there is no benefit in the most beneficial laws, even when these have been approved by all those engaging in politics, if they are not going to be habituated and educated in the regime—if the laws are popular, in a popular spirit, if oligarchic, in an oligarchic spirit. If lack of self-control exists in the case of an individual, it exists also in the case of a city. (13) But to be educated relative to the regime is not to do the things that oligarchs or those who want democracy enjoy, but rather the things by which the former will be able to run an oligarchy and the latter to have a regime that is run democratically. At present, however, in oligarchies the sons of the rulers live luxuriously, while those of the poor undergo exercise and exertion, so that they are both more inclined to attempt subversion and more capable of it; (14) on the other hand, in those democracies which are held to be most particularly democratic, what has become established is the opposite of what is advantageous. The cause of this is that they define freedom badly. For there are two things by which democracy is held to be defined: the majority having authority, and freedom. (15) Justice is held to be something equal; equality requires that whatever the multitude resolves is authoritative, and freedom and equality [85] involve doing whatever one wants. So in democracies of this sort everyone lives as he wants and "toward whatever [end he happens] to crave," as Euripides says. [86] (16) But this is a poor thing. To live with a view to the regime should not be supposed to be slavery, but preservation. 35

Such, then, simply speaking, are the things that cause regimes to undergo revolution and destruction and those through which they are preserved and made to last. 15 20 25 30

CHAPTER 10

(1) It remains to address monarchy, and the things that are naturally apt to cause its destruction and its preservation. What happens in the case of kingships and tyrannies is very close to what 40 1310b1

has been spoken of in connection with [republican] regimes.[87] (2) Kingship accords with aristocracy, while tyranny is composed of the ultimate sort of oligarchy and of democracy—hence it is the most harmful to the ruled, inasmuch as it is composed of two bad regimes and involves the deviations and errors of both of them. (3) The origin of each of these sorts of monarchy lies in exactly opposite circumstances. Kingship arose with a view to providing assistance to the respectable against the people; kings are selected from the respectable on the basis of preeminence in virtue or in the actions that come from virtue, or on the basis of preeminence of a family of this sort. The tyrant, however, arises from the people or the multitude against the notables, in order that the people not be done injustice by them. (4) This is evident from events: most tyrants arose from popular leaders who were trusted because of their slanders of the notables. (5) Some tyrannies were established in this fashion when cities had already grown in size; some arose prior to these through kings who deviated from traditional ways and strove for the sort of rule characteristic of a master; some from persons elected to the authoritative offices, as in ancient times the people selected magistrates and ambassadors for long periods of time; and some in oligarchies that elected a single person with authority over the greatest offices. (6) It was easy for them to work their will in all of these modes if only they wanted to do so, on account of the power they already had, whether through kingly office or the power of their prerogative. For example, Pheidon of Argos and others established themselves as tyrants where a kingship already existed, those in Ionia and Phalaris as a result of their prerogatives, and Panaetius at Leontini, Cypselus at Corinth, Pisistratus at Athens, and Dionysius at Syracuse and others in the same manner as a result of their popular leadership.[88]

(7) Now as we said, kingship is an arrangement that accords with aristocracy. For it accords with merit, whether based on individual virtue, virtue of family, benefactions, or these things together with capacity. (8) For all those who obtained this prerogative had benefited or were capable of benefiting their cities or nations. Some kept them from being enslaved in war, such as Codrus; others, such as Cyrus, liberated them, or founded [a city] or acquired territory, such as the kings of the Lacedaemonians, Macedonians, and Molossians.[89] (9) A king tends to be a guardian, seeing to it that those possessing property suffer no injustice, and that the people are not treated with arrogance. Tyranny, as has often been said, looks to nothing common, unless it is for the sake of private benefit. The tyrant's goal is pleasure; the goal of a king is the noble. (10) Hence, of the objects of aggrandizement,

goods are characteristic of tyranny, while what pertains to honor is characteristic of kingship. It is characteristic of kingship that its defense is carried out by citizens; of tyranny, that it is carried out by foreigners.

(11) That tyranny has the evils both of democracy and of oligarchy is evident. Having wealth as its end comes from oligarchy (for of necessity it is only in this way that it can both defend itself and provide luxury), as does its distrust of the multitude. Hence the sequestration of [heavy] arms, and the fact that common to both—to tyranny as well as oligarchy—is ill-treatment of the mass and its expulsion from town and resettlement.[90] (12) From democracy comes their war on the notables—doing away with them secretly and openly, and exiling them as rivals in the art [of ruling] and impediments to their rule. For it is from these that conspiracies arise—both of those who wish to rule themselves and those who do not want to be enslaved. (13) Hence the piece of advice that Periander gave to Thrasyboulus, the lopping off of the preeminent ears, the assumption being that it is necessary always to eliminate the preeminent among the citizens.[91]

As has in effect been said, one should consider the beginning points of revolutions to be the same in the case of monarchies as in that of [republican] regimes. For it is through injustice, fear, and contempt that the ruled in many cases attack monarchies (with respect to injustice it is through arrogance above all, but sometimes also through seizure of private [possessions]). (14) The ends are also the same there as in connection with tyrannies and kingships; for the wealth and honor belonging to monarchs are of such a magnitude that all strive after them. Some attacks are carried out against the person of the rulers, some against the office. Those owing to arrogance are against the person. (15) Though arrogance is of many sorts, each of them gives rise to anger, and most of those who are angry attack for the sake of revenge rather than preeminence. The attack on the Pisistratids, for example, took place because of the abusive treatment of Harmodius' sister and the insult of Harmodius (for Harmodius attacked because of his sister, and Aristogeiton because of Harmodius).[92] (16) They also conspired against Periander, the tyrant in Ambracia, because when drinking with his favorite he asked whether he was yet pregnant by himself. The attack on Philip by Pausanias was because Philip let him be treated arrogantly by Attalus and those around him; that on Amyntas the Little by Derdas because Amyntas made fun of his youth; that of the eunuch against Euagoras of Cyprus on the grounds of arrogant treatment, because Euagoras' son had taken away his wife.[93] (17) Many attacks have also occurred be-

10

15

20

25

30

35

40

1311b1

5

cause of the disgraceful behavior of certain monarchs toward the person of others. For example, the attack of Crataeus on Archelaus—he was always resentful of their relationship, so that

10 even a lesser excuse would have been adequate, but he did it because Archelaus gave none of his daughters to him although he had agreed to do so, but the eldest he gave to the king of Elimeia when he was hard pressed in the war against Sirras and Arrabaeus, and the younger to his son Amyntas, supposing that this

15 would be likely to prevent him from quarreling with his son by Cleopatra; but the beginning point of their estrangement was his resentment at the sexual favors [he provided Archelaus]. (18) Hellanocrates of Larisa joined him in the attack for the same reason: because Archelaus made use of his youth and yet kept refusing to restore him to his home although he had promised to do so, he supposed the relationship had come about as a result of arro-

20 gance rather than erotic desire.[94] Python and Heracleides of Aenus did away with Cotys to avenge their father, and Adamas revolted against Cotys on the grounds of arrogant treatment, because he had been castrated by him as a child.[95] (19) And many, in anger at physical outrages against their person, as being arrogantly

25 treated, have done away with, or attempted to do away with, those connected with offices or with kingly dynasties. For example, when the Penthilids at Mytilene went around and struck people with clubs, Megacles and his friends attacked and eliminated them; and later, Smerdis did away with Penthilus after being beaten and dragged away from his wife.[96] (20) Decamnichus be-

30 came leader of the attack on Archelaus, having been the first to stir up the attackers; the reason for his anger was that Archelaus had handed him over to the poet Euripides for flogging—Euripides was enraged at something he had said about the smell of his breath.

35 (21) And many others have been eliminated or conspired against for reasons of this sort. And similarly through fear (for this was one of the causes, in the case of monarchies as in the case of [republican] regimes). Artapanes, for example, [killed] Xerxes out of fear of being accused in connection with Darius, whom he had had hanged without orders from Xerxes, but on the supposition that he would forgive him on account of his forgetfulness

40 when carousing.[97]

1312a1 (22) Other [attacks have been undertaken] through contempt, as when someone saw Sardanapalus carding wool with the women, if what the retailers of stories say is true (though if not of him, this might well be true of another); (23) and Dion attacked Dionysius the Younger because of his contempt for him, when he saw the

170

citizens in the same condition and Dionysius himself always
drunk.[98] Even certain of their friends attack them through contempt, for they feel contempt because they are trusted and will
escape notice [when conspiring]. (24) Those who suppose they
are capable of taking control of the office also in a manner attack
through contempt: they make the attempt easily, as they feel themselves capable and feel contempt for the danger on account of
their capacity. Thus generals attack their monarchs—as Cyrus attacked Astyages, for example, out of contempt both for his way of
life and his power, because his power had deteriorated while he
himself lived luxuriously, and the Thracian Seuthes attacked
Amadocus when he was his general.[99] (25) Some also attack for
several of these [reasons,] for example, both out of contempt and
through profit, as Mithridates attacked Ariobarzanes.[100] The attempt is made for this reason above all by those who are bold in
their nature and hold a military prerogative from their monarchs;
courage coupled with power produces boldness, and it is on account of both of these that they attack, on the assumption that they
will conquer easily.

Of those who attack through ambition the cause operates in a
different manner than in the case of those spoken of before. (26)
Some make an attempt against tyrants because they see both great
profits and great prerogatives in store for them, but this is not why
each of those attacking through ambition deliberately chooses to
court danger: the former do it for the reason mentioned, the latter
make an attempt against monarchs because they want not a monarchy but reputation, just as in the case of any other extraordinary
action from which [men] acquire a name and become notable in
the eyes of others. (27) Those who are impelled by this sort of
reason are, to be sure, very few in number, for underlying this
there must be a lack of all thought for preservation in the event the
action is not successful. (28) Accompanying them should always
be the conception of Dion, though it is not easy for this to arise in
many persons: he set off on the campaign against Dionysius with
a few followers and asserting that matters stood with him in such
a way that, however far he was able to proceed, it was enough for
him to have that much of a share in the action—for example, if it
should happen that he met his end after just setting foot on land,
that death would be a noble one for him.

(29) One mode in which tyranny is destroyed, just as in the
case of each of the other regimes, is from outside, if there is some
regime opposed to it which is superior. The wish to destroy it will
be present on account of the opposition of intention; and what
[men] want to do, all do who are capable of it. (30) Moreover, the

5

10

15

20

25

30

35

40

1312b1

regimes are opposed—[rule of] the people to tyranny in accordance with Hesiod's "potter against potter,"[101] since the extreme sort of democracy is a tyranny; kingship and aristocracy because of the opposition of the regime. Hence the Lacedaemonians overthrew very many tyrannies, as did the Syracusans during the period they were governed finely.

(31) Another mode [in which tyranny is destroyed] is from within itself, when those sharing [power] fall into factional conflict, as in the tyranny of Gelo and his family, and in that of Dionysius and his family today. The tyranny of Gelo [was destroyed] when Thrasyboulus, the brother of Hiero, sought popularity with Gelo's son and impelled him toward pleasures, so that he might rule himself; [though succeeding in this, Thrasyboulus aroused the opposition of others in the family. When this conflict became evident to the notables, some began to take up arms; the result was that] the kin combined together so that the tyranny would not be entirely overthrown, but only Thrasyboulus, while those among [the notables] who had combined, having the occasion, expelled all of them.[102] (32) Dion, who was connected by marriage with Dionysius, campaigned against him and, getting the people on his side, expelled him, and was himself killed.

There are two reasons for which they attack tyrannies above all, hatred and contempt. The former of these, hatred, always exists for tyrants, and many have been overthrown as a result of contempt. An indication of this is that most of those who acquired their offices also defended them, while their successors all perished immediately, so to speak. For because they live a life of gratification they fall easily into contempt and provide many occasions for others to attack them. Anger too should be regarded as a part of hatred, for in a certain manner it acts as a cause of the same actions. (34) Often, indeed, it is more conducive to action than hatred: they attack in more determined fashion on account of the passion not using calculation (it particularly happens that they let themselves follow their spiritedness as a result of arrogance, which is the reason the tyranny of the Pisistratids was overthrown and many others), while hatred does this to a greater extent. (35) For anger is accompanied by pain, so that it is not easy to calculate, while enmity is without pain.

To speak summarily, whatever causes we spoke of in the case both of the unmixed and final sort of oligarchy and of the extreme sort of democracy are to be regarded as causes in the case of tyranny as well; for these [regimes] happen to be tyrannies divided [among many persons].

(36) Kingship is destroyed least of all by things outside itself, and hence is long-lasting; most of the sources of destruction are

internal. It is destroyed in two modes: one when those sharing in the kingship fall into factional conflict, the other mode when they try to administer it in more tyrannical fashion, and claim to merit authority over more matters and contrary to the law. (37) Kingships no longer arise today; if monarchies do arise, they tend to be tyrannies. This is because kingship is a voluntary sort of rule, with authority over relatively great matters, but [today] there are many persons who are similar, with none of them so outstanding as to match the extent and the claim to merit of the office. So on this account [men] do not voluntarily endure it; and if someone should rule through deceit or force, this is already held to be a sort of tyranny. (38) In kingships based on family one should regard as a cause of destruction, in addition to the ones spoken of, the fact that many [kings] are easy to hold in contempt, and that they behave arrogantly in spite of possessing only a kingly prerogative and not tyrannical power. For their overthrow used to be easy: [one ruling] unwilling persons will immediately cease to be king, while the tyrant [rules] even over unwilling persons. Monarchies are destroyed, then, through these and other such causes.

40
1313a1

5

10

15

CHAPTER 11

(1) It is clear that they are preserved, on the other hand, by opposite things simply speaking, and in the case of kingships in particular, by drawing them toward greater moderateness. For the fewer the things over which [kings] have authority, the greater the period of time their rule as a whole will necessarily last: they themselves are less like masters and more equal in their characters, and are less envied by those they rule. (2) It is on this account that the kingship of the Molossians has lasted for a long time, and also that of the Lacedaemonians, both because the office was divided from the beginning into two parts and because Theopompus moderated it, among other things by establishing in addition the office of the overseers. By taking away from its power, he increased the duration of the kingship, and so in a certain manner made it not less but greater. (3) This is just what he is supposed to have answered his wife when she asked him whether he was not ashamed to hand over to his sons a kingship that was lesser than the one he had received from his father, and he said: "Not at all—I am handing over one that will be longer lasting." [103]

(4) Tyrannies are preserved in two modes that are quite opposite to one another. One is the mode that has been handed down,

20

25

30

35 according to which most tyrants administer their rule. Most of these [tyrannical methods] are said to have been established by Periander of Corinth; many such things may also be seen in the rule of the Persians. (5) These include both what was spoken of some time ago as relating to the preservation (so far as this is pos-

40 sible) of tyrannies—lopping off the preeminent and eliminating those with high thoughts—and also not permitting common messes, clubs, education, or anything else of this sort, but guarding

1313b1 against anything that customarily gives rise to two things, high thoughts and trust. Leisured discussions are not allowed, or other meetings connected with leisure,[104] but everything is done to make

5 all as ignorant of one another as possible, since knowledge tends to create trust of one another. (6) Also, residents [of the city] are made to be always in evidence and pass their time about the doors [of the tyrant's palace];[105] in this way their activities would escape notice least of all, and they would become habituated to having

10 small thoughts through always acting like slaves. And there are other such features of tyranny, in Persia and among the barbarians, which have the same power. (7) Also, to attempt to let nothing that is done or said by any of those he rules escape his notice, but to have spies, like the women called "inducers" at Syracuse, and the "eavesdroppers" Hiero sent out whenever there was some meeting or gathering (for men speak less freely when

15 they fear such persons, and if they do speak freely they are less likely to escape notice).[106] (8) Also [a feature of tyranny is] to slander them to one another, and set friends at odds with friends, the people with the notables, and the wealthy with themselves. It is also a feature of tyranny to make the ruled poor, so that they

20 cannot sustain their own defense,[107] and are so occupied with their daily [needs] that they lack the leisure to conspire. (9) Examples of this are the pyramids in Egypt, the monuments of the Cypselids, the construction of the temple of Olympian Zeus by the Pisistratids, and the work done by Polycrates on the [temples] at Samos.[108] All of these things have the same effect—lack of leisure

25 and poverty on the part of the ruled. (10) There is also the matter of taxes, as in Syracuse, where in the time of Dionysius it happened that they were taxed for their entire property over a period of five years. The tyrant is also a warmonger, so that they will always be kept lacking in leisure and in need of a leader. Kingship

30 is preserved by friends [of the king], but it is characteristic of the tyrant to distrust his friends, on the assumption that all wish [to overthrow him], but these are particularly capable of it.

(11) Everything that happens in connection with democracy of the extreme sort is characteristic of tyranny—dominance of

women in the household, so that they may report on their husbands, and laxness toward slaves for the same reasons. Slaves and   35
women do not conspire against tyrants, and as they prosper [under
such circumstances] they necessarily have a benevolent view both
of tyrannies and of democracies (for, indeed, the people wish to
be a monarch). (12) Hence also the flatterer is held in honor by
both—the popular leader by peoples, as the popular leader is a   40
flatterer of the people, and by tyrants, persons approaching them
in obsequious fashion, which is the work of flattery. On this account tyranny is friendly to the base, for they delight in being flat-   1314al
tered, and no one would do this who had free thoughts: respectable persons may be friends, but they will certainly not flatter.
(13) And the base are useful for base things: "nail [is driven out]
by nail," as the proverb has it. It is also a feature of tyranny not to   5
delight in anyone who is dignified or free; for the tyrant alone
claims to merit being such, and one who asserts a rival dignity
and a spirit of freedom takes away the preeminence and the element of mastery of tyranny; hence these are hated as persons un-
dermining [the tyrant's] rule. (14) It is also characteristic of the
tyrant to have foreigners rather than persons from the city as com-   10
panions for dining and entertainment, the assumption being that
the former are enemies, while the latter do not act as rivals.

Such things are, then, characteristic of tyrants and help preserve their rule—though in no respect do they fall short in depravity. All of these things are encompassed, so to speak, under
three heads. (15) For tyranny aims at three things: one, that the   15
ruled have only modest thoughts (for a small-souled person will
not conspire against anyone); second, that they distrust one another (for a tyranny will not be overthrown before some persons
are able to trust each other—hence they make war on the respectable as being harmful to their rule not merely because they claim
not to merit being ruled in the fashion of a master, but also be-   20
cause they are trustworthy, both among themselves and with respect to others, and will not denounce one another or others); (16)
and third, an incapacity for activity,[109] for no one will undertake
something on behalf of those who are incapable, so that not even
a tyranny will be overthrown where the capacity is lacking. The   25
defining principles to which the wishes of tyrants may be reduced
are, then, these three. For one might reduce all things characteristic of tyranny to these presuppositions—that they not trust one
another, that they not be capable, that they have modest thoughts.

(17) The one mode of preservation for tyrannies, then, is of this   30
sort; the other involves a sort of superintendence that is practically the opposite of what has been spoken of. (18) One may

175

grasp this in connection with the destruction of kingships. For just as one mode of destruction for kingship is to make the rule more tyrannical, so it is a source of preservation for tyranny to make it more kingly, provided one thing only is safeguarded—his power,[110] so that he may rule not only willing persons, but also those who are unwilling; for if this is thrown away, so is the tyranny. (19) This must remain as a presupposition, then, but in whatever else he does or is held to do he should give a fine performance of the part of the kingly [ruler]. In the first place, he should be held to take thought for the common [funds], not only by not making expenditures on gifts which enrage the multitude (when they take from persons working and exerting themselves in penury, and give lavishly to prostitutes, foreigners, and artisans), but also by rendering an account of what has been taken in and what expended, as some tyrants have in fact done in the past. One administering matters in this way might be held a manager [of the city] rather than a tyrant. (20) There is no need to be afraid of running short of funds, since he has authority in the city; and, in any event, for tyrants who are campaigning away from their own territory this is even more advantageous than leaving behind a great hoard, as in that case those safeguarding [the city] would be less likely to attack his position (such persons are more fearsome to tyrants when they are away from home than the citizens, for the latter are away with him, but the former remain behind). (21) Next, he should make a show of collecting taxes and public services for the sake of management [of the city], particularly if something should be needed for use in times of war, and he should generally present himself as guardian and treasurer of common rather than private [funds].

He should appear not harsh but dignified, and further, of such a sort that those encountering him feel awe rather than fear. (22) This is not easy to achieve, however, for one who is readily held in contempt. Hence, though he may concern himself with none of the other virtues, he must concern himself with military[111] virtue, and create a reputation of this sort for himself. Further, not only should he himself avoid any appearance of arrogant behavior toward any of those he rules, including youths and girls, but so also should those around him. (23) Their women, too, should stand in a similar relation to other women, for many tyrannies have perished on account of the arrogant behavior of women. In connection with bodily gratifications, they should do the opposite of what certain tyrants now do: not only do they engage in this beginning at dawn and continuing for many days, but they wish to be seen doing so by others, so that they will be admired as persons who are happy and blessed. (24) On the contrary, he ought to be moderate in such matters, or if not, at least he should avoid appearing so to others. It is the drunkards, not the sober, the drowsy, not the wakeful, who are readily attacked and held in contempt.

Indeed, what must be done is the opposite in nearly every case of the things mentioned previously. He must furnish and adorn the city as if he were a steward rather than a tyrant. (25) Further, he must always show himself to be seriously attentive to the things pertaining to the gods. For [men] are less afraid of being treated in some respect contrary to the law by such persons, if they consider the ruler a god-fearing sort who takes thought for the gods, and they are less ready to conspire against him as one who has the gods too as allies. In showing himself of this sort, however, he must avoid silliness. (26) He should also honor those who have proven themselves good in some respect, and in such a way that they consider they would not have been honored more by citizens living under their own laws. He should distribute such honors himself; but punishments [should be administered] through others—through officials and courts.

(27) A precaution common to every sort of monarchy is to make no single person great but [where necessary to elevate] several persons, as they will watch one another. Or if it is necessary after all to make one person great, it should at least not be someone who is of a bold character; such a character is most ready for the attack in connection with every sort of action. And if it is held necessary to remove someone from power, this should be done gradually—his functions should not all be taken away at once. (28) Further, he should refrain from every sort of arrogance, and from two above all the rest: that involving bodily abuse, and that involving [taking sexual advantage of] youth. This precaution is to be taken particularly in connection with ambitious persons. A slight affecting their goods bears heavily on the greedy; a slight involving dishonor bears heavily on the ambitious and the respectable among human beings. (29) Hence he must either not engage in such things, or else be seen to administer punishments in a paternal spirit rather than in order to slight, to engage in relations with the young for erotic reasons and not because of [a desire to flaunt] the license [he enjoys], and generally to compensate for any acts that are held to involve dishonor with greater honors.

(30) Of those who make attempts at assassination, the ones who are most to be feared and require the most precautions are those who deliberately choose not to try to save their lives once they have carried out the assassination. (31) Hence he must beware particularly of those who consider him to have behaved ar-

35

40

1315a1

5

10

15

20

25

30

rogantly either toward themselves or toward those they cherish; for those who undertake [such a deed] out of spiritedness are not sparing of themselves. As Heraclitus said, "it is hard to fight with spiritedness," as it "pays the price of soul." [112]

(32) Since cities are constituted out of two parts, human beings who are poor and others who are well off, both should conceive that they are being preserved and that neither is being treated unjustly by the other on account of the [tyrant's] rule. But whichever is superior, these he should particularly attach to his rule, so that, his position being enhanced in this way, there will be no necessity for the tyrant to effect a freeing of slaves or a sequestration of [heavy] arms. For the addition of one of these parts to his power is enough to make them superior to any attackers.

35

40

(33) To speak of such matters in detail would be superfluous. The aim is evident: he should appear to the ruled not as a tyrannical sort but as a manager and a kingly sort, not as an appropriator [of the things of others] but as a steward. He should pursue moderateness in life, not the extremes; further, he should seek the company of the notables, but seek popularity with the many. (34) As a result of these things, not only will his rule necessarily be nobler and more enviable by the fact that he rules over persons who are better and have not been humbled and does so without being hated and feared, but his rule will also be longer lasting; further, in terms of character he will either be in a state that is fine in relation to virtue or he will be half-decent—not vicious but half-vicious.

1315b1

5

10

CHAPTER 12

(1) Oligarchy and tyranny are, however, the most short-lived regimes. The tyranny of Orthagoras' sons and of Orthagoras himself at Sicyon existed for the longest period; it lasted a hundred years. The reason for this was that they treated the ruled moderately and in many respects were slaves to the laws; also, because Cleisthenes was a warlike sort he could not readily be held in contempt, and in many respects they sought popularity by acts of concern. [113] (2) It is said of Cleisthenes, at any rate, that he gave a crown to the person who denied him victory [in a competition]; some assert that the statue of a seated person in the marketplace there is a representation of the one who gave this judgment. They

15

20

178

also assert that Pisistratus once put up with being summoned as defendant in a suit before the Areopagus.[114]

(3) The second longest was that of the Cypselids at Corinth. This went on for seventy-three years and six months. Cypselus was tyrant for thirty years, Periander for forty and a half,[115] and Psammetichus the son of Gorgus for three years. (4) The reasons are the same in this case: Cypselus was a popular leader, and went without a bodyguard throughout his entire rule; Periander, though a tyrannical sort, was at the same time warlike.[116]

(5) The third was that of the Pisistratids at Athens, though it was not continuous. Pisistratus twice went into exile when tyrant, so that in thirty-three years he was tyrant for seventeen of these; his sons [ruled] for eighteen years, so that altogether it existed for thirty-five years.[117]

(6) Of those remaining, the longest was that connected with Hiero and Gelo at Syracuse. Yet not even this lasted long, only eighteen years altogether. Gelo was tyrant for seven years and died in the eighth; Hiero for ten years; Thrasyboulus went into exile after ten months. Most tyrannies have been quite short-lived, however.[118]

(7) The things connected both with [republican] regimes and with monarchies that lead to their destruction and their preservation have nearly all been spoken of. Now in the *Republic* there is a discussion of revolutions by Socrates,[119] but he does not argue rightly. In the case of the regime that is best and first he does not speak of a revolution proper to it. (8) He asserts the reason is that nothing is lasting, but everything undergoes revolution over a certain cycle, and the beginning point lies in those things where "a basic ratio of four to three, yoked to five, produced two modes," saying [that this happens] when the number of this figure is cubed,[120] the assumption being that nature sometimes brings into being persons who are mean and beyond education. Now in saying this he is perhaps not wrong, for there may be persons who are incapable of being educated and becoming excellent men. (9) But why should this be a sort of revolution peculiar to the regime he calls the best, rather than belonging to all the others and to all [persons] coming into existence? And is it because of time, through which he says all things undergo revolution, that even things not beginning simultaneously should undergo revolution simultaneously? If something came into being on the day before the turning point, will it then undergo revolution simultaneously?

(10) In addition to these things, what is the reason for its undergoing revolution in the direction of the Spartan regime? All re-

gimes undergo revolution more frequently into their opposite than into a regime of a neighboring sort. The same argument also applies to the other revolutions. He asserts that from the Spartan regime there is a revolution in the direction of oligarchy, from this to democracy, and from democracy to tyranny. (11) Yet revolution may also go the other way—from [rule of] the people to oligarchy, for example; and this [is more likely to happen] than revolution in the direction of monarchy. Further, in the case of tyranny he does not say either if there will be a revolution or, if there will not, what the reason is for this, or into which sort of regime. The reason for this is that it would not have been easy for him to say, as it is impossible to determine. According to him it should be in the direction of the first and best, for in this way there would be a continuous circle. (12) But tyranny also undergoes revolution into tyranny, for example the one at Sicyon, where the tyranny of Myron [was replaced by] that of Cleisthenes; into oligarchy, like that of Antileon at Chalcis; into democracy, like that of Gelo and his family at Syracuse; and into aristocracy, like that of Charilaus in Lacedaemon, and at Carthage.[121] (13) There can also be a revolution from oligarchy to tyranny, as happened with most of the ancient oligarchies in Sicily—to the tyranny of Panaetius at Leontini, to that of Cleander at Gela, to that of Anaxilaus at Rhegium, and similarly in many other cities.[122]

(14) It is also odd to suppose that there is a revolution in the direction of oligarchy because those holding the offices are greedy and involved in business, and not because those who are very pre-eminent by the fact of their property suppose it is not just for those possessing nothing to have a share in the city equal to that of the possessors. In many oligarchies, to engage in business is not permitted, and there are laws preventing this; on the other hand, at Carthage they engage in business although it is run timocratically,[123] and have not yet undergone a revolution. (15) It is also odd to assert[124] that an oligarchic city is really two cities, of the wealthy and the poor. For why should it have this characteristic more than the Spartan or any other [sort of regime] where all do not possess equal things or are not good men in a similar way? (16) Without anyone's becoming poorer than before, regimes can nonetheless undergo revolution from oligarchy to democracy, if the poor become a majority, or from [rule of] the people to oligarchy, if the well-off element is superior to the multitude and the latter neglect [politics] while the former put their mind to it.

(17) Though there are many reasons for revolutions occurring [from oligarchy to democracy], he only speaks of one—their becoming poor by extravagant living and paying out interest on

loans,[125] the assumption being that all or most were wealthy from the beginning. But this is false. Rather, when certain of the leaders have squandered their properties, these engage in sedition, but in the case of others nothing terrible happens, and even if it should, revolutions would be no more likely to occur in the direction of [rule of] the people than in that of any other sort of regime. (18) Further, [men] engage in factional conflict and effect revolution in regimes if they have no share in prerogatives or if they are treated unjustly or arrogantly, even where they have not consumed all their property on account of the license to do whatever they want, the cause of which he asserts is too much freedom. Although there are many sorts of oligarchies and democracies, Socrates speaks of the revolutions as if there were only one sort of each.[126]

20

25

BOOK 6

CHAPTER 1

(1) How many varieties there are, and which they are, both of the deliberative and authoritative element of the regime and of the arrangement connected with the offices; concerning courts, which sorts are organized with a view to which sort of regime; further, concerning the destruction and preservation of regimes, from what things these arise and through what causes—this was spoken of earlier.[1] (2) But since it turned out that there are several kinds of democracy as well as of the other regimes in similar fashion, it is not a bad thing to investigate anything that remains to be said about the former, and at the same time to identify the mode that is proper and advantageous to each. (3) Further, aggregates of all the modes that have been spoken of must also be investigated; for when [modes proper to different regimes are] conjoined, these make regimes overlap, so that there are oligarchic aristocracies and polities of a more democratic cast. (4) I mean that there are conjunctions which should be investigated, but at present have not been investigated—for example, if the deliberative element and what is connected with the selection of officials is organized oligarchically, but matters connected with the courts aristocratically; or these and what is connected with the deliberative element oligarchically, and what is connected with the selection of officials aristocratically; or if in some other manner not all of what is combined is proper to the regime.[2]

(5) What sort of democracy is suitable for what sort of city, and in the same way too what sort of oligarchy is suitable for what sort of multitude, and of the remaining regimes which is advantageous for which [peoples], was spoken of earlier.[3] (6) Yet [since] it should be made clear not only which of these sorts of regimes is best for cities, but also how one should institute both these and others, let us address this in succinct fashion. Let us speak first of democracy—for [how one should do this] will become evident also for the regime that corresponds to it, the one some call oligarchy.

(7) With a view to this inquiry, it is necessary to grasp all the things that are characteristic of popular rule or that are held to

accompany democracies. For it is as a result of the combination of these that the kinds of democracy arise, and that there are several sorts of democracy which differ, and not a single sort. (8) There are two reasons for which there are several sorts of democracy. First, there is the one spoken of earlier, that peoples are different.[4] For one multitude is of the farming sort, another of the vulgar and laboring sort; and if the first of these is added to the second, or again the third to both, these create a difference not only with respect to the democracy being better or worse, but even with respect to its being the same sort of democracy. The second reason is the one we are speaking of now. (9) For the things that accompany democracies and are held to belong to this sort of regime make democracies different when they are [differently] combined: one sort will be accompanied by fewer, another by more, another by all of them. It is useful to be familiar with each of these things both with a view to instituting whichever sort [of democracy] one happens to want and with a view to reforming [existing ones]. (10) Those who establish regimes seek to aggregate everything that belongs to the presupposition [of the regime], but they err in so doing, as was said earlier in the [discourses] on the sources of destruction and preservation of regimes.[5] Let us now speak of the claim and character [of the kinds of democracy] and what they strive for.

CHAPTER 2

(1) Now the presupposition of the democratic sort of regime is freedom. It is customarily said that only in this sort of regime do [men] share in freedom, for, so it is asserted, every democracy aims at this. One aspect of freedom is being ruled and ruling in turn. (2) The justice that is characteristically popular is to have equality on the basis of number and not on the basis of merit; where justice is of this sort, the multitude must necessarily have authority, and what is resolved by the majority must be final and must be justice, for, they assert, each of the citizens must have an equal share. The result is that in democracies the poor have more authority than the well off, for they are the majority, and what is resolved by the majority is authoritative. (3) This, then, is one mark of freedom, and it is regarded by those of the popular sort as the defining principle of the regime. Another is to live as one wants. For this is, they assert, the work of freedom, since not liv-

25

30

35

40

1317b1

5

10

ing as one wants is characteristic of a person who is enslaved. (4) This, then, is the second defining principle of democracy. From it has come [the claim to merit] not being ruled by anyone, or failing this, [to rule and be ruled] in turn. It contributes in this way to the freedom that is based on equality.

(5) These things being presupposed and [democratic] rule being of this sort, the following are characteristically popular: election to all offices from among all [the citizens]; rule of all over each, and of each over all in turn; having all offices chosen by lot, or those not requiring experience and art; having offices not based on any assessment, or based on the smallest possible; the same person not holding any office more than once, or doing so rarely, or in few cases, apart from those relating to war; having all offices of short duration, or those where this is possible; having all adjudicate or [persons chosen] from all, and concerning all matters or most, and these the greatest and most authoritative (for example, concerning audits, or the regime, or private transactions); the assembly having authority over all matters or the greatest, and no office having authority over any, or having it over as few as possible (6) (of the offices the most popular is the council, when there is not a ready supply of pay for all—when there is, the power even of this office is eliminated, for if the people are well supplied with pay they have all decisions referred to themselves, as was said earlier in the inquiry preceding this[6]); (7) next, providing pay—particularly for all, for the assembly, courts, and offices, but failing this, for the offices, courts, council, and assemblies that are authoritative, or for those offices where it is necessary to have common messes with one another.[7] Further, since oligarchy is defined by family, wealth, and education, the opposites of these things are held to be characteristically popular—lack of birth, poverty, and vulgarity.[8] (8) With regard to the offices, [another popular characteristic is] having none of them be for life, and if any such remain out of a previous revolution, stripping them of their power and making [the holders] chosen by lot rather than by election.[9]

(9) These things are common to democracies, then. But what is held to be democracy or [rule of the] people above all is what results from the sort of justice that is agreed to be democratic, which is all having an equal share on the basis of number. For it is equality if the poor rule no more than the well off and do not have authority alone, but all do equally on the basis of number. For in this way they might consider both equality and freedom as being present in the regime.

CHAPTER 3

(1) The question that arises after this is how they will come to have equality. Should assessments be distinguished [in such a way that the total property of the poor and the well off is equal—for example, that][10] of five hundred persons to a thousand, and the thousand given power equal to the five hundred? Or is equality on this basis not to be sought in this way, and should one not rather make this distinction and then take an equal number of persons from the five hundred and from the thousand and give them authority over elections and the courts? (2) Is this, then, the most just sort of regime that accords with popular justice, or rather the one that is based on the multitude? Those of the popular sort assert that justice is whatever is resolved by the majority, while those of the oligarchic sort assert it is whatever is resolved by [those with] the greater property (for they assert that decisions ought to be made on the basis of the amount of property). (3) Both involve inequality and injustice. For if [justice is] whatever the few [decide], it is [indistinguishable from] tyranny, for if a single individual has more than others who are well off, on the basis of oligarchic justice it is just for him alone to rule. But if it is what the majority [decide] on the basis of number, they will act unjustly by confiscating the [property] of the rich few, as was said earlier.[11] (4) What sort of equality there might be that both sides will agree on must be investigated in connection with the definition of justice given by both. For they [both] say that whatever is resolved by the majority of the citizens should be authoritative. This may be allowed to stand, though not entirely. Rather, since it happens that there are two parts of which the city [is constituted], rich and poor, whatever is resolved by both or by a majority [of both] should stand as authoritative; and if each resolves on opposite things, whatever [is resolved] by a majority which also has the greater assessment. (5) For example, if there are ten of the former and twenty of the latter, and something was resolved [differently] by six of the wealthy and fifteen of the poorer, four of the wealthy had joined the poor and five of the poor the wealthy. Whichever [group's] assessment predominates when those of both on either side are counted up, then—this is authoritative. (6) If it falls out equally, this must be considered a problem common to [the way things are done] now, if the assembly or the court is split; in such a case there must be resort to lot, or something else of this sort must be done.

15

20

25

30

35

40

1318b1

185

But concerning equality and justice, even though it is very difficult to find the truth about these matters, it is still easier to hit on it
than it is to persuade those who are capable of aggrandizing themselves. The inferior always seek equality and justice; those who
5   dominate them take no thought for it.

CHAPTER 4

(1) Of the four sorts of democracy, the best is the one that is first in
the arrangement spoken of in the discourses preceding these; it is
also the oldest of them all.[12] But I call it first in the sense that one
might distinguish among peoples. The best people is the farming
10   sort, so that it is possible also to create [the best] democracy
wherever the multitude lives from farming or herding. (2) For on
account of not having much property it is lacking in leisure, and
so is unable to hold frequent assemblies. Because they do not[13]
have the necessary things, they spend their time at work and do
not desire the things of others; indeed, working is more pleasant
15   to them than engaging in politics and ruling, where there are not
great spoils to be gotten from office. (3) For the many strive more
for profit than for honor. A sign of this is that they used to put up
with the ancient tyrannies and still put up with oligarchies, if no
one prevents them from working or takes away anything from
them: before long some of them become rich, while others cease
20   to be poor. (4) Further, if they have any element of ambition, having authority to elect and audit would satisfy their need. Indeed,
among some peoples it is sufficient for the many if they have no
share in election to the offices but certain persons are elected [to
do this] from all by turns, as at Mantinea, provided they have au-
25   thority over deliberation. (5) One should consider even this a certain form of democracy, as it once existed at Mantinea.[14]
Hence it is both advantageous and customarily belongs to the
sort of democracy spoken of earlier to have all elect to the offices
and audit and adjudicate, but for persons elected on the basis of
30   assessments to hold the offices, and the greater from the greater
assessments—or else to elect none on the basis of assessments,
but rather capable persons. (6) Those who govern themselves in
this way must necessarily be finely governed. The offices will al-
35   ways be in the hands of the best persons, the people being willing
and not envious of the respectable, while the arrangement is satisfactory for the respectable and notable. These will not be ruled by

others who are their inferiors, and they will rule justly by the fact that others have authority over the audits. (7) For to be under constraint and unable to do everything one might resolve to do is advantageous. The license to do whatever one wishes cannot defend against the mean element in every human being. So it necessarily results that the respectable rule without falling into error, while the multitude does not get less than its due—something that is most beneficial for regimes.

(8) That this is the best sort of democracy, then, is evident, and the reason for this—that it is because the people are of a certain quality. With a view to instituting a farming people, certain of the laws that existed among many in ancient times are entirely useful—laws either generally forbidding the possession of land beyond a certain measure or forbidding it between a certain location and the town or city. (9) In ancient times there also used to be legislation forbidding the sale of the original allotments; there is also the law they say derives from Oxylus, which has the same sort of power, forbidding borrowing against any part of the land belonging to an individual. [Given things as they are] at present, one should attempt reform through the law of the Aphytaeans as well, for it is useful in relation to what we are speaking of. (10) Though there are many of them and they possess little land, the Aphytaeans nevertheless all engage in farming. For they are not assessed on the basis of whole estates [as originally allotted], but they divide these into parts of such a size that even the poor have enough to enable them to exceed the assessment [that is required for citizenship].[15]

(11) After the farming multitude, the best sort of people exists where they are herdsmen and live from livestock. These are in a condition very similar to farmers, and in what relates to military activities they are particulary well exercised with respect to their dispositions as well as useful with respect to their bodies and capable of living in the open. (12) The other sorts of multitude out of which the remaining sorts of democracy are constituted are almost all much meaner than these: their way of life is a mean one, with no task involving virtue among the things that occupy the multitude of human beings who are vulgar persons and merchants or the multitude of laborers. (13) Further, on account of their always frequenting the marketplace and the town, nearly all persons of this type can easily attend the assembly, while those engaged in farming, on account of their being scattered in the country, do not come together in this way and have no need of doing so. (14) But where it happens that the position of the territory is such that the country is far removed from the city, it is easy to create a decent

40
1319a1

5

10

15

20

25

30

35   democracy or a polity. For the multitude is compelled to have its dwelling places in the fields; so that even where there is a mass of merchants, one should not hold assemblies in democracies without the multitude from the country.

(15) How the best and first sort of democracy should be instituted, then, has been spoken of; how the others should be instituted is also evident. They should deviate progressively, always
40   separating out a worse multitude [for citizenship]. The final sort,
1319b1   on account of all participating in it, is one that not every city can support, nor is it easy for it to last, as it is not well composed with respect to its laws and customs. (As to what results in the destruction both of this and of the other regimes, this was for the most
5   part spoken of earlier.) (16) With a view to establishing this sort of democracy, those at the head of affairs customarily make the people stronger by adding as many persons as possible, admitting as citizens not only those who are legitimate but even bastards and those descended from a citizen either way, I mean either from the
10   father or the mother; for this whole element is proper to this sort of people. (17) Popular leaders customarily institute it in this way, then. In fact, however, one should add [citizens] up to the point where the multitude predominates over the notables and the middling elements and not proceed beyond this. For if [the lower elements] are in excess, they introduce disorder into the regime, and
15   goad the notables into looking harshly on the democracy and not putting up with it—something which turned out to be a cause of the factional conflict at Cyrene.[16] A base element is tolerated if it is few, but as it becomes more numerous it is more in front of
20   one's eyes. (18) Also useful with a view to a democracy of this sort are the sort of institutions that Cleisthenes used at Athens when he wanted to enhance the democracy, or those at Cyrene who established [rule of] the people.[17] (19) Other and more numerous tribes and clans are to be created, private rites incorporated into a few common rites, and everything devised so that all
25   are mixed together to the greatest possible extent, and their previous familiar [associations] broken up. (20) Further, tyrannical institutions too are held to be characteristic of popular rule—I mean, for example, lack of rule over slaves (which might be advantageous [to a democracy] up to a certain point) as well as over women and children, and tolerating everyone living as he wants.
30   For the element assisting a regime of this sort will be considerable; living in a disorderly way is more pleasant to the many than living with moderation.

188

CHAPTER 5

(1) But instituting it is not the greatest or the only task of the legislator or of those wanting to constitute some regime of this sort, but rather to see that it is preserved; for it is not difficult to be governed in one fashion or another for one, two, or three days. (2) Hence one should take what was studied earlier, the sources of preservation and destruction of regimes, and try to institute stability, avoiding what destroys regimes and enacting laws—both written and unwritten—of a sort that will encompass above all what preserves regimes; and one should not consider as characteristic of popular rule or of oligarchy something that will make the city democratically or oligarchically run to the greatest extent possible, but something that will do so for the longest period of time. (3) The popular leaders of the present, seeking to win the favor of the people, undertake many confiscations through the courts. Those who cherish the regime should take action against this, legislating that nothing that is confiscated in a case affecting common matters should become public [property], but rather sacred [property]. Those acting unjustly will be no less cautious, for they will be fined in the same way, but the mass will less frequently vote against those who are being tried, as they are not going to get anything out of it. (4) Further, public suits should always be kept as few as possible, those prosecuting in a frivolous way being curbed by large penalties. For they customarily bring these against the notables rather than the popular sort; but all the citizens should feel benevolent toward the regime, or failing this, they should at least not consider those in authority as their enemies.

(5) Since the ultimate sorts of democracy have a considerable population and it is difficult for them to attend the assembly without pay, this [state of affairs]—where there do not happen to be [external sources of] revenues—is inimical to the notables; for it must necessarily be got from taxes and confiscations and corruption of the courts, things which have before now brought down many democracies. Where there do not happen to be revenues, then, one should hold few assemblies, and the courts should have many members but meet only for a few days. (6) This contributes to the wealthy's not fearing the expenditure, if the well off do not receive pay for attending court but the poor do; and it contributes to a much better judgment of suits, for the well off are unwilling to be away from their private affairs for many days, but are willing for a brief period of time. (7) Where there are revenues, however, one should not do what popular leaders do at present. They dis-

35

40
1320a1

5

10

15

20

25

30   tribute any surplus; [the people] take it and at the same time ask for more of the same. This sort of assistance to the poor is the [proverbial] "punctured jar." [18] But one who is genuinely of the popular sort should see to it that the multitude is not overly poor;

35   (8) for this is the reason for democracy being depraved. Measures must therefore be devised so that there will be abundance over time. Since this is advantageous also for the well off, what ought to be done is to accumulate what is left over of the revenues and distribute accumulated [sums] to the poor. This should particularly be done if one could accumulate enough for the acquisition of a plot of land, or failing this, for a start in trade or farming. (9)

1320b1   If this is not possible for all, it should be distributed on the basis of tribes or some other part [of the city] by turns; and in the meantime the well off should be taxed to provide pay for necessary meetings, while at the same time being released from pointless sorts of public service. It is by governing in such a manner that

5   the Carthaginians have acquired the friendship of the people: they are constantly sending out some of the people to the subject [cities] and making them well off. [19] (10) Also, notables who are refined and sensible will divide the poor among themselves and pro-

10   vide them with a start in pursuing some work. It is also right to imitate what the Tarentines do. By making their possessions common for use by the poor, they maintain the benevolence of the multitude. [20] (11) Further, they also created all the offices in a double form, the ones chosen by election, the others by lot—those chosen by lot so that the people could have a share in them, those chosen by election so that they would be better governed. (This same thing can be done by splitting the same office between [dif-

15   ferent] persons chosen by lot and by election. [21])

    How democracies should be instituted, then, has been spoken of.

CHAPTER 6

    (1) How one should do this in connection with oligarchies is very

20   nearly evident from these things as well. Each sort of oligarchy should be aggregated out of the opposite elements, reasoning in relation to the sort of democracy opposite to it. The first and most well blended of the sorts of oligarchy [is related to the first sort of democracy]; this is the one that is very close to so-called polity. (2) In this there should be a distinction among assessments, some

being lesser and others greater: on the basis of the lesser they will share in the necessary offices, on the basis of the greater, in the more authoritative; it should be open to anyone possessing the assessment to share in the regime—bringing in through the assessment as many of the people as will allow them to be superior to those not sharing; (3) and they should always take from the better [part] of the people those who are to be partners [in the regime].

The next sort of oligarchy should be instituted in a similar way, with a slight tightening [of the qualifications for citizenship]. As regards the sort that corresponds to the extreme sort of democracy, the most dynastic and tyrannical of the sorts of oligarchy, to the degree that it is the worst, it requires the greater defense. (4) For just as bodies that are in a good state with respect to health, or ships that are in a fine condition for a voyage with respect to their crews, admit of more errors without being destroyed by them, while bodies that are in a diseased condition and ships with loosened timbers and a poor crew cannot bear up even under small errors, so too in the case of regimes the worse need the most defense.

(5) Democracies generally are preserved by their considerable populations; this is the antithesis of the sort of justice that is based on merit. But it is clear that oligarchy must, on the contrary, obtain its preservation by being well arranged.

25

30

35

1321a1

CHAPTER 7

(1) Since there are four parts of the multitude, the farming element, the vulgar element, the merchant element, and the laboring element, and four parts [of the city] that are useful with a view to war, the horse [-rearing] element, the heavy-armed element, the light-armed element, and the seafaring element, wherever it happens that the country is suitable for horses, conditions are naturally apt for instituting a strong oligarchy (for the preservation of the inhabitants derives from a force of this sort, and horse-rearing is done by those possessing large properties); where it is suitable for heavy arms, the next sort of oligarchy (for the heavy-armed element is made up of the well off more than the poor). (2) Light-armed and naval forces, on the other hand, are wholly popular. At present, therefore, wherever this sort of multitude is numerous and there is a factional split, [the oligarchs] often get the worst of the contest. A remedy for this should be sought from those gener-

5

10

15

als who are expert in war, who join to the cavalry and the heavy-armed force an appropriate light-armed force. (3) This is the way the people prevail over the well off in factional splits: being light-armed, they can easily contend against a force of cavalry and heavy-armed troops. To establish such a force from these, therefore, is to establish one against themselves. Rather, there being a distinction of age, the older on one side and the young on the other, they should teach their sons the working of auxiliary and light arms when still young, and some should be picked out from among the boys to be themselves practitioners of these tasks.[22]

(4) Giving a share in the governing body to the multitude can occur either in the way spoken of earlier, to those possessing the assessment, or as among the Thebans, to those abstaining for a certain period of time from vulgar tasks, or as at Massilia, where they make a judgment as to who merits [office], whether those within the governing body or those outside it.[23]

(5) Further, with respect to the most authoritative offices, which should be retained by those in the regime, public services should be attached to them, so that the people may be willing to forego sharing in them, and may feel indulgence for their rulers as having paid heavily for the office. (6) It is also appropriate for them both to offer magnificent sacrifices when they enter office and to institute something common,[24] so that the people, in sharing in what is connected with these festivities and seeing the city adorned with votive statues and buildings, are glad to see the regime endure; and it will also result that the notables have a memorial of their expenditure. (7) At present, however, those connected with oligarchies do not do this, but rather the opposite: they are in search of spoils no less than honor. Hence it is well to speak of them as small democracies.

As to how one ought to establish democracies and oligarchies, then, let our discussion stand in this manner.

CHAPTER 8

(1) It follows on what has been said to distinguish finely among the matters connected with offices, how many and which there are and over which matters, as was said earlier.[25] Without the necessary offices it is impossible for a city to exist; without those that relate to its good arrangement and order, it is impossible for it to be finely administered. (2) Further, in small cities there must of

necessity be fewer offices, and in large cities more, as was said earlier.[26] Which offices can suitably be aggregated, then, and which separated, should not be overlooked.

(3) First, then, of the necessary [offices] there is the superintendence connected with the market, for which there should be an office which has oversight in connection both with agreements and with orderliness. For very nearly all cities must of necessity buy and sell certain things with a view to each other's necessary requirements, and this is the readiest way to self-sufficiency, on account of which [men] are held to join together in one regime.

(4) Another sort of superintendence, connected with this sort and close to it, is that over public and private [property] in town, to ensure orderliness, and over the preservation and repair of decaying buildings and roads, and to ensure that accusations do not arise concerning the boundaries between [the properties of the citizens] themselves, and whatever else belonging to this sort of superintendence is similar to these things. (5) Most call this sort of office "town management"; it has a number of parts, and in more populous states different officials are established for the different parts—for example, wall builders, superintendents of wells, and harbor guards.

(6) Another office is necessary and quite similar to this. It is concerned with the same things, but is connected with the country and matters outside the town; they call these officials "field managers" in some places, in others "foresters."

There are three sorts of superintendence over these matters, then. Another office is that by which revenues from common things are received, guarded, and split up among each administrative element. They call these "receivers" and "treasurers."

(7) Another office is that with which one registers both private agreements and judgments from the courts. Before these same officials should also come indictments and initiations of suits. In some places they split this office too among several [persons], but a single office has authority over all these matters.[27] They call them "sacred recorders," "supervisors," "recorders," and other terms that resemble these.

(8) Next after this is one which is very nearly the most necessary as well as the most difficult of the offices, that connected with actions taken against persons found guilty or those whose names have been posted in notices,[28] and with the guarding of prisoners. (9) It is difficult by the fact that it involves much odium, so that unless it is possible to make great profits, [men] will either not put up with being officials of this sort or, if they do, they will be unwilling to act in accordance with the laws; but it is necessary,

10

15

20

25

30

35

40

1322a1

5 because there is no benefit in having suits about matters of justice
if these do not achieve their end, so that if it is impossible [for
men] to be partners where there are no suits, so also is it where
there are no actions [taken against those found guilty]. (10) Hence
it is better for this not to be a single office, but rather [for it to be
carried out by] persons drawn from different courts, and in con-
10 nection with the posting of notices to try to distinguish in the same
way; and further, to have some actions taken by officials [rather
than by functionaries of the courts], and in particular to have in-
coming officials take action in suits decided by outgoing ones, or
in the case of serving officials to have one determine guilt and another take the action—for example, the town managers would
take action in cases coming from the field managers, and the latter
in cases from the former. (11) The less the odium that attaches to
15 the actions taken, the more will the actions achieve their end. To
have the same persons determining guilt and taking action involves a double odium, and to have the same [taking action] in all
cases [makes them] inimical to everyone.[29] In many places the
office that guards [prisoners] is distinguished from that which
20 takes actions, as at Athens in the case of the so-called Eleven.[30]
(12) Hence it is better to make this separate too, and to seek the
[same] device here as well. This office is no less necessary than
the one spoken of, but it happens that the respectable avoid it
above all, while it is not safe to give authority over it to the de-
25 praved, as these are more in need of being guarded themselves
than capable of guarding others. (13) Hence there should not be a
single office assigned to them, nor should the same one do it continuously, but they should be superintended by different persons in
turn—by the young, where there is a body of cadets or garrison
troops, and by [other] officials.

30 These offices must be set first, then, as being the most necessary. After these are others which are no less necessary, but higher
in rank arrangement, as they require much experience and trust.
(14) These would be the ones connected with the defense of the
city, and any that are arranged with a view to military requirements. Both in peace and in war alike there should be superinten-
35 dents of the defense of gates and walls, and of the scrutiny and
organization of the citizens. In some places there are more offices
for all of these things, in others fewer—in small cities, for example, there might be a single one concerned with all. (15) They call
1322bl such persons "generals" and "war officials." Further, if there are
cavalry, light-armed troops, archers, or a naval element, an official is sometimes established for each of these, which they call
"admirals," "cavalry commanders," and "regimental command-

ers," and for the parts under them, "warship commanders," "leaders of companies," and "tribal commanders," and [others are appointed to command] any parts belonging to these. The entirety of these things makes up a single kind [of office], superintendence of military matters.

(16) In connection with this office, then, things stand in this manner. Now since some of the offices, if not all of them, handle substantial quantities of common [funds], it is necessary for there to be a different office to receive the accounts and to do an additional audit, one which does not itself handle any other matter. Some call these "auditors," others "accountants," others "scrutinizers," and others "advisers."

(17) Besides all these offices, there is the one that is most particularly authoritative in all matters. For the same office often has [authority over] the final [disposition] as well as the introduction [of all measures], or else it presides over the multitude, wherever the people have authority; for there should be something which convenes the authoritative element in the regime. In some places it is called "preliminary councillors," because it engages in preliminary deliberation; where there is a [ruling] multitude, it is called a "council" instead.

(18) Those of the offices that are political are very nearly this many. Another kind of superintendence is that connected with the gods—for example, priests and superintendents of matters connected with sacred things, including the preservation of existing buildings and the restoration of those that are in decay, and whatever other arrangements there are related to the gods. (19) Sometimes it happens, as for example in small cities, that there is a single superintendence for this; sometimes there are many officials who are separate from the priesthood—for example, sacrificers, temple guardians, and treasurers of sacred funds. (20) Next after this is the office that specializes in all the common sacrifices which the law does not assign to the priests, but which they have the prerogative [of celebrating] from the [city's] common hearth. These officials are called "kings" by some, "presidents" by others.

(21) The necessary sorts of superintendence are, then, to speak in summary fashion, the following. They are those connected with divine matters, military matters, revenues, expenditures, the market, the town, harbors, and the country; and further, those connected with courts, the registration of agreements, actions [against offenders,] guarding [of prisoners, receiving] accounts, and the scrutinizing and auditing of officials; and finally, those connected with the element that deliberates about common mat-

ters. (22) Peculiar to those cities which enjoy greater leisure and are more prosperous, and which in addition take thought for orderliness, are the offices of manager of women, law guardian, manager of children, and exercise official, and in addition to these the superintendence connected with gymnastic and Dionysiac contests, as well as any other spectacles of this sort there may happen to be. (23) Some of these offices are evidently not of a popular sort—for example, management of women and management of children: the poor must necessarily treat both their women and children as attendants on account of their lack of slaves.

(24) There are three sorts of offices under the direction of which election to the authoritative offices is made—law guardians, preliminary councillors, and council; law guardians are aristocratic, preliminary councillors oligarchic, and a council popular.

Concerning offices, then, almost all of them have been spoken of in outline. . . .[31]

BOOK 7

CHAPTER 1

(1) Concerning the best regime, one who is going to undertake the investigation appropriate to it must necessarily discuss first what the most choiceworthy way of life is. As long as this is unclear, the best regime must necessarily be unclear as well; for it is appropriate for those who govern themselves best on the basis of what is available to them to act in the best manner, provided nothing occurs contrary to reasonable expectation. (2) Hence there should first be agreement on which is the most choiceworthy way of life for all, so to speak, and after this, whether the same or a different way of life is choiceworthy [for men] in common and separately [as individuals]. Considering as adequate, then, much of what is said in the external discourses concerning the best way of life,[1] we must use that here as well.

(3) For in truth no one would dispute that, there being a distinction among three groups [of good things], those that are external, those of the body, and those of the soul, all these things ought to be available[2] to the blessed. (4) No one would assert that a person is blessed who has no part of courage, moderation, [the virtue of] justice, or prudence, but is afraid of the flies buzzing around him, abstains from none of the extremes when he desires to eat or drink, destroys his dearest friends for a trifle, and similarly regarding the things connected with the mind, is as senseless and as thoroughly deceived [by a false perception of things] as a child or a madman. (5) Yet while all would admit what has been said, they differ in regard to how much [of each type of good is desirable] and their [relative degree of] preeminence. For [men] consider any amount of virtue to be adequate, but wealth, goods, power, reputation, and all such things they seek to excess without limit. (6) We shall say to them that it is easy to convince oneself concerning these matters through the facts as well [as through argument], when one sees that men do not acquire and safeguard the virtues by means of external things, but the latter by means of the former, and that living happily—whether human beings find it in enjoyment or in virtue or in both—is available to those who have to excess the adornments of character and mind but behave mod-

15

20

25

30

35

40

1323b1

erately in respect to the external acquisition of good things, rather than to those who possess more of the latter than what is useful but are deficient in the former. Yet this can also be readily seen by those investigating on the basis of argument.

(7) External things, like any instrument, have a limit: everything useful belongs among[3] those things an excess of which must necessarily be either harmful or not beneficial to those who have them. In the case of each of the good things connected with the soul, however, the more it is in excess, the more useful it must necessarily be—if indeed one should attribute to these things not only nobility but utility as well. (8) In general, it is clear, we shall assert, that the best state of each thing in relation to other things corresponds with respect to its preeminence to the distance between the things of which we assert that these are states. So if the soul is more honorable than both possessions and the body both simply and for us, the best state of each must necessarily stand in the same relation as these things [among themselves]. (9) Further, it is for the sake of the soul that these things are naturally choiceworthy and that all sensible persons should choose them, and not the soul for the sake of them.

(10) That the same amount of happiness falls to each person as of virtue and prudence and action in accordance with these, therefore, may stand as agreed by us. We may use the god as testimony to this: he is happy and blessed, yet not through any of the external good things but rather through himself and by being of a certain quality in his nature. And it is on this account that good fortune necessarily differs from happiness. Of the good things that are external to the soul the cause is chance and fortune; but no one is just or sound by fortune or through fortune.

(11) Next, and requiring the same arguments, is [the assertion] that the best city is happy and acts nobly.[4] It is impossible to act nobly without acting [to achieve] noble things; but there is no noble deed either of a man or of a city that is separate from virtue and prudence. (12) The courage, justice, and prudence of a city have the same power and form as those things human beings share in individually who are called just, prudent, and sound.

(13) These things, so far as they go, may stand as a preface to our discourse. For it is not possible either not to touch on them or to exhaust all of the arguments pertaining to them (these things are a task for [an inquiry belonging to] another sort of leisure). For the present let us presuppose this much, that the best way of life both separately for each individual and in common for cities is that accompanied by virtue—virtue that is equipped to such an extent as to [allow them to] share in the actions that accord with

198

virtue. (14) With regard to those who dispute [such an argument], we must pass over them for the purposes of the present inquiry, but shall make a thorough investigation later, if anyone happens not to be persuaded by what has been said.[5]

CHAPTER 2

(1) Whether happiness must be asserted to be the same both for a single individual human being and for a city or not the same, however, remains to be spoken of. But this too is evident: all would agree it is the same. (2) For those who ascribe living well to wealth in the case of a single person also call the city as a whole blessed if it is wealthy; those who honor the tyrannical way of life above all would also assert that the city is happiest which rules the greatest number of persons; and if anyone accepts that the individual [is happy] on account of virtue, he will also assert that the more excellent city is the one that is happier.

(3) But the following two things are in need of investigation: one, which is the more choiceworthy way of life, that which involves engaging jointly in politics and participating in a city, or rather that characteristic of the foreigner and divorced from the political partnership; and further, which regime and which state of the city are to be regarded as best (regardless of whether participating in a city is choiceworthy for all or only for most and not for certain persons).

(4) Since this [question]—but not [that concerning] what is choiceworthy for the individual—is a task for political thought and study, and since at present we have intentionally chosen [to limit ourselves to] this sort of investigation, the former is incidental to, the latter a task for, this inquiry.

(5) Now that the best regime must necessarily be that arrangement under which anyone might act in the best manner and live blessedly is evident. Yet there is a dispute among those who agree that the most choiceworthy way of life is that accompanied by virtue as to whether the political and active way of life is choiceworthy, or rather that which is divorced from all external things—that involving some sort of study, for example—which some assert is the only philosophic way of life. (6) For it is evident that these two ways of life are the ones intentionally chosen by those human beings who are most ambitious with a view to virtue, both in former times and at the present; the two I mean are the political and

5

10

15

20

25

30

the philosophic. It makes no small difference on which side the truth lies, for a sensible person, at any rate, must necessarily organize matters with a view to the better aim both in the case of human beings individually and for the regime in common. (7) There are some who consider rule over one's neighbors, if undertaken after the fashion of a master, to be accompanied by injustice of the greatest sort, and if in political fashion, not to involve injustice but to be an impediment to one's own well-being. Others hold opinions that are virtually the opposite of these. [They believe] that the active and political way of life is the only one for a man,[6] and that in the case of each sort of virtue there is no more room for action on the part of private individuals than on the part of those who are active with respect to common matters and engage in politics. (8) This is the conception some of them have; but others assert that the mode of regime involving mastery and tyranny is the only happy one. Indeed, among some [peoples] this is the defining principle of the regime and the laws—that they exercise mastery over their neighbors. (9) Hence while most of the usages existing among most [peoples] are, so to speak, a mere jumble, nevertheless if the laws anywhere look to one thing, it is domination that all of them aim at. In Sparta and Crete, for example, it is with a view to wars[7] that education and the greatest part of the laws are organized. (10) Further, among all nations that are capable of aggrandizing themselves, power of this sort is honored—for example, among the Scythians, the Persians, the Thracians, and the Celts. Among some of them there are also certain laws stimulating [men] to this sort of virtue; for example at Carthage, so it is asserted, they receive armlets to adorn themselves for each campaign they go on. (11) There was once a law in Macedonia as well that any man who had not killed an enemy had to wear a tether for a belt; among the Scythians one who had not killed an enemy was not permitted to drink from the cup passed around at a banquet; among the Iberians, a warlike nation, they fix in the ground a tomb as many spits as the number of enemies [the deceased] has destroyed; (12) and there are many other things of this sort among other [peoples], some of them prescribed by laws, others by customs.

Yet it may perhaps seem overly odd to those wishing to investigate [the matter] that this should be the task of the expert in politics, to be able to discern how to rule and exercise mastery over those nearby, whether they wish it or not. (13) How could this be characteristic of the political expert or the legislator when it is not even lawful? It is not lawful to rule [a city in this fashion] justly, let alone unjustly; and it is possible to dominate unjustly. Yet not

even in the other sciences do we see this: it is not the task of the
doctor or the pilot to either persuade or [failing that] compel persons [to submit to their rule]—patients in the case of the one,
voyagers in the case of the other. (14) But the many seem to suppose that expertise in mastery is [the same as] political expertise,
and they are not ashamed to train [to do] in relation to others what
they deny is just or advantageous for themselves. For among
themselves they seek just rule, but they care nothing about justice
toward others. (15) It would be odd if there did not exist by nature
that which exercises mastery and that which does not exercise
mastery,[8] so that if matters stand in this manner, one should not
try to exercise mastery over all things but only over those that are
to be mastered, just as one should not hunt human beings for a
feast or sacrifice, but rather that which is to be hunted for this
(that which is to be hunted is any wild animal that is edible). (16)
But even by itself a single city could be happy—one that is finely
governed (if indeed it is possible for a city to be settled by itself
somewhere using excellent laws)—and the organization of its
regime will not be with a view to war and the domination of
enemies; for [under this assumption] nothing of this sort would
exist.

(17) It is clear, therefore, that all of the concerns that are with a
view to war are to be regarded as noble, but not as the highest end
of all, but rather as being for the sake of that. It belongs to the
excellent legislator to see how a city, a family of human beings,
and every other sort of partnership will share in the good life and
in the happiness that is possible for them. (18) There will be different arrangements, however, with regard to certain usages [in
accordance with differing circumstances]; and where neighboring
[peoples] are present, it belongs to legislative expertise to see
what sorts of training are to be undertaken with a view to what
sorts [of neighboring peoples] or how the things suitable for each
sort are to be practiced. But this [question]—toward what end the
best regime should be directed—may be appropriately investigated later.[9]

CHAPTER 3

(1) In regard to those who agree that the most choiceworthy way
of life is the one accompanied by virtue but differ about the practice of it, we must say to both—on the one side they reject [the

holding of] political offices, since they consider the way of life of
20 the free person to be different from that of the political [ruler] and
the most choiceworthy of all; on the other, they consider the latter
the best, [arguing that] it is impossible for one who acts in nothing
to act well, and that acting well and happiness are the same thing—
that they both argue correctly in some respects and incorrectly in
others. (2) The one side is correct in saying that the way of life of
the free person is better than that involving mastery. This is true:
25 there is nothing dignified about using a slave as a slave; giving
commands concerning necessary things has no share in the noble
things. But to consider every sort of rule as mastery is not correct.
There is no less distance between rule over free persons and rule
over slaves than between what is by nature free and what is by
nature slavish. But these things were discussed adequately in the
30 initial discourses.[10]

(3) To praise inactivity more than activity is also not true. Happiness is a sort of action, and the actions of just and moderate persons involve an end for many noble things. Now when such matters are discussed in this way, one might perhaps conceive that
35 having authority over all [persons] is best, for in this way one
would have authority over the greatest number and the noblest of
actions. (4) So [on this understanding] one who is capable of doing so should not leave those nearby to rule themselves but should
deprive them of it, and a father should take no account of his children nor children of their father nor a friend for his friend nor take
40 any thought for this: the best is what is most choiceworthy, and
acting well is best. Perhaps they argue truly in this if the most
choiceworthy of existing things will be available to those who
1325b1 plunder and use force. (5) But perhaps it is impossible that it be
available, and this presupposition of theirs is false. For actions
can no longer be noble for one who does not differ as much [from
those he rules] as husband differs from wife, father from children,
5 or master from slaves. So the transgressor could never make up
later for the deviation from virtue he has already committed.
Among similar persons nobility and justice are found in [ruling
and being ruled] in turn, for this is something equal and similar:
(6) [to assign] what is not equal to equal persons and what is not
similar to similar persons is contrary to nature, and nothing con-
10 trary to nature is noble. Hence when another person is superior on
the basis of virtue and of the power that acts [to achieve] the best
things, it is noble to follow this person and just to obey him. (7)
(Not only virtue should be present but also power, on the basis of
which he will be active.) But if these things are argued rightly and
happiness is to be regarded as [the same as] acting well, the best

way of life both in common for every city and for the individual would be the active one.

(8) Yet the active way of life is not necessarily to be regarded as being in relation to others, as some suppose, nor those thoughts alone as being active which arise from activity for the sake of what results, but rather much more those that are complete in themselves, and the sorts of study and ways of thinking that are for their own sake. Acting well is the end, so it too is a certain action; and even in the case of external actions we speak of those who by means of their thoughts are master craftsmen as acting in the authoritative sense. (9) Indeed, not even cities that are situated by themselves and intentionally choose to live in this way are necessarily inactive. For this [activity] can come about on the basis of [a city's] parts: there are many sorts of partnership that belong to the parts of the city in relation to one another. (10) This is available in a similar way to any individual human being as well. For otherwise the god and the entire universe could hardly be in a fine condition, since they have no external actions beyond those that are proper to themselves. That the same way of life must necessarily be the best both for each human being individually and for cities and human beings in common, then, is evident.

CHAPTER 4

(1) Since this has been said by way of preface about these things, and since the other sorts of regimes were studied earlier,[11] the beginning point of what remains is to speak in the first instance of the sorts of presuppositions there should be concerning the city that is to be constituted on the basis of what one would pray for. (2) For it is impossible for the best regime to arise without equipment to match. Hence there are many things that we should presuppose for ourselves in advance, like persons offering prayer; yet none of these things should be impossible. I mean, for example, concerning the number of citizens and the amount of territory. (3) For just as in the case of the other craftsmen—the weaver, for example, or the shipbuilder—material should be available that is suitable to work on (for to the extent that this has been better prepared, what is brought into being by the art is necessarily finer), so too in the case of the political expert and the legislator the proper material should be available in a suitable condition. (4) To the equipment characteristic of the city belongs in the first in-

stance both the multitude of human beings—how many should be available and of what quality by nature—and the territory in the same way—how much there should be and of what quality. Now most persons suppose that it is appropriate for the happy city to be great. To the extent that this is true, they are ignorant of what sort of city is great and what sort small. (5) They judge one to be great on the basis of the magnitude of the number of inhabitants, but one should look not to their number but to their capacity. For there exists a certain task of a city too, so that the city most capable of bringing this to completion is the one that must be supposed the greatest—just as one might assert that Hippocrates is greater not as a human being but as a doctor than someone excelling him in bodily size. (6) Yet even if one should judge by looking to number, this must not be done on the basis of any chance multitude (for perhaps of necessity there is present in cities a large number of slaves as well as aliens and foreigners), but only those who are a part of the city—of those proper parts out of which a city is constituted. It is the preeminence of these things in a multitude that is an indication of a great city. One that can send out a large number of the vulgar but few heavy-armed troops cannot possibly be great. To be a great city and a populous one is not the same thing.

(7) This too, at any rate, is evident from the facts: that it is difficult—perhaps impossible—for a city that is too populous to be well managed. Of those that are held to be finely governed, at any rate, we see none that is lax in regard to [restricting the] number [of citizens]. This is clear also through the proof afforded by arguments. (8) For law is a certain sort of arrangement, and good management must of necessity involve good arrangement.[12] But an overly excessive number is incapable of sharing in arrangement. This is, indeed, a task requiring divine power, which is what holds together the whole itself. [At the same time, too small a number is also inadequate for a good or beautiful arrangement,[13]] since the beautiful, at any rate, comes to exist customarily in [things having a certain] number and size. (9) Hence that city too must necessarily be the finest where, together with size, the defining principle mentioned is present. But there is a certain measure of size in a city as well, just as in all other things—animals, plants, instruments: none of these things will have its own capacity if it is either overly small or excessive with respect to size, but it will sometimes be wholly robbed of its nature, and at other times in a poor condition. A ship that is a foot long, for example, will not be a ship at all, nor one of twelve hundred feet, and as it approaches a certain size it will make for a bad voyage,

in the one case because of smallness, in the other because of excess. (11) Similarly with the city as well, the one that is made up
of too few persons is not self-sufficient, though the city is a self-
sufficient thing, while the one that is made up of too many persons is with respect to the necessary things self-sufficient like a
nation, but is not a city; for it is not easy for a regime to be 5
present. Who will be general of an overly excessive number, or
who will be herald, unless he has the voice of Stentor?[14]

Hence the first city must necessarily be that made up of a multitude so large as to be the first multitude that is self-sufficient with
a view to living well in the context of the political partnership.
(12) It is possible for one that exceeds this on the basis of number
to be a greater city, but this is not possible, as we said, indefi- 10
nitely. As to what the defining principle of the excess is, it is easy
to see from the facts. The actions of the city belong on the one
hand to the rulers, on the other to the ruled. The task of a ruler is
command and judgment. (13) With a view to judgment concerning the just things and with a view to distributing offices on the
basis of merit, the citizens must necessarily be familiar with one 15
another's qualities; where this does not happen to be the case,
what is connected with the offices and with judging must necessarily be carried on poorly. For in connection with both it is not
just to improvise—the very thing that manifestly happens in an
overly populous city. (14) Further, [in such cities] it is easy for 20
aliens and foreigners to assume a part in the regime: it is not difficult for them to escape notice on account of the excess of number.
It is clear, therefore, that the best defining principle for a city is
this: the greatest excess of number with a view to self-sufficiency
of life that is readily surveyable. Concerning the size of a city,
then, let the discussion stand in this manner. 25

CHAPTER 5

(1) Something very similar holds as well in the case of what concerns the territory. As far as its being of a certain quality is concerned, it is clear that everyone would praise the territory that is
the most self-sufficient. That which bears every sort of thing is of
necessity such, for self-sufficiency is having everything available
and being in need of nothing. In number[15] and size [the territory
should be] large enough so that the inhabitants are able to live at 30
leisure in liberal fashion and at the same time with moderation.

35

40

1327a1

5

10

(2) Whether regarding this defining principle we are arguing rightly or not must be investigated with greater precision later, when there will be an opportunity to give an account of possessions generally and of [what is involved in] being well off in terms of property—how and in what manner this should stand in relation to use itself.[16] For there are many disputes in connection with this investigation on account of those who invite us toward either sort of excess in a way of life, the ones toward penury, the others toward luxury.[17]

(3) It is not difficult to speak of the kind of territory (regarding certain matters one should also be persuaded by those who are experienced in generalship)—that it ought to be difficult for enemies to enter, but readily exited by [the citizens] themselves, and further, just as we asserted that the multitude of human beings should be readily surveyable, that the territory too ought to be: being readily surveyable, the territory is readily defended. If the position of the city is to be fixed according to what one would pray for, it is appropriate for it to lie rightly in relation both to the sea and the land. (4) One defining principle is that mentioned—the city should have access to all localities with a view to defensive sallies. The remaining one is that it should be accessible with a view to the conveyance of crops, and further of materials for lumber, and any other product of this sort the territory might happen to possess.

CHAPTER 6

15

20

(1) Concerning access to the sea, there is much dispute as to whether it is beneficial or harmful for well-managed cities. To have persons raised under other laws present as foreigners, it is asserted, is disadvantageous with respect to good management, as is overpopulation; for, [it is asserted,] as a result of their use of the sea for exporting and importing, a multitude of traders comes into existence, and this is contrary[18] to their being finely governed. (2) Now it is not unclear that, if these things do not result, it is better both with a view to safety and with a view to having a ready supply of necessary things for the city and the territory to have a share of the sea. (3) With a view to bearing up under enemies more easily, they should be capable of a ready defense in both elements—both on land and at sea—if they are to preserve themselves. And with a view to injuring the attackers, if this is

not possible in both elements, to do so in one element will still be easier for those who share in both. (4) It is also necessary [for cities] both to import the things that happen not to be available at home and to export what exists in surplus. But the city should be involved in trade for itself, not for others: those who set themselves up as a market for all do so for the sake of revenue; a city that should not share in this sort of aggrandizement should not possess a trading center of this sort. (5) Since we see at present many territories and cities having ports and harbors that are naturally well positioned in relation to the city, so that they neither form part of the same town nor are overly far away, but are dominated by walls and other fortifications of this sort,[19] it is evident that if any good thing results from such access, this will be available to the city, while anything harmful can be guarded against easily by means of laws that stipulate and define which sorts of persons should and which should not have dealings with one another.

(6) Concerning naval power, it is not unclear that it is best to have a certain amount of it. They should be formidable and capable of putting up a defense by sea as well as by land not only for themselves but also for certain of their neighbors. (7) Concerning the amount and size of this force, one must look to the way of life of the city. If it is going to lead a way of life that involves leadership and is political, it must necessarily have this sort of power available as well to match its actions. Cities will not necessarily have the overpopulation that occurs in connection with the seafaring mass: these should be no part of the city. (8) The marine element is free and belongs to the infantry; this is in authority and dominates the crew. And if there is available a multitude of subjects who farm the territory, there will necessarily be an abundance of sailors too. We see this too in certain [cities] at present, as for example the city of the Heracleots, which sends out many warships in spite of being more modest in size than other cities.[20]

Concerning territory, harbors, cities, and the sea, and concerning naval power, then, let our discussion stand in this manner.

CHAPTER 7

(1) Concerning the political multitude, we spoke earlier of what its defining principle ought to be; let us speak now of what quality of persons they should be in their nature. Now one may ascertain

this merely by looking both at those cities among the Greeks that are held in repute and at the entire inhabited [world] as divided among nations. (2) The nations in cold locations, particularly in Europe, are filled with spiritedness, but relatively lacking in thought and art; hence they remain freer, but lack [political] governance and are incapable of ruling their neighbors. Those in Asia, on the other hand, have souls endowed with thought and art, but are lacking in spiritedness; hence they remain ruled and enslaved. (3) But the stock of the Greeks shares in both—just as it holds the middle in terms of location. For it is both spirited and endowed with thought, and hence both remains free and governs itself in the best manner and at the same time is capable of ruling all, should it obtain a single regime. (4) The nations of Greeks also display the same difference in relation to one another. Some have a nature that is one-sided, while others are well blended in relation to both of these capacities. It is evident, therefore, that those who are to be readily guided to virtue by the legislator should be both endowed with thought and spirited in their nature. (5) For as to what some assert should be present in guardians,[21] to be affectionate toward familiar persons but savage toward those who are unknown, it is spiritedness that creates affectionateness; for this is the capacity of soul by which we feel affection. An indication of this is that spiritedness is more aroused against intimates and friends than against unknown persons when it considers itself slighted. (6) Hence Archilochus, when complaining of his friends, appropriately addressed his spiritedness: "Yes, it is among friends you are choked with rage."[22] Both the element of ruling and the element of freedom stem from this capacity for everyone: spiritedness is a thing expert at ruling and indomitable. (7) But it is not right to say that they are harsh toward those who are unknown. One ought not to be of this sort toward anyone, nor are magnanimous persons savage in their nature, except toward those behaving unjustly. And, further, they will feel this rather toward their intimates, as was said earlier, if they consider themselves treated unjustly. (8) Moreover, it is reasonable that this should happen. For when it is among those they suppose should be under obligation to return a benefaction, in addition to the injury they consider themselves deprived of this as well. Thus it has been said: "harsh are the wars of brothers," and "those who have loved extravagantly will hate extravagantly too."[23]

(9) Concerning those engaging in politics, then, how many there should be and of what quality in their nature, and further with respect to the territory, how much and of what quality it

should be, there has been enough discussion. The same precision should not be sought through arguments as through what depends on perception.   20

CHAPTER 8

(1) Just as in other things constituted according to nature those things without which the whole could not exist are not parts of the constitution [of the thing] as a whole, it is clear that those things must not be regarded as parts of a city which are present in cities of necessity, nor of any other partnership out of which [there is constituted] something single in type. (2) For there should be one   25
single thing that is both common and the same for all partners, whether they share equally or unequally—in sustenance, for example, or an amount of territory, or anything else of this sort. (3) When one thing is [something] for the sake of which [other things exist][24] and another thing is for the sake of this, there is nothing common to these things except that one acts and the other re-   30
ceives. I mean, for example, as between any instrument or the craftsmen and the work produced: there is nothing in common between a house and a house builder, but the house builders' art is for the sake of the house. (4) Hence while cities need possessions, possessions are no part of the city. Many animate things are part of possessions. But the city is a partnership of similar persons, for   35
the sake of a life that is the best possible. (5) Since happiness is the best thing, and this is the actualization of virtue and a certain complete practice of it, and since it happens that some persons are able to share in it while others are able to do so only to a small degree or not at all, it is clear that this is the cause of there being several kinds and varieties of city and several sorts of regime. For   40
it is through hunting for this in a different manner and by means   1328b1
of different things that [groups of] individuals create ways of life and regimes that differ.

(6) We must also investigate how many things there are without which a city could not exist; what we speak of as being parts of a city would also be among those things which must necessarily be present.[25] We must therefore have a grasp of the number of tasks [the city requires]; it will be clear from these things. (7) First,   5
then, sustenance must be available; next, arts, for living requires many instruments; third, arms, for those who are partners must

necessarily also have arms among themselves both with a view to ruling for the sake of those who disobey and with a view to outsiders who attempt to do them injustice; further, a ready supply of funds, so that they may have [what suffices] with a view both to their needs among themselves and to military needs; fifth, and first, the superintendence connected with the divine, which they call priestcraft; sixth in number, and the most necessary thing of all, judgment concerning the advantageous things and the just things—those [affecting the citizens] in relation to one another. (8) These, then, are the tasks that virtually every city needs. For the city is not any chance multitude, but one self-sufficient with a view to life, as we assert; and if any of these things happens to be omitted, it is impossible for this partnership to be simply self-sufficient. (9) A city must necessarily be constituted, therefore, on the basis of these tasks. Accordingly, there must be a multitude of farmers who will provide sustenance, artisans, a fighting element, a well-off element, priests, and judges of things necessary[26] and advantageous.

CHAPTER 9

(1) These things having been discussed, it remains to investigate whether all are to participate in all of these things (for it is possible that the same persons should all be farmers, artisans, and those who deliberate and adjudicate), or different persons are to be presupposed for each of the functions mentioned, or some of these are of necessity special and others common. It is not the same in every regime. (2) For, as we said, it is possible both for all to participate in everything and for all not to participate in everything, but some in some things [and not in others]. These things too make regimes different: in democracies all share in everything, while in oligarchies it is the opposite. (3) Since we happen to be investigating concerning the best regime, and this is the one in accordance with which the city would be happy above all, and since it was said earlier[27] that happiness cannot be present apart from virtue, it is evident from these things that in the city that is most finely governed—one possessing men who are just unqualifiedly and not in relation to a presupposition—the citizens should not live a vulgar or a merchant's way of life, for this sort of way of life is ignoble and contrary to virtue. (4) Nor, indeed, should those who are going to be [citizens in such a regime] be

farmers; for there is a need for leisure both with a view to the   1329al
creation of virtue and with a view to political activities. But since
both the military element and the element that deliberates concerning the advantageous things and judges concerning the just
things inhere in the city and are evidently parts of it above all,
must these too be regarded as different, or are both to be assigned   5
to the same persons? (5) This too is evident: in a manner it should
be to the same persons, and in a manner to different persons. Insofar as each of these tasks belongs to a different prime of life, the
one requiring prudence, the other power, it should be to different
persons; but insofar as it is impossible that those who are capable
of using compulsion and preventing [its being used against them]   10
will always put up with being ruled, to this extent they should be
the same persons. For those who have authority over arms also
have authority over whether the regime will last or not. (6) What
remains is for this regime to assign both things to the same persons,[28] though not at the same time, but as it is natural for power
to be found among younger persons and prudence among older
persons, it is advantageous and just to distribute them to both, for   15
this division involves what accords with merit.

(7) Possessions too should [be assigned] in connection with
these persons.[29] For a ready supply must necessarily be available
to the citizens, and these are the citizens. For the vulgar element
does not share in the city, nor any other type that is not a "crafts-   20
man of virtue."[30] This is clear from the presupposition: happiness
must necessarily be present together with virtue, and one should
call a city happy by looking not at a certain part of it, but rather at
all the citizens. (8) It is also evident that possessions must belong
to these persons if the farmers must necessarily be slaves or bar-   25
barian subjects.[31]

Of the things enumerated there remains the stock of priests. (9)
The arrangement of these too is evident. No farmer or vulgar person is to be appointed priest, for it is proper for the gods to be
honored by citizens. Since the political element is divided into   30
two parts—these being the armed element and the deliberative
element—and since it is proper that those worn out with age
should both render worship to the gods and find rest for themselves, it is to these that priesthoods are to be assigned.

(10) We have spoken of the things without which a city cannot be
constituted and of how many parts of a city there are. Farmers,   35
artisans, and the entire laboring element must necessarily be present in cities; the armed element and the deliberative element are
parts of the city; and each of these is separate from the others,
some permanently, the others by turns.

CHAPTER 10

40

1329b1

(1) That the city should be divided among separate types [of persons], and that the fighting and farming elements should be different, seems not to be something that is familiar to those philosophizing about the regime only at present or in recent times. Things stand in this manner in Egypt even today, and also in Crete, Sesostris having legislated in this fashion for Egypt, so it is asserted,[32] and Minos for Crete. (2) The arrangement of common messes also seems to be ancient, those at Crete having arisen in connection with the kingship of Minos, while those in Italy are much older than these. (3) For the chroniclers who live there assert that a certain Italus became king of Oenotria, and that on account of him they changed their name and were called Italians instead of Oenotrians, and the name of Italy was acquired by that promontory of Europe which is within the gulfs of Scylletium and Lametius, these being a half-day's journey apart.[33] (4) Now they say that this Italus made farmers of the nomadic Oenotrians and enacted laws for them, in particular instituting—for the first time— common messes. Hence even now some of those who are descended from him still use common messes and some of the laws. (5) In the direction of Tyrrhenia there lived the Opicans, who were then (and are at present) called by the surname Ausonians; and in the direction of Iapygia and the Ionian Gulf, in the so-called Siritis, lived the Chonians—the Chonians too being Oenotrians by stock.[34] (6) It was there, then, that the arrangement of common messes first arose, while the separation of the political multitude according to type originated in Egypt (for the kingship of Sesostris long precedes that of Minos). (7) One should therefore consider that practically everything has been discovered on many occasions—or rather an infinity of occasions—in the course of time. For it is likely that the necessary [discoveries] are taught by need, while those relating to elegance and superfluity may be reasonably expected to begin increasing once these are already present; and one should suppose that the things connected with regimes stand in the same manner. (8) That all [such] things are ancient is indicated by those connected with Egypt. For [the Egyptians] are held to be the most ancient [of peoples], yet they have obtained laws and a political arrangement. Hence one should use what has been adequately discovered[35] while attempting to seek out what has been passed over.[36]

5

10

15

20

25

30

35

(9) That the territory should belong to those who possess [heavy] arms and those who share in the regime, then, was said earlier,

and why the farmers should be different from these and how much
and of what sort the territory ought to be [was also discussed]. We
must now speak first about the distribution [of land] and, with re-   40
gard to the farmers, who and of what sort they ought to be, since
we assert both that possessions should not be common, as some
have said, but rather should become common in use after the fash-   1330a1
ion of friends, and that none of the citizens should be in want of
sustenance.[37] (10) Regarding common messes, all hold that it is
useful for them to be present in well-instituted cities; the reason
for our holding the same opinion will be spoken of later.[38] All the
citizens should participate in these, but it is not easy for the poor   5
to contribute the required amount from their private [funds] and
administer the rest of their household. Further, expenditures relating to the gods should be common to the entire city.

(11) It is necessary, therefore, to divide the territory into two
parts, one being common and the other for private individuals,   10
and to divide each of these in two again. One part of the common
territory should be for public service relating to the gods, the
other for the expense of the common messes. Of the territory that
belongs to private individuals, one part should be toward the fron-
tiers, the other toward the city, so that, with two allotments as-   15
signed to each individual, all share in both locations. This provides equality and justice, as well as greater concord with a view
to wars with their neighbors. (12) For wherever things do not
stand in this manner, some make light of an enmity toward those
on the border, while others are concerned with it overly much and
contrary to what is noble. Hence among some [peoples] there is a   20
law that those who are neighbors of a bordering [people] may not
share jointly in deliberation concerning wars against them, the assumption being that they are not capable of deliberating finely on
account of their private [interest].

(13) It is necessary to divide the territory in this manner, then,
for the reasons just spoken of. As for the farmers, it is necessary   25
above all—if one should [speak] on the basis of what one would
pray for—that they be slaves who are neither all of the same stock
nor of spirited ones, as in that way they would be useful with a
view to the work and safe as regards engaging in subversion; or,
second, they should be barbarian subjects resembling in their nature those just mentioned. (14) Of these, the ones in private hands
should belong privately to those possessing the properties, while   30
those on the common land should be common. In what manner
slaves should be treated, and why it is better to hold out freedom
as a reward for all slaves, we will speak of later.[39]

213

CHAPTER 11

(1) That the city should have access to the mainland and the sea as well as to the territory as a whole, so far as circumstances allow, was said earlier.[40] As for its position relative to itself, one should pray to obtain this looking to four things.[41] The first, as being something necessary, is health. (2) Those cities are healthier which slope toward the east and toward the winds that blow from the direction of the rising sun; second are those sloping in the direction the north wind blows, as these have better winters. Of the remaining things, [one should look to see that the city] is in a fine condition with a view to political and military activities. (3) With a view to military activities, it ought to be ready of exit for [the citizens] themselves but difficult for their adversaries to approach and besiege. It should have available above all a multitude of pools and springs of its own; but failing this, a way has been discovered to construct great and ample receptacles for rain water, so that they will never run short when they are cut off from their territory by war. (4) Since one should take thought for the health of the inhabitants, this consists in the location being finely situated on [ground of] this sort and toward [an exposure of] this sort, and second, in using healthy sorts of water, and making this more than an incidental concern; for the things we use most of and most often for the body are what contribute most to health, and the capacity of waters and wind has such a nature. (5) Hence in all sensible cities, if all the springs are not similar or those of such a [healthy] sort are not ample, a distinction should be made between those for sustenance and those for other needs.

With regard to fortified places, what is advantageous is not the same for all regimes. For example, a fortified height[42] is characteristic of oligarchy and monarchy; levelness is characteristic of democracy; neither of these is characteristic of aristocracy, but rather a number of strong places. (6) The disposition of private dwellings is considered more pleasant and more useful for other activities if it involves straight rows in the newer manner of Hippodamus,[43] but for safety in war the opposite manner that prevailed in ancient times; for this made it difficult of exit for foreign [troops garrisoned in the city] and difficult for attackers to find their way around. (7) Hence it should share in both of these. If one institutes [the sort of arrangement] that among farmers some call "clumps" of vines, it is possible to avoid having the city as a whole disposed in straight rows, but for certain parts and places to be; in this way it will be in a fine condition with a view to safety as well as ordered beauty.[44]

214

(8) As regards walls, those who deny that cities laying claim to virtue should have them have overly old-fashioned conceptions—especially when they see the cities that have pretensions of that sort refuted by fact.[45] (9) Possibly it is not a noble thing to seek preservation from [attackers who are] similar and not much greater in numbers by means of the fortification of walls. But since it happens—and is [always] possible—that the preeminence of the attackers is greater than virtue that is [only] human and resident in a few [who make up the citizen body], the safest fortification of walls must be supposed to be what most accords with military expertise, if [the city] is to be preserved and not suffer any ills or be arrogantly treated, particularly given the inventions of the present connected with missiles and machines for improved proficiency in sieges.[46] (10) To claim that cities do not merit having walls around them is like seeking to have the territory ready of access and mountainous places removed—it is like not having walls for private houses on the grounds that the inhabitants will become unmanly. (11) This too should not be overlooked, that it is open to those who have walls around the city to treat their cities in either fashion, as having walls and as not having them, while this is not open to those who do not possess them. If things stand in this manner, not only must there be walls around a city, but they should be taken care of in such a way that they should be in an appropriate condition both with a view to order and beauty and with a view to military requirements, in particular those that have arisen only recently. (12) For just as it is the modes of aggrandizement that are of concern for the attackers, so in the case of the defenders some things have been discovered already, while others should be sought out and investigated[47] by them. For [men] will not even attempt an attack in the first place against those who are well prepared.

CHAPTER 12

(1) Since the multitude of the citizens should be distributed in common messes, and since the walls should have guardhouses and towers at intervals in convenient places, these things clearly suggest setting up some of the common messes in these guardhouses. (2) One might order these things, then, in this manner. As for the buildings assigned to divine matters and the common messes for the most authoritative official boards, it is fitting for them to be located together in a proper place, at least in the case of

35

40

1331a1

5

10

15

20

25

those temples which the law or some prophecy of the Delphic oracle does not require to be separate. (3) This would be the sort of place whose position is adequate for the manifestation of virtue[48] and at the same time better fortified in relation to the neighboring parts of the city. Below this place it is proper to institute a market of the sort they call by that term in Thessaly—the one they call "free"; (4) this is one that is kept clear of wares and where no vulgar person or farmer or anyone else of this sort can enter unless summoned by the officials. The place would have added appeal if there was an arrangement there for the exercises of the older [men]. (5) For it is proper to distinguish this order as well on the basis of age, and to have some of the officials spend time with the younger [men], and the older with the officials; for being before the eyes of officials most of all engenders respect and the fear that belongs to free persons. (6) The market for wares should be different from this and have a separate location, one that is convenient for bringing together both the things that are sent in from the sea and all the things from the country.

Since the multitude of the city is divided into priests, officials, [and soldiers, and since common messes have been provided on sacred ground for officials,] it is proper that there should be an arrangement to have common messes for the priests too in the vicinity of the sacred buildings.[49] (7) Those of the official boards that superintend agreements, suits of indictment, summonses, and other administration of this sort, and further, management of the market and so-called town management, should be stationed near the market or some accessible meeting place, this being one that is located near the necessary market. For the upper market we regard as the one for being at leisure, and this one as being with a view to necessary activities. (8) The arrangement just spoken of ought to be imitated in matters pertaining to the country. For there too with a view to guarding there must necessarily be guardhouses and common messes for those officials some call "foresters" and others "field managers," and further, temples must be distributed throughout the country, some for gods and others for heroes.

(9) But it is pointless to spend time at present giving a detailed account and speaking of such things. It is not difficult to understand such things, but more so to do them: speaking about them is a work of prayer, having them come about, a work of chance. Hence anything further concerning such things may be dismissed at present.

CHAPTER 13

(1) We must [now] speak of the regime itself, and of which and what sort of things the city that is going to be blessed and finely governed should be constituted from. (2) There are two things that [living] well consists in for all: one of these is in correct positing of the aim and end of actions; the other, discovering the actions that bear on the end. These things can be consonant with one another or dissonant, for sometimes the aim is finely posited but in acting they miss achieving it, and sometimes they achieve everything with a view to the end, but the end they posited was bad. And sometimes they miss both. In connection with medicine, for example, [doctors] sometimes neither judge rightly what the quality of a healthy body should be nor achieve what is productive in relation to the object they set for themselves. But in all arts and sciences both of these should be kept in hand, the end and the actions directed to the end.

(3) Now that everyone strives for living well and for happiness is evident. It is open to some to achieve these things, but to others not, on account of some sort of fortune or nature; for living nobly requires a certain equipment too—less of it for those in a better state, more for those in a worse one. (4) Some, on the other hand, seek happiness incorrectly from the outset although it is open to them to achieve it. Since our object is to see the best regime, and this is one in accordance with which a city would be best governed, and it would be best governed in accordance with one that would make it possible for the city to be happy most of all, it is clear that one should not overlook what happiness is.

(5) We assert—and we have defined it thus in the [discourses on] ethics, if there is anything of benefit in those discourses[50]— that happiness is the actualization and complete practice of virtue, and this not on the basis of a presupposition but unqualifiedly. (6) By "not on the basis of a presupposition" I mean necessary things, by "unqualifiedly," nobly. In the case of just actions, for example, just retributions and punishments derive from virtue, but they are necessary, and have the element of nobility only in a necessary way (for it would be more choiceworthy if no man or city required anything of the sort); but actions directed to honors and to what makes one well off are very noble in an unqualified sense. (7) For the one is the choice[51] of an evil, but actions of this [latter] sort are the opposite; they are providers and generators of good things. An excellent man would deal in noble fashion with poverty, disease, and other sorts of bad fortune, but blessedness is

25

30

35

40

1332a1

5

10

15

20   in their opposites. Indeed, it was defined thus in the ethical discourses[52]—that the excellent person is one of a sort for whom on
account of his virtue the things that are good unqualifiedly are
good; (8) and it is clear that his uses of these [good things] must
necessarily also be excellent and noble in an unqualified sense.
25   Hence human beings consider the causes of happiness to be those
good things that are external—as if the lyre rather than the art
were to be held the cause of brilliant and beautiful lyre playing.
Necessarily, therefore, some of the things mentioned must be
present, while others must be supplied by the legislator. (9) Hence
30   we pray for the city to be constituted on the basis of what one
would pray for[53] in those matters over which fortune has authority
(we regard it as having authority [over the external things we regard as being desirable for the best city to have present[54]]); but the
city's being excellent is no longer the work of fortune, but of
knowledge and intentional choice. But a city is excellent, at any
rate, by its citizens'—those sharing in the regime—being excel-
35   lent; and in our case all the citizens share in the regime. (10) This,
then, must be investigated—how a man becomes excellent. Now
even if it is possible for all to be excellent but not each of the
citizens individually, the latter is more choiceworthy; for all [be-
ing excellent] follows from [all] individually [being excellent].
40   Now [men] become good and excellent through three things.
(11) These three are nature, habit, and reason. For one must first
develop naturally as a human being and not some one of the other
animals, and so also be of a certain quality in body and soul. But
there is no benefit in certain [qualities] developing naturally, since
1332b1   habits make them alter: certain [qualities] are through their nature
ambiguous, through habits [tending] in the direction of worse or
better. (12) The other animals live by nature above all, but in some
slight respects by habit as well, while man lives also by reason
5   (for he alone has reason); so these things should be consonant
with the other. For [men] act in many ways contrary to their habituation and their nature through reason, if they are persuaded that
some other condition is better. (13) Now as to the sort of nature
those should have who are going to be readily taken in hand by
the legislator, we discussed this earlier.[55] What remains at this
point is the work of education. For [men] learn some things by
10   being habituated, others by listening.

CHAPTER 14

(1) Since every political partnership is constituted of rulers and ruled, this must then be investigated—if the rulers and the ruled should be different or the same throughout life; for it is clear that education too will have to follow in accordance with this distinction. (2) Now if the ones were as different from the others as we believe gods and heroes differ from human beings—much exceeding them in the first place in body, and then in soul, so that the preeminence of the rulers is indisputable and evident to the ruled—it is clear that it would always be better for the same persons to rule and the same to be ruled once and for all. (3) But since this is not easy to assume, there being none so different from the ruled as Scylax says the kings in India are,[56] it is evident that for many reasons it is necessary for all in similar fashion to participate in ruling and being ruled in turn. For equality is the same thing [as justice[57]] for persons who are similar, and it is difficult for a regime to last if its constitution is contrary to justice. (4) For the ruled [citizens] will have with them all those [serfs] in the countryside who want to subvert it, and it is impossible that those in the governing body will be numerous enough to be superior to all of these. Nevertheless, that the rulers should differ from the ruled is indisputable. How this will be the case and how they will share [in ruling and being ruled], then, should be investigated by the legislator.

(5) This was spoken of earlier. Nature has provided the distinction by making that which is the same by type have a younger and an older element, of which it is proper for the former to be ruled and the latter to rule. No one chafes at being ruled on the basis of age or considers himself superior, particularly when he is going to recover his contribution[58] when he attains the age to come. (6) In one sense, therefore, it must be asserted that the same persons rule and are ruled, but in another sense different persons. So education too must necessarily be the same in a sense, and in another sense different. For, so it is asserted, one who is going to rule finely should first have been ruled.[59] Now rule, as was said in our first discourses,[60] is on the one hand for the sake of the ruler, and on the other for the sake of the ruled. Of these [sorts of rule] we assert the former to be characteristic of a master, and the latter to belong to free persons.[61] (7) Now certain commands differ not by the works [involved] but by the [end] for the sake of which [they are carried out]. Hence it is noble for the free among the young to

219

serve in many of the tasks that are held to be characteristic of servants; for, with a view to what is noble and what not noble, actions do not differ so much in themselves as in their end and that
10 for the sake of which [they are performed].

(8) Since we assert that the virtue of citizen and ruler is the same as that of the good man,[62] and the same person must be ruled first and ruler later, the legislator would have to make it his affair to determine how men can become good and through what pur-
15 suits, and what the end of the best life is.

(9) The soul is divided into two parts, of which the one has reason itself, while the other does not have it in itself, but is capable of obeying reason. To these belong, we assert, the virtues in accordance with which a man is spoken of as in some sense good.[63] As to which of these the end is more to be found in, what must be
20 said is not unclear to those who distinguish in the way we assert should be done. (10) The worse is always for the sake of the better—this is evident in a similar way both in what accords with art and in what accords with nature; and the element having reason is better. This is divided in two in the manner we are accustomed to distinguish: there is reason of the active sort on the one hand and
25 reason of the studying sort on the other.[64] (11) It is clear, therefore, that this part [of the soul] must also be divided in the same fashion. And we shall say that actions stand in a comparable relationship: those belonging to that [part] which is better by nature are more choiceworthy for those who are capable of achieving either all of them or [those belonging to] the two [lower parts]. For what is most choiceworthy for each individual is the highest it is pos-
30 sible for him to achieve.

(12) Life as a whole is divided, too, into occupation and leisure and war and peace, and of matters involving action some are directed toward necessary and useful things, others toward noble things. (13) Concerning these things there must of necessity be the same choice as in the case of the parts of the soul and their ac-
35 tions: war must be for the sake of peace, occupation for the sake of leisure, necessary and useful things for the sake of noble things. The political [ruler] must legislate, therefore, looking to all [these] things in the case both of the parts of the soul and of their actions, but particularly to the things that are better and [have more the
40 character of] ends. (14) And [he must do so] in the same manner in connection with the ways of life and the divisions[65] among activities; for one should be capable of being occupied and going to
1333b1 war, but should rather remain at peace and be at leisure, and one should act [to achieve] necessary and useful things, but noble things more so. So it is with a view to these aims that they must be

educated when still children as well as during the other ages that
require education.

(15) Those of the Greeks who are at present held to be the best
governed and the legislators who established these regimes evidently did not organize the things pertaining to the regime with a
view to the best end, or the laws and education with a view to all
the virtues, but inclined in crude fashion toward those which are
held to be useful and of a more aggrandizing sort. (16) Certain
persons writing later in a spirit similar to this have expressed the
same opinion: in praising the regime of the Lacedaemonians they
admire the aim of the legislator, because he legislated everything
with a view to domination and war—[views] which are readily
refutable on the basis of reason, and have now been refuted by the
facts. (17) For just as most human beings envy mastery over many
persons because it provides much equipment in the things of fortune, so Thibron and each of the others who write about their regime[66] evidently admire the Spartans' legislator because they
ruled over many persons as a result of having exercised themselves with a view to dangers. (18) And yet since now at least ruling [an empire] is no longer available to the Spartans, it clearly
follows that they are not happy, and that their legislator was not a
good one. But[67] this is ridiculous—that they should have lost [the
chance for] living nobly even while abiding by his laws, and in the
absence of any impediment to putting the laws into practice. (19)
Nor do they have a correct conception concerning the sort of rule
that the legislator should be seen to honor: rule over free persons
is nobler and accompanied to a greater extent by virtue than ruling in the spirit of a master. Further, it is not on this account that
one should consider the city happy and praise the legislator, that
he trained it to dominate for the purpose of ruling those nearby;
these things involve great harm. (20) For it is clear that any citizen who is capable of doing so must attempt to pursue the ca-
pability to rule his own city—the very thing the Spartans accuse
their king Pausanias of, even though he held so great a prerogative.[68] There is, indeed, nothing in such arguments and laws that
is either political, beneficial, or true. (20) The same things are
best [for men] both privately and in common, and the legislator
should implant these in the souls of human beings. Training in
matters related to war should be practiced not for the sake of re-
ducing to slavery those who do not merit it, but in the first place in
order that they themselves will not become slaves to others; next,
so that they may seek leadership for the sake of benefiting the
ruled, but not for the sake of mastery over everyone; and third, to
be master over those who merit being slaves. (22) That the legis-

221

lator should give serious attention instead to arranging that legislation, and particularly that connected with matters related to
5 war, is for the sake of being at leisure and of peace, is testified to
by events as well as arguments. Most cities of this sort preserve
themselves when at war, but once having acquired [imperial] rule
they come to ruin; they lose their edge, like iron, when they remain at peace. The reason is that the legislator has not educated
10 them to be capable of being at leisure.

CHAPTER 15

(1) Since the end is evidently the same for human beings both in
common and privately, and there must necessarily be the same defining principle for the best man and the best regime, it is evident
that the virtues directed to leisure should be present; for, as has
15 been said repeatedly, peace is the end of war, and leisure of occupation. (2) The virtues useful with a view to leisure and pastime
are both those of which the work is in leisure and those of which it
is in occupation. For many of the necessary things should be
present for it to be open to them to be at leisure. Hence it is appropriate that the city have moderation, courage, and endurance, for
as the proverb has it, "there is no leisure for slaves," and those
20 who are incapable of facing danger in a courageous spirit are
slaves of whomever comes along to attack them. (3) Now courage
and endurance are required with a view to occupation; philosophy, with a view to leisure; moderation and [the virtue of] justice,
at both times, and particularly when they remain at peace and are
25 at leisure. For war compels [men] to be just and behave with moderation, while the enjoyment of good fortune and being at leisure
in peacetime tend to make them arrogant. (4) There is, then, a
need for much [of the virtue of] justice and much moderation on
the part of those who are held to act in the best way and who have
30 all the gratifications that are regarded as blessings, like those—if
there are such—whom the poets assert are "in the islands of the
blessed." [69] For these will be most particularly in need of philosophy and moderation and [the virtue of] justice to the extent that
they are at leisure in the midst of an abundance of good things of
this sort.
35 (5) Why a city that is going to exist happily and be excellent
should share in these virtues, then, is evident. For if it is disgrace-

ful not to be capable of using good things, it is still more so to be incapable of using them in leisure, but to be seen to be good [men] while occupied and at war but servile when remaining at peace and being at leisure. (6) Hence one should not train in virtue as the city of the Lacedaemonians does. For it is not in this way that they differ from others, by not considering the greatest of good things to be the same things others do, but by considering that these things are got through some sort of virtue. But since [they consider] these good things and the gratification deriving from them to be greater than that deriving from the virtues, [the sort of virtue in which they are trained is only that useful and necessary for the acquisition of good things. That the sort of virtue is rather to be cultivated that governs the use of these good things, that this is preeminently the sort of virtue that is cultivated in leisure, and that it is to be cultivated[70]] on its own account, is evident from these things. How and through what things it will exist is what must be studied now.

(7) We made a distinction earlier [to the effect] that there is a need for nature, habit, and reason. Of these things, what quality [the citizens] ought to be in their nature was discussed earlier; what remains is to study whether they are to be educated first by means of reason or by means of habits. These should be consonant with one another, and the consonance should be the best; for it is possible for one or both to have missed the best presupposition in respect of reason and to have been similarly guided by habits. (8) This, then, is evident at any rate in the first instance, [with men] just as among other things—that birth derives from a beginning point, and the end from some beginning point that is an end of something else;[71] but reason and intellect are the end of our nature, so that it is with a view to these that birth and the concern with habits should be handled. (9) Next, just as soul and body are two things, so also do we see two parts of the soul, the irrational and that having reason, and the dispositions belonging to these are two in number, one of which is appetite and the other intellect; and just as the body is prior in birth to the soul, so is the irrational part to that having reason. (10) This too is evident, for spiritedness and will, and furthermore desire, are present in children immediately on their being born, while reasoning and intellect develop naturally in them as they go along. Hence in the first instance the superintendence of the body must necessarily precede that of the soul; next comes that of appetite; but that of appetite is for the sake of intellect, and that of the body for the sake of the soul.

40

1334b1

5

10

15

20

25

CHAPTER 16

(1) If, therefore, the legislator should see to it from the beginning
that the bodies of those being reared are to become the best possible, care must be taken in the first place in connection with the
union [of men and women, to determine] when and with what
quality of persons marital relations with one another ought to be
brought about. (2) One should legislate with respect to this partnership with a view to [the partners] themselves and the length of
time of their lives [together], in order that they arrive together in
terms of their ages at the same juncture and their capacities not be
dissonant, the male still being capable of generation and the female not capable, or the female capable and the male not; for
these things create conflicts and differences among them. Next,
one should legislate with a view to the succession of the offspring,
for the offspring should neither fall too short of their fathers in
terms of age—since older fathers get no benefit from the gratitude
of offspring, nor their offspring from the assistance rendered by
fathers—nor be too close; (4) this involves many difficulties: less
respect is present in those of this sort as being contemporaries [of
their fathers], and closeness gives rise to accusations in connection with management of the household. Further, to return to
where we began digressing to this point, one should legislate so
that the bodies of offspring in the process of generation become
available [in a way that answers] to the will of the legislator.

Now virtually all of these things result from a single sort of superintendence. (5) Since the age of seventy at the outside defines
in most cases the end of generation for men, and the age of fifty
for women, the beginning of their union in terms of their ages
should be such as to arrive at its conclusion at these times. (6) The
mating of young persons is a poor thing with a view to procreation: among all animals the issue of the young is incomplete,
likely to bear females, and small of figure, so this same thing
must necessarily result in the case of human beings as well. A
proof of it is that in those cities where the union of young men and
women is the local fashion, [the citizens] are incomplete and
small of body. (7) Further, young women labor more in childbirth,
and more of them die—hence some assert it was for such a reason
that the oracular response was given to the Troezenians, that it
was as a result of always marrying off younger women that so
many [children] were dying, not anything related to the harvest-
ing of the crops.[72] (8) Further, it is advantageous with a view to
moderation for women to be given in marriage when they are

224

older, for they are held to be more licentious if they have practiced intercourse when young. Also, the bodies of males are held to be injured with respect to growth if they have intercourse while the seed is still growing; for there is a definite length of time for this as well, after which it is no longer plentiful. (9) Hence it is fitting for women to unite in marriage around the age of eighteen, and for men at thirty-seven or a little [before].[73] At such an age, union will occur when their bodies are in their prime, and will arrive at its conclusion conveniently for both of them with respect to the cessation of procreation. (10) Further, the succession of the off-spring—if birth occurs shortly after marriage, as can reasonably be expected—will be for them at the beginning of their prime, while for [the fathers] it will be when their age has already run its course toward the seventieth year. When a union should take place, then, has been spoken of. As regards time with respect to the season, the practice of most people at present is a fine one, setting apart winter as the time to begin cohabitation. (11) [Married persons] themselves should study what is said by doctors and ex-perts in natural [science] in relation to procreation. Doctors give an adequate account of the occasions [best suited to procreation with respect to the condition] of bodies, and experts in natural [science] of winds, praising northerly rather than southerly ones.

(12) As regards the quality of body that would be of most bene-fit to offspring in the process of generation, we must stop to speak of it more at length in the [discourses] concerning management of children; at present it is enough to speak of it in outline.[74] The [bodily] disposition of athletes is not useful either with a view to the good condition required of the citizen or with a view to health and procreation, and neither is one that is overly valetudinarian and ill-suited for exertion, but a middling sort between these. (13) One should have a disposition formed by exertion, but not by vio-lent exertion, and not with a view to one thing only, like the ath-letes' disposition, but with a view to the actions belonging to lib-eral persons. And these things should be present in similar fashion in men and women. (14) Even pregnant women ought to take care of their bodies, not remaining idle or taking meager sustenance. This is easy for the legislator to do by mandating that they make a trip every day to worship the goddesses who have been granted the prerogative connected with birth.[75] (The mind, however, un-like their bodies, may fittingly spend time in more idle fashion.) For offspring in the process of generation evidently draw re-sources from the one bearing them, just as plants do from the earth.

(15) Concerning exposure and rearing of offspring when they are born, let there be a law that no deformed [child] should be

25

30

35

40

1335b1

5

10

15

20

raised, but that none should be exposed after they are born on account of number of offspring, where the arrangement of customs forbids [procreation beyond a certain number]. A number should indeed be defined for procreation,[76] but in cases of births in consequence of intercourse contrary to these, abortion should be induced before perception and life arises (what is holy and what is not will be defined by reference to perception and life).

(16) Since the beginning point of the age when a man and a woman ought to begin their union has been defined, let us define also for how much time it is fitting for them to do public service with respect to procreation. The issue of older persons, like that of younger persons, is born incomplete both in body and mind, while that of persons in old age is weak; hence [the time may be defined] on the basis of the mind's prime. (17) In most persons this comes—as some of those poets have said who measure age in periods of seven years[77]—around the time of the fiftieth year. So within four or five years after this age they should be released from generation for public purposes, and for the time remaining it should be evident that they are having relations for the sake of health or some other reason of this sort. (18) Concerning relations with another man or another woman, let it be [considered] simply not a fine thing to indulge in it at all in any way when one is or is referred to as spouse; if someone should be found doing some such thing during the period of procreation, let the person be punished with a loss of honor appropriate to the error.

CHAPTER 17

(1) Once offspring are born, [one should] suppose that it makes a great difference with a view to the power of the body what sort of sustenance they get. It is evident to those investigating the other animals as well as those nations that are concerned to cultivate a military disposition that sustenance of a sort rich in milk is most particularly suited to their bodies—and one that is relatively free of wine, on account of the diseases [it produces]. (2) Further, it is advantageous to have them engage in whatever movements are possible for those of that age. With a view to preventing distortion of their limbs due to their softness, however, some nations even now use certain instruments devised to make the bodies of such persons straight. It is also advantageous to habituate them to the cold immediately from the time they are small children: this is

226

most useful with a view both to health and to military activities. (3) Hence among many barbarians it is customary either to plunge the newly born into a cold river or to give them light clothing, as for example among the Celts. In all those matters where habituation is possible, it is better to habituate immediately from the beginning, not to habituate gradually. And the disposition of children is naturally apt on account of its warmth for training to bear cold.

(4) In connection with the first age, then, it is advantageous to have a superintendence of this sort or nearly so. During the age following up to five years, which one should not apply to any sort of learning or to necessary exertions, so that their growth is not impeded, they should engage in enough movement that they avoid bodily idleness. This should be provided them through play, as well as through other activities. (5) The sorts of play, too, should neither be illiberal nor involve too much exertion or laxness. Concerning the quality of the stories and tales those of this age should hear, let this be a matter of concern to the officials who are called managers of children. For all such things should prepare the road for their later pursuits. Hence most sorts of play should be imitations of the things they give serious attention to later. (6) Those who in the *Laws* forbid the screaming and crying of children[78] are not correct in this prohibition: these things are advantageous with a view to growth; in a certain manner they provide exercise for bodies, for holding the breath gives strength to those exerting themselves, and it is this very thing that results from children screaming.

(7) The managers of children must investigate their pastime, particularly so as to ensure that as little of it as possible will be with slaves. For this age, up to seven years, must necessarily have its rearing at home; it is therefore reasonable to expect that even at such an age they will acquire an element of illiberality from what they hear and see [on account of the proximity of slaves]. (8) Generally, then, the legislator should banish foul speech from the city more than anything else (for by speaking readily about some foul matter one comes closer to doing it), and particularly from among the young, so that they neither say nor hear anything of this sort. (9) One who is found speaking or doing something that is forbidden, if he is a free person who cannot yet claim to merit reclining at table, should be punished with dishonor and with beating, and if an older person of this age, with dishonor of an illiberal sort, because of the slavishness [he has manifested]. Since we are banishing speaking about anything of this sort, it is evident that looking at unseemly paintings or stories also [must be

15

20

25

30

35

40

1336b1

5

10

banished]. (10) Let it be a concern of the officials, then, that no
statue or painting be an imitation of such actions, except in the
case of [the temples of] certain gods—those to whom the law also
assigns scurrilous mockery.[79] In addition to these things, the law
permits those still of a suitable age[80] to do homage to the gods on
behalf of themselves, their offspring, and their women. (11) And
there must be legislation that younger persons not be spectators
either of lampoons[81] or of comedy, until they reach the age at
which they will be able to participate in reclining at table and
drinking,[82] and education will make them all immune to the harm
that arises from such things.

(12) At present we have given an account of these things in
passing. Later we must stop to discuss it more at length, raising
the question first of all whether one should or should not [exclude
the young from such performances], and how it should be done;
on this occasion we have made mention of it as far as is necessary.[83] (13) For the remark of the tragic actor Theodorus was not a
bad one—that he never allowed anyone to come out on stage before him, not even a poor actor, because the spectators make their
own what they hear first.[84] This same thing results in regard both
to relations with human beings and to those with objects; we are
fonder of the first things [we encounter]. (14) Hence everything
mean should be made foreign to the young, particularly things of
this sort that involve either depravity or malice. Once they have
passed through the first five years, during the two up to seven they
should become onlookers of the sorts of learning that they themselves will be required to learn.

(15) There are two ages with a view to which it is necessary to
distinguish education, that following the age from seven up to
puberty, and again that following the age from puberty up to
twenty-one. Those who distinguish ages by periods of seven years
argue for the most part not badly,[85] but one should follow the distinction of nature, for all art and education wish to supply the element that is lacking in nature. (16) First, then, we must investigate whether some arrangement is to be created in connection
with children; next, whether it is advantageous for the superintendence of them to be in common or on a private basis, which is
what happens even now in most cities; and third, what quality this
should have.

BOOK 8

CHAPTER 1

(1) That the legislator must, therefore, make the education of the young his object above all would be disputed by no one. Where this does not happen in cities it hurts the regimes. (2) One should educate with a view to each sort, for the character that is proper to each sort of regime both customarily safeguards the regime and establishes it at the beginning—the democratic character a democracy, for example, or the oligarchic an oligarchy; and the best character is always a cause of a better regime. Further, in relation to all capacities and arts there are things with respect to which a preparatory education and habituation is required with a view to the tasks of each, so that is clear that this is so also with a view to the actions of virtue.

(3) Since there is a single end for the city as a whole, it is evident that education must necessarily be one and the same for all, and that the superintendence of it should be common and not on a private basis—the mode in which each individual at present superintends his own offspring privately and teaches them whatever private sort of learning he holds best. For common things the training too should be made common. (4) At the same time, one ought not even consider that a citizen belongs to himself, but rather that all belong to the city; for each individual is a part of the city. But the superintendence of each part naturally looks to the superintendence of the whole. One might well praise the Lacedaemonians for this: they most all pay serious attention to their children, and do so in common.

CHAPTER 2

(1) That there must be legislation concerning education, then, and that this must be made common, is evident. But what education is, and how one ought to educate, should not be neglected. For at present there is a dispute concerning its tasks. Not everyone conceives that the young should learn the same things either with a

view to virtue or with a view to the best way of life, nor is it evident whether it is more appropriate that it be with a view to the mind or with a view to the character of the soul. (2) Investigation on the basis of the education that is current yields confusion, and it is not at all clear whether one should have training in things useful for life, things contributing to virtue, or extraordinary things; for all of these have obtained some judges [willing to decide in their favor]. Concerning the things relating to virtue, nothing is agreed. Indeed, to start with, not everyone honors the same virtue, so it is reasonable to expect them to differ as well in regard to the training in it.

(3) Now that those of the useful things that are necessary should be taught is not unclear, and also that not all should be taught: free tasks being distinguished from unfree ones, it is evident that they should share in those of the useful things that will not make the one sharing in them vulgar. (4) One should consider a vulgar task, art, or sort of learning to be any that renders the body, the soul, or the mind of free persons useless with a view to the practices and actions of virtue. (5) Hence we call vulgar both the sorts of arts that bring the body into a worse state and wage-earning sorts of work, for they make the mind a thing abject and lacking in leisure. But it is also the case that, while it is not unfree to share in some of the liberal sciences up to a certain point, to persevere overly much in them with a view to proficiency is liable to involve the sorts of injury just mentioned. (6) It makes a difference, too, for the sake of what one does or learns something. What is for one's own sake or for the sake of friends or on account of virtue is not unfree, while the person who does the same thing on account of others would often be held to do something characteristic of the laborer or the slave.

CHAPTER 3

(1) Now the accepted sorts of learning are, as was said earlier, ambiguous. Essentially, there are four things they customarily educate in: letters, gymnastics, music, and fourth, some in expertise in drawing—expertise in letters and drawing as being useful for life and having many uses, gymnastic as contributing to courage; but about music one might already raise a question. (2) At present most people share in it for the sake of pleasure; but those who arranged to have it in education at the beginning did so because

nature itself seeks, as has been said repeatedly, not only to be oc- 30
cupied in correct fashion but also to be capable of being at leisure
in noble fashion. For this is the beginning point of everything—if
we may speak of this once again.[1] (3) If both are required, but
being at leisure is more choiceworthy than occupation and more
an end, what must be sought is the activity they should have in 35
leisure. Surely it is not play: play would then necessarily be the
end of life for us. (4) But if this is impossible, and the sorts of
play are rather to be practiced in occupation (for a person who
exerts himself requires rest, and play is for the sake of rest, while
occupation is accompanied by exertion and tension), on this account those introducing play should observe the occasions for its 40
use, the assumption being that they are administering it as a remedy. For this sort of motion of the soul is a relaxation and rest
effected by pleasure. Being at leisure, on the other hand, is held 1338a1
itself to involve pleasure, happiness, and living blessedly. (5) This
is not available to those who are occupied, but rather to those at
leisure, for the person who is occupied is occupied for the sake of
some end that is assumed not to be available, while happiness is
an end, and something all suppose to be accompanied not by pain 5
but by pleasure. This pleasure, however, is not regarded as the
same by all, but by each individual in accordance with themselves
and their own disposition; but the best sort regards it as the best
pleasure and that deriving from the noblest things.

(6) So it is evident that certain things should be learned and
there should be education with a view to the leisure that is spent in 10
pastime[2] as well, and that these subjects of education and these
sorts of learning should be for their own sake, those with a view
to occupation being necessary and for the sake of other things. (7)
Hence those of earlier times arranged that music too would be in
education, not as being something necessary, for it involves nothing of the sort, nor as being something useful, as letters are with a 15
view to business, management of the household, learning, and
many political activities (and drawing too is held to be useful with
a view to judging more finely the works of artisans), nor again as
gymnastic is with a view to health and vigor, for we see neither of 20
these arising from music. (8) What remains is that it is with a
view to the pastime that is in leisure; and it is evidently for just
this purpose that they bring it in. For they arrange to have it in
what they suppose to be the pastime of free persons. Hence Homer wrote thus: "but him alone it is needful to invite to the rich
banquet," and then goes on to say that there are certain persons 25
(9) "who invite a singer, that he may bring delight to all."[3] And
elsewhere Odysseus says that this is the best pastime, when hu-

man beings are enjoying good cheer and "the banqueters seated in order throughout the hall listen to a singer."[4]

30 (10) That there is a certain sort of education, therefore, in which children are to be educated, not as being useful or necessary but as being liberal and noble, is evident. As to whether this is of one or several sorts, and which these are and how [they should be taught], we must speak of these things later.[5] (11) At present we have come this far along the road, that from the an-

35 cients too we have some testimony deriving from the subjects of education. Music makes this clear. It is also clear, further, that children should be educated in some of the useful things not only on account of the element of utility, as for example in the learning of letters, but also because many other sorts of learning become

40 possible through them. (12) Similarly, they should be educated in drawing not so that they may not make errors in their private purchases and avoid being deceived in the buying and selling of wares,

1338b1 but rather because it makes them expert at studying the beauty connected with bodies. To seek everywhere the element of utility is least of all fitting for those who are magnanimous and free.

(13) Since it is evident that education through habits must come

5 earlier than education through reason, and education connected with the body earlier than education connected with the mind, it is clear from these things that children must [initially] be given over to gymnastic and to sports training. The first of these makes the disposition of the body of a certain quality, the other [gives instruction in particular] tasks.

CHAPTER 4

(1) At present, of those cities that are most particularly held

10 to superintend children, some inculcate an athletic disposition, thereby damaging the forms and growth of their bodies, while the Spartans, although they have not made this error, turn out children resembling beasts by [imposing severe] exertions, the assumption being that this is the most advantageous thing with a view to courage. (2) As has been said repeatedly, however, this

15 superintendence must not look to a single [virtue], and particularly not to this one;[6] yet even if it did, they have not discovered [how to secure] even this. For neither among the other animals nor in the case of [barbarian] nations do we see courage accompanying the most savage, but rather those with tamer and lionlike char-

acters. (3) There are many nations that are ready to engage in kill- 20
ing and cannibalism, such as the Achaeans and Heniochi of the
Black Sea and others among the nations of the continent, some of
them in similar fashion and others more so: these are expert at
banditry, but have no share in courage. (4) Further, we know that
the Spartans themselves, so long as they persevered in their love
of exertion, had preeminence over others, while at present they 25
fall short of others in both gymnastic and military contests.[7] For it
was not by exercising the young in this manner that they stood
out, but merely by the fact of their training against others who did
not train. (5) The element of nobility, not what is beastlike, should
have the leading role. For it is not the wolf or any of the other 30
beasts that would join the contest in any noble danger, but rather a
good man. (6) Those who are overly lax with their children in this
direction and leave them untutored in the necessary things turn
out [citizens] who are in the true sense vulgar, making them useful
for political expertise with a view to one task only—and with a 35
view to this, as the argument asserts, worse than others. (7) One
should not judge on the basis of their earlier deeds, but on the
basis of those of the present; for now they have rivals in the contest of education, whereas before they did not.

That gymnastic is to be practiced and how it is to be practiced,
then, has been agreed. Up to puberty lighter exercises are to be 40
employed; reduced sustenance and compulsory exertions should
be forbidden, in order that nothing impede their growth. (8) No
small indication that they are capable of having this effect is that 1339a1
in the Olympic games one would only find two or three persons
who won victories both as men and boys, because training in
youth impairs their capacity through its compulsory exercises. (9)
When during the three years following puberty they have devoted
themselves to other subjects of learning, then it is fitting that the 5
next age be taken up both with exertion and with compulsory diet-
ing. For one should not exert oneself with the mind and the body
at the same time. Each of these acts of exertion is naturally apt to
produce opposite things, the exertion of the body impeding the
mind, that of the mind the body. 10

CHAPTER 5

(1) Concerning music, we raised certain questions earlier in the
argument, and it will be well to take these up again now and de-

velop them, in order to provide a sort of prelude to the arguments one might make in expressing views about it. (2) For it is not easy to distinguish what its power is or for the sake of what one should share in it, whether for the sake of play and rest, as in the case of sleep and drinking (for in themselves these do not belong among excellent things, but are pleasant and at the same time "put a stop to care," as Euripides has it;[8] (3) hence music too is arranged among them and all—sleep, drinking, and music—are treated in similar fashion; and some place dancing among them as well); or whether it is rather to be supposed that music contributes something to virtue, the assumption being that, just as gymnastic makes the body of a certain quality, so also is music capable of making the character of a certain quality by habituating it to be capable of enjoying in correct fashion; (4) or whether it contributes in some way to pastime and prudence; for this is to be posited as the third of the things mentioned.

Now that the young should not be educated for the sake of play is not unclear. They do not play when they are learning, as learning is accompanied by pain. On the other hand, neither is it fitting to assign pastime to children or those of such ages; for the end is not suited to anything incomplete. (5) But perhaps it might be held that what children seriously attend to is for the sake of their play once they have become men and complete. But if something of this sort is the case, for the sake of what would they have to learn it themselves, and not partake of the learning and the pleasure through others performing it, like the kings of the Persians and the Medes? (6) Indeed, what results will necessarily be better if performed by those who have made this very thing their work and art than by those who are concerning themselves with it only for so much time as is required for learning. And if they should exert themselves in such matters, they would themselves have to take up the activity of cooking; but this would be odd.

(7) The same question arises even if it is capable of making their characters better. For why should they learn these things themselves, and not both enjoy correctly and be capable of judging by listening to others, like the Spartans? For these, although they do not learn themselves, nevertheless are capable of judging correctly, so they assert, which tunes are decent and which are not. (8) The same argument applies as well if it is to be practiced with a view to well-being and liberal pastime: why should they learn themselves, and not have the benefit of others practicing it? We may permit ourselves to investigate the conception we have about the gods: Zeus himself does not sing and play the lyre for our poets. But we even call persons of this sort vulgar, and the

234

activity one not belonging to a man, unless one who is drunk or playing.

(9) But perhaps these things must be investigated later.[9] What we must first seek to answer is whether music is to be placed in education or not, and what power it has of the three we raised questions about—whether education, play, or pastime. It is reasonable to arrange it under all of them; it evidently shares in all. (10) For play is for the sake of rest, and rest must necessarily be pleasant, as it is a sort of healing of the pain coming from exertions; and pastime, it is agreed, should involve not only the element of nobility but also pleasure, for being happy derives from both of these. (11) But all of us assert that music belongs among the most pleasant things, both by itself and with melody (Musaeus, at any rate, asserts that "singing is the pleasantest thing for mortals"; hence it is reasonable to expect it to be brought into [social] gatherings and pastimes, as being capable of providing good cheer),[10] so that on this account as well one might conceive that younger persons should be educated in it. (12) For those pleasures that are harmless are fitting not only with a view to the end but also with a view to rest; and since it happens that human beings rarely attain the end, but frequently rest and make use of play not only for some purpose beyond but also on account of the pleasure, it would be a useful thing to have them rest on occasion in the midst of the pleasures that derive from this.

(13) But it has happened to human beings that they make play an end. For the end too involves a certain pleasure—though not any chance pleasure; and while seeking the former they take the latter for it, on account of its having a certain similarity to the end of actions. For the end is choiceworthy not for the sake of anything that will be, and pleasures of this sort are not for the sake of anything that will be, but of things that have been, such as exertions and pain. (14) One might plausibly conceive this to be the reason, then, for their seeking happiness through these pleasures, though as far as participating in music is concerned, it is not on this account only, but also because music is useful with a view to rest, as it seems.

(15) Yet we must investigate whether this result is not accidental and its nature is not more honorable than what accords with the need mentioned, and one should not only share in the common pleasure that derives from it, of which all have a perception—for music involves a natural pleasure, hence the practice of it is agreeable to all ages and characters—but see whether in some way it contributes to the character and the soul. (16) This would be clear if we become of a certain quality in our characters on account of

10

15

20

25

30

35

40

1340a1

5

10

15

20

25

30

35

40

1340b1

5

it. But that we do become of a certain quality is evident through many things, and not least through the tunes of Olympus; for it is agreed that these make souls inspired, and inspiration is a passion of the character connected with the soul.[11] (17) Further, all who listen to imitations come to experience similar passions, even apart from rhythms and tunes themselves.[12] Since music belongs accidentally among pleasant things, and virtue is connected with enjoying in correct fashion and feeling affection and hatred, it is therefore clear that one should learn and become habituated to nothing so much as to judging in correct fashion of, and enjoying, respectable characters and noble actions. (18) For in rhythms and tunes there are likenesses particularly close to the genuine natures of anger and gentleness, and further of courage and moderation and of all the things opposite to these and of the other things pertaining to character. This is clear from the facts: we are altered in soul when we listen to such things. (19) But habituation to feel pain and enjoyment in similar things is close to being in the same condition relative to the truth. For example, if someone enjoys looking at the image of something for no other reason than the form itself, then the very study of the thing the image of which he studies must necessarily be pleasant. (20) It happens that no likeness of characters is present in other perceptible things—in things touched or tasted, for example, while in visible things it is present only to a slight degree. For there are figures of this sort, though only to a small extent, and all participate in this sort of perception; and further, these things are not likenesses of characters, but the figures and colors that exist of this sort are rather indications of characters, (21) and these only as manifested by the body when it is in the grip of the passions. But to the extent that there is a difference in connection with the study of these things as well, the young should not study the [paintings] of Pauson but those of Polygnotus or of any other painter or sculptor who is expert in character.[13] In tunes by themselves, however, there are imitations of characters. (22) This is evident: the nature of the harmonies diverged at the outset, so that those listening are in a different state and not in the same condition in relation to each of them. In relation to some—for example, the so-called Mixed Lydian— they are in a state more of grief and apprehension; in relation to others—for example, the relaxed harmonies—they are softer of mind; they are in a middling and settled state in relation to one above all, this being what Dorian alone among the harmonies is held to make them; and Phrygian makes them inspired. (23) This is what those who have philosophized in connection with this sort of education argue, and rightly; they find proofs for their arguments in the facts themselves.[14] Things stand in the same manner in connection with rhythms as well: some of them have a character that is more steadfast, others a character marked by movement, and of these some have movements of a cruder, others of a more liberal sort.

(24) It is evident from these things, then, that music can render the character of the soul of a certain quality. If it is capable of doing this, clearly it must be employed and the young must be educated in it. (25) The teaching of music is fitting in relation to the nature of those of such an age, for on account of their age the young do not voluntarily put up with anything that is not sweetened, but music by nature belongs among the sweetened things. Moreover, there seems to be a certain affinity [on their part] for harmonies and rhythms; hence many of the wise assert either that the soul is a harmony or that it involves harmony.[15]

CHAPTER 6

(1) But whether they themselves should learn through singing and playing instruments or not—the question we raised earlier—must now be spoken of. It is not unclear that it does indeed make a great difference with a view to becoming of a certain quality if one participates in the work oneself; for it is an impossible or a difficult thing for them to become excellent judges without participating in the works. (2) At the same time, children should also have some pursuit: "the rattle of Archytas,"[16] which they give to children so they will use this and not break anything around the house, should be supposed a fine thing; anything young is incapable of keeping still. This, therefore, is fitting for children in infancy, while education is a rattle for the young when they are bigger.

(3) That there is to be education in music in such a way that they will participate in the works, therefore, is evident from such things. What is appropriate and inappropriate for [different] ages is not difficult to define and resolve, in response to those who assert that the concern is a vulgar one. (4) In the first place, since one should share in the works for the sake of judging, on this account they should practice the works when they are young, and when they become older leave off the works, and be able to judge the noble things and to enjoy in correct fashion through the learning that occurred in their youth. (5) Concerning the criticism of

40

1341a1

some that music makes people vulgar, it is not difficult to resolve by investigating up to what point those who are being educated to political virtue should participate in the works and which sorts of tunes and rhythms they should participate in, and further, on which sorts of instruments they are to learn, for it is likely that this too makes a difference. (6) The resolution of the criticism lies in these things, for nothing prevents certain modes of music from producing the effect mentioned. It is evident that the learning of it

5

should neither be an impediment with a view to later activities, nor make the body vulgar and useless with a view to military and political training—with a view on the one hand to the uses now, and on the other to the sorts of learning [to be undertaken] later.

(7) This would result in connection with the learning [of music]

10

if they did not exert themselves to learn either what contributes to contests involving expertise in the art or those works that are difficult and extraordinary (which have now come into the contests, and from the contests into education), (8) but [learned] such things as well [as other works of music only] up to the point where they are capable of enjoying noble tunes and rhythms and

15

not merely the common element of music, as is the case even for some of the other animals, and further for the multitude of slaves and children.

It is clear from these things also which instruments are to be used. (9) Flutes are not to be brought into education, nor any other instrument involving expertise in the art, such as the lyre or any other that may be of this sort, but only those that will make

20

them good listeners either of music education or of the other [sort of education]. Further, the flute is an instrument involving not character but rather frenzy, and so is to be used with a view to those occasions when looking on has the power of [effecting] purification rather than learning. (10) Let us add that the fact that the

25

flute prevents speech also tells against its use in education. Hence those of earlier times rightly rejected the use of it by the young and free, although they had used it before. (11) For when [Greeks] came to have more leisure through being better off and were more magnanimous in regard to virtue, and further, being full of high

30

thoughts on account of their deeds both before and after the Persian Wars, they put their hand to every sort of learning, making no discrimination between them but seeking to advance further in all. Hence expertise in the flute was also brought in among the sorts of learning. (12) Indeed, in Sparta a certain chorus leader himself played the flute for the chorus, and at Athens it became so much

35

the local fashion that most free persons had a share in it (this is clear from the tablet that Thrasippus, the chorus leader, set up for

Ecphantides).[17] Later, it was rejected as a result of the experience of it, when they were better able to judge what contributes to virtue and what does not. (13) The same thing happened also with many of the ancient instruments, such as the pectis, the barbitos, and those contributing to the pleasure of those who listen to their practitioners, the heptagon, the trigon, and the sambuca,[18] and all those requiring professional knowledge. And the tale told by the ancients about flutes is a reasonable one. They assert that Athena, though she had invented the flute, threw it away. (14) Now it is not bad to assert that the goddess did this out of annoyance at the distortion of her face; but it is more likely that it was because education in flute playing has nothing to do with the mind, for we ascribe to Athena knowledge and art.

(15) Since we reject the education involving expertise in the art both in instruments and in performance—we regard as involving expertise in the art that with a view to contests, for one who is active in this does not undertake it for the sake of his own virtue but for the sake of the pleasure of his listeners, and this a crude pleasure; hence we judge the performance as not belonging to free persons but being more characteristic of the laborer; (16) and indeed the result is that they become vulgar, for the aim with a view to which they create the end for themselves is a base one; the spectator, being crude himself, customarily alters the music, so that he makes the artisans engaging in it with a view to him of a certain quality themselves and with respect to their bodies on account of the movements. . . .

CHAPTER 7

(1) We must investigate further in connection with harmonies and rhythms, both [whether the same harmonies and rhythms are appropriate for citizens and noncitizens and] whether all harmonies and all rhythms are to be used with a view to education or a distinction is to be made, and next, whether we shall posit the same definition for those exerting themselves with a view to education or some other third definition is needed.[19] Since we see that music depends on tune composition and rhythms, one should not overlook the power that each of these has with a view to education, and whether one should intentionally choose music with good tune over music with good rhythm.[20] (2) Considering as right, then, much of what has been said about these things by some of

40

1341bl

5

10

15

20

25

the current experts in music and by those in philosophy who have experience with the education connected with music,[21] we shall refer to them anyone who seeks a detailed account of each particular, and for the present we shall make distinctions in legal fashion and speak about these things only in outline.

(3) Since we accept the distinction of tunes as they are distinguished by certain persons in philosophy,[22] regarding some as relating to character, some to action, and some to inspiration (and they regard the nature of harmonies as akin to each of these, one of them to one part[23]), and since we assert that music should be practiced not for the sake of a single sort of benefit but for the sake of several (for it is for the sake both of education and of purification—as to what we mean by purification, we will speak of it simply at present, but again and more elaborately in the [discourses] on poetic expertise[24]—and third, [it is useful] with a view to pastime, rest, and the relaxation of strain), it is evident that all the harmonies are to be used, but that all are not to be used in the same manner, but with a view to education those most relating to character, and with a view to listening to others performing those relating to action and those relating to inspiration as well.[25]

(4) For the passion that occurs strongly in connection with certain sorts of souls is present in all, but differs by greater and less—for example, pity and fear, and further, inspiration. For there are certain persons who are possessed by this motion, but as a result of the sacred tunes—when they use the tunes that put the soul in a frenzy—we see them calming down as if obtaining a cure and purification.[26] (5) This same thing, then, must necessarily be experienced also by the pitying and the fearful as well as by the generally passionate, and by others insofar as each individual has a share in such things, and there must occur for all a certain purification and a feeling of relief accompanied by a pleasure.[27] In a similar way the purificatory tunes as well provide harmless delight to human beings.

(6) Hence it is to be set down that contestants undertaking theatrical music [should use[28]] harmonies of this sort and tunes of this sort. But as the spectator is twofold, the one free and educated, the other crude and composed of vulgar persons and laborers and others of this sort, contests and spectacles are to be assigned to such persons as well with a view to rest. (7) Just as their souls are distorted from the disposition that accords with nature, so too there are deviations among the harmonies, and tunes that are strained and highly colored; and what is akin according to nature is what creates pleasure for each sort of individual. Hence license is to be given to those contesting with a view to this sort of spectator to use a certain sort of music of this type.[29]

(8) With a view to education, as was said, those of the tunes that relate to character are to be used and harmonies of this sort. The Dorian is of this sort, as we said before, and one should accept any other that is approved for us by those participating in the pursuit of philosophy and in the education connected with music. (9) The Socrates of the *Republic* is not right in leaving Phrygian alone [in education] together with Dorian, especially as he rejects the flute among the instruments.[30] For Phrygian has the same power among the harmonies as the flute among the instruments: both are characteristically frenzied and passionate. (10) Poetry makes this clear. For all excitement and all motion of this sort belongs particularly to the flute among the instruments, while among the harmonies these things find what is appropriate to them in Phrygian tunes. The dithyramb, for example, is held by agreement to be Phrygian. (11) Many instances of this are mentioned by those who understand these matters, but particularly the fact that Philoxenus attempted to compose a dithyramb in Dorian—*The Mysians*—but was unable to do it, but because of its very nature he fell back on Phrygian again, the harmony appropriate to it. (12) Concerning Dorian, all agree that it is the most steadfast and has most of all a courageous character. Further, since we praise the middle between extremes and assert it ought to be pursued, and since Dorian has this nature relative to the other harmonies, it is evident that it is appropriate for younger persons to be educated particularly in Dorian tunes.

(13) There are two aims, the possible and the appropriate; individuals should undertake things possible and appropriate [for them]. These things too are defined by ages. It is not easy for those exhausted with age, for example, to sing the strained harmonies, but nature suggests the relaxed ones instead for persons of such an age. (14) Hence some of those connected with music rightly criticize Socrates for this as well, that he would reject for purposes of education the relaxed harmonies,[31] taking them to have an effect related to drinking—not of drunkenness, as drunkenness gives rise rather to excitement, but of exhaustion. So one should take up both harmonies of this sort and tunes of this sort with a view to the age to come when they are older. (15) Further, if there is among the harmonies one of a sort that is appropriate to the age of children on account of its capacity to involve simultaneously both order and play,[32] as appears to be the case most particularly with Lydian among the harmonies, it is clear that these three are to be made defining principles for purposes of education—the middle, the possible, and the appropriate.[33]

NOTES

Introduction

1. The case has been argued principally by Anton-Hermann Chroust, *Aristotle: New Light on His Life and on Some of His Lost Works* (Notre Dame and London, 1973), 1:83–176. A comprehensive inventory of the evidence may be found in Ingemar Düring, *Aristotle in the Ancient Biographical Tradition* (Göteborg, 1957).

2. See Chroust, 1:96–102. Plato was not actually present in Athens at the time of Aristotle's arrival, returning from his Sicilian journey only in 365/64. The central place of rhetoric in the intellectual preoccupations of Aristotle's early years will be discussed below.

3. *II Vita Aristotelis Syriaca* 2–4. See Chroust, 1:117–24.

4. The orator Demochares, supporting the motion of a certain Sophocles, alleged among other things that letters Aristotle had sent to Macedonia at this juncture were intercepted by the Athenians. See Chroust, 1:121–22.

5. A later writer (Demetrius, *On Style* 29 = Aristotle, fr. 669 Rose) cites Aristotle as remarking in a letter: "I went from Athens to Stagira on account of the great king, and from Stagira to Athens on account of the great winter." Aristotle is said to have interceded with Philip or Alexander to have Stagira reconstructed, and may have done so at this time. The phrase "the great king" may allude ambiguously to Philip and the king of Persia. Aristotle's diplomatic role with respect to Hermias is accepted by J. R. Ellis, *Philip and Macedonian Imperialism* (London, 1976), pp. 97–98.

6. See Chroust, 1:125–32.

7. See, for example, W. W. Tarn, *Alexander the Great* (Cambridge, 1948), Ernst Badian, "Alexander the Great and the Unity of Mankind," *Historia* 7 (1958): 425–44.

8. The location of the school appears to have been at a site near the city of Mieza (in the mountains southwest of the Macedonian capital of Pella) known as the Nymphaion. See the account of Ellis, pp. 160–62.

9. *IV Vita Aristotelis Arabica* (Ibn Abi Usaibia): 17–19. See Chroust, 1:133–44.

10. A crisis in the relationship between Alexander and his father was created by Philip's decision in 337 to contract a new marriage with the Macedonian noblewoman Cleopatra. Although polygamy seems to have been an accepted practice in the royal family, Alexander and his mother Olympias apparently saw this step as a threat to their position. That Olympias was in any way implicated in the assassination of Philip in the year following, as some sources claim, is unlikely, but it is not impossible that the later factional struggle between Olympias and the family of Antipater had its roots in this period, and that Aristotle's close identification with Philip and Antipater had placed him in an awkward position. The remark ascribed to Aristotle by Demetrius (note 5 above), that he left Stagira for Athens on account of the "great winter" (or "great storm"), perhaps contains a masked reference to these events, though it could also allude to the rapid and violent entry of Alexander into central Greece in 336.

11. *Politics* 4. 11. 1296a32–b2. The identification with Philip is made by a number of scholars; see, for example, Wilhelm Oncken, *Die Staatslehre des Aristoteles* (Leipzig, 1875), 2:267, Maurice Defourny, *Aristote: Études sur la politique* (Paris, 1932), pp. 534ff. Assuming that books 4 and 5 were written at roughly the same time, Philip could be appropriately referred to in the past. Various figures prominent in the domestic politics of the Greek cities have been suggested, but the context clearly refers to interstate relations. Particularly revealing is the phrase "now even among those in the cities," the contrast apparently being between contemporary Greek politicians, their earlier counterparts, and the barbarian world. The terms of the peace agreed to at the Congress of Corinth in 338/37 appear from [Demosthenes] 17. 15; see the account of Ellis, pp. 204–8. Cities were enjoined from actions such as unlawful executions or banishments, confiscation of property, dispersal of land, cancellation of debts, or emancipation of slaves, where these might endanger the existing regime.

12. *Politics* 7. 7.1327b32–33.

13. Plutarch, *On the Fortune of Alexander* 1. 6 = Aristotle, fr. 658 Rose. See, for example, Defourny, pp. 488, 494–95, 527–45, Oncken, 2:287ff., and Hans Kelsen, "The Philosophy of Aristotle and the Hellenic-Macedonian Policy," *Ethics* 48 (1937): 1ff.

14. *Politics* 7. 2–3, 14–15 (particularly 14. 1333b38–34a2). For a full discussion of these passages, see Carnes Lord, *Education and Culture in the Political Thought of Aristotle* (Ithaca and London, 1982), pp. 189–96.

15. Aristotle makes clear, for example, that at least certain barbarians are abundantly endowed with a psychological disposition that leads them to desire freedom from foreign domination and even rule over others (*Politics* 7. 2. 1324b5–22, 7. 1327b23–27). Carthage is discussed in 2. 11.

16. I follow here the account of Ellis, pp. 227–34.

17. See Philip Merlan, "Isocrates, Aristotle and Alexander the Great," *Historia* 3 (1954–55): 76–81, Chroust, 1:83–91.

18. Wolfgang Wieland, "Aristoteles als Rhetoriker und die exoterischen Schriften," *Hermes* 86 (1958): 323–46.

19. Ingemar Düring, *Aristotle's Protrepticus: An Attempt at Reconstruction* (Göteborg, 1961).

20. Kurt von Fritz and Ernst Kapp, *Aristotle's Constitution of Athens* (New York, 1950).

21. The lists also contain works that were probably not used for lecture purposes—in addition to the catalogue material, collections of "theses" for training in dialectic and rhetoric and of "problems" reflecting the results of advanced research in various fields; it is sometimes difficult to distinguish these works as listed from the specialized treatises. The lists have been analyzed in detail by Paul Moraux, *Les listes anciennes des ouvrages d'Aristote* (Louvain, 1951).

22. Aulus Gellius 20. 5, Plutarch, *Alexander* 7, Clement of Alexandria, *Stromata* 5. 9.

23. See George Boas, "Ancient Testimony to Secret Doctrines," *Philosophical Review* 62 (1953): 79–92, Düring, *Aristotle in the Ancient Biographical Tradition*, pp. 432–43.

24. Aulus Gellius 20. 5.

25. *Nicomachean Ethics* 1. 3. 1095a2–11.

26. *Nicomachean Ethics* 1. 2. 1094a18–28, 9. 1099b29–32, 2. 2. 1103b26–31, 10. 9. 1179a35–b4, *Eudemian Ethics* 1. 5. 1216b11–25.

27. Philodemus, *On Rhetoric, Volumina Rhetorica* 2:50–63 Sudhaus; see Düring, *Aristotle in the Ancient Biographical Tradition*, pp. 299–311, Chroust, 1:105–16. According to Philodemus, who seems to be paraphrasing a lost Aristotelian work either directly or as reported in an earlier polemical writing (perhaps the treatise entitled *Against Aristotle* that is ascribed to Isocrates' student Cephisodorus), Aristotle taught that "political science is a part of philosophy" and spoke of the differences between it and rhetoric (50–51), encouraging the study of political science on the grounds that too early an involvement in political activity would cut one off from "purer pursuits," while the pursuit of theoretical knowledge would not provide a basis for "engaging in politics, bringing an end to disorder and establishing a decent regime unless after a very long time" (60–61).

28. For Aristotle's view of rhetoric and his relationship to the Platonic critique of rhetoric, see Carnes Lord, "The Intention of Aristotle's *Rhetoric*," *Hermes* 109 (1981): 326–39.

29. Even in the *Protrepticus*, an early work praising the philosophic life after the manner of Plato, Aristotle is at pains to show that "theoretical wisdom" is directly beneficial for human life and for political life in particular (consider *Protrepticus*, frs. B46–B51 Düring).

30. Strabo 13. 1. 54 and 4. 2, Plutarch, *Sulla* 26.

31. The evidence concerning Andronicus' edition is collected and discussed by Düring, *Aristotle in the Ancient Biographical Tradition*, pp. 412–25. The crucial source is Porphyry, *Life of Plotinus* 24.

32. The most radical exponent of this position is Joseph Zürcher, *Aristoteles' Werk und Geist* (Paderborn, 1952). See also Felix Grayeff, *Aristotle and His School* (New York, 1974), pp. 9–85, and Chroust, 1:ix–xv.

33. See the careful and authoritative account of Paul Moraux, *Der Aristotelismus bei den Griechen* (Berlin, 1973), pp. 3–94.

34. See Moraux, *Listes*, pp. 211–47. Moraux identified the source as Ariston, scholarch of the Athenian Peripatos at the end of the third century, but other scholars continue to favor the Alexandrian librarian Hermippus (cf. Moraux, *Aristotelismus*, pp. 4–5).

35. There is no reason to suppose that the reference to "political [discourses]" in Aristotle's *Rhetoric* (1366a21 and ff.) is to anything other than our *Politics*.

36. Werner Jaeger, *Aristoteles: Grundlegung einer Geschichte seiner Entwicklung* (Berlin, 1923); *Aristotle: Fundamentals of the History of His Development*, trans. Richard Robinson (Oxford, 1948²).

37. *Politics* 4. 1. 1288b10–89a7.

38. That Aristotle's audience must be assumed to have been not only predominantly Athenian but predominantly aristocratic must be kept in mind if the full bearing of the discussion of the merits of the practical or political life in 7. 2–3 is to be understood. For the practical intention underlying this apparently "Platonizing" passage, see Lord, *Education and Culture*, pp. 180–90.

39. *Politics* 2. 9. 1270b7–13 and 10. 1272b19–22 probably refer, respectively, to a meeting of Spartan officials with a Persian fleet at the island of Andros, and the subjugation of Crete by the Spartan Agesilaus, both of which occurred in 333. These are the latest datable references in the *Politics* as a whole.

40. Diogenes Laertius 5. 51–52. The chief objection to transposing the books is the apparent summary of the contents of the *Politics* given at the end of the *Nicomachean Ethics* (10. 9. 1181b12–24). For further discussion of this passage and related matters, see Carnes Lord, "The Character and Composition of Aristotle's *Politics*," *Political Theory* 9 (1981): 472–74, from which much of the treatment here is drawn.

41. At the end of his account of Plato's *Laws*, Aristotle refers to a later discussion of "this sort of regime" (2. 6. 1266a23–25). Although generally referred to book 7, the fact that Aristotle explicitly associates the regime of the *Laws* with polity rather than aristocracy (1265b26–31) indicates that he has in mind the account of polity in 4. 7–9.

42. *Politics* 1. 13. 1260b8–13. It is not clear whether the phrase refers to 2–8 or 4–8; the latter is perhaps more likely. There is a reference to 3. 6–13 in 4. 2. 1289a26–27 as "our first inquiry concerning the regimes."

43. *Politics* 4. 2. 1289a30–33, 3. 1290a1–3, 7. 1293b1–7. When Aristotle says that "aristocracy and kingship have been spoken of—for to study the best regime is the same as to speak about [the regimes designated by] these terms as well, as each of them wishes to be established on the basis of virtue that is furnished with equipment," it is evident that the reference can be only to the best regime of the later books and not to any of the passing references to aristocracy as a general regime type in book 3. Aristocracy as a general type of regime "wishes" to rest on virtue that is suitably equipped, but in practice it is usually diluted by the presence of powerful elements (the few rich and the many) whose claim to participation in the regime derives from the "equipment" they provide (money and manpower) rather than from virtue; by contrast, the best regime is aristocracy in the strict sense—the undiluted rule of the virtuous few. It is sometimes argued that the best regime is not in fact an aristocracy at all but a variant of polity, and that the discussion of

aristocracy referred to here must therefore be considered to be missing from our *Politics*. This view overlooks Aristotle's indications that a multitude as such is incapable of complete or genuine virtue (consider 3. 7. 1279a40–b1, 15. 1286a25–38), and misses the significance of the serf class of the best regime (consider 7. 9. 1329a17–26).

44. *Politics* 1. 13. 1260b8–13, 2. 9. 1271a23–26, 7. 10. 1330a4–5, 1330a31–33, 16. 1335b2–5, 17. 1336b24–26, 8. 3. 1338a30–34, 7. 1341b38–40. The reference at 1341b38–40 to a discussion of musical catharsis "in the [discourses] on poetic expertise" (*en tois peri poiētikēs*) is almost universally assumed to be to Aristotle's *Poetics*, or more precisely, to a discussion supposed to have been provided in its now lost second book, but other similar expressions appear to designate passages that originally belonged to the *Politics* itself. See Lord, *Education and Culture*, pp. 146–50.

45. The case against the final paragraph of book 8 is argued in Lord, *Education and Culture*, pp. 213–17. Of the many questionable features of 1. 11, most striking are its inconsistent use of the term "expertise in business" (*chrēmatistikē*) and its uncritical attitude toward something Aristotle has just sharply criticized; its effort to describe the "practice" of household management would seem to reveal a lack of understanding of the character of Aristotle's argument generally.

46. *Metaphysics* E. 1. 1025b18–28, *Topics* 6. 6. 145a15–18, *Nicomachean Ethics* 7. 2. 1139a26–b4, 4. 1140a1–23.

47. The key passages are *Nicomachean Ethics* 1. 3. 1094b11–27, 4. 1095a30–b13, 7. 1098a26–b8, *Eudemian Ethics* 1. 5–6. 1216b11–17a18. For recent discussion of these issues, see Otfried Höffe, *Praktische Philosophie: Das Modell des Aristoteles*, Epimeleia XVIII (Munich/Salzburg, 1971), and Günther Bien, *Die Grundlegung der praktischen Philosophie bei Aristoteles* (Freiburg/Munich, 1973), pp. 59–69, 103–37.

48. *Nicomachean Ethics* 1. 3. 1094b11–27, 7. 1098a26–33.

49. "There are certain persons who, it being held to belong to a philosopher to say nothing randomly but rather to use reasoned argument, make arguments that are alien to the subject and empty (they do this sometimes out of ignorance and sometimes from charlatanry) and are not detected, thus taking in those who are experienced and capable of acting, though they themselves neither have nor are capable of architectonic or practical thinking" (*Eudemian Ethics* 1. 6. 1217a1–6).

50. These considerations go some way toward refuting the notion that Aristotle's political science is invalidated by its association with an outmoded teleological or metaphysical natural science. Whether or to what extent Aristotle may be supposed to have recognized the possibility of a theoretical "anthropology" that would serve as the foundation for a practical science of politics is not easy to say. Of interest in this connection is Stephen R. L. Clark, *Aristotle's Man* (Oxford, 1975).

51. *Nicomachean Ethics* 6. 8. 1141b23–33. For political science as the "architectonic" science and the subordination of ethics to it, see *Nicomachean Ethics* 1. 2. 1094a26–b11, *Magna Moralia* 1. 1. 1181a23–b28, *Rhetoric* 1. 2. 1356a25–28.

52. *Politics* 3. 12. 1282b14–23. The phrase "political philosophy" occurs only here in Aristotle's writings; cf. 8. 1279b12–25, where it is indicated that the inquiry of the *Politics* is in some sense philosophical and "not merely looking toward action." Compare, however, *Eudemian Ethics* 1. 1. 1214a9–14, where Aristotle indicates that "what involves theoretical philosophy alone" will be brought in only when proper to the inquiry, as well as 6. 1216b35–39, where he suggests that "discourses philosophically argued" will have at best a restricted role.

53. I have attempted to argue elsewhere ("The Character and Composition of Aristotle's *Politics*," pp. 472–74) that the work described there is not the *Politics* at all but the similar treatise known to have been written by Theophrastus.

54. Assuming that the common books (*Nicomachean Ethics* 5–7 = *Eudemian Ethics* 4–6) originally belonged to the *Eudemian Ethics*. The case is made by, among others, Jaeger, pp. 283–85.

55. *Nicomachean Ethics* 6. 8. 1141b24–29.

56. *Rhetoric* 1. 4. 1359b19–23 and ff.

57. *Rhetoric* 1. 4. 1360a19–23. Aristotle proceeds to recommend the study of works of geography or ethnography with a view to "legislation," and of works of history with a view to "political deliberations" (1360a30–37).

58. Consider particularly *Politics* 3. 15. 1286a2–7, 4. 1. 1289a10–25; for the interpretation of the latter passage, see note 3 to book 4 below.

59. *Nicomachean Ethics* 10. 9. 1181a12–19. Isocrates is no doubt particularly meant.

60. See the discussion in Lord, "The Intention of Aristotle's *Rhetoric*," pp. 337–38.

61. *Politics* 2. 6. 1265a1–2, b26–33.

62. Julian, *Letter to Themistius* 260d–61c, 263d; Proclus, *Commentary on Plato's Republic* 2:360–67 Kroll. See generally Alois Dreizehnter, *Aristoteles' Politik* (Munich, 1970), pp. xv–xxi.

63. At the beginning of his commentary on Plato's *Republic*, for example, Averroes explains that he has chosen to write on this work because "Aristotle's book on governance has not yet fallen into our hands" (*Averroes on Plato's Republic*, ed. Ralph Lerner [Ithaca, N.Y., 1974], p. 4).

64. See Quentin Skinner, *The Foundations of Modern Political Thought* (Cambridge, 1978), 1:3–12, 49–65.

65. The fullest account is Alan Gewirth, *Marsilius of Padua: The Defender of the Peace* (New York, 1951).

66. For the influence of the *Politics* in modern Europe, see particularly Joachim Ritter, *Naturrecht bei Aristoteles* (Stuttgart, 1961), and Manfred Riedel, *Metaphysik und Metapolitik: Studien zu Aristoteles und zur politischen Sprache der neuzeitlichen Philosophie* (Frankfurt am Main, 1975).

NOTES TO THE POLITICS

Book 1

1. The reference appears to be particularly to Plato, *Statesman* 258e–59d; consider also Xenophon, *Memorabilia* 3. 4. 12 (cf. 6. 14) and *Oeconomicus* 13. 5.

2. That there is a single "science" of political and kingly rule is asserted in *Statesman* 295c.

3. The meaning of "our normal sort of inquiry" (*hē hyphēgēmenē methodos*) is not certain; the analytic approach alluded to here is by no means rigidly followed throughout Aristotle's writings. Cf. 1. 8. 1.

4. Probably a kind of knife used at the religious center of Delphi for a variety of sacrificial purposes, but the meaning is uncertain.

5. Euripides, *Iphigenia in Aulis* 1400–401.

6. Hesiod, *Works and Days* 405.

7. The legislator Charondas of Catana is mentioned again in 3. 12 and 4. 11 and 13. Epimenides of Crete is said to have written poetry as well as a prose work on the Cretan regime (Diogenes Laertius 1. 109–15).

8. The latter phrase is Homeric in origin (*Iliad* 20. 308; cf. Plato, *Laws* 681b); both expressions seem to have designated the extended family or clan (*genos*). The word "extension" (*apoikia*) derives from a phrase meaning "from the household;" it is the normal term for a colonial settlement.

9. The reference is to the Homeric Cyclopes: "These have no assemblies to take counsel nor customary laws [*themistes*], but dwell in the heights of lofty mountains / in hollow caves: each acts as law to [*themisteuei*] his children and wives, and pays no attention to the others" (*Odyssey* 9. 112–15). Cf. *Nicomachean Ethics* 1180a24–32, Plato, *Laws* 680b–e.

10. Homer, *Iliad* 9. 63–64: "Without clan, without law [*athemis*], without hearth is the man / who longs for chilling war among his people." It is not certain exactly what game Aristotle is referring to; the piece is apparently given a technical name or description, "unyoked" (*azyx*), suggesting an unprotected position.

11. Aristotle probably means to allude to incest, cannibalism, and similar phenomena; cf. *Nicomachean Ethics* 1145a15–33, 1148b15–49a20.

12. Or "justice [*dikē*] is an ordering [*taxis*] of the political association," as it is usually understood. *Taxis* here appears to have the sense of "institution."

13. Reading *technopoiētikē* ("expertise in parental [rule]") with the MSS rather than Dreizehnter's conjectural *patrikē* ("expertise in paternal [rule]"), based on the use of that term in 12. 1.

14. Homer, *Iliad* 18. 376. Daedalus was a legendary sculptor who was held to have the power of creating animated statues.

15. The phrase *exōterikōtera skepsis* appears to refer to a type of written composition intended for circulation outside the Lyceum (the *exōterikoi logoi* or "external discourses"; see p. 9 above), but it is sometimes taken to mean merely "an investigation external to the subject."

16. Reading *logou* with Π² instead of *logōi* with Π¹ and Dreizehnter. The latter reading produces the more usual translation: "The other animals do not obey reason, though perceiving it, but their passions." Aristotle appears to suggest that the slave differs from even a tame animal by perceiving and obeying reason as distinct from force or habit (cf. 13. 2–3, 12–14).

17. Reading *monon* ("only") here with the MSS instead of at the end of the previous sentence with Dreizehnter and most editors.

18. "Motion of illegality" (*graphē paranomōn*) is a technical term of Athenian jurisprudence for a suit brought against anyone proposing in the public assembly a measure contravening the fundamental laws of the city.

19. This passage has been variously interpreted. The phrase "the other arguments" (*hateroi logoi*) is usually referred to one or both of "these arguments" (the view that conventional slavery is just only if accompanied by benevolence and the view that it is just because of the superiority implied in the very fact of mastery) when "set against" or opposed to one another (*diastantōn chōris*). I take "the other arguments" to refer to the view that conventional slavery is just simply by the fact of resting on force, and understand the words *diastantōn chōris* ("set on one side") as distinguishing this view from the view—common to both of "these arguments"—that conventional slavery is just because it rests on some form of superiority in virtue. As suggested by his earlier reference to the opinions of "the wise," the "other arguments" that Aristotle has in mind are probably sophistic arguments of the kind presented, for example, by Thrasymachus in the first book of Plato's *Republic*.

20. Theodectes, fr. 3 Nauck.

21. Philemon, fr. 53 Kock.

22. Reading *chrēmatistikēs* with the MSS rather than the conjectural *oikonomikēs* ("of expertise in household management") adopted by Dreizehnter.

23. Reading this sentence with the MSS rather than as punctuated and supplemented by Dreizehnter.

24. Reading *ho* with the MSS rather than *hōi* with Dreizehnter in b27. I understand *chrēmatōn* in 29 to depend on *ktētikēs* in 27.

25. Solon, fr. 1, 71 Diehl.

26. Reading *chrēseōs ktēsis* in b37 with the MSS rather than the conjectural *ktēseōs chrēsis* ("use is of the same property") adopted by Dreizehnter.

27. The word for "interest," *tokos*, also means "offspring."

28. The work of Apollodorus is cited and used in the agricultural writings of Varro and Pliny; Chares is otherwise unknown. The suggestion concerning collecting accounts of business success appears to be taken up in the second book of the pseudo-Aristotelian *Economics*.

29. Thales, the founder of Greek philosophy, lived in the late sixth and early fifth centuries.

30. It is not clear whether Dionysius I (405–367 B.C.) or Dionysius II (367–44 B.C.) of Syracuse is meant.

31. Dreizehnter marks a lacuna at this point in the text; I have supplied what I take to be the sense.

32. Amasis, an Egyptian king of lowly origin, had his subjects worship a statue of a god fashioned from a golden footpan. Cf. Herodotus 2. 172.

33. The reference is to Plato, *Meno* 71d ff.

34. Sophocles, *Ajax* 293.

35. There is no discussion of this sort in the remainder of the *Politics* as we have it. What is meant by "the [discourses] connected with the regimes" is not certain; the reference would seem to be to books 2–8 or 4–8 of the *Politics*.

Book 2

1. Plato, *Republic* 449a ff.

2. The meaning of this sentence has been much disputed. Aristotle's argument seems to presuppose a distinction between nations (*ethnē*) consisting simply of autonomous villages and nations consisting of villages subject to some central authority: the relatively primitive Arcadians had been organized in a kind of federal state since the founding of the fortified center of Megalopolis in 362 B.C. Aristotle suggests that a state of this sort differs from a city by being merely an alliance of elements (villages) not differing in kind.

3. *Nicomachean Ethics* 1132b33–34 and ff.

4. The text is uncertain at this point. Dreizehnter brackets the sentence following as a gloss; none of its variant forms yields a satisfactory sense, but the general idea appears merely to elaborate the remark that alternation of rule among equals imitates the permanent differentiation of rulers and ruled in a society of unequals.

5. See *Sophistic Refutations* 166a33 ff.

6. An apparent reference to the geographer Eudoxus of Cnidos (cf. frs. 322, 323, and 360 Lasserre); see also Herodotus 4. 180.

7. Plato, *Republic* 403b.

8. The best regime of the early books of the *Republic* consists fundamentally of two classes, a producing class (farmers and artisans) and a ruling and military class (called by Plato "guardians"). It is left unclear in the *Republic* whether communism is meant to be extended to the lower class.

9. In Plato's *Symposium* (191a ff.).

10. Accepting the reading of the MSS here rather than the conjectural alterations adopted by Dreizehnter.

11. I follow many editors in marking a lacuna here, and supply what I take to be the sense.

12. The holding of property in common by brothers was an accepted practice in Athens and elsewhere, and the reference is probably to this.

13. Greek meters typically admit of much variation in the feet or units that make up a line of poetry.

14. This seems to refer specifically to the discussion of the education of philosophers in *Republic* 6–7.

15. These "common messes" (*syssitia*), which also served as a form of social organization, are discussed further below.

16. The Spartan ruling class was supported by the labor of agricultural serfs, the so-called helots.

17. Literally, "suffering what will they submit," reading *pathontes* with some MSS and Susemihl instead of the *mathontes* ("learning") accepted by Dreizehnter.

18. Cf. *Republic* 415d–17b, 419a–20a, 543b–c.

19. *Republic* 425c–d.

20. *Apophora*: the term used at Sparta to designate the tax or rent in kind provided by the helots to their masters. Cf. *Republic* 416e.

21. The term "serf" (*penestēs*) was usually applied specifically to the agricultural serfs of Thessaly, as the term "helot" was to the serfs of Laconia and Messenia.

22. *Republic* 451d ff.

23. *Republic* 415a ff.

24. *Republic* 420b ff.

25. *Republic* 451e–52a.

26. In the *Republic* (458c–d) women are included in the common messes of the male guardians; in the *Laws* (780d–81d, 806d) they are assigned separate messes. On the size of the citizen body see *Republic* 423a and *Laws* 737e, 740a–41a.

27. Cf. 3. 3. 5.

28. This is not clearly stated in the *Laws*, but see 704a ff.

29. *Laws* 737d ff.

30. *Laws* 740d–e.

31. 7. 10. 9–13.

32. *Laws* 734e–35a.

33. *Laws* 744d–e.

34. *Laws* 745e. The second house is evidently intended for the use of a married son (776a).

35. *Laws* 753b.

36. See *Laws* 739a–e. The "first regime" described in the *Laws* is evidently that of the *Republic*.

37. *Laws* 693d.

38. *Laws* 756b–e, 763d ff., 765b ff.

39. Or "those who are from the highest assessments will be more numerous and better."

40. The reference would appear to be to 4. 7–9. Cf. p. 00, n. 41 above.

41. Nothing else is known of Phaleas.

42. 2. 6. 8–9.

43. The Athenian legislator who abolished the debts of the poor and established a moderate democracy; see 2. 12. 1–6.

44. What evidently happened was that permitting division of the original allotments created a shortage of individuals with the requisite property qualification for office, and the qualification was then reduced to allow poorer men to serve. Cf. 6. 4. 10.

45. Homer, *Iliad* 9. 319.

46. Reading *an epithymoien* with the MSS rather than bracketing the phrase with Dreizehnter.

47. Or perhaps "that some amount of possessions is advantageous."

48. Atarneus, a strongly fortified town on the coast of Asia Minor, together with other territory in the area, formed an independent state under Euboulus—originally a wealthy moneychanger—and his successor Hermias; the incident involving the Persian general Autophradates probably occurred during the 350s.

49. The "two obol allowance" (*diōbolia*) was a subsidy paid Athenian citizens out of a special fund for attendance at the theater, and later at all public festivals.

50. Or "A beginning point in such matters is. . . ." I read *archē* with the MSS instead of Dreizehnter's conjecture.

51. Text and meaning are somewhat uncertain; I read *eiper dei dēmosious einai, tous ta koina ergazomenous dei, kathaper . . . , touton echein ton tropon* with Welldon. We have no other information about the arrangement at Epidamnus or the scheme (or identity) of Diophantus.

52. Hippodamus seems to have gone to Italy as a colonist around the middle of the fifth century, where he planned the city of Thurii (Diodorus Siculus 12. 10. 7); nothing is known of his activity in Piraeus, the port of Athens. He apparently introduced the division of cities into regular quarters and straight streets, which Aristotle will later criticize (7. 11. 6–7). Hippodamus' interest in natural philosophy seems to be reflected in his predilection for threefold divisions; this suggests the influence of Pythagoreanism (cf. *On the Heavens* 268a10–20).

53. This division was a relatively common one in Greek cities.

54. This division is roughly congruent with the categories of Greek private law, but it omits all offenses relating to the city or to religion (cf. Plato, *Laws* 853b–64e).

55. *Politophylakes:* the term is probably Hippodamus' own; it is uncertain what kind of officials are meant.

56. Aristotle suggests that the legislation would provide opportunities for judicial "harassment" or blackmail (*sykophantia*) of the wealthy or politically powerful—a common phenomenon in democratic Athens—through pretended "discovery" of various kinds of malfeasance.

57. This perhaps alludes to Plato, *Statesman* 272b–d. For the traditional view of the earliest men as "earthborn," see Plato, *Statesman* 271a ff. and *Menexenus* 237d–38b; for the view that they were survivors of a universal cataclysm, *Laws* 676a ff.

58. This subject does not appear to be dealt with further in the remainder of the *Politics* as we have it.

59. Aristotle follows general Greek practice in using "Lacedaemonian" to refer to the Spartan state as a whole and "Spartan" (*Lakōn*) or "Spartiate" to refer to the Spartan citizen class. There were several categories of free persons—freed helots and the semiautonomous "subjects" (*perioikoi*) primarily—who did not enjoy political rights or share the way of life of full citizens, yet played some role in the state, particularly militarily.

60. Thessaly, Sparta, and Crete (and probably a number of other Greek cities) had systems of agricultural serfdom for which there were different names, the Thessalian name (*penestēs*) being closest to a generic term "serf." These serfs probably consisted largely of pre- or proto-Greek peoples who had been brought into subjection at the time of the Dorian invasions. In the case of Sparta, however, a considerable proportion of the helots were neighboring Messenians who had been conquered in the recent past and remained extremely restive. They sustained a revolt for ten years following a severe earthquake in 464, and were a constant preoccupation of the Spartans during the Peloponnesian War (see Thucydides 1. 101, 4. 41, 80, 5. 14, 23). After their decisive defeat at Leuctra and a Theban invasion of the Peloponnese in 370, the Spartans were forced to restore to Messenia its independence.

61. "Subjects" (*perioikoi*) was the specific term for the serfs of Crete.

62. These territories were subsequently reduced to subjection by the Thessalians. Thessalian serfdom is alleged to have originated in mutual agreement (Athenaeus 264a).

63. Lycurgus was traditionally regarded as the founder of Sparta's characteristic institutions and way of life, and Aristotle appears elsewhere to have accepted this tradition (10. 2; cf. Plutarch, *Lycurgus* 1). However, it should not be assumed that Aristotle's references to "the legislator" are in all cases to Lycurgus (cf. n. 73). There remains considerable uncertainty as to the historicity of Lycurgus and the date and character of the Lycurgan reforms; these are most commonly connected with the circumstances of the Second Messenian War (probably mid-seventh century).

64. The story is told by Hesiod (*Theogony* 933–37), but it is uncertain whether the reference is intended to be a precise one.

65. This seems to refer to the period of Spartan hegemony following the end of the Peloponnesian War.

66. For these events see Xenophon, *Hellenica* 6. 5. 28 and Plutarch, *Agesilaus* 31.

67. This account appears to place the Lycurgan reforms at the end of the First Messenian War (late eighth century). Cf. Plutarch, *Lycurgus* 14.

68. The nature of the Spartan system of land tenure and inheritance is controversial. Generally speaking, land was not owned by the citizens but held under a system of entail based on an original distribution (on what basis is highly uncertain) of "allotments." Aristotle seems to suggest that alienation of the allotments was not strictly illegal but only carried disgrace. There is (disputed) evidence concerning a change in the law effected earlier in the fourth century: the overseer Epitadeus is said to have introduced a bill that would "permit a man during his lifetime to give his estate and allotment to anyone he wished or to leave it so in his will" (Plutarch, *Agis* 5). It is possible that Aristotle is here alluding to this change, which would appear to have involved merely a liberalization of restrictions on the persons permitted to receive gifts or inheritances in land (cf. 5. 8. 20). Also involved may have been the disposition of heiresses in cases where no will existed: previously, it would seem, this had been a prerogative of the kings (Herodotus 6. 57).

69. The blow in question is the defeat at Leuctra in 371. The figures given by Aristotle appear to apply to Spartan territory prior to the loss of Messenia in 370, and seem related to Plutarch's claim (*Lycurgus* 8) that Lycurgus distributed thirty thousand allotments to the Spartan "subjects" and nine (or perhaps six) thousand to the citizens. Prior to Leuctra, the Lacedaemonian army

(which included an unknown number of "subjects" serving as regular heavy-armed troops) seems to have amounted to about six thousand men.

70. Or perhaps "exempt from normal military service" (*aphrouron*)—*phroura* being a Spartan word for a military levy or expedition.

71. Reading *pantes* with the MSS rather than *pantos* with Dreizehnter ("from the entire people").

72. The reference is uncertain, but probably concerns Spartan intrigues with Persia just prior to the victory of Alexander at Issus in 333. A Persian fleet active in the Aegean at this time appears to have put in at Andros and may have been met there by certain Spartan overseers; King Agis is supposed to have met the Persians at the island of Siphnos and entered into negotiations concerning a subsidy and military aid against Macedon (Arrian 2. 13. 4 ff., Quintus Curtius 4. 1. 37).

73. It seems to have been widely believed that the board of "overseers" (*ephoroi*) was not part of the original Lycurgan regime; Aristotle himself later (5. 11. 2–3) ascribes its institution to the early Spartan king Theopompus, as does Plutarch (*Lycurgus* 7; cf. *Cleomenes* 7). Other explanations (none are mutually exclusive) are that the overseers evolved from a college of priests or a council of headmen of the five Spartan tribes; the facts of the matter remain quite uncertain.

74. This is our only information on the mode of selection of the overseers, and its meaning is uncertain. It is often assumed that the overseers were elected by a vote of the popular assembly in the same manner as the senators (cf. n. 76); in a later remark (4. 9. 9), however, Aristotle seems to imply this was not the case. It has been suggested (on the basis of Plato, *Laws* 692a; cf. 690c) that their selection somehow involved the taking of auspices.

75. Cf. 3. 1. 10.

76. Senators were chosen in the popular assembly by an archaic process of acclamation (Plutarch, *Lycurgus* 26).

77. 3. 14–18.

78. Sparta had a system of dual kingship, each king being drawn from a separate hereditary line; factional conflict between the kings and their partisans was thus a natural development. The kings were regularly accompanied by several overseers when on military expeditions, but kings did not as a rule undertake diplomatic missions. Aristotle perhaps has in mind "the Andros matter" (see n. 72).

79. *Phiditia*: the etymology of the term is uncertain, but it may derive from a dialect form of the word "friend" (*philos*).

80. This suggests that a certain number of Spartan citizens were excluded from full political rights on account of their failure to support the expense of the common messes; this may be the class of "inferiors" (*hypomeiones*) referred to by Xenophon (*Hellenica* 3. 3. 6.) which figured in the conspiracy of Cinadon early in the fourth century.

81. Originally occupied periodically by the kings themselves, the office of admiral (*nauarchos*) had come under the control of the overseers by the late fifth century. Though subject to renewal every year, the office accumulated considerable power, particularly in the field of foreign policy, during the tenure of Lysander and subsequently.

82. Plato, *Laws* 625c–38b and passim.

83. This expression refers to a type of regime that was evidently common to most or all of the (independent) Cretan cities. Crete was not politically unified in historical Greek times.

84. For the derivation of the Spartan regime from the Cretan see Herodotus 1. 65 and Ephorus, *FGH* 70F148 ff. (an account which Aristotle here seems to draw on in other respects as well). Aristotle's argument is that the Spartan colonists in Crete adopted the institutions of the original inhabitants—the people who subsequently became their "subjects" or serfs; that the "subjects" still retained most of these ancestral institutions was indicated at an earlier point (2. 5. 19).

85. This paragraph is detached from the main argument, and probably represents an annotation by a later reader. Crete had been the seat of the maritime empire established by the semimythical Minos (cf. Thucydides 1. 15), but played little role in the politics of the Greek world during the classical period.

86. There is no discussion of this question in the remainder of the *Politics* as we have it.

87. It is not entirely clear whether Aristotle is thinking of the Spartan senators or the overseers: deciding at discretion had been criticized in connection with the overseers (9. 23).

88. Apparently the entire office could be declared to be in abeyance, though how this was done is not known. It would seem that the orderers acted as public prosecutors in the senate for certain types of crimes involving "the powerful."

89. The Spartans were well known for their strict control and periodic expulsion of aliens present in Spartan territory. See, for example, Xenophon, *Constitution of the Lacedaemonians* 14. 4.

90. This could refer to either or both of the following events: the operations conducted in Crete by the Phocian adventurer Phalaecus in 345–43 B.C.; the subjugation of the island by Agesilaus, brother of the Spartan king Agis, in 333.

91. Almost nothing is known of the political institutions of early Carthage apart from the information Aristotle provides.

92. Text and meaning are uncertain here. I assume a lacuna with Conring and others rather than accepting the conjectural reconstruction of Dreizehnter, and supply what I take to be the sense.

93. It is not completely certain that this is the same body referred to earlier.

94. Or "all cases tried by all official bodies [*archeia*] and not some by some and some by others [*allas hyp' allōn*]," as it is sometimes understood. But it is difficult to see how the arrangement could be aristocratic unless a distinction is being drawn between trials by select "boards" and trials by larger bodies such as a senate or popular assembly. The Spartan assembly appears to have functioned as a court at least in cases involving disputed royal succession. Cf. 3. 1. 10–11.

95. Or "by many": it is not clear whether the expression refers to the Carthaginian lower class or to non-Carthaginians generally.

96. Or "each of the same things." I read *tōn autōn* with the MSS rather than *tōn archōn* ("of the offices") with Dreizehnter. The reference would seem to be to 2. 4–7.

97. Cf. 6. 5. 9. Carthage was an imperial city, and Aristotle appears to refer to "cities" that were subject to it. Whether the people were sent out as officials or colonists or for trading purposes of some sort is unknown.

98. Solon was traditionally regarded as the founder of the democratic regime in Athens in the early sixth century. The identity of the proponents of the views described here is not certain; Aristotle himself later (3. 11. 8–9, 4. 11. 15) indicates approval of the Solonian legislation.

99. These reforms were effected around 460 B.C.

100. The aristocratic party in Athens following the Persian Wars was headed by Cimon; Ephialtes and Pericles were the chief popular leaders. For the significance of Athenian naval power for the internal political struggle see 5. 4. 8.

101. A key element of the Solonian reforms was the establishment of a system of four assessment classes based on landed wealth as distinct from birth. See *Constitution of Athens* 7.

102. Charondas and Zaleucus (seventh century B.C.) were sometimes connected with the circle of Pythagoras. Onomacritus is probably the Orphic soothsayer who was influential in Athens at the time of the Pisistratid tyranny; the Thales in question is the poet Thales (or Thaletas) of Gortyn in Crete.

103. Nothing else is known of Philolaus.

104. Plato, *Laws* 671d–72a, 794d–95d.

105. Draco was considered the author of the first Athenian legal code (late seventh century B.C.).

106. Pittacus was elected dictator of Mytilene during a period of civil strife there in the early sixth century; he was later enrolled (together with Solon) among the "seven wise men" of Greece.

107. Nothing else is known of Androdamas.

108. Much or all of this chapter is regarded by many scholars as of doubtful authenticity.

Book 3

1. Those beyond a certain age were apparently relieved of political as well as military duties; cf. Plato, *Republic* 498c.

2. 3. 6. 11.

3. Aristotle appears to be thinking of consultative bodies such as the Council of Five Thousand which formed part of the moderate oligarchic regime established in Athens in 411 B.C. (Thucydides 8. 67. 3).

4. Cf. 2. 11. 7. Aristotle's argument is that regimes like those of Sparta and Carthage handle judicial business primarily through tribunals of officials rather than large popular juries, as was the case in democracies like Athens; he had previously indicated that Carthage is even more restrictive in this respect than Sparta.

5. Gorgias puns on the word *dēmiourgos*, which means both "craftsman" and "magistrate." Larisa was a town in Thessaly; the occasion of the remark is unknown, but would appear to have involved a wholesale enfranchisement of noncitizens.

6. The democratic reforms effected by Cleisthenes after the overthrow of the Pisistratid tyranny (510 B.C.) involved abolishing the original four tribes of Athens and creating ten new ones in order to accommodate the new citizens. The text and the exact meaning of Aristotle's description of these citizens is controversial.

7. "City" (*polis*) has both a physical and a political sense: two cities "disjoined" in place or geography might nevertheless form part of a single city in the political sense. Aristotle may have in mind island cities that possessed territory and towns on the mainland (such as Lesbos or Samos) or cities with substantial dependent ports (such as Athens or Megara).

8. Babylon was captured by the Persians under Cyrus in the sixth century. Cf. Herodotus 1. 191.

9. 7. 4. ff.

10. The text is uncertain here. I follow Dreizehnter in considering the accepted reading *ethnos* a conjectural addition, but prefer the version of Π² (*hen ē pleiō*) to his own conjecture (*genē pleiō*); possibly the original text was *ton topon hen ē pleiō*, though this would not seem necessary for the sense. Aristotle seems to have in mind the advantages of a separate port city (cf. 7. 6. 5).

11. Reading *legoimen* with the MSS ("we would say") rather than *legomen* ("we say") with Dreizehnter. The point of the comparison seems to depend on the considerable overlap between the notes utilized for the Dorian and Phrygian modes as well as the very different spirit of these modes (cf. 8. 5. 22, 7. 9–12).

12. Or "name" (*onoma*); but Aristotle seems to refer not to the names of cities (there is in any case little evidence of change in these) but to the terms for regimes.

13. I follow Bernays in bracketing *ktēsis* in a8. Translating the text of the MSS: "and a household of man and woman, and possessions of master and slave. . . ."

14. Euripides, fr. 16. Nauck. The lines are from the *Aeolus*, and were apparently spoken by the king about his sons.

15. Jason of Pherae, in Thessaly, was a notorious tyrant of the early fourth century.

16. The text is somewhat uncertain: I read *dokimou ⟨dokei⟩* with Bernays and Newman instead of *dokei pou* ("the virtue of a citizen is surely held") with Jackson and Dreizehnter.

17. Aristotle seems to allude in particular to Athens, where the exclusion of laborers (the assessment class of Thetes) from office (Plutarch *Solon* 18) seems to have persisted through much of the fifth century.

18. A saying of this sort was ascribed to Solon (Diogenes Laertius 1. 60).

19. Accepting Bernays's supplement *archontos kai* in 18.

20. For the relationship of "making" and "using" arts see 1. 8. 1–2; for the example see Plato, *Republic* 601d.

21. Aristotle seems to anticipate the subsequent introduction (5. 4) of "laborers" as a distinct "sort" of persons excluded from office.

22. This appears to be a reference to 1. 8–9, but the exact sense is uncertain.

23. Homer, *Iliad* 9. 648, 16. 59.

24. For Aristotle's "external discourses" see pp. 00–00 above.

25. These remarks seem to be directed at Athens in particular.

26. *Nicomachean Ethics* 1131a14–24.

27. Or, as the phrase is generally translated, "whether of the original sum or of the accruing profits." I take the remark to be the oligarchic response to a (democratic or aristocratic) argument for special treatment in consequence of descent from the original settlers.

28. The territory of Megara bordered that of Corinth, though the cities themselves were relatively distant.

29. The argument depends on the technical use of the word *atimoi* (literally, "those without honor") to designate persons judicially deprived of certain prerogatives of citizenship.

30. Or, as it is most generally understood, "[is a position giving rise to objections which] could be held to be refutable." The meaning and syntax of the phrase *doxeien an luesthai* are uncertain, and the soundness of the MSS here has been questioned. I share Newman's suspicion that something has dropped out of the text—at least the word *dei* ("in need of being"), and perhaps an entire line; I have supplied what I take to be the overall sense.

31. Cf. 2. 12. 2–3, 5–6.

32. Food in a raw or crude state; cf. *Generation of Animals* 728a26 ff.

33. Apparently a reference to *Nicomachean Ethics* 1131a9 ff. See pp. 00–00 above.

34. Reading *ei gar mallon to ti megethos* with the MSS rather than the conjectural *ei gar symballoito ti megethos* ("if height contributed something") adopted by Dreizehnter. The phrase, which is awkward in any event, has been variously understood.

35. Or "and height generally is more preeminent than virtue," as it is usually understood.

36. An apparent allusion to *Nicomachean Ethics* 1129b25–30a5.

37. "Where are your claws and teeth?" (Aesop, *Fables* 241). It is not known to what work of Antisthenes Aristotle here refers.

38. Ostracism was particularly employed in Athens in the fifth century, but appears to have fallen into disuse by Aristotle's time; see the account in *Constitution of Athens* 22. The fixed period seems to have been ten years originally, later five.

39. In the version of the myth to which Aristotle seems to be alluding, the ship Argo refused (through its speaking mast) to accept Heracles on account of his great weight.

40. The story is recounted at greater length in Herodotus 5. 92, though there it is Thrasyboulus (tyrant of Miletus) who gives the advice to Periander (tyrant of Corinth). Cf. 5. 11. 4–5.

41. It is not certain to what events Aristotle is referring. As the most powerful of the island states in the alliance formed by Athens after the Persian wars, Lesbos, Chios, and Samos were treated more favorably than the others (cf. *Constitution of Athens* 24). Samos was crushed by Athens in 440 B.C. when it revolted in protest against an Athenian prohibition of its prosecution of a local war; the humiliations in question were most probably similar attempts by Athens prior to this time to limit the autonomy of these allies.

42. A proverbial expression meaning "second best."

43. Or "is advantageous [for each regime] individually," as it is generally understood; but the phrase in question (*idiai sympherei*) seems to look back to 13. 20.

44. The meaning is somewhat uncertain. The phrase "splitting the offices" (*merizōn tas archas*) seems to refer to rotation in office (cf. 6. 5. 11); "this is almost as if they should claim to merit ruling over Zeus" is sometimes taken as a parenthetical remark.

45. Homer, *Iliad* 2. 391–93. The last phrase of the quotation is not found in our texts of Homer.

46. Aristotle uses the term *aisymnētai* (which probably derives from an expression meaning "those mindful of the auspices"), a magistracy that was generally (though not invariably) comparable to the dictatorship in Rome. It was usually created under unusual circumstances of civil disorder or external threat.

47. Alcaeus, fr. 87 Diehl.

48. Kingship of the "times of the heroes" (the period of the Trojan War as described in the poetry of Homer) was limited monarchy of a feudal type reflecting a predominantly rural and aristocratic society.

49. In later times all adjudication was done under oath; the remark seems intended to point to kingly prerogatives which had since disappeared.

50. For an account of the origins of the tyranny of Dionysius at Syracuse, see Diodorus Siculus 13. 85–94.

51. Reading *basileias* with the MSS rather than the conjectural *politeias* ("of regime") adopted by Dreizehnter. This was strongly implied, if not precisely said, in 15. 2–3.

52. Reading *panta* with the MSS rather than *pantōn* ("over all persons") with Dreizehnter (on the basis of a citation by Julian).

53. I follow Susemihl in suspecting a lacuna at this point in the text.

54. Or "for one person to have authority over all the citizens," as it is generally understood. But the phrase *kyrios pantōn* seems regularly used elsewhere (consider 14. 3) in the sense "have authority over all matters," and a limitation of kingly sovereignty over persons is nowhere discussed by Aristotle.

55. An allusion to the oath sworn by jurors at Athens.

56. Homer, *Iliad* 10. 224, 2. 372.

57. Reading this passage (a10–15) with the MSS rather than as rearranged by Dreizehnter. Aristotle's argument is intelligible as it stands if the word "multitude" (*plēthos*) is understood in a narrower as well as a wider sense—as the equivalent of the "governing body" in a polity or aristocracy (consider 13. 6, 15. 9, 18. 1).

58. Reading *pantes* with Π² rather than *pantēi* ("entirely") with Π¹ and Dreizehnter.

59. 3. 13. 24–25.

60. The comparison seems to be suggested by the fact that the same word (*meros*) means both "turn" and "part."

61. 3. 4–5.

62. This sentence, which is incomplete in the MSS, is repeated vebatim at the beginning of book 7. See pp. 00–00 above.

Book 4

1. Possibly a reference to 2. 1. 1, though it is generally taken to be to the immediate context.

2. Reading *hekastēs* with Dreizehnter; but *hekastois* ("for each individually") has some manuscript authority, and is perhaps right.

3. Or, as this clause is generally understood, "but laws are distinct from the things that are indicative of the regime [*nomoi de kechōrismenoi tōn dēlountōn tēn politeian*], and it is in accordance with them that the rulers must rule and guard against those transgressing them." But the general argument is concerned to establish the *connection* between laws and the regime; and Aristotle seems to be thinking specifically here of "constitutional" laws regulating the tenure of officials (cf. 3. 16. 3) and protecting against legislative subversion of the regime (cf. 1. 6. 2).

4. 3. 6–8.

5. This is often referred to 3. 14–18, but the only real discussion of aristocracy as the best regime occurs in 7. See pp. 00–00 above.

6. Or, as it is generally understood, "when kingship should be established." My rendering gives the normal meaning of *nomizein*.

7. The reference would seem to be particularly to 3. 15–16.

8. Or "from polity," as it is sometimes taken; but both alternatives pose difficulties. What is wanted instead is a reference to kingship, and it is just possible that something of this kind has dropped out of the text here.

9. Plato, *Statesman* 302e–03a.

10. These topics appear to correspond respectively to 4. 3–6, 4. 7–11, 4. 12–13, 4. 14–16, and 5.

11. This is often referred to 3. 12. 8–9, but the reference would seem rather to be to 7. 7–9.

12. This clause, sometimes bracketed as an interpolation, is usually understood to mean "[some equality common to] the badly off or the well off, or some [equality] common to both"; it has also been explained as "[the power of] the badly off or the well off, or [the power] common to both."

13. This view seems to underlie Plato's treatment of the modes or harmonies (*Republic* 399a–c), which is generally taken as reflecting the musical doctrines of the school of Damon.

14. The interpretation of this passage has been much disputed. I retain *harmonias* in a26 instead of bracketing the word with Immisch and Dreizehnter ("from the well-blended regime as well as from the best regime"); and I understand the final clause as referring to harmonies instead of regimes, as it is generally assumed to do, and take the word *despotikōteras* ("closer to rule of a master") as predicate rather than subject. The "well-blended harmony" would seem to be Mixed Lydian, which forms a mean between the extremes of "taut" Lydian (*syntonolydisti*) and Phrygian on the one hand and the "relaxed" Lydian and Ionian harmonies on the other; and the second of the "one or two" well-constituted harmonies would seem to be Dorian (see 8. 5. 22). The implicit comparison, then, would appear to be between Mixed Lydian and polity—a "mixture" of oligarchy and democracy (4. 8. 3); and the "one or two" well-constituted regimes would seem to be (at least if the parallel is meant to be exact) polity and aristocracy.

15. Herodotus 3. 20.

16. The war between Colophon and the kingdom of Lydia occurred in the first half of the seventh century. Cf. Herodotus 1. 14.

17. Reading *eidē* with the MSS rather than the conjectural *eiē* adopted by Dreizehnter.

18. Cf. 2. 2. 3, 3. 1. 2, 7. 8. 7–9.

19. Cf. Plato, *Republic* 369d–71e.

20. The omission of a sixth element in the enumeration suggests a lacuna in the text at this point; the parallel account in 7. 8. 7–9 points to the priesthood as the missing element. Another possibility is that the deliberative and judicial functions are implicitly considered a single element, as they seem to be in 4. 17 (and in 7. 8. 7 and 9).

21. Or "certain political men who share in virtue," or possibly "certain persons who share in virtue as it relates to political things."

22. Homer, *Iliad* 2. 204.

23. Probably a reference to Plato, *Republic* 557c–58c.

24. Something may be wrong with the text here. *Politeia* is often explained as meaning "citizen body," but it is doubtful whether Aristotle elsewhere uses the word in this sense.

25. This sentence has been differently understood. The words *autoi hairontai* ("they themselves elect") appear to refer to a process of cooptation by which the officials themselves would choose their successors (in contrast to the first variety, where election to office is by the entire citizen body). But they have sometimes been taken to refer to the entire citizen body, and the process interpreted (in the light of 6. 9) as involving the admission of noncitizens to citizenship.

26. Text and meaning are uncertain. I follow the text of Dreizehnter (apart from his unnecessary supplement) rather than the reconstruction of Rassow, but suspect a lacuna following *to men* at the end of b31; I have supplied what I take to be the sense. There would seem to be little question that the term *prosodoi* refers to state revenues.

27. Or possibly "they make the law a thing of this sort," i.e., the ruling authority.

28. Or perhaps "they use only the four, as Plato does in the [section of his work treating] regimes," i.e., *Republic* 8–9. Plato's enumeration includes, beside an aristocracy of philosophers, timocracy (or "so-called aristocracy" on the model of Sparta), oligarchy, democracy, and tyranny. It is not known to what other authorities Aristotle is here referring.

29. The reference appears to be to the discussion of the best regime in 7–8, rather than to the various allusions to aristocracy in 3 (consider particularly 7. 3, where the definition given of aristocracy seems clearly intended to be a generic one).

30. This is usually referred to 3. 7. 5, but the reference seems to be rather to 4. 2, if the translation given here (which accepts the interpretation though not the supplement of Thurot) is correct.

31. Text and meaning are uncertain. The expression *to tēs politeias eidos kaleitai* is explained by Newman as "the form which is called polity exists," but it is hardly clear how this idiomatic sense of *kalein* helps to make sense of the larger context; others have suggested a variety of emen-

dations, none very satisfying. I believe something has dropped out of the text, and supply what I take to be the sense.

32. Or "disputing for equal treatment in the regime," as it is usually translated; but the reference appears to be to the fundamental discussion of democratic and oligarchic views of the *meaning* of equality in 3. 9.

33. A "tally" (*symbolon*) was one of two halves of a token which two contracting parties broke between them for purposes of identification.

34. Bracketing *exothen* with Thurot.

35. 3. 14–17.

36. E.g., *Nicomachean Ethics* 1101a14–16.

37. Text and meaning are uncertain. I accept Bernays's conjectural *phygarchousi* ("avoid ruling") for the *phylarchousi* or *philarchousi* of the MSS; but the verbs *phygarchein* and *boularchein* (in the sense of "wish to rule") are found nowhere else, and the entire clause may be corrupt or out of place (it is bracketed by Dreizehnter as a gloss). It is perhaps possible to take it to mean that both rich and poor (and not the middle class, the apparent antecedent of "these") shun public service as cavalry commander (*phylarchos*) or head of council (*boularchos*), but this is not very satisfactory in its immediate context.

38. Phocylides, fr. 12 Diehl.

39. The reference appears to be to 5. 8. 7.

40. For Solon see *Constitution of Athens* 5 and Plutarch, *Solon* 1 and 14; the view that Lycurgus was king at Sparta and therefore a wealthy man appears, for example, in Plutarch, *Lycurgus* 3 and *Solon* 16 (but cf. *Cleomenes* 10).

41. The reference is to the Athenians and the Spartans respectively.

42. The identity of this individual has been much disputed. Solon and Theramenes are commonly cited as possibilities, but what seems wanted is the leader of a hegemonial state; the most plausible candidates would appear to be Philip of Macedon and Antipater, both of whom could have been exposed to "persuasion" in this connection by Aristotle himself. Cf. p. 00 above.

43. Here and in the rest of this chapter, *politeia* is frequently taken to be used in its generic sense of "regime" rather than in its specific sense of "polity," though I think wrongly (consider particularly the reference to polities which seems implicit in the text in a6–7).

44. *Politeia* is here frequently taken in its generic sense. But the reference back to this passage in 5. 8. 2–4 confirms what is indicated at the end of 4. 12, that the use of such devices is characteristic of "well-blended" regimes—polities and aristocracies that approach polities.

45. That is, to decline office with an oath supporting the claim that it would be unduly burdensome for financial or other reasons.

46. The practice of governing through joint official boards (*synarchiai*) seems to have become fairly common by Aristotle's day. The "smallest parts" referred to here would seem to be political subdivisions of the type of the "quarters" (*dēmoi*) of Athens. Nothing else is known of Telecles of Miletus.

47. Text and meaning are somewhat uncertain. I read *politōn* ("among the citizens") with one MS rather than *politikōn* with most MSS and Dreizehnter. Retaining *politikōn*, the meaning could be either "where the popular sort greatly exceed the political sort in number," or "where the popular sort among political [men] greatly exceed [the notables] in number." The parts of the city referred to here would seem to be administrative divisions such as tribes or quarters rather than social classes. All of these devices are intended to increase the participation of the upper classes in decision making in democracies.

48. Probably an office created on an occasional basis for rationing purposes.

49. Apparently, a spit that could also serve as a lamp holder, i.e., with a dual purpose.

50. Reading *dei* with the MSS rather than the conjecture adopted by Dreizehnter.

51. Reading *poiōn* and *polla* with Thurot and Dreizehnter rather than *poia* and *pollōn* with the MSS ("what sort of boards should supervise many matters").

52. Reading *euporia tis ēi ē misthos* with the MSS rather than *euporia tis ēi misthou* ("are well off through pay") with Spengel and Dreizehnter.

53. Reading *treis* with the MSS rather than *duo* ("two") with Schneider and Dreizehnter. In each case there are two simple varieties and a third formed by combining them.

54. Possibly a reference to the overthrow of the democracy at Megara in 424 B.C. (Thucydides 4. 66–74), but this is not certain.

55. Bracketing *ē* with Newman. Throughout this much-disputed passage I adhere to the order of the MSS rather than to the reconstructions offered by Dreizehnter or others.

56. Accepting the supplement of Dreizehnter.

57. Reading *kai* with Π² rather than *kai ē* with Π¹ and Dreizehnter.

58. The twelve modes are: all selecting from all by election or lot or both, all selecting from some by election or lot or both, some selecting from all by election or lot or both, some selecting from some by election or lot or both. The other two conjunctions are when selection is done by both some and all, and when it is done from both some and all.

59. Bracketing *ginesthai* with Dreizehnter. It seems possible that a line has dropped out of the text at this point.

60. Accepting the supplement of Newman.

61. The text and meaning of this sentence (all of which is bracketed by Dreizehnter) are uncertain and much disputed. But the basic argument seems clear: what is being discussed are the nondemocratic variants of polity. The minimum supplement would appear to be *ē pantas hairesei* ("or offices are selected by election") in b1.

62. Accepting the supplement of Lambinus.

63. 6. 8.

64. These four courts closely correspond to Athenian practice. All unpremeditated murders (as well as killings of slaves and foreigners) fell under the jurisdiction of the second court; the third dealt with cases where the killing could be argued to be accidental or otherwise "just" or justified. In the court at Phreatto the defendant argued his case from a boat anchored off shore. See *Constitution of Athens* 57. 3–4.

65. Retaining *kai* rather than bracketing it with Spengel and Dreizehnter; the reference would seem to be to the earlier discussion of officials.

66. Something appears to have dropped out of the text here; I translate the supplement of Newman.

67. Bracketing *ē* ("or") with Susemihl and Dreizehnter.

Book 5

1. 3. 9. 1–4, 12. 1–2.

2. Aristotle alludes to the etymology of *pleonektein* ("to aggrandize themselves"), which literally means "to seek to have more," "to take a greater share."

3. It is not clear whether Lycurgus sought to abolish the monarchy simply or only the hereditary rule of the Heracleidae. The Pausanias in question is apparently the victor of the battle of Plataea during the Persian Wars (cf. 7. 4, 7. 14. 20).

4. The change described, of which nothing further is known, appears to have been from a restricted oligarchy to a moderate oligarchy or polity.

5. The reference is probably to an oligarchical revolution in 390 B.C. (cf. Diodorus Siculus 14. 97).

6. The battle of Oenophyta occurred in 457 B.C.; it is not known when the democracy at Thebes was replaced by the oligarchy that governed there during the Peloponnesian War. Gelon seized power at Syracuse in 491 B.C. It is not known to what events the allusion to Megara refers.

7. This occurred in 473 B.C.; see Diodorus Siculus 11. 52, Herodotus 7. 70.

8. Probably a reference to the day of the month on which the battle was fought (cf. Plutarch, *On the Virtues of Women* 4), but the meaning is uncertain. For the wars of Cleomenes against Argos (early fifth century) see Herodotus 6. 76–83.

9. During the Peloponnesian War, the Athenian army was drawn from a list of citizens of the wealthier classes, while the navy was manned by the poorer citizens. In Aristotle's time the army consisted primarily of mercenaries.

10. Nothing is known of this event.

11. Accepting the standard view of *kai* as epexegetic; but something may be wrong with the text here. Oreus (also known by its older name Hestiaea; cf. 4. 4), a town in Euboea, revolted from Sparta and joined the Second Athenian League in 377 B.C.; the change in regime may have been connected with this event.

12. Nothing else is known of this revolution at Ambracia.

13. Literally, "until they draw breath together," like horses in harness; cf. Plato, *Laws* 708d.

14. Nothing else is known of these events, or of the curse (presumably connected with the destruction of Sybaris in 510 B.C.).

15. For this incident see Diodorus Siculus 12. 11. 1, Strabo 6. 1. 13.

16. Nothing is known of the events at Byzantium or Antissa. The factional struggle at Zancle (Messina) was the result of the influx of refugees there following the suppression of the revolt of the Ionians against Persian rule in 494 B.C.; see Herodotus 6. 22–24.

17. Nothing is known of the events at Apollonia; the reference to Syracuse is to the period following the fall of the tyrant Thrasyboulus in 467 B.C. (cf. Diodorus Siculus 11. 72. 3); the expulsion of the original Athenian colonists of Amphipolis and the incorporation of the city into the Chalcidian Confederation probably occurred around 370 B.C.

18. This paragraph seems out of place here; Newman has suggested transposing it to follow 1. 5 (1301a39).

19. Chytrus was evidently a mainland dependency of the island city of Clazomenae; Notium was the port of Colophon. Nothing is known of the events referred to.

20. The episide is usually referred to the period of the oligarchy of the Gamori at Syracuse shortly before its overthrow by the people and the subsequent seizure of power by the tyrant Gelon in 485 B.C. Cf. Plutarch, *Precepts for Governing a Republic* 32.

21. This sentence turns on an untranslatable pun on the word *archē*, which means both "beginning" and "rule" or "government." "The beginning is half of the whole" was a common Greek proverb.

22. The episode, of which nothing else is known, must have occurred between 479 B.C. and the absorption of Hestiaea by Athens in 446.

23. More details are given by Plutarch, *Precepts for Governing a Republic* 32.

24. For the revolt of Mytilene against Athens during the Peloponnesian War, see Thucydides 3. 2.

25. Nothing else is known of this conflict or its relationship to political events in Phocis or to the outbreak of the Sacred War between Phocis and the Amphictyonic League in 356 B.C. Mnason is said to have been a friend of Aristotle's.

26. It is not certain whether this is the same revolution referred to in 1. 10–11.

27. The lowest class of Athenians (the so-called Thetes) had been excluded from all military pursuits prior to their enlistment as rowers in the fleet at the time of the battle of Salamis in 480 B.C. Cf. *Constitution of Athens* 23; Plutarch, *Themistocles* 10.

28. For this oligarchic revolution at Argos (418 B.C.), which was short-lived, see Thucydides 5. 72. 3, Diodorus Siculus 12. 75. 79–80.

29. The responsibility of the Syracusan people for the victory over Athens in 413 B.C. does not emerge clearly from the account of Thucydides, but Aristotle may have in mind particularly the showing of the Syracusan fleet (Thucydides 7. 41, 55). The primary democratic development occurring at this time appears to have been the use of the lot in the selection of officials; cf. Diodorus Siculus 13. 34. 6.

30. Nothing is known of this event.

31. This occurred around 580 B.C. (Plutarch, *Amatorius* 23); see further 10. 16.

32. The reference is to the oligarchic regime of 411 B.C. in Athens.

33. Nothing is known of this event.

34. Cf. 3. 4. Apparently, the popular leaders used money that was to be used for ship construction or repair to provide subsidies to the people for attendance at the assembly or similar activities.

35. The city is probably Heracleia on the Black Sea, colonized from Megara in the middle of the sixth century; nothing else is known of these events.

36. Nothing is known of this event, which is evidently the same one referred to in 3. 5.

37. Nothing is known of this event.

38. Possibly the tyranny of Thrasyboulus (Herodotus 1. 20), but the reference is uncertain.

39. Pisistratus became tyrant of Athens in 560 B.C. after making himself champion of the popular faction ("those of the hill") against the oligarchic faction ("those of the plain"); see Herodotus 1. 59–64, *Constitution of Athens* 13 ff.

40. Nothing is known of the incident involving Theagenes, tyrant of Megara in the seventh century. For the events connected with the accession of Dionysius as tyrant of Syracuse in 405 B.C., see Diodorus Siculus 13. 85–96.

41. Lygdamis became tyrant of Naxos around 540 B.C.; see Herodotus 1. 61 and 64, *Constitution of Athens* 15.

42. That is, apparently, from persons or groups other than the oligarchs themselves.

43. Little is known of the internal history of these cities. For Massilia (Marseilles) cf. 6. 7. 4; the Heracleia in question is probably the one on the Black Sea (cf. 5. 3), where Istrus was also located.

44. Nothing else is known of these events; the occasion referred to in 6. 16 would appear to be different.

45. Nothing is known of this event. The Basilid family was presumably descended from the original kings of the city.

46. The regime of the Thirty Tyrants ruled Athens in 404/3 B.C., that of the Four Hundred in 411. See *Constitution of Athens* 28–38.

47. Nothing is known of the nature of these officials. For the term *politophylakes*, see 2. 8. 9.

48. Regimes based on oligarchic "clubs" (*hetairiai*) were set up by the Spartan admiral Lysander after the battle of Aegospotami (Plutarch, *Lysander* 13). A regime of this sort may have arisen at Abydus at the time of its revolt from Athens in 411 B.C.

49. Nothing is known of this event. Cf. 5. 3, 6. 2–3.

50. See Diodorus Siculus 13. 92–94.

51. Nothing is known of these events. Amphipolis had been originally settled by Athenians, who remained few in comparison with inhabitants drawn from the region.

52. Chares was an Athenian mercenary commander; the attempted subversion of the Aeginetan government may have occurred while he was stationed in Corinth in 367 B.C., but nothing else is known of the incident.

53. Nothing is known of this event.

54. Nothing is known of the oligarchy of Pharsalus in Aristotle's time; the city had had a recent history of factional conflict (cf. Xenophon, *Hellenica* 6. 1. 2 ff.), and was a political dependency of Macedon after 350 B.C.

55. Little else is known of the internal politics of Elis.

56. Timophanes made himself tyrant of Corinth during the war with Argos (350 B.C.); he was subsequently killed by his brother Timoleon (Plutarch, *Timoleon* 4).

57. The Aleuads were one of the great feudal clans of Thessaly; Simus is probably the Simus of Larissa who helped bring Thessaly into subjection to Philip of Macedon in 342 B.C. (Demosthenes, *On the Crown* 48, *Philippics* 3. 26). Nothing is known of the incident in Abydus.

58. The earlier discussion is 4. 5–7. Nothing else is known of the overthrow of the Eretrian oligarchy (cf. *Constitution of Athens* 15).

59. Nothing is known of these events.

60. Nothing is known of the revolution in Chios; for Cnidus cf. 6. 4.

61. The Partheniae are variously said to have been the illegitimate offspring of Spartan fathers or Spartan mothers or disenfranchised citizens at the time of the First Messenian War in the late eighth century B.C. "Peers" (*homoioi*, literally "similars") was a term used of the Spartiates, the Spartan citizen class.

62. Lysander was the outstanding Spartan admiral of the final stage of the Peloponnesian War; for these incidents, see Xenophon, *Hellenica* 2. 4. 29, Plutarch, *Lysander* 23. For the conspiracy of Cinadon in 398 B.C., see Xenophon, *Hellenica* 3. 3. 4–11.

63. The reference is to the Second Messenian War in the seventh century B.C. Tyrtaeus' "Good Management" (*Eunomia*) is extant (frs. 2–5 Diehl).

64. For Pausanias cf. 1. 10 and 7. 14. 20. Hanno is probably the Carthaginian general who fought in Sicily against the elder Dionysius of Syracuse around 400 B.C. (Justin 20. 5. 11 ff., 22. 7. 10), but this is not certain.

65. A line appears to have dropped out of the text at this point; I have supplied what I take to be the sense.

66. Nothing else is known of these events at Thurii (which are probably unrelated to those mentioned in 3. 12). I follow Dreizehnter in assuming a lacuna, and supply what I take to be the sense.

67. Cf. 2. 9. 13 ff.

68. The reference is to the tyranny exercised at Locri (in southern Italy) during the 350s by Dionysius the Younger, son of Dionysius the Elder of Syracuse and a Locrian woman. See Diodorus Siculus 14. 44. 6.

69. The last phrase is probably a later gloss. Cf. 3. 10.

70. Nothing else is known of these events. Cf. 7. 9, 3. 12.

71. The reference is to the period of the Peloponnesian War. Cf. 4. 11. 18–19.

72. These expressions were commonly used to refer to the world or the universe.

73. Cf. 4. 13. 1–5.

74. Cf. 6. 5–6.

75. Reading *koinou* ("common") with the MSS rather than *kainou* ("new") with Coraes and Dreizehnter: the "common assessment" is clearly a valuation of the total assets of the citizen body. What the passage as a whole argues primarily is the need to adjust property qualifications to take account of inflation or deflation in the currency.

76. The first case reflects a deflationary, the second an inflationary situation.

77. The words *kai en monarchiai* are omitted in Π²; Dreizehnter brackets them as a gloss, probably rightly.

78. Or possibly "but rather to attempt to give small prerogatives over a long period of time or great ones briefly," reading *brachy* instead of the odd *tachy* ("quickly") of the MSS. It is also conceivable that something has dropped out of the text here.

79. The meaning of the word *parastaseis* ("sojourns") is not entirely certain: though usually considered to involve some form of ostracism (cf. Plato, *Laws* 855c), it could perhaps refer merely to official missions such as embassies or military commands.

80. The term *lochos* is usually found in military contexts; here it perhaps refers to an organization of the common messes (cf. 2. 5. 17).

81. Or simply "a question arises," if Dreizehnter is correct in bracketing *pōs chrē poieisthai tēn hairesin* as a gloss.

82. The argument is that knowledge and the proper disposition do not guarantee the proper action because men lacking in virtue will be unable to control their passions. There is a further question, however, as to whether even an education to virtue can guarantee control of the passions. For an extended treatment of "lack of self-control" (*akrasia*) see *Nicomachean Ethics* 1145a15–52a36.

83. Cf. 4. 9. 10, 12. 1.

84. This sentence has been variously understood. The awkward language may conceal textual corruption; an easy emendation (*tous* for *tois* in 1310a1) would provide some improvement: "in destroying by laws those who enjoy preeminence [*phtheirontes tous kath' hyperochēn nomois*] they destroy the regimes." The implicit argument would seem to be that the destruction of the well off in democracies invariably prepares the way for tyranny.

85. Reading *kai ison* ("and equality") with the MSS rather than bracketing the phrase with Spengel and Dreizehnter.

86. Euripides, fr. 891 Nauck[2] (from an unknown play).

87. Throughout this chapter, a distinction is implied between "monarchies"—personal rule whether kingly or tyrannical—and "regimes" (*politeiai*) in the sense of republican or constitutional political orders. Cf. 3. 15. 11.

88. Pheidon was tyrant of Argos in the middle of the seventh century. Thrasyboulus of Miletus, one of the best known of the Ionian tyrants, had risen from general, as was also the case with Phalaris of Agrigentum (cf. *Rhetoric* 1393b10 ff.).

89. According to legend, Codrus saved Athens from a Dorian invasion while already king; whether some other event is referred to is uncertain. The elder Cyrus liberated the Persians from the rule of the Medes and became the first king of the Persian Empire in the middle of the sixth century. The territory acquired by Sparta to which reference is made is most probably Messenia. For the origins of Macedonia see Herodotus 8. 138; for the Molossian kingdom, see Plutarch, *Pyrrhus* 1.

90. This was done, for example, by the Thirty at Athens (Xenophon, *Hellenica* 2. 4. 1).

91. Cf. 3. 13. 17.

92. For the fall of the Pisistratid tyranny at Athens, see *Constitution of Athens* 18, Thucydides 6. 54.

93. For Periander cf. 4. 9. Philip of Macedon was murdered by the youth Pausanias in 336 B.C. (Diodorus Siculus 16. 91–94); nothing is known of the incident involving Derdas and Amyntas, who was almost certainly another Macedonian king; a fuller account of the murder of Euagoras of Cyprus in 374/3 B.C. is provided by Theopompus (*FGH* 115F103. 12).

94. For the murder of Archelaus of Macedon in 399 B.C., see Diodorus Siculus 14. 37. 5, Aelian 8. 9, Plutarch, *Amatorius* 23.

95. Cotys, king of the Thracians, was murdered in 359 B.C.

96. The Penthilids were apparently the leading family in the oligarchy of Mytilene; these events (which date from the seventh century) are alluded to in the poetry of Alcaeus (fr. 22 ff. Diehl).

97. For the murder of Xerxes, the Persian king, in 465 B.C., see Diodorus Siculus 11. 69, Justin 3. 1, Ctesias, *FGH* 688F13.33.

98. The reference to "retailers of stories" (*hoi mythologountes*) would seem to be particularly to Ctesias, the historian of the Persian court (see *FGH* 688F1. 23–27 for his account of Sardanapalos). For the fall of Dionysius II of Syracuse in 357 B.C., see Plutarch, *Dion* 22 ff.

99. Aristotle appears to assume, contrary to most authorities, that Cyrus was not also the grandson of Astyages, the king of the Medes; cf. Herodotus 1. 107–30, Ctesias, *FGH* 688F9. For Seuthes and Amadocus, king of the Odrysians, cf. Xenophon, *Hellenica* 4. 8. 26.

100. Probably a reference to the Ariobarzanes who was satrap of the Persian province of Pontus in the mid-fourth century, but this is not certain. A lacuna or some dislocation in the text has been suspected here.

101. A proverbial expression for the rivalry of like with like (*Works and Days* 22 ff.).

102. This compressed and obscure account of the fall of the dynasty of Gelon in Syracuse (466 B.C.) almost certainly involves textual corruption: probably several lines have been lost describing the intervention of other elements in the city in the quarrel between Thrasyboulus and the adherents of Gelon's son; I have tried to supply the sense. It is stated in 12. 6 that Thrasyboulus ruled as tyrant for ten months following the death of Hiero; it would seem that he was able to eliminate Gelon's son from the succession, but only at the price of fatally weakening the position of the entire family with respect to the notables or some section of them, who rose up and instituted an aristocracy or polity. Cf. Diodorus Siculus 11. 66–67.

103. Cf. 2. 9. 29–30, 3. 14. 3–4. The attribution of the establishment of the overseers to Theopompus, king of Sparta in the late eighth century B.C., is not found before Aristotle; cf. Plato, *Laws* 692a. Little is known of the political institutions of the relatively primitive Molossians; cf. Plutarch, *Pyrrhus* 5.

104. The term *scholai* ("leisured discussions") is probably meant to apply to gatherings for philosophical and literary discussion of the sort represented in many Platonic dialogues, as well

as to "schools" such as Aristotle's Lyceum; other "meetings connected with leisure" (*syllogoi scholastikoi*) probably include gatherings at gymnasia and social and religious functions.

105. A practice of Persian origin; see Xenophon, *Education of Cyrus* 8. 1. 6–8, 16–20.

106. This was also a well-known Persian practice (Xenophon, *Education of Cyrus* 8. 2. 10–12). For its use by the tyrants of Syracuse, see Plutarch, *Dion* 28.

107. The meaning of this phrase is uncertain; it seems to refer to the ability of the citizens to afford heavy arms, but the word *phylakē* has sometimes been interpreted as implying some sort of standing military force. Absence of heavy arms would seem to be the "incapacity" referred to in 16.

108. The monuments of the Cypselids (the family of Periander of Corinth) were votive statues erected in the sanctuaries in Olympia and Delphi, the most noteworthy being a colossal golden statue of Zeus at Olympia (cf. Plato, *Phaedrus* 236b). The temple of Olympian Zeus at Athens was begun by Pisistratus (cf. Pausanias 1. 18. 6–9). The exact sense of the reference to Polycrates is uncertain; I take it to refer to statuary rather than temple structures (cf. Herodotus 3. 60).

109. The meaning of the phrase "incapacity for activity" (*adynamia tōn pragmatōn*) is uncertain, but Aristotle seems to have in mind economic and military as well as political weakness; cf. 10 and n. 101 above.

110. The word *dynamis* ("power") can also refer to a military force, and it is possible that Aristotle thinks primarily or exclusively of the tyrant's bodyguard.

111. Accepting Madvig's conjectural *polemikēs* for the *politikēs* ("political") of the MSS.

112. That is, spiritedness seeks satisfaction even if the price is death. Heraclitus, fr. 85 Diels-Kranz.

113. The tyranny of Orthagoras at Sicyon was instituted in 670 B.C.; Cleisthenes was his great-grandson. Cf. Herodotus 6. 126.

114. Cf. *Constitution of Athens* 16, Plutarch, *Solon* 31.

115. Accepting the conjectural *hemisy* ("half") in place of the *tettara* ("four") of the MSS.

116. The tyranny at Corinth was instituted in about 657 B.C. Cf. Herodotus 5. 92, Aristotle, fr. 611. 20 Rose.

117. Cf. *Constitution of Athens* 17 and 19.

118. For the tyranny at Syracuse see 10. 31. This entire passage (1–6) has often been bracketed by editors as an interpolation.

119. Plato, *Republic* 545c ff.

120. Plato, *Republic* 546c. The allusion is to the notorious riddle of the "nuptial number," which Socrates claims should define the periods for breeding in his best regime. Interpretation of the mathematics involved is highly uncertain.

121. Cleisthenes was apparently the brother of Myron (Nicolaus of Damascus, *FGH* 90F61); nothing is known of Antileon. In 10. 30, Aristotle indicates that the regime succeeding Gelo's tyranny at Syracuse was an aristocracy or polity rather than a democracy. For Charilaus cf. 2. 10. 2 and Aristotle, fr. 611. 10 Rose. That a tyranny once existed at Carthage is often held to contradict 2. 11. 2; but there Aristotle seems to refer to tyrants arising after the establishment of the republican regime. Loss of the name of the Carthaginian tyrant in the present passage has often been suspected.

122. Panaetius is also mentioned in 10. 6. For Cleander, see Herodotus 7. 154 ff.; for Anaxilaus, Herodotus 6. 23, 7. 165, 170. Rhegium was actually on the Italian mainland opposite Sicily.

123. Accepting Newman's conjectural *timokratoumenēi* for the *dēmokratoumenēi* ("democratically run") of the MSS. Cf. 6. 5. 9 as well as the thematic discussion of the Carthaginian regime in 2. 11. It would be natural for Aristotle to use the Platonic term for (conventional) aristocracy in this context.

124. Plato, *Republic* 551d ff.

125. Plato, *Republic* 555c–d.

126. The text here is almost certainly corrupt. A lacuna is probably to be marked after *ousian* ("property") in 23, as is done by Susemihl, Immisch, and others, as the latter part of this sentence seems to refer not to the transition from oligarchy to democracy but to that from democracy

to tyranny (cf. *Republic* 557b). The abrupt ending of the book has led to the suspicion that additional material may have been lost as well.

Book 6

1. 4. 14–5. 12.

2. Two themes appear to be announced here: the varieties of democracy and the (institutional) "modes" appropriate to them, and possible "aggregations" of such modes forming hybrid "conjunctions" of a variety of different regimes. A discussion of democracy (and derivatively of oligarchy) occupies chapters 1–7. Chapter 8, which deals with the varieties and functions of offices, would appear to be preparatory to a discussion of the second theme, which is missing from book 6 and the *Politics* as we have it.

3. 4. 12.

4. 4. 4. 20–21.

5. 5. 9.

6. 4. 15. 12–13.

7. This was an established practice in democratic Athens; see, for example, *Constitution of Athens* 43. 3, 62. 2.

8. This sentence is bracketed by Dreizehnter as an interpolation, almost certainly rightly.

9. This was notably the case in regard to the institution of kingship, at Athens and elsewhere; cf. 3. 14. 13.

10. It seems necessary to assume a lacuna in the text at this point.

11. 3. 10. 1–2.

12. 4. 6. 1–6. Five varieties of democracy are listed in 4. 4. 22–25; but one of these appears to be the democracy based on equality of rich and poor that is discussed in 5. 2. 9–3.

13. Reading *mē* ("not") with the MSS rather than bracketing the word with Bojesen and Dreizehnter.

14. Nothing further is known of this arrangement at Mantinea.

15. Oxylus was an ancient legislator of Elis. Nothing else is known of the legislation of Aphytis, and the meaning of the text is somewhat uncertain: the town, like its neighbor Potideia, had probably been settled as a colony, with citizenship restricted to those owning the equivalent of an original allotment of land; later, as a result of an increasing population, the assessment was evidently reduced to ownership of some small fraction of this allotment.

16. The reference is perhaps to civil disturbances at Cyrene in 401 B.C. (Diodorus Siculus 14. 34).

17. For the reforms of Cleisthenes, see *Constitution of Athens* 21. The reference to Cyrene is probably to the establishment of democracy there around 462 B.C.

18. The allusion is to the myth of the daughters of Danaus, who were punished in Hades for murdering their husbands by having to pour water into a leaking jar.

19. Cf. 2. 11. 15.

20. Nothing is known of this arrangement. As Tarentum was a colony of Sparta, however, it is likely that the practice of common use of property there was similar to the Spartan practice (2. 5. 7–8).

21. The meaning is somewhat uncertain. Aristotle is generally taken to argue that the offices at Tarentum were of two kinds, those chosen by election and those chosen by lot; yet such an arrangement would not have been particularly distinctive. The precise language used would seem to suggest instead that each office had both an elective component and one chosen by lot—presumably, a popular "overseer" on the Spartan model. If this interpretation is correct, Aristotle's parenthetical remark would also have to be understood as referring to rotation in office rather than to a simultaneous sharing of office by officials chosen by election and by lot.

22. Particularly in the hands of skilled mercenary commanders, "light-armed" (*psiloi*) troops had become of increasing military significance during the fourth century; most commonly their armament consisted of a javelin and a small shield, but specialized forces of archers and slingers also existed in certain areas. Aristotle appears to counsel training in such specialities (which may

be the "auxiliary" (*koupha*) arms referred to here; cf. 8. 15) for all of the oligarchic youth, and the establishment of a select force drawn from the oligarchs themselves.

23. For Thebes cf. 3. 5. 6–7. Nothing else is known of the arrangement at Massilia.

24. That is, apparently, to erect a public building or monument.

25. 4. 15. 22.

26. 4. 15. 7–8.

27. Reading *estin de* with the MSS rather than *estin d' hou* with Thurot and Dreizehnter ("while in others a single office has authority").

28. That is, with the collection of fines and of public debts. The official chiefly concerned with these matters at Athens was called an "actioner" (*praktōr*).

29. Accepting the reading of the MSS rather than the emendation of Dreizehnter; but something may have dropped out of the text here.

30. Reading *diēirētai* ("distinguished from") with the MSS rather than the conjecture of Niemeyer and Dreizehnter. It is true that the Eleven at Athens (the officials in charge of prisons) do appear to have had some role in the collection of public debts, but the "actioners" nevertheless constituted a separate magistracy.

31. This sentence is clearly incomplete in the original.

Book 7

1. It is not known to what work Aristotle refers. For the general problem of the "external discourses," see pp. 00–00 above.

2. Reading *hyparchein* with the MSS and *chrē* with Π^1 ("ought to be available") rather than bracketing *chrē* on the basis of its omission in Π^2 and reading *hyparchei* ("are available") with Dreizehnter.

3. Reading *estin hōn* with the MSS ("belongs among those things an excess of which") rather than *eis ti ·hon* ("is for some purpose; of these an excess") with Immisch and Dreizehnter.

4. Here and throughout this discussion, the phrases "act finely" (*kalōs prattein*) and "act well" (*eu prattein*) bear their idiomatic meaning "do well" or "prosper."

5. The reference would appear to be to 7. 13, but this is not certain.

6. That is, a "real man": *anēr* here clearly carries a strong connotation of maleness or manliness.

7. Π^1 has *tous polemious* ("enemies") instead of *tous polemous* ("wars"), perhaps rightly.

8. Reading *despozon* (twice) with the MSS rather than *desposton* ("that which is to be mastered and that which is not to be mastered") with Schneider and Dreizehnter.

9. 7. 13–15.

10. 1. 4–7.

11. The reference would seem to be to the discussion of candidate best regimes in book 2.

12. The term "good management" (*eunomia*) is etymologically related to the term "law" (*nomos*), but is suggestive of a condition of orderliness going beyond the observance of legal norms as such.

13. A line appears to have dropped out of the text at this point; I have supplied what I take to be the sense.

14. The proverbial Stentor was one of Homer's warriors (*Iliad* 5. 785–86).

15. Or "in magnitude" (*plēthei*); but Aristotle is perhaps thinking of the size of individual land holdings as well as the overall size of the territory. The awkwardness of the transition here and the fact that the question of the quality of the territory is not clearly exhausted (it appears to be returned to in 3–4) suggest that something may have been omitted from the text.

16. There is no discussion of this kind in the remainder of the *Poltics* as we have it. A plausible emendation (*autēs* for the *autēn* of the MSS) would give "the use of it" instead of "use itself."

17. The reference is probably to different systems of laws and customs concerning property (the Spartan and the Carthaginian?); but Aristotle may also have in mind differing philosophical views—in particular those of the Cynics and Cyrenaics (consider, for example, Diogenes Laertius 2. 68–69, 6. 8).

18. Reading *hypenantion* with a few MSS rather than *hypenantian* with the other MSS and with

Dreizehnter and most editors. I take *emporōn plēthos* as the subject of this clause rather than *tēn polyanthrōpian*, as is commonly done. If *hypenantian* is retained, the meaning would be: "which arises as a result of a multitude of traders using the sea for exporting and importing, and which is contrary to their being finely governed."

19. Piraeus, the port of Athens, stood some five miles from the city, but was connected to it by long walls, and its harbors were fortified against attack by sea. Megara, Corinth, and other cities with important maritime interests had similar arrangements.

20. This argument is meant to answer a possible objection to the possession of naval power deriving from the experience of Athens, where the manpower requirements of the fleet had greatly increased the political strength of the lower classes (cf. 4. 4. 21, 5. 4. 8).

21. An allusion to the warrior class of Plato's *Republic* (375b–c).

22. Archilochus, fr. 67b Diehl.

23. The quotations are from tragedies by Euripides (fr. 975 Nauck [2]) and an unknown author (fr. 78 Nauck [2]).

24. "The for the sake of which" (*to hou heneka*) is a technical Aristotelian term synonymous with "end" or "final cause."

25. Reading *en toutois an eiē ha* with Newman. The text of Π[1] has *en toutois an eiē dio* ("would be among these things, hence"), which does not seem satisfactory. Newman's conjectural *ha* (presupposing the omission of *dio* in Π[2]) is much preferable to Dreizehnter's bracketing of *an eiē dio*.

26. Some editors read *dikaion* ("just") in place of *anankaion* ("necessary"), perhaps rightly.

27. 7. 1.

28. Reading *amphotera* with Susemihl rather than *amphoterois* with the MSS and taking *tēn politeian tautēn* as the subject of *apodidonai*. The text of the MSS is usually translated: "What remains is to assign these political rights to both groups of persons."

29. At least one word appears to have dropped out of the text at this point.

30. Apparently an allusion to Plato, *Republic* 500d.

31. Bracketing the *ē* of the MSS ("barbarians or subjects") with Dreizehnter; cf. 10. 13.

32. See Herodotus 2. 164.

33. The modern gulfs of Squillace and S. Eufemia. The material referred to may derive from the chronicler Antiochus of Syracuse.

34. Tyrrhenia corresponds roughly to modern Tuscany; Iapygia is modern Puglia, the southeastern extremity of the Italian peninsula.

35. Reading *heurēmenois* with Lambinus and Dreizehnter instead of the *eirēmenois* ("what has been mentioned") of the MSS.

36. Many editors consider part or all of this passage (1329a40–b25) to be a later interpolation.

37. Cf. 2. 5. 6–7.

38. There is no discussion of this sort in the remainder of the *Politics* as we have it.

39. There is no discussion of this sort in the remainder of the *Politics* as we have it.

40. Cf. 7. 5.

41. Text and meaning are somewhat uncertain. I read *katatynchanein* with the MSS rather than Dreizehnter's conjectural *kata tychēn*.

42. Many cities—notably Athens—had grown up around a "fortified height" (*akropolis*) where citizens could take refuge during an invasion.

43. For Hippodamus, see 2. 8.

44. A "clump" (*systas*, literally, a "close standing") of vine plants consisted of five plants arranged like the five spots of a die. Aristotle appears to suggest that houses could be grouped more or less irregularly in this fashion in the city's outlying parts, while large boulevards and public areas would be reserved for the protected center.

45. The allusion is to Sparta and its humiliation by Thebes during the invasion of Epaminondas.

46. Catapults, battering rams, and movable towers were introduced into Greek warfare by the Carthaginians in the course of their struggle with Dionysius I of Syracuse; Philip of Macedon used them extensively (cf. Demosthenes, *Philippics* 3. 50).

47. Literally, "philosophized about."

48. Reading *thesin te echei pros tēn tēs aretēs epiphaneian* with Thomas instead of *epiphaneian te echei pros tēn tēs aretēs thesin* ("has conspicuousness in respect to the position of virtue") with the MSS and Dreizehnter.

49. Text and meaning are uncertain. I assume a lacuna after *archontas* rather than bracketing the word with Dreizehnter, or reading *proestos* ("the directing element") instead of the *plēthos* ("the multitude") of the MSS with a number of editors.

50. The reference appears to be to *Eudemian Ethics* 1219a38, b2; cf. *Nicomachean Ethics* 1098b29–31, 1099b26, 1129b31.

51. Reading *hairesis* with the MSS rather than *anairesis* ("removal") with Dreizehnter and many editors; cf. Newman ad loc.

52. The reference appears to be to *Eudemian Ethics* 1248b26 ff.

53. Reading *kat' euchēn* with the MSS rather than *kata tychēn* ("according to fortune") with Dreizehnter.

54. The text is somewhat uncertain; I assume a lacuna following *gar* in a30.

55. 7. 7.

56. Scylax of Caryianda was a geographical writer of the late sixth century.

57. Accepting Thurot's supplement *tōi dikaiōi*.

58. A "contribution" (*eranos*) is a gift or loan for which repayment in some form is anticipated.

59. Both the structure of this sentence (*te* is unanswered) and the abrupt abandonment of the just introduced subject of education suggest that a substantial passage may have dropped out of the text at this point.

60. 3. 4. 10–13.

61. A lacuna at this point in the text has been suspected by Immisch and others, perhaps rightly.

62. 3. 4–5.

63. Compare particularly *Nicomachean Ethics* 1102a23–3a10.

64. For the difference between "practical" and "theoretical" reason, see *Nicomachean Ethics* 1138b35–39b13 and the discussion that follows.

65. Reading *diaireseis* with the MSS instead of *haireseis* ("choices") with Coraes and Dreizehnter.

66. Apart from Thibron, about whom nothing is known, Aristotle may have in mind Xenophon's extant treatise on the Spartan regime; but he appears to indicate that such treatises were numerous.

67. Reading *esti de* with Congreve instead of *eti de* ("further") with the MSS and Dreizehnter.

68. Presumably the Pausanias who attempted to become tyrant of Sparta after the Persian War, although he was never technically king; but some have identified him with a Pausanias who was king during the Peloponnesian War. Cf. 5. 1. 10, 7. 4.

69. A dwelling place for the souls of dead heroes; cf. Hesiod, *Works and Days* 170 ff.

70. A lacuna of indeterminate and possibly substantial length occurs in the text at this point; I supply what I take to be the basic sense.

71. The meaning is somewhat uncertain, and the text may be corrupt. The argument appears to be that just as birth is not a beginning simply but derives from a prior beginning point in the act of generation, so the end or completion of a human being does not derive from one simple beginning point but proceeds through a number of stages, the end of one being the beginning point of the next.

72. The oracle was "do not plough the young furrow"—in its literal meaning, a prohibition against the ploughing of fallow land.

73. Reading *ē mikron* with the MSS; one or more words appear to have dropped out of the text here.

74. There is no discussion of this sort in the remainder of the *Politics* as we have it; no other Aristotelian writing of this sort is attested.

75. The goddesses Artemis and Eileithyia are particularly referred to.

76. Text and meaning are somewhat uncertain. I read *hōristhai gar dē dei* rather than *hōristhō dē* with Dreizehnter.

77. Solon, fr. 19 Diehl.

78. Plato, *Laws* 791e–92a.

79. Dionysus seems to be particularly meant; "scurrilous mockery" (*tōthasmos*) was also characteristic of the rites of Demeter and Core.

80. The text is somewhat uncertain. The phrase "those still of a suitable age" is omitted in Π² and is bracketed by Newman; *eti* ("still") is bracketed by Dreizehnter. *Pros toutous* ("in regard to these") should perhaps be read instead of the *pros toutois* ("in addition to these things") of the MSS.

81. "Lampoons" (*iamboi*) were indecent and abusive verses recited by actors at festivals of Dionysus. Cf. *Poetics* 1448b24–49a15.

82. The age of twenty-one is probably intended; it seems to have been at this age that a young Spartan became a member of one of the common messes.

83. There is no further discussion of this sort in the *Politics* as we have it.

84. Theodorus was a famous actor of the fourth century. What is meant is probably that he insisted on appearing in the first play of every tragic tetralogy.

85. Reading *legousin ou kakōs* with Dreizehnter and most editors rather than *legousin ou kalōs* ("argue not rightly") with the MSS.

Book 8

1. Cf. 7. 14–15.

2. Reading *tēn en tēi diagōgēi scholēn* with the MSS instead of *tēn en tēi scholēi diagōgēn* ("the pastime that is in leisure") with Coraes and Dreizehnter. A distinction seems intended between leisure for political and military activities and leisure for pastime.

3. Homer, *Odyssey* 17. 382–85. The first line quoted does not appear in our text of the *Odyssey*, but appears to have followed line 382 in the version used by Aristotle.

4. Homer, *Odyssey* 9. 5–6.

5. There is no further discussion of this question in the *Politics* as we have it.

6. Cf. 2. 9. 34, 7. 14. 15–20, 15. 6.

7. The reference would seem to be particularly to Thebes (cf. Plutarch, *Pelopidas* 7), but Aristotle may also have Macedon in mind.

8. Euripides, *Bacchae* 381.

9. 8. 6.

10. Musaeus was a semilegendary figure to whom various archaic poems and sayings were ascribed. In the epic language of the quotation, "singing" (*aeidein*) almost certainly refers to the recitation of poetry (to a simple musical accompaniment) by a professional "bard" (*aoidos*), but Aristotle seems to use the quotation in support of the view that singing in the ordinary sense is most pleasant. The view he is implicitly correcting would seem to be the view that poetry as such—that is, music "by itself" (*psilē ousa*, literally "bare") is the truly pleasant element of music generally. Most translations of this passage wrongly assume that the phrase "music by itself" refers to purely instrumental music. The term "melody" (*melōidia*, literally "tune singing") here appears to mean "musical setting"; it connotes primarily choral song—the sort of singing characteristic of social gatherings in classical Greek times.

11. Olympus was a semilegendary personage who is said to have lived in Phrygia in the eighth century B.C.; the "tunes" ascribed to him were solo pieces for the flute, apparently in the Phrygian mode. Cf. 6. 9, 7. 4 and Plato, *Symposium* 215c.

12. The text and meaning of this sentence have been disputed, but it seems most likely that poetic imitations in the broadest sense are what is meant. Cf. *Poetics* 1447a8–16.

13. Little is known of the works of Polygnotus or Pauson, who were active in the fifth century. Cf. *Poetics* 1448a1–6, 1450a26–29.

14. Greek music in the classical period was based not on a uniform scale but on a modal system deriving originally from the divergent characteristics of different sorts of musical instruments. The word "harmony" (*harmonia*) originally meant the tuning or scale of a particular sort of instrument; it was then applied derivatively to the musical style associated with particular instru-

ments as used for particular occasions. A "tune" (*melos*) is properly a melodic realization of a particular harmony (the common translation "song" is misleading in its implication that a vocal element is necessarily present). The notion that different harmonies affect the soul differently seems to have originated among the Pythagoreans; it was further developed by Damon, the musical authority for Plato, and Aristoxenus, a student of Aristotle. Little is otherwise known of the characteristics of the various harmonies; perhaps the fullest ancient accounts are Plato, *Republic* 398d–99c and [Aristotle] *Problems* 19. 48.

15. The views of the Pythagoreans and of Plato's Simmias (*Phaedo* 92a–95a) respectively.

16. The invention of the rattle was proverbially ascribed to Archytas of Tarentum, the Pythagorean philosopher.

17. The "chorus leader" (*chorēgos*)—the producer—of a dramatic performance sometimes set up a votive tablet to Dionysus recording the victory of the poet whose play had been produced. (Ecphantides was an early Athenian comic poet.) The tablet in question presumably recorded the flute player as well.

18. These were all types of stringed instruments.

19. Text and meaning of this sentence have been much disputed. I believe a line has dropped out containing reference to the noncitizen class of the best regime, and that the three "definitions" apply to the harmonies used by the citizens simply, the harmonies used by the citizens for education simply, and the harmonies used by the citizens for the education of the young in singing and the playing of instruments.

20. This remark may refer to the difference between lyric and epic poetry respectively.

21. The musical experts referred to are probably persons associated with the school of Damon; to the latter category belong Aristoxenus and Plato.

22. The distinction very probably derives from Aristoxenus; it appears to be presupposed in the discussion in [Aristotle,] *Problems* 19. 48. What little evidence is available suggests that the tunes "relating to character" (*ēthika*) corresponded to the harmonies of the Lydian group as well as to Dorian, those "relating to action" (*praktika*) to the Hypophrygian (Ionian) and Hypodorian (Aeolian) harmonies, and those "relating to inspiration" (*enthousiastika*) to the Phrygian harmony.

23. A plausible emendation would give "tune" (*melos*) for the "part" (*meros*) of the MSS.

24. This phrase is usually taken to be a reference to the treatment of "purification" (*katharsis*) in Aristotle's *Poetics*; but the matter is only alluded to in the text of that work as it stands (6. 1449b26–28). A plausible alternative is that it refers to a later discussion in the *Politics* itself which was subsequently lost.

25. The Dorian harmony can be identified as that "most relating to character." Aristotle appears to accept implicitly the use of this and other harmonies in the same category—notably Mixed Lydian, which was the mode characteristic of tragic choruses—for purposes of "listening to others perform." The Hypophrygian and Hypodorian modes were associated particularly with the heroes of tragedy.

26. Aristotle appears to refer to "melancholics"—persons susceptible to episodes of "enthusiastic" madness because of a physiological condition involving an excess of black bile (see [Aristotle,] *Problems* 30. 1). He indicates that a "purification" of such persons could occur throughout the application of "sacred tunes" (probably to be identified with the "tunes of Olympus" mentioned in 5. 16) in the context of Dionysian ritual, where their normal effect was precisely to induce religious inspiration or frenzy.

27. This sentence seems intended to describe the effect of tragic performances on their audience.

28. One or more words appear to have dropped out of the text at this point; I translate the supplement of Dreizehnter.

29. The deviant harmonies are probably the "relaxed" and the "strained" Lydian; the former was associated with feasting and drinking, the latter with funeral celebrations. The "strained and highly colored tunes" are probably Phrygian tunes of the chromatic or "colored" variety associated with the dithrambic poetry of the fourth-century poet Philoxenus.

30. Plato, *Republic* 399a–c.

31. Plato, *Republic* 398e.

32. Reading *paidia* ("play") with Schneider rather than *paideia* ("education") with the MSS and Dreizehnter. The notion of "order" (*kosmos*) would seem to encompass education of character.

33. This paragraph is regarded by some scholars as an interpolation, I believe rightly. The association of the (relaxed) Lydian mode with education is contrary to Aristotle's earlier argument, as is the notion that old men should sing (cf. 6. 4); both appear to have been characteristic of the Damonian school.

GLOSSARY

Action (*praxis*): purposive human action or activity, particularly moral or political activity. The related term *praktikos*, "active," is frequently used by Aristotle with reference to the practical or political way of life (see particularly 7. 2–3) as well as the form of reasoning associated with it. The verb *prattein* is rendered "to act." The expressions *eu prattein* ("to act well") and *kalōs prattein* ("to act finely") carry the idiomatic meaning "to do well" or "to prosper."

Adjudication (*dikē*): the process of determining what is lawful or just. In its narrow sense *dikē* is rendered "trial" or "lawsuit"; in a larger sense, it refers to the system of adjudication which is characteristic of any civilized community (consider 1. 2. 16). Of related terms, *dikazein* is rendered "to adjudicate," *dikastēs* as "juror," *dikastērion* as "court." See **Justice.**

Administer (*oikein*): dwell in and govern after the fashion of a household (*oikos*). Also rendered simply "to settle" or "to inhabit." See **Manager**.

Affection (*philia*): friendship, friendly feeling, or (nonsexual) love. The related word *philos* is translated "friend"; "affectionateness" renders *to philētikon*. See *Nicomachean Ethics* 8–9.

Aggrandizement (*pleonexia*): taking more than one's share (literally, "having more"); greedy or unjust behavior.

Ambition (*philotimia*): see **Honor.**

Aristocracy (*aristokratia*): any form of regime in which virtue is taken into account in the selection of officials; more properly, rule of the few who are best (*aristoi*) on the basis of virtue, or a regime centrally concerned with the cultivation and practice of virtue. Cf. 3. 7. 3, 4. 7, 8. 7–9.

Arms (*hopla*): arms or weapons generally; the armament of a "heavy-armed soldier" (*hoplitēs*), the mainstay of most Greek citizen armies (this sense is rendered "[heavy] arms").

Arrangement (*taxis*): order or an ordered arrangement; a measure, regulation or institution. The related verb *tattein* is translated "to arrange"; the compound words *syntaxis* and *syntattein* are rendered "organization" and "to organize."

Arrogance (*hybris*): arrogant, insulting, or violent behavior, particularly if such behavior is unprovoked and in disregard or defiance of conventional restraints; as a term of law, unprovoked physical or sexual assault.

Art (*technē*): any practical or productive activity based on a body of communicable knowledge or expertise. The related term *technitēs* is rendered "artisan."

Assembly (*ekklēsia*): a gathering (literally, "calling out") of the citizenry; the popular assembly, the dominant political institution in a democracy.

Assessment (*timēma*): a property valuation serving to distinguish classes of citizens for various civic purposes. The phrase *apo timēmatōn* ("on the basis of assessments") denotes a political arrangement involving some form of property qualification.

Authoritative (*kyrios*): dominant or controlling in a political sense (the more common translation "sovereign" misleadingly suggests a purely legal form of authority). Also used of the controlling or most proper sense of a term.

Barbarian (*barbaros*): anyone of non-Greek stock, including relatively civilized peoples such as the Persians or the Phoenicians of Carthage.

Business (*chrēmatismos*): the activity of making money; more generally and properly, the activity of acquiring "goods" (*chrēmata*) "to use" (*chrēsthai*) in support of the needs of the household (cf. 1. 8–10). *Chrēmata* is an elastic term that can denote things or objects very generally as well as money in an abstract sense; it is translated "funds" as well as "goods." More frequent than *chrēmatismos* is *chrēmatistikē*, "business expertise"; "businessman" renders *chrēmatistēs*.

Character (*ēthos*): the character or customary behavior of a living being or group; the character, in particular the moral character, of an individual.

Choice (*hairesis*): choice or election, particularly in a political sense; also translated "election." The related verb *haireisthai* is rendered "to choose" or "to elect." The compound words *proairesis* and *proaireisthai* are rendered "intentional choice" (or "intention") and "to choose intentionally"; for this term, which has a technical meaning in Aristotle's thought, see *Nicomachean Ethics* 3. 2.

Citizen (*politēs*): a free person who is entitled to participate in the political life of a city through the holding of deliberative and judicial office. Cf. 3. 1–2.

City (*polis*): a political community characterized by social and economic differentiation, the rule of law, and republican government; the chief urban center of such a community. Cf. 1. 1. 1–2, 2. 2. 3–7, 3. 3. 3–5, 3. 9. 6–14, 7. 8. 6–9.

Common (*koinos*): accessible to or shared by all (this sense is sometimes rendered "accessible" or "attainable"); the public as opposed to the individual or private. The expression *ta koina*, translated "common [funds]," denotes the public treasury of a city; *to koinon*, "community," denotes the public in a general sense, or the central authority of a political organization. See **Partnership.**

Council (*boulē*): a body of restricted membership with primarily deliberative functions, which often shared supreme authority with a popular assembly. A "preliminary council" (*proboulē*) was a smaller body, characteristic of oligarchies. Cf. 4. 15. 11–12, 6. 8. 17.

Custom (*ethos*): the custom of a city or the habit of an individual; also translated "habit." The related verb *ethizein* is rendered "to habituate."

Defining principle (*horos*): principle, standard, limit, characteristic feature. Of related terms, *horismos* is rendered "definition," *horizein* "to define," and *diorizein* "to discuss" or "to determine."

Democracy (*dēmokratia*): any regime in which the "people" (*dēmos*) rule or control the authoritative institutions of the city; more properly, rule of the poor or the majority in their own interest. Cf. 3. 8, 4. 4, 6, 6. 2–4. *dēmokrateisthai* is rendered "to be run democratically." See **People.**

Dominate (*kratein*): to conquer through force, to master or control; also rendered "to conquer." The verb derives from the noun *kratos*, "bodily strength"; a related term is *kreittōn*, "superior."

Dynasty (*dynasteia*): a form of oligarchy characterized by the dominance of a few "powerful men" (*dynastoi*) and their families and retainers. Cf. 2. 10. 14–15.

Education (*paideia*): the education of children (*paides*); the education or culture of man in general.

End (*telos*): the character of a thing when fully formed, its completion or perfection. Of related terms, *teleios* is rendered "complete," *teleisthai* "to be completed."

Equality (*to ison*): equality or fairness.

Equipment (*chorēgia*): the expenditure required of a chorus leader (*chorēgos*) or producer of dramas; material preconditions, supplies, equipment. Used by Aristotle as a quasi-technical term to denote the external requirements or preconditions of the virtuous life.

Error (*hamartia*): a failing generally involving a moral as well as intellectual dimension, but less than full moral culpability.

Expertise (*-ikē*): proficiency in any human activity, art or science (the adjectival form is frequently used by itself as a substantive).

Factional conflict (*stasis*): political unrest, agitation, or sedition aimed at overturning a regime or altering its character in various ways (cf. 5. 1. 8–10); the factional conflict or state of civil disorder resulting from this. "To engage in factional conflict" renders *stasiazein*; *diastasis* is translated "factional split."

Few (*hoi oligoi*): the upper classes, particularly the wealthy, as distinct from the common people.

Fine (*kalos*): morally, or physically beautiful, noble, fine, right; also translated "noble" and "right." The related term *kallos* is rendered "beauty" or "good looks." See **Action.**

Gentleman (*kaloskagathos*): a person of good family and established position (literally, a "noble and good man"); a person distinguished by education, refinement, and virtue.

Govern (*politeuesthai*): to govern oneself or to be governed as a free citizen (the verb generally appears in the middle voice; both reflexive and passive translations are used according to context); more generally, to live as a free citizen in a city and participate in public life (this sense is regularly rendered "to engage in politics").

Governing body (*politeuma*): the group or class that holds effective political power in a city (cf. 3. 6. 1–2). See **Regime.**

Habit (*ethos*): see **Custom.**

Happiness (*eudaimonia*): happiness as a settled condition and state of mind, well-being. See *Nicomachean Ethics* 1. "Blessed" (*makarios*) is a stronger term connoting an extraordinary degree of happiness comparable to that associated with the gods.

Helotry (*heilōteia*): the institution of agricultural serfdom at Sparta based on the ethnically distinct class of persons known as Helots (*heilōtai*). See **Subjects**.

Honor (*timē*): honor, esteem, value; mark of honor, prerogative (this sense is rendered "prerogative"). *Atimos*, "deprived of prerogatives," is a technical term for loss of civic rights or disenfranchisement. "Ambition" renders *philotimia* (literally, "love of honor"). See **Assessment**.

Household management (*oikonomia*): governance of the household, including rule over women, children, and slaves, and the provision of material necessities. Occasionally, *oikonomia* is used (as the related verb *oikonomein* generally is) in a broader sense, rendered "management." See **Manager**.

Judge (*krinein*): to distinguish, judge, decide, usually but not exclusively in a judicial context; sometimes translated "to decide." Of related terms, *kritēs* is translated "judge," *krisis* as "judgment" or "trial."

Justice (*to dikaion*): what is right, fair, or morally justifiable; a right or rightful claim (this sense is generally rendered "[claim to] justice"). Of related terms, the adjective *dikaios* is translated "just," the adverb *dikaiōs* "justly" or "justifiably": *dikaiosynē* is rendered "[the virtue of] justice." See **Adjudication**.

Kind (*eidos*): distinctive appearance (this sense is translated "look" or "mark"); form, character, species.

Kingship (*basileia*): rule of one man in the common interest. "Absolute kingship" (*pambasileia*) is a form of kingship resembling paternal rule in the household. Cf. 3. 14–17.

Laborer (*thēs*): an unskilled worker or day laborer. Laborers or "the laboring element" (*to thētikon*) constituted the lowest social stratum among free persons; their participation in politics was generally limited at best, even in democratic regimes.

Law (*nomos*): written or unwritten law, custom, or convention. *Nomos* in the broad sense (often translated elsewhere as "convention") is frequently understood in opposition to *physis*, "nature." Related terms are *nomimos*, "lawful," *ta nomima*, "usages" or "ordinances," *nomisma*, "money," and *nomizein*, "to consider."

Leader (*hēgemōn*): head of a largely voluntary alliance or association. The term is particularly used of cities maintaining hegemony (as distinct from imperial rule) over other cities.

Leisure (*scholē*): freedom from the need of working for a living; free time, leisure. See **Occupation**.

Liberal (*eleutherios*): pertaining to a free man (*eleutheros*) as distinct from a slave; free from the constraints of economic necessity, generous or liberal. Cf. *Nicomachean Ethics* 4. 1.

Man (*anēr*): the male of the species in general; a manly or spirited type of man. "Man" also renders *anthrōpos* in its generic sense; this term is otherwise translated "human being." *Anēr* is sometimes rendered "male"; in some contexts, the translation "husband" is often equally appropriate. A related term is *andreia*, "courage."

Manager (-*nomos*): governor, regulator, supervisor, manager. The term is found only in compound forms; it derives from the verb *nemein* (to dispense or distribute; to shepherd or lead to pasture), which is itself related to *nomos*, "law." Apart from "household manager" (*oikonomos*), the head of household as ruler and provider, terms ending in -*nomos* generally refer to city officials having supervisory duties of various sorts. The verb *oikonomein* is translated "to manage"; *oikonomia* is on occasion also used in this broader sense, and is rendered "management" simply. "Good management" renders *eunomia*, a word connoting social order and competent government.

Many (*hoi polloi*): most people in a generic sense; the common people as distinct from the educated or wealthy "few."

Mass (*ochlos*): an unruly crowd of people; the lower classes.

Master (*despotēs*): the head of household in his capacity as master of slaves.

Mean (*phaulos*): mean, contemptible, base, bad (also rendered "bad" and "poor"); as a social term, a person of the lower classes.

Merit (*axia*): worth, desert, merit; also rendered "worth." The verb *axioun* is translated "to merit," "to claim to merit," or "to claim"; *axiōma* is rendered "claim."

Mode (*tropos*): manner, mode, style, temper; also rendered "manner."

Moderation (*sōphrosynē*): the virtue that controls the desires, particularly bodily desires; its opposite is the vice of "licentiousness" (*akolasia*). See *Nicomachean Ethics* 3. 10–12. The related adjective *sōphrōn* is translated "sound"; it connotes soundness of mind or good sense as well as self-control. "Moderate" and "moderateness" render *metrios* and *metriotēs* respectively, terms which connote a measured or balanced condition.

Money (*nomisma*): coined money, currency. The drachma, the mina (100 drachmas), and the talent (60 minas) were the basic units of Greek coinage; one talent was a substantial sum of money to be held by a private individual. See **Law.**

Multitude (*plēthos*): any aggregation of independent units; an association of similar persons; in a political context, the body of the citizens, and in particular the majority of the citizens, or the lower classes. Also translated "number," "amount," and "bulk."

Nation (*ethnos*): a tribal or ethnically based state, usually organized as a loose confederation of villages under a hereditary king, but also extending to substantial empires such as the Persian.

Nature (*physis*): origin, growth, development (the related verb *phyein* is translated "to grow" or "to develop"); the character of a thing when fully developed, its nature; nature or the universe. For Aristotle and the Greeks generally, "nature" is a term of distinction (it is frequently found in opposition to "chance," "art" or "law"), implying a standard of value independent of human thought or action.

Necessary (*anankaios*): compulsory; related to economic or material needs. The related verb *anankazein* is rendered "to compel."

Noble (*kalos*): see **Fine.**

Notables (*hoi gnorimoi*): well-known or distinguished persons; a common term for the upper classes, particularly the hereditary aristocracy.

Occupation (*ascholia*): necessary activity, business, work, occupation; literally, "lack of leisure."

Oligarchy (*oligarchia*): rule of the rich who are few (*oligoi*) in their own interest. Cf. 3. 8, 4. 5–6, 6. 6–7.

Order (*kosmos*): order, beauty, adornment (also rendered "ordered beauty"); the visible universe or cosmos (rendered "universe"). "Orderers" (*kosmoi*) was the term for a magistracy in Crete similar to the Spartan overseers. "Orderliness" renders *eukosmia*, a term connoting public order or decency. The verb *kosmein* is translated "to adorn."

Part (*meros*): part, section, group, class. The common expression *kata merē* is rendered "in turn," "by turns" or "by groups."

Participate (*koinōnein*): see **Common; Partnership.**

Pastime (*diagōgē*): any voluntary pursuit or occupation; the serious or cultivated pursuits of leisure.

People (*dēmos*): the body of the people, the public; the common people or lower classes of a city; the government of the common people, or democracy (this sense is translated "[rule of] the people"). *Dēmos* was also an administrative unit (rendered "quarter") of Athens. See **Popular; Public.**

Philosophy (*philosophia*): theoretical investigation or study (literally, "love of wisdom"); culture (for this sense consider particularly 2. 5. 15).

Political (*politikos*): pertaining to or characteristic of the city, or of political life generally; also, pertaining to or characteristic of polity (translation of the adjective varies according to context). As a substantive, *politikos* denotes a person actively engaged in politics, a politician or statesman; it is translated "expert in politics," "political [man]," or "political [ruler]." The substantive *politikē*, denoting the art or science of politics, is rendered "political expertise."

Polity (*politeia*): a form of popular rule involving oligarchic features and directed to the common interest; more properly, any regime combining oligarchy and democracy. Cf. 3. 7, 4. 8. See **Regime.**

Poor (*aporos*): a person not materially well off (literally, "lacking a supply"), though not destitute; as a political category, the majority in most cities. "Poor" in a morally pejorative sense translates *phaulos* (see **Mean**).

Popular (*dēmotikos*): characteristic of or pertaining to the people (*dēmos*). "Those of the popular sort" (*hoi dēmotikoi*) is an expression designating the active supporters of a democratic regime, or a democratic party in a loose sense of that term (which could and frequently did include persons not belonging to the people as a class). "Popular leader" translates *dēmagōgos*; the verb *dēmagōgein* is rendered "to seek popularity with."

Possession (*ktēma*): what one has acquired and owns. The related verb *ktasthai* is rendered "to acquire" or "to possess"; *ktēsis* is rendered "possessions."

Power (*dynamis*): the capacity or potential of a thing in a general sense (*dynamis* derives from the common verb *dynasthai*, "to be able"); the nature or character of a thing as expressed in its potential; power in a specifically political and military sense; a military force; also rendered "capacity." *Dynastoi,* a term referring to exceptionally wealthy and powerful men, is translated "the powerful"; cf. **Dynasty.**

Preeminence (*hyperochē*): superiority, predominance; political power, position, or influence.

Prerogative (*timē*): see **Honor.**

Presupposition (*hypothesis*): a qualifying condition or assumption.

Private (*idios*): proper or peculiar to a person or thing (this sense is generally translated "peculiar"); the private or individual as opposed to the public or "common" (*koinos*). The related term *idiōtēs* is translated either "private individual" or "nonprofessional."

Property (*ousia*): property in an abstract sense (the word derives from the verb *einai,* "to be," and is also used as a technical term in metaphysics; compare English "substance"); a property or estate.

Prudence (*phronēsis*): good sense or soundness of mind; wisdom or intelligence; prudence. In Aristotle's thought, *phronēsis* is the virtue associated with the active or practical portion of the rational part of the soul, prudence or practical wisdom. See *Nicomachean Ethics* 6. 5, 8–13.

Public (*dēmosios*): pertaining to the people (*dēmos*) as a whole; official, public. *Dēmoseuein,* "to confiscate," means literally "to make public." The phrase "public service" renders *leitourgia,* a term frequently applied to large expenditures by private individuals for public purposes such as the building of warships (a form of indirect taxation), but used generally of any official function, including worship of the gods (cf. 7. 10. 11).

Refined (*charieis*): graceful, elegant, appealing; a term used euphemistically of the upper or educated classes.

Regime (*politeia*): the organization of offices in a city, particularly the most authoritative; the effective government or governing body of a city; the way of life of a city as reflected in the end pursued by the city as a whole and by those constituting its governing body (the common translation "constitution" is misleading insofar as it connotes a formal legal order). Cf. 3. 6. 1, 4. 1. 10, 3. 5, 11. 3. Sometimes *politeia* bears the meaning of a specifically constitutional or republican regime as distinct from personal monarchic rule. See **Governing body; Polity.**

Resolution (*dogma*): an official decision reflecting the general "opinion" (*doxa*) of a deliberative body. The related verb *dokein* is translated "to hold" or "to resolve."

Respectable (*epieikēs*): decent, fair, reasonable, equitable; as a substantive, a person of the upper or educated classes.

Revolution (*metabolē*): change or alteration (this sense is sometimes rendered "alteration"); change—not necessarily sudden or violent—in the essential character of a regime. The related verb *metaballein* is rendered "to be altered" or "to undergo revolution."

Right (*kalos*): see **Fine.**

Rule (*archē*): the activity or institutions of governance; in particular, the executive magistracies of a city (this sense is generally rendered "office").

Archē in the sense of governance of other cities is translated "[imperial] rule." A different sense of the term is rendered "beginning point" or "ruling principle."

Science (*epistēmē*): knowledge in a general sense; an organized body of knowledge, a science (generally used of theoretical sciences as distinct from applied sciences or "arts").

Seditious (*kainotomos*): innovative or novel (this sense is translated "original"—cf. particularly 2. 6. 6); seeking innovation or revolution in a city or its institutions.

Senate (*gerousia*): council of "elders" (*gerontes*), an aristocratic deliberative body particularly associated with Sparta.

Spiritedness (*thymos*): anger; more generally, the part of the soul or complex of passions (extending to anger, ambition, arrogance, and affection) connected with man's sociality. Cf. 7. 7.

Study (*theōrein*): to look at, study, or contemplate; also rendered "to look at" and (in the aorist) "to discern." Of related words, *theōria* is translated as "looking on," "study," or "spectacle," *theōros* as "onlooker," and *theatēs* as "spectator."

Subjects (*perioikoi*): dependent peoples (literally, "dwellers around"); used of the class of agricultural serfs (similar to the Spartan Helots) in Crete, and of non-Spartiate free Lacedaemonians.

Superintendence (*epimeleia*): supervision, care, concern, practice; also translated "care" and "concern."

Sustenance (*trophē*): what is required to sustain physical life; food; support or maintenance; nurturing or rearing (this sense is translated "rearing").

Task (*ergon*): function, work; characteristic activity or result; deed, fact; also rendered "work," "deed," and "fact." The related word *energeia* (literally, "at work"), rendered "actualization," is a technical term in Aristotelian metaphysics denoting the realization or completion of a potential.

Traditional (*patrios*): deriving from one's forefathers, ancestral. The related term *patrikos* is translated "hereditary."

Type (*genos*): family, stock, class, type; also rendered "family" and "stock" (usually in reference to a large social grouping—a clan or people—closely related by blood).

Use (*chrēsthai*): to use, employ, or practice; also translated "to treat." Of related words, *chrēsimos* is translated "useful," *chrēstos* (a term of moral approbation) "decent," *chrēsis* "use" or "usage." Cf. **Business.**

Vice (*kakia*): badness, baseness, viciousness, vice. The adjective *kakos* is rendered "bad" or "wrong," the substantive *kakon* as "ill."

Virtue (*aretē*): the goodness, excellence, or right operation of a person or thing. See *Nicomachean Ethics* 2. 1–6.

Vulgar (*banausos*): characteristic of craftsmen engaged in manual work (as distinct from laborers, farmers, or merchants); more properly, characteristic of any work, art, or kind of learning incompatible with the education of free persons in virtue (cf. 8. 2. 4–5).

Well off (*euporos*): a materially affluent person (literally, "having a ready supply"). While sometimes used as a synonym of "wealthy" (*plousios*), the term seems to have a wider application, probably extending to all citizens capable of affording heavy arms. (cf. 3. 17. 4).

INDEX OF NAMES

Index of Names